DIEGO SIMEONE DEFENDING TACTICS

Tactical Analysis and Sessions from Atlético Madrid's 4-4-2

Written by
ATHANASIOS TERZIS

Published by

DIEGO SIMEONE DEFENDING TACTICS

Tactical Analysis and Sessions from Atlético Madrid's 4-4-2

First Published July 2020 by SoccerTutor.com

info@soccertutor.com | www.SoccerTutor.com

UK: 0208 1234 007 | **US:** (305) 767 4443 | **ROTW:** +44 208 1234 007

ISBN: 978-1-910491-39-3

Copyright: SoccerTutor.com Limited © 2020. All Rights Reserved.

All rights reserved. No part of this publication may be reproduced, stored in a retrieval system, or transmitted in any form or by any means, electronic, mechanical, photocopy, recording or otherwise, without prior written permission of the copyright owner. Nor can it be circulated in any form of binding or cover other than that in which it is published and without similar condition including this condition being imposed on a subsequent purchaser.

Author
Athanasios Terzis © 2020

Edited by
Alex Fitzgerald - SoccerTutor.com

Cover Design by
Alex Macrides, Think Out Of The Box Ltd.
Email: design@thinkootb.com Tel: +44 (0) 208 144 3550

Diagrams
Diagram designs by SoccerTutor.com. All the diagrams in this book have been created using SoccerTutor.com Tactics Manager Software available from www.SoccerTutor.com

Note: While every effort has been made to ensure the technical accuracy of the content of this book, neither the author nor publishers can accept any responsibility for any injury or loss sustained as a result of the use of this material.

CONTENTS

Meet The Author: Athanasios Terzis 9
Diego Simeone's Achievements 10
Simeone's Incredible Success with Atlético Madrid Against the Odds 11
Atlético Madrid's 4-4-2 Formation (2017-18 Season) 13
Atlético Madrid's 4-4-2 Formation (2018-19 Season) 14
Atlético Madrid Players 15
Coaching Format 16

THE DEFENSIVE PHASE 17
The Defensive Phase (When The Opposition Have Possession) 18

TACTICAL SITUATION 1: Positioning and Defensive Movements of the Forwards 19
Balanced Defensive Positioning of the 2 Forwards Against 2 Centre Backs 20
Unbalanced Defensive Positioning of the 2 Forwards Against 2 Centre Backs 21
Balanced Defensive Positioning of the Forwards Mirrored by Central Midfielders 22

Practice for "Positioning and Defensive Movements of the Forwards" 23
Forwards Retain Balance and Deny Space Between the Lines in a 4v5 (+GK) Functional Practice ... 24

TACTICAL SITUATION 2: Defensive Reactions when the Positioning of 1 Forward is Incorrect 25
Controlling Opposing Midfielders (Against 2 Centre Backs and 2 Central Midfielders) 26
Correct Defensive Reaction When the Centre Back Moves Forward with the Ball 28
Bad Timing in Pressing the Ball Creates Space in the Centre 29
Good Timing Pressing the Ball (Against 2 Centre Backs and 2 Central Midfielders) 30
Bad Timing Pressing the Ball (Against 2 Centre Backs and 3 Central Midfielders) 31

Practice for "Defensive Reactions when the Positioning of 1 Forward is Incorrect" 34
Defensive Reactions when the Positioning of 1 Forward is Incorrect in a Zonal Practice 35

TACTICAL SITUATION 3: Positioning of the Forwards to Prepare for Counter Attacks 37
Positioning of the Forwards to Prepare for Counter Attacks Against 2 Centre Backs 38
The Forwards Cannot Prepare for Counter Attacks and Must Control 3 Centre Backs 41

Practice for "Positioning of the Forwards to Prepare for Counter Attacks" 42
Positioning of the Forwards to Prepare for Counter Attacks in a 4v5 (+GK) Functional Practice 43

TACTICAL SITUATION 4: Positioning and Defensive Movements of the Midfielders 45
Shape, Distance and Defensive Cohesion of the Midfield Line (Ball in Centre) 46
Defensive Reactions of the Midfield Line when the Centre Back Dribbles Forward 48
Shape, Distance and Defensive Cohesion of the Midfield Line (Ball Near Side-Line) 49

Practice for "Positioning and Defensive Movements of the Midfielders" 50
Compact Midfield Line Blocking Through Passes in a Functional Game 51

TACTICAL SITUATION 5: Positioning and Defensive Movements of the Defenders 53
Positioning and Defensive Movements of the Defenders 54
Positioning and Defensive Movements Against 3 Forwards (4-3-3) 55
Defensive Positioning with the Ball in the Centre Against 2 Forwards (4-4-2) 58
Defensive Positioning with the Ball Out Wide Against 2 Forwards (4-4-2) 59
Defensive Positioning Against 1 Forward and 1 Attacking Midfielder (4-2-3-1) 61
Advantages of 2 Centre Backs Against 1 Forward in the Centre (4-2-3-1) 62

3 Practices for "Positioning and Defensive Movements of the Defenders" 66
1. Appropriate Positioning and Defending Medium and Long Passes Against 1 Forward (4-3-3) 67
2. Appropriate Positioning and Defending Medium and Long Passes Against 2 Forwards (4-4-2) 69
3. Appropriate Positioning and Defending Medium and Long Passes Against 2 Forwards (4-2-3-1) 71

TACTICAL SITUATION 6: Wide Positioning of the Full Backs to Contest the Opposing Wingers 73
Advantages of the Wide Positioning of the Full Backs 74

2 Practices for "Wide Positioning of the Full Backs to Contest the Opposing Wingers" 77
1. Wide Positioning and Shifting Across of Full Backs to Contest the Wingers Against the 4-3-3 78
2. Positioning and Shifting Across of Full Backs to Contest Wingers Against the 4-4-2 and 4-2-3-1 ... 80

TACTICAL SITUATION 7: Controlling the Large Gaps Between the Centre Backs and Full Backs 82
Disadvantages of the Wide Positioning of the Atlético Full Backs 83
Controlling Gaps Between the Centre Backs and Full Backs Against the 4-3-3 84
Controlling Gaps Between the Centre Backs and Full Backs Against the 4-2-3-1 86
Full Back's Movement to Control the Gap Between the Centre Back and Full Back 89

Session (3 Practices) for "Controlling the Large Gaps Between the Centre Backs and Full Backs" 92
1. Centre Backs Controlling the Gaps to the Full Backs in a Functional Practice vs 4-3-3 93
2. Full Backs Controlling the Gaps to the Centre Backs in a Functional Practice vs 4-3-3 95
3. Defensive Line Controlling the Gaps Between the Centre Backs and Full Backs in a Functional Practice. 97

TACTICAL SITUATION 8: Positioning and Defensive Movements of the Front Block 98
How the Opposition Can Exploit the "Crucial Central Area" 99
Main Aim of the Front Block 100
1st Aim: Narrowing the Passing Lanes to Prevent Through Passes 100
2nd Aim: Limiting the Available Space Between the Forward and Midfield Lines. 102
Defensive Reactions of the Front Block when the Opposition Break Through Pressure 110

Session (3 Practices) for "Positioning and Defensive Movements of the Front Block" 113
1. Block Through Passes with the Front Block in a Functional Practice (6 v 6 +GK) 114
2. Block Through Passes with the Front Block in a Functional Practice (6 v 8 +GK) 115
3. Block Through Passes and Defend the Crucial Central Area with the Front Block in a Tactical 11v11 Game 117

TACTICAL SITUATION 9: Rear Block's Positioning and Movements to Control Wide Areas 118
Space Created Out Wide Due to Atlético's Compact Midfield Line. 119
Positioning of the Rear Block 122
Main Aims of the Rear Block 123
1st Aim: Controlling the Wide Areas. 124
Controlling the Movements of the Opposing Full Backs and Wingers. 125
2nd Aim: Controlling Long Passes Out Wide to the Wingers. 128

Practice for "Rear Block's Positioning & Movements to Control Wide Areas" .. 132
Controlling Wide Areas with the Rear Block in a Functional Practice. 133

TACTICAL SITUATION 10: Rear Block Controlling Passes within Wide Areas 135
Zones of Responsibility in Wide Areas (Full Backs and Wide Midfielders). 136
Importance and Benefits of the Full Back's Good Starting Position 137
Problems that Occur if the Full Back Has a Bad Starting Position 141
Reaction of the Full Back when the Opposing Winger Drops Back 144
Collective Reactions of the 2 Wide Players to Win the Ball. 146

Session (3 Practices) for "Rear Block Controlling Passes within Wide Areas" ... 148
1. Rear Block Controlling Passes within Wide Areas in a Functional Practice. ... 149
2. Rear Block Controlling Passes within Wide Areas in a Functional Zonal Small Sided Game. ... 150
3. Rear Block Controlling Passes within Wide Areas in a Functional 9v9 Game. ... 152

TACTICAL SITUATION 11: Rear Block's Reaction After the Extensive Shift of the Centre Back ... 153
Rear Block's Reaction After the Extensive Shift of the Centre Back ... 154

Session (3 Practices) for "Rear Block's Reactions After the Extensive Shift of the Centre Back" ... 158
1. Rear Block's Reaction After the Extensive Shift of the Centre Back in a 4v6 Functional Practice ... 159
2. Rear Block's Reaction After the Extensive Shift of the Centre Back in a 6v8 Functional Practice ... 160
3. Rear Block's Reaction After the Extensive Shift of the Centre Back in a Functional Game ... 162

TACTICAL SITUATION 12: Rear Block's Defensive Reactions After Wide Players Receive ... 163
The Central Midfielder Covers the Space Behind the Full Back Against the 4-3-3 ... 164
Compact Lines Prevent Inside Passes from Wide Areas Against the 4-2-3-1 or 4-4-2 ... 167
Compact Lines Prevent Inside Passes from Wide Areas Against the 4-3-3 ... 169
The Opposing Full Back Receives in an Advanced Position Against the 4-2-3-1 ... 170
Controlling the Full Back who Receives in an Advanced Position Against the 4-2-3-1 ... 173
Controlling the Winger when the Centre Back is Close to the Strong Side ... 176
Controlling the Winger when the Centre Back is Away from the Strong Side ... 180

Session (2 Practices) for "Rear Block's Defensive Reactions After Wide Players Receive" ... 182
1. Rear Block's Defensive Reactions After Wide Players Receive in a Structured Functional Practice ... 183
2. Rear Block's Defensive Reactions After Wide Players Receive in a Dynamic Game ... 185

TACTICAL SITUATION 13: How the Centre Backs Defend the Forwards' Movements (Rear Block) ... 186
How the Centre Backs Defend the Forwards' Movements ... 187

Session (2 Practices) for "How the Centre Backs Defend the Forwards' Movements (Rear Block)" ... 193
1. The Centre Backs Defend the Forwards' Movements in a Structured Functional Practice. ... 194
2. The Centre Backs Defend the Forwards' Movements in a Dynamic Game. ... 195

TACTICAL SITUATION 14: Pressing High Up the Pitch (from the Goalkeeper) ... 196
Pressing High Up the Pitch (From the GK) Against the 4-3-3 ... 197

Practice for "Pressing High Up the Pitch (from the Goalkeeper)" 203
Pressing High Up the Pitch (from the GK) and Forcing Play Wide in a Dynamic Game with a Central Zone.. 204

TACTICAL SITUATION 15: Pressing After the Goalkeeper's Pass 205
Pressing After the Goalkeeper's Pass Against the 4-3-3 206
Forcing Play to One Side and Creating an Ideal Pressing Situation Against the 4-3-3 210
Pressing when the Defensive Midfielder Drops Very Deep Against the 4-3-3..................... 214
Pressing After the Goalkeeper's Pass Against the 4-4-2 218
Pressing After the Goalkeeper's Pass Against the 4-2-3-1 220
The Central Midfielder Drops into a Deep Position Against the 4-4-2 221

Practice for "Pressing After the Goalkeeper's Pass" 224
Pressing After the Goalkeeper's Pass in a Dynamic Game with Central Zones vs the 4-3-3 225

THE TRANSITION FROM ATTACK TO DEFENCE 227
The Transition from Attack to Defence (Negative Transition) 228

TACTICAL SITUATION 1: Retaining a Numerical Advantage at the Back During Build-up Play 229
Retaining a Numerical Advantage at the Back During Build-Up Play........................... 230
Retaining a Numerical Advantage at the Back During Build-Up Against the 4-4-2................ 231
Retaining a Numerical Advantage at the Back During Build-Up Against the 4-2-3-1.............. 236
Retaining a Numerical Advantage at the Back During Build-Up Against the 4-3-3 or 4-1-4-1....... 237
Retaining a Numerical Advantage at the Back During Build-Up Against the 3-5-2................. 238

Session (2 Practices) for "Retaining a Numerical Advantage at the Back During Build-up Play" 240
1. Retaining a Numerical Advantage at the Back During Build-up Play in a Passive Practice......... 241
2. Retaining a Numerical Advantage at the Back During Build-up Play in a Conditioned 7v8 (+GK) Game 243

TACTICAL SITUATION 2: Negative Transition After Losing Possession from a Long Pass 244
Negative Transition After Losing Possession.. 245
Negative Transition After Losing Possession from a Long Pass 246

Practice for "Negative Transition After Losing Possession from a Long Pass"... 249
Negative Transition After Losing Possession from a Long Pass in a Conditioned Game with a Central Zone.. 250

TACTICAL SITUATION 3: Negative Transition After Losing Possession During a Switch of Play 251
Negative Transition After Losing Possession During a Switch of Play 252

Practice for "Negative Transition After Losing Possession During a Switch of Play" 255
Negative Transition After Losing Possession During a Switch of Play in a Conditioned Game vs 4-4-2 256

TACTICAL SITUATION 4: Counter-Pressing After Losing Possession During Combination Play 257
Counter-Pressing After Losing Possession During Combination Play in the Centre 258
Counter-Pressing After Losing Possession During Combination Play Out Wide 260

Practice for "Counter-Pressing After Losing Possession During Combination Play" 262
Counter-Pressing After Losing Possession During Short Combination Play in a Conditioned Game 263

MEET THE AUTHOR: ATHANASIOS TERZIS

- **UEFA 'A' Coaching Licence**
- **M.S.C. in Coaching and Conditioning**
- **Greek Football Federation Instructor (HFF)**
- **Former Coach of Professional Teams in Greece**
- **Former Coach of Semi-Pro Teams in Greece**
- **Former Technical Director of DOXA Dramas Academy** (Greek 2nd division)
- **Former Professional Football Player**

Athanasios Terzis is a football tactics expert and is regularly invited as an instructor to many coaching seminars and workshops around the world.

Athanasios has written many successful football coaching books published by **SoccerTutor.com**, which have sold thousands of copies worldwide in multiple languages (English, Spanish, German, Italian, Greek, Japanese, Korean, and Chinese):

- **Pep Guardiola Attacking Tactics - Tactical Analysis and Sessions from Manchester City's 4-3-3** (2019)
- **Creative Attacking Play - From the Tactics of Conte, Allegri, Simeone, Mourinho, Wenger & Klopp** (2017)
- **Marcelo Bielsa - Coaching Build Up Play Against High Pressing Teams** (2017)
- **Coaching the Juventus 3-5-2 - Tactical Analysis and Sessions: Attacking and Defending** (2016)
- **Jürgen Klopp's Attacking and Defending Tactics: Tactical Analysis and Sessions from Borussia Dortmund's 4-2-3-1** (2015)
- **FC Barcelona Training Sessions: 160 Practices from 34 Tactical Situations** (2014)
  * Winner of Italian FA Award for "Best Coaching Book" 2014
- **Jose Mourinho's Real Madrid - A Tactical Analysis: Attacking and Defending in the 4-2-3-1** (2012)
- **FC Barcelona - A Tactical Analysis: Attacking and Defending** (2012)

DIEGO SIMEONE'S ACHIEVEMENTS

Coaching Roles

- Atlético Madrid (2011 - Present)
- Racing Club (2011)
- Catalania (2011)
- San Lorenzo (2009 - 2010)
- River Plate (2007 - 2008)
- Estudiantes La Plata (2006 - 2007)
- Racing Club (2006)

Honours

- Spanish La Liga Primera División (2014)
- UEFA Champions League Runner-up (2014 & 2016)
- UEFA Europa League (2012 & 2018)
- UEFA Super Cup (2012 & 2018)
- Argentine Primera División (2006 & 2008)
- Copa Del Rey (2013)
- Supercopa de España (2014)

Individual Awards

- European Coach of the Season (2012)
- La Liga Coach of the Year (2013, 2014 & 2016)
- IFFHS World's Best Club Coach (2016)
- Miguel Muñoz Trophy (2014 & 2016)
- Globe Soccer Master Coach Special Award (2017)

SIMEONE'S INCREDIBLE SUCCESS WITH ATLÉTICO MADRID AGAINST THE ODDS

LA LIGA

2014 CHAMPION

Fewest Goals Conceded:
- 2012-13 (31)
- 2013-14 (26)
- 2015-16 (18)
- 2016-17 (27)
- 2017-18 (22)
- 2018-19 (29)

Most Clean Sheets:
- 2012-13 (20)
- 2013-14 (20)
- 2015-16 (24)
- 2016-17 (20)
- 2017-18 (23)
- 2018-19 (20)

UEFA CHAMPIONS LEAGUE

 +

2014 RUNNER-UP **2016 RUNNER-UP**

UEFA EUROPA LEAGUE

 +

2012 CHAMPION **2018 CHAMPION**

UEFA SUPER CUP

 +

2012 CHAMPION **2018 CHAMPION**

COPA DEL REY

2013 CHAMPION

* Trophy images from **PIXSECTOR.com**

©SOCCERTUTOR.COM

DIEGO SIMEONE'S DEFENDING TACTICS

The Winning Culture at Atlético Madrid Under Diego Simeone

During his years at Atlético Madrid, Diego Simeone has managed to build an extraordinarily strong team which has won or been the runners-up of the most significant titles against all odds.

The Argentine coach brought with him a culture of commitment, passion, aggressiveness, and determination. From the first moment of his arrival at Atlético Madrid, he made it clear that nobody and nothing is above the team and in order to achieve greatness, the players have to give everything and work all together within a strong team spirit.

This culture was, from the first day, transferred to the players and since the beginning of Diego Simeone's era, it is more than obvious that they fight in every match like warriors and are willing to support each other until the very end.

Teamwork is paramount as Atlético Madrid lack superstars like Messi and Ronaldo, who they have consistently competed against.

Even though they are forced to sell every big player like Falcao, Diego Costa and Griezmann and their budget is relatively low compared to other top clubs, they still remain the same ultra-competitive side that refuses to surrender.

Diego Simeone's Atlético Madrid era may not have produced a team which plays attractive and free-flowing football, but nobody can deny that they are often the toughest team to play against in the whole of Europe.

Diego Simeone's Atlético Madrid Tactics

The tactical organisation has had a lot to do with the culture that Diego Simeone has created at Atlético Madrid. Simeone built a game plan which relied on good defensive organisation.

The players must carry out their basic defensive tasks with commitment, passion, aggressiveness, and determination (elements of the culture brought by the Argentine).

This has made them extremely difficult to break down, even by the very top attacking sides, while Atlético have found great success in scoring goals with a counter attacking style and by exploiting set pieces.

ATLÉTICO MADRID'S 4-4-2 FORMATION
(2017-18 SEASON)

Atlético Madrid's First XI

Diego Simeone's Atlético Madrid team mainly use the 4-4-2 formation.

There were some matches where Simeone adapted and used the 4-1-4-1, 4-4-1-1 and 4-3-3 formations. However, this book will focus solely on how Atlético implemented the 4-4-2.

This was the first XI for Atlético during the 2017-18 season, with **Thomas (5)** the most regular change, making 50 appearances in central midfield.

Squad Players

Thomas (5) often played with **Saúl (8)** or in place of him if he moved into the right midfield position.

Lucas (19) made 44 appearances as cover at left back and centre back. **Savić (15)** and **Vrsaljko (16)** also played many games at centre back and right back respectively.

D. Costa (18) was bought in January 2018 and became a starter, while **Gameiro (21)** made 36 appearances as cover and often as a substitute.

ATLÉTICO MADRID'S 4-4-2 FORMATION
(2018-19 SEASON)

Atlético Madrid's First XI

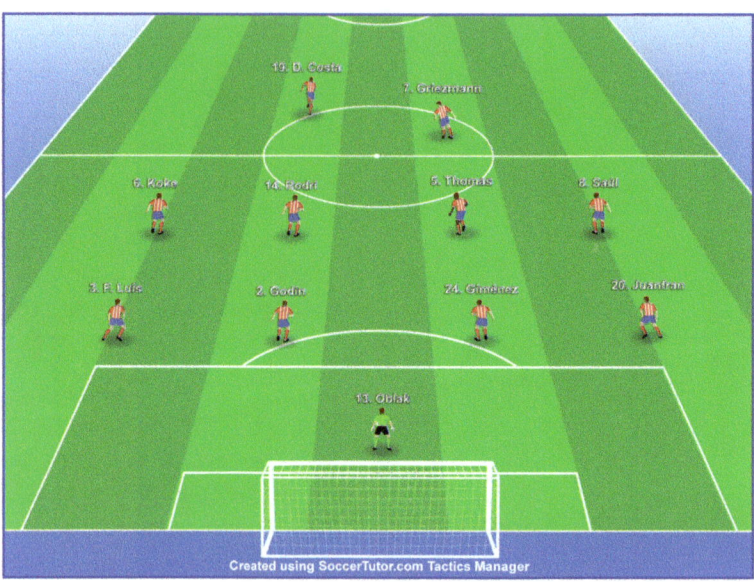

This was the first XI for Atlético during the 2018-19 season.

However, the wide midfielders were changed often:

- **Lemar (11)** made 43 appearances mainly as a left midfielder.
- **Correa (10)** made 49 appearances mainly as a right midfielder.

Squad Players

As explained above, **Lemar (11)** and **Correa (10)** often played as wide midfielders. They would play in place of **Koke (6)** or **Saúl (8)** if either of them was playing in central midfield and sometimes purely just because it was Diego Simeone's preference for a particular game.

Arias (4) made 33 appearances as cover at right back and **Morata (22)** made 17 appearances as a forward.

DIEGO SIMEONE'S DEFENDING TACTICS

ATLÉTICO MADRID PLAYERS

GOALKEEPER

Jan Oblak (13) has been one of Europe's most outstanding goalkeepers in the last few years, providing a high level of consistency and security for Atlético's goal.

CENTRE BACKS

Diego Godín (2) was a top class defender for Atlético, together with **Stefan Savić (15)** or the younger **Jose Giménez (24)**. Either would form a strong duo with **Godín (2)** in the centre of defence. All 3 centre backs are highly effective in aerial duels, as well as in duels on the ground.

FULL BACKS

Juanfran (20) and **Simo Vrsaljko (16)** at right back, together with **Filipe Luis (3)** and **Lucas Hernandez (19)** on the left, are very quick, good in 1v1 situations and are all capable of contributing well in the attacking phase too.

CENTRAL MIDFIELDERS

Gabi (14) was the player who could always play at a high tempo and with full energy for the entirety of the 90 minutes. His contribution was outstanding as he could fill every possible gap in midfield, as well as in the defensive line. **Gabi (14)** could also block through passes and apply heavy pressure in every single attempt. His tactical awareness was fantastic as well, as he read the game perfectly and applied the appropriate tactical response in each moment.

Gabi's (14) partner was the versatile **Saúl Niguez (8)** who is exceptionally good tactically and technically, as well as extremely hard-working, perfectly matching the demands of Simeone. **Thomas (5)** was often used in central midfield as well, playing a mainly defensive role.

During the 2018-19 season, **Rodri (14)** took over **Gabi's (14)** role and was partnered with **Saúl (8)** or **Thomas (5)** if **Saúl (8)** played as a right midfielder.

WIDE MIDFIELDERS

Angel Correa (11) and especially **Koke (6)** are not "winger-type" wide midfielders, and mainly play as inside midfielders. They are Atlético Madrid's most creative players. They can dribble, make key passes, and shoot well from long distance. In addition, during the defensive phase they are very hard-working players who provide a great contribution. **Saúl (8)** also played as a wide midfielder, mostly during the 2018-19 season.

FORWARDS

Antoine Griezmann (7), **Diego Costa (18/19)**, **Fernando Torres (9)** and **Kevin Gameiro (21)** are all quick and capable of playing on the counter attack. They are highly effective in dribbling and finishing. During the defensive phase, they played a crucial role as they controlled their zone of responsibility effectively using well-coordinated movements.

COACHING FORMAT

1. TACTICAL SITUATION AND ANALYSIS

- The analysis is based on recurring patterns of play observed within **Diego Simeone's Atlético Madrid** team. Once the same phase of play occurred several times (at least 10), the tactics would be seen as a pattern.
- Each action, pass, individual movement (with or without the ball) and the positioning of each player on the pitch including their body shape, are presented with a full description.

2. FULL TRAINING SESSION FROM THE TACTICAL SITUATION

- Technical and Functional Practices, Tactical Practices and Games
- Objective and Full Description
- Restrictions, Progressions, Variations & Coaching Points (if applicable)

KEY

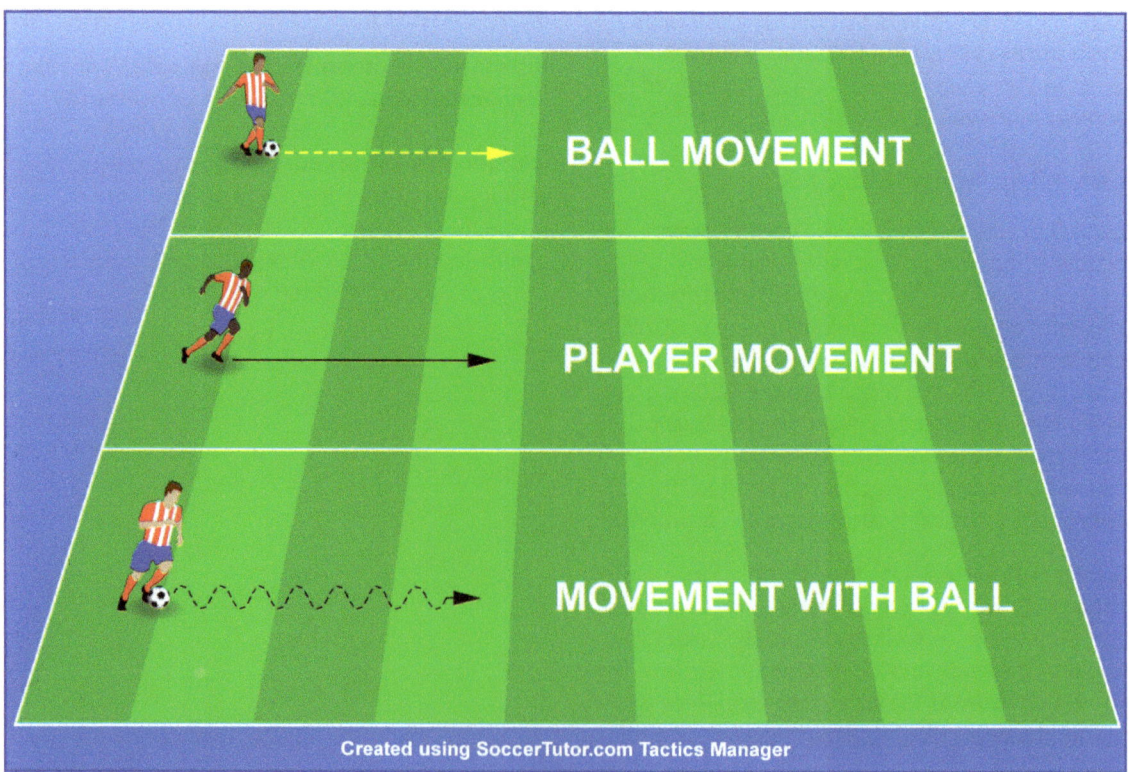

THE DEFENSIVE PHASE

THE DEFENSIVE PHASE (WHEN THE OPPOSITION HAVE POSSESSION)

Atlético Madrid's success under Diego Simeone is mainly based on their tactics in the defensive phase and the transition from defence to attack.

Atletico have some basic aims to carry out during the defensive phase. These aims are achieved through specific tactical behaviour and are as follows:

1. Forcing the Ball Wide to Limit Available Options, Block Inside Passes and Win Possession

- Controlling the opposing centre backs by preventing them from receiving in free space and moving forward with the ball to play through passes

- Blocking defenders' through passes from central and wide areas towards opponents positioned within the **Crucial Central Area**

- Keeping the space between the forwards and midfielders limited

- Preventing the opposing midfielders from receiving in between the forward and midfield lines, turning, and playing through passes

2. Forcing the Ball Wide to Limit Available Options and Block Inside Passes to Win Possession

- Control wide areas to prevent passes towards the inside when the full backs receive in advanced positions

- Block passes towards the inside when the full backs receive with intelligent positioning

- Win possession by applying double marking when wide midfielders receive within limited space

- Intercepting long passes directed to wide midfielders during switches of play by wide positioned full backs

3. Dealing with Opponents that Receive Inside the Crucial Central Area

- Keep the space between the defenders and midfielders limited

- Double mark opponents who receive and prevent them from turning towards the inside, with good cooperation of the defenders and the midfielders

4. Neutralising Long Passes Played to the Forwards

- Tight marking of the forwards within each defender's zone of responsibility, which neutralises passes or limits their time and space immediately

NOTE: To analyse the tactics applied by Diego Simeone's Atletico Madrid team in this book, we will firstly present the tactical behaviour of each line separately and then we will move on to how the players of each block (front block and rear block) cooperate to deal with the tactical problems created by the opposition.

TACTICAL SITUATION 1

Positioning and Defensive Movements of the Forwards

The content in this section is from analysis of Diego Simeone's Atlético Madrid teams during the 2017/2018 and 2018/2019 seasons.

The analysis is based on recurring patterns of play observed within the Atlético Madrid team. Once the same phase of play occurred several times (at least 10), the tactics would be seen as a pattern. The analysis on the following pages are examples of the team's tactics being used effectively.

Each action, pass, individual movement with or without the ball, and the positioning of each player on the pitch including their body shape, are presented.

The analysis is then used to create a practice to coach this specific tactical situation.

Tactical Situation 1 - Positioning and Defensive Movements of the Forwards

BALANCED DEFENSIVE POSITIONING OF THE 2 FORWARDS AGAINST 2 CENTRE BACKS

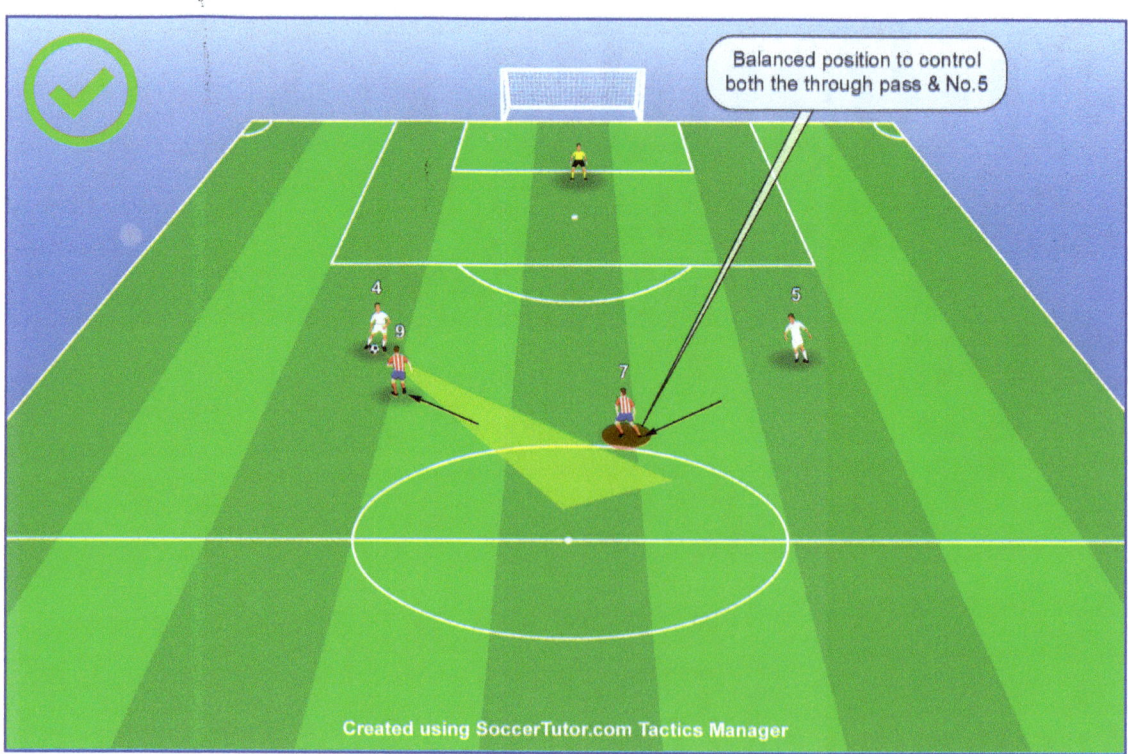

The 2 Atlético Madrid forwards work together with the aim of keeping the space between them and the midfielders limited.

The closest forward to the player in possession **Torres (9)** moves to press the ball and the other forward **Griezmann (7)** drops back at a diagonal angle.

Griezmann (7) takes a balanced position while shifting across to control a potential through pass (narrowing the passing lane) and control the other white centre back No.5.

Tactical Situation 1 - Positioning and Defensive Movements of the Forwards

UNBALANCED DEFENSIVE POSITIONING OF THE 2 FORWARDS AGAINST 2 CENTRE BACKS

Unbalanced Positioning Creates Problems with Space Created for Opposing Centre Back to Receive and Dribble Forward

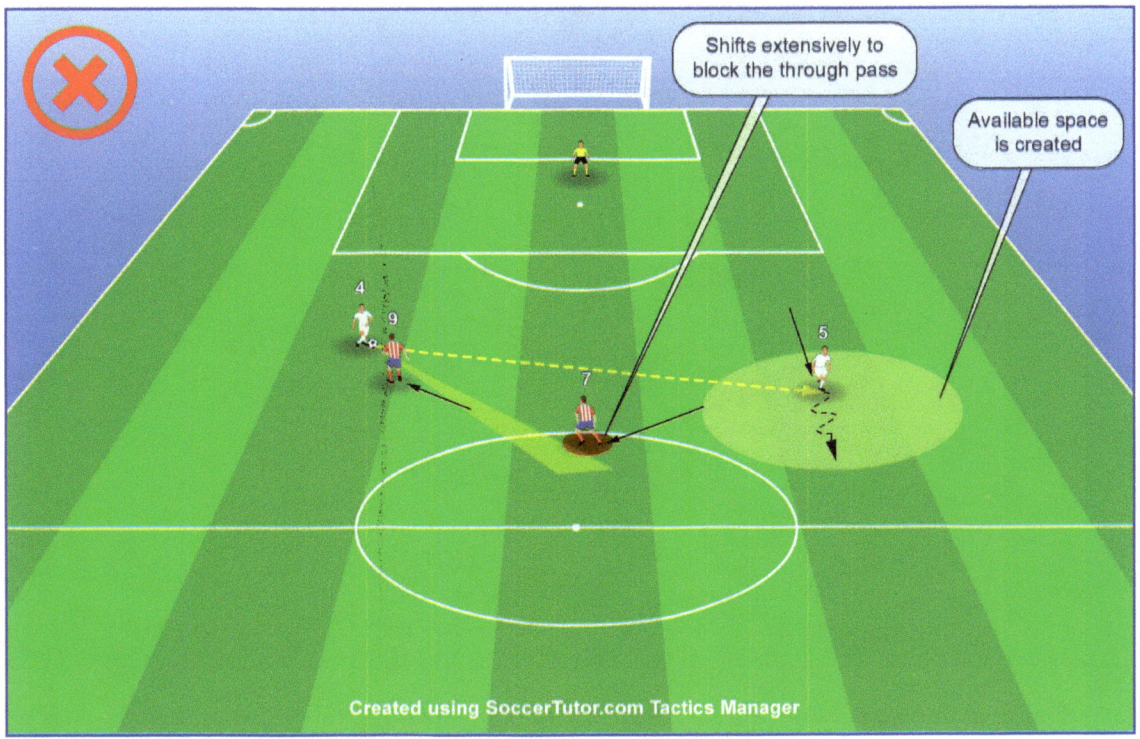

If the deepest forward **Griezmann (7)** shifts across further to focus on narrowing the passing lane (preventing a through pass), then available space is created for the white left centre back No.5 to receive from his team-mate.

The white No.5 is able to receive easily from No.4 and move forward with available time and space. This then enables the ball carrier to play successful through passes, as there is no longer a safety distance between him and the Atlético midfielders (this will be fully analysed later on in the book).

As balance is lost for Atlético, the forward **Griezmann (7)** will have to sprint a few yards across to restore it and close white No.5 down.

Tactical Situation 1 - Positioning and Defensive Movements of the Forwards

BALANCED DEFENSIVE POSITIONING OF THE FORWARDS MIRRORED BY CENTRAL MIDFIELDERS

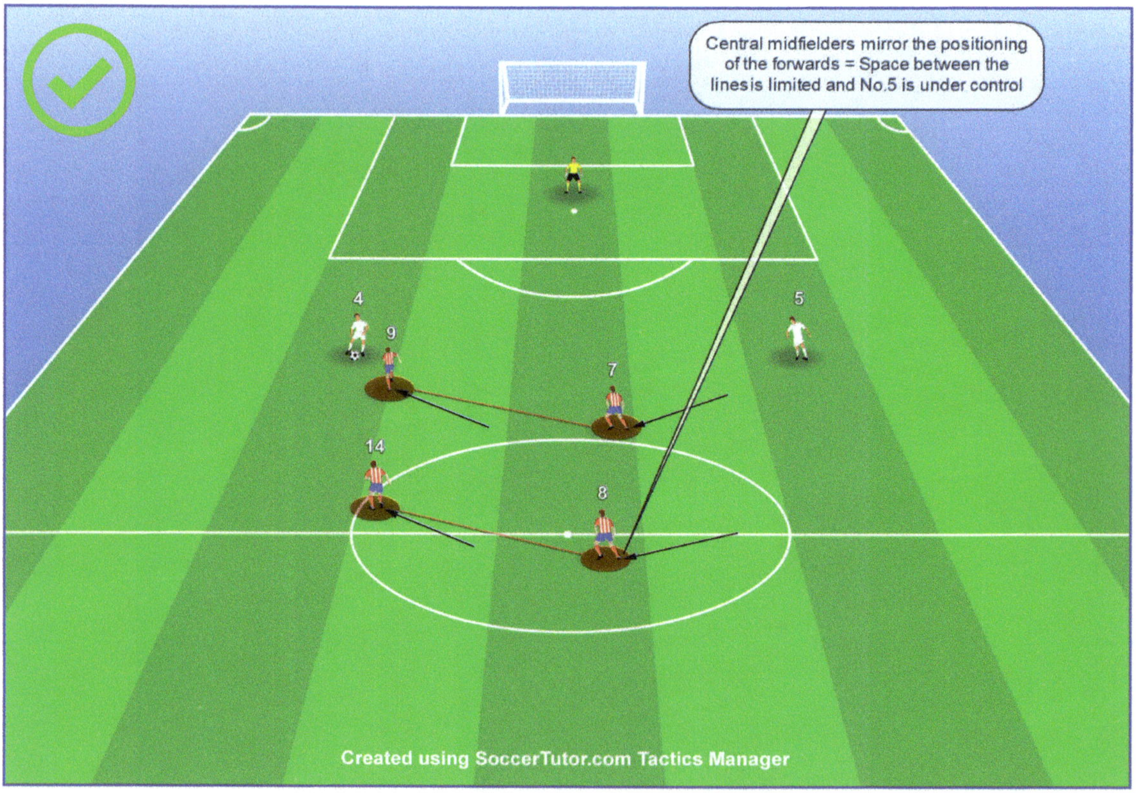

Cohesion in Positioning Between the Forwards and the Central Midfielders Restricts Space Between the Lines

As long as the position of the deepest forward **Griezmann (7)** is balanced and the positioning of both forwards is mirrored by the positioning of the 2 central midfielders **Gabi (14)** & **Saúl (8)**, the opposing white centre back without the ball (No.5) is under control.

At the same time, the space between the lines (attack and midfield) is kept limited.

©SOCCERTUTOR.COM

DIEGO SIMEONE'S DEFENDING TACTICS

PRACTICE FOR "POSITIONING AND DEFENSIVE MOVEMENTS OF THE FORWARDS"

DIEGO SIMEONE'S DEFENDING TACTICS

Tactical Situation 1 - Positioning and Defensive Movements of the Forwards

PRACTICE FOR THIS TACTICAL SITUATION
Forwards Retain Balance and Deny Space Between the Lines in a 4 v 5 (+GK) Functional Practice

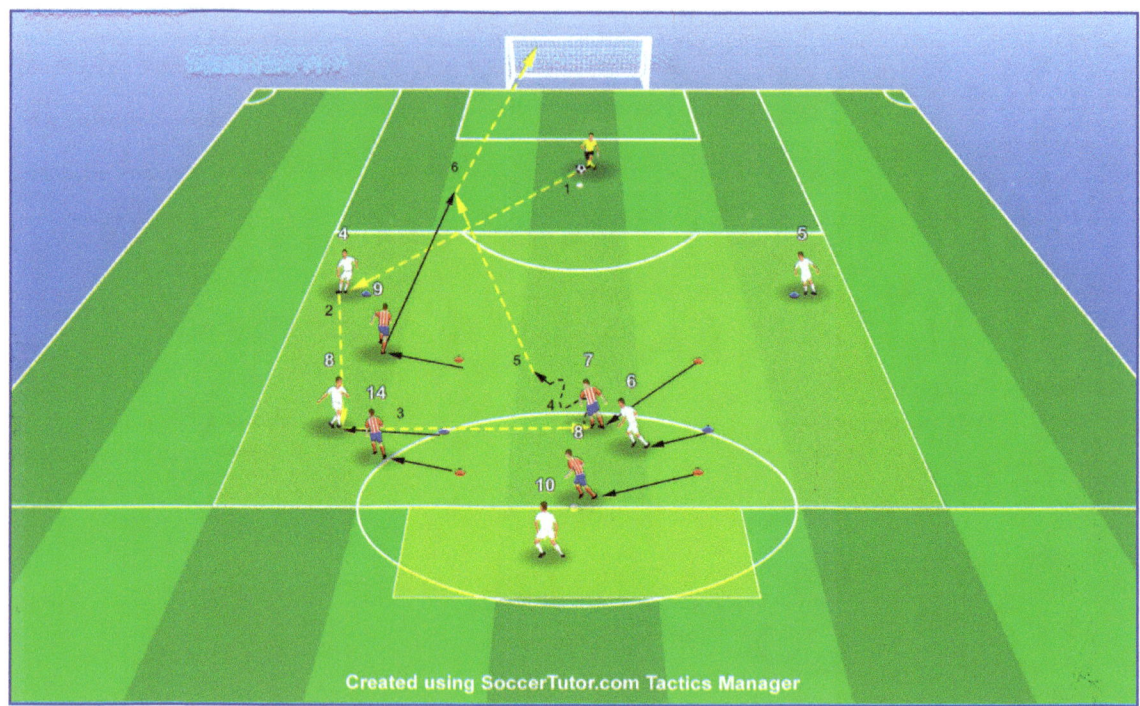

Objective: Prevent through passes or a switch of play with correct positioning when the opposition build-up play from the back.

Description
- We have a 4v4 situation inside the main area, with 2 red forwards **(7 & 9)** and 2 red central midfielders **(14 & 8)** against 2 white centre backs and 2 white central midfielders.
- There is an extra white player (No.10) in the yellow target area.
- The practice starts with the GK's pass and the players start on their respective cones.
- The whites aim to move the ball to No.10 (yellow area) either with a direct pass from the defenders or with help from the midfielders.
- The reds aim to stop the white team playing into the yellow area by using the correct positioning of the 2 forwards, who shift together with synchronised movements, limit the space between the lines and control the players on the weak side.
- After winning possession, the reds try to score past the GK via a counter attack within 8 seconds.

Coaching Points
1. Use the correct angles and body shape to block through passes.
2. Deny space between the lines.
3. Launch a quick counter attack as soon as the ball is won (go direct to goal).

DIEGO SIMEONE'S DEFENDING TACTICS

TACTICAL SITUATION 2

Defensive Reactions when the Positioning of 1 Forward is Incorrect

The content in this section is from analysis of Diego Simeone's Atlético Madrid teams during the 2017/2018 and 2018/2019 seasons.

The analysis is based on recurring patterns of play observed within the Atlético Madrid team. Once the same phase of play occurred several times (at least 10), the tactics would be seen as a pattern. The analysis on the following pages are examples of the team's tactics being used effectively.

Each action, pass, individual movement with or without the ball, and the positioning of each player on the pitch including their body shape, are presented.

The analysis is then used to create a practice to coach this specific tactical situation.

Tactical Situation 2 - Defensive Reactions when the Positioning of 1 Forward is Incorrect

CONTROLLING OPPOSING MIDFIELDERS (AGAINST 2 CENTRE BACKS AND 2 CENTRAL MIDFIELDERS)

a. Reaction of the Forward when his Team-mate is in an Incorrect Position

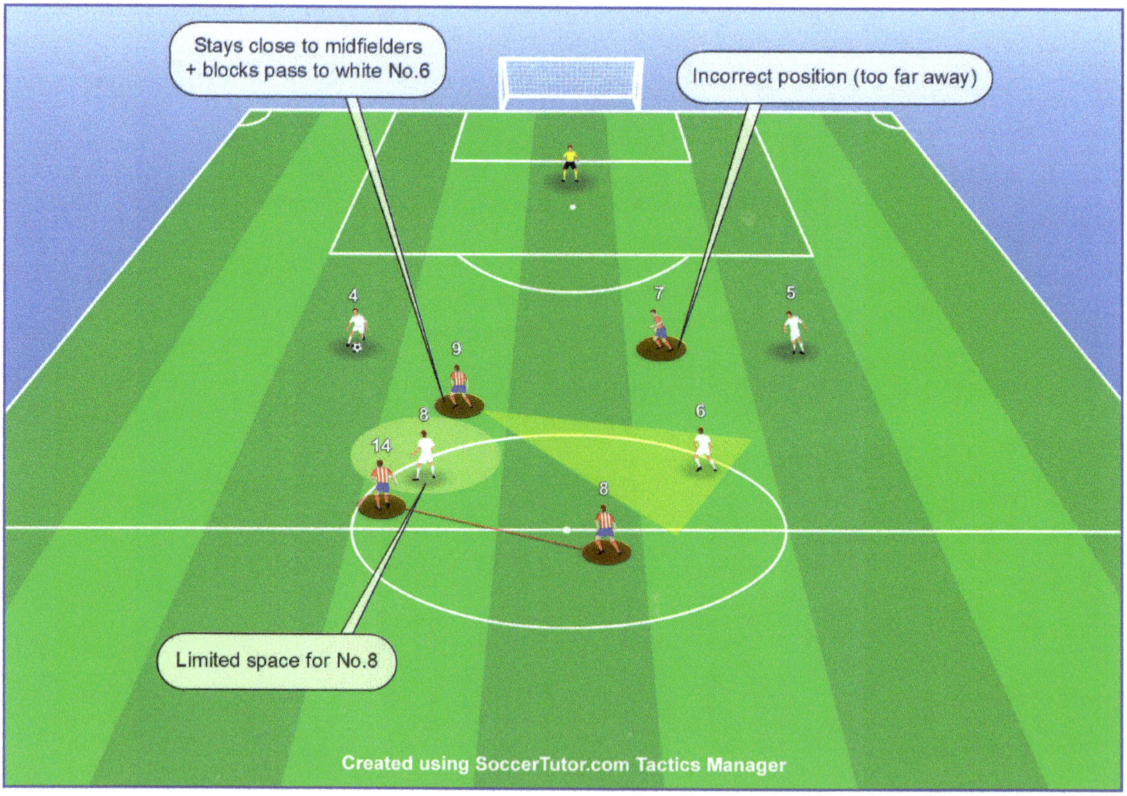

When an opposing centre back is in possession, the forward closest to him should normally move to press the ball and limit the available space and time. However, it is not always the right time to move forward to put the man in possession under pressure.

In this situation, **Griezmann (7)** is too far away (advanced) to quickly drop back diagonally behind his team-mate, so it is better for the deepest forward **Torres (9)** to stay close to the midfielders.

The aim is to prevent the pass to the opposing central midfielder (No.6) by narrowing the passing lane and keeping the available space for No.8 limited.

Torres (9) has to wait until **Griezmann (7)** drops back. As soon as he is in a suitable defensive position, it is the right time for **Torres (9)** to move forward and put pressure on the player in possession.

DIEGO SIMEONE'S DEFENDING TACTICS

Tactical Situation 2 - Defensive Reactions when the Positioning of 1 Forward is Incorrect

b. Applying Double Marking when the Opposing Centre Back Passes to the Central Midfielder on the Strong Side

In this tactical example, **Torres' (9)** positioning enables him to block the pass to the central midfielder on the weak side (No.6).

This forces the white centre back No.4 to pass to the central midfielder on the strong side (No.8).

As there is limited space available in the centre of the pitch, the deepest Atlético forward **Torres (9)** and the central midfielder on that side **Gabi (14)** are able to quickly apply double marking on the new ball carrier.

Tactical Situation 2 - Defensive Reactions when the Positioning of 1 Forward is Incorrect

CORRECT DEFENSIVE REACTION WHEN THE CENTRE BACK MOVES FORWARD WITH THE BALL

The 2 Forwards Block the Inside Pass and Keep the Space Between the Lines Limited

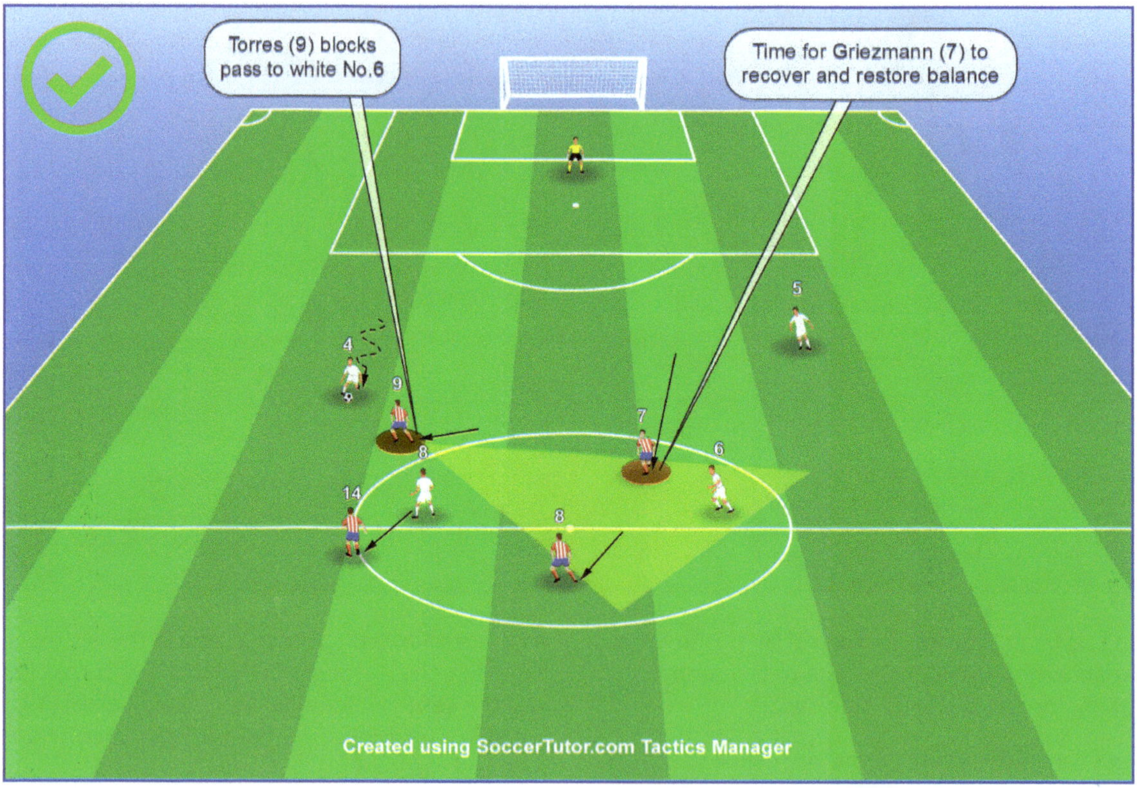

If the opposing centre back in possession (No.4) moves forward with the ball, the deepest forward **Torres (9)** drops back and across to cover the ball carrier, stays close to the midfield line and prevents the pass to white No.6 on the weak side.

This defensive reaction gives time for **Griezmann (7)** to drop back, take up an effective defensive position and restore balance in the positioning of the Atlético midfielders and forwards.

DIEGO SIMEONE'S DEFENDING TACTICS

Tactical Situation 2 - Defensive Reactions when the Positioning of 1 Forward is Incorrect

BAD TIMING IN PRESSING THE BALL CREATES SPACE IN THE CENTRE

Forward Moves to Press Ball with the Other Forward in an Incorrect Position and Space is Created in the Centre

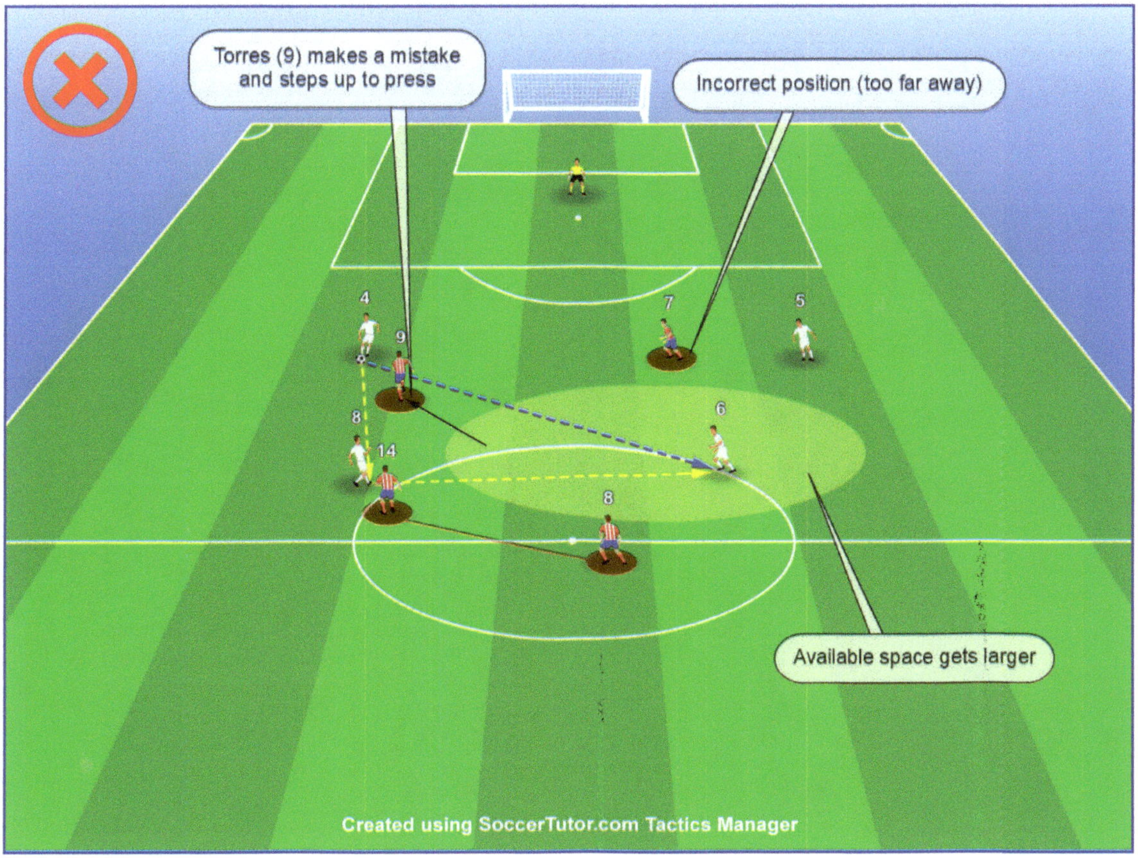

In this variation of the previous tactical example, **Griezmann (7)** again starts in an incorrect advanced position.

Torres (9) makes a mistake and decides to step up and press the white centre back No.4 before **Griezmann (7)** has been able to drop back.

As a consequence, the available space for the opposing central midfielders and especially for the white No.6 gets larger.

The ball can be directed to No.6 through a direct pass or via a link player (No.8).

As soon as white No.6 receives, both forwards are neutralised (out of the game) and the opposing midfielder has available time and space on the ball to find the next pass, which is highly likely to be a through pass.

DIEGO SIMEONE'S DEFENDING TACTICS

Tactical Situation 2 - Defensive Reactions when the Positioning of 1 Forward is Incorrect

GOOD TIMING PRESSING THE BALL (AGAINST 2 CENTRE BACKS AND 2 CENTRAL MIDFIELDERS)

Forward Moves to Press Ball Once the Other Forward is Able to Drop Back and Block All Passing Options

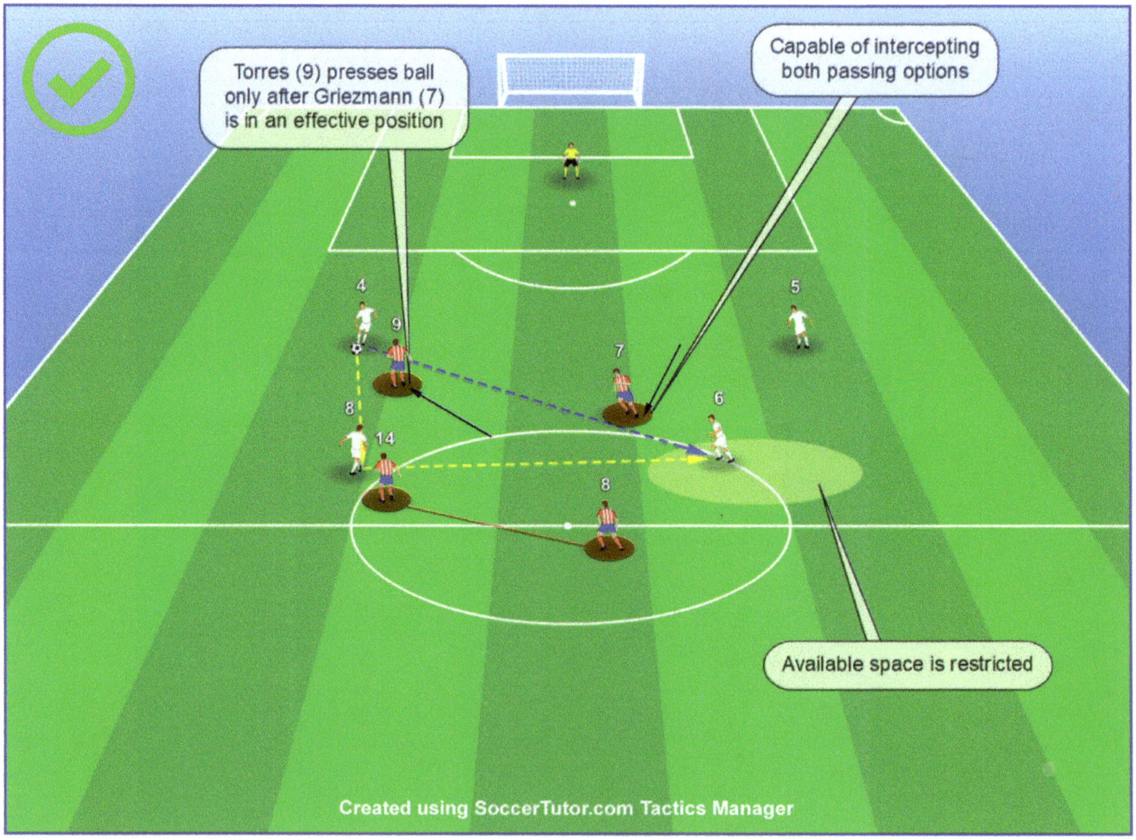

In this variation of the previous example, both Atlético forwards react quickly in this tactical situation.

Torres (9) waits until the other forward **Griezmann (7)** has dropped back into a suitable position, and then moves forward to close white No.4 down.

Griezmann's (7) position restricts the space between the lines and enables him to be capable of intercepting either the direct pass to white No.6 or the pass to him via No.8.

Even if white No.6 manages to receive, he will be immediately pressed by **Griezmann (7)**.

Tactical Situation 2 - Defensive Reactions when the Positioning of 1 Forward is Incorrect

BAD TIMING PRESSING THE BALL (AGAINST 2 CENTRE BACKS AND 3 CENTRAL MIDFIELDERS)

1. Forward Moves to Press Ball with Other Forward in an Incorrect Position and the Defensive Midfielder Receives in the Centre

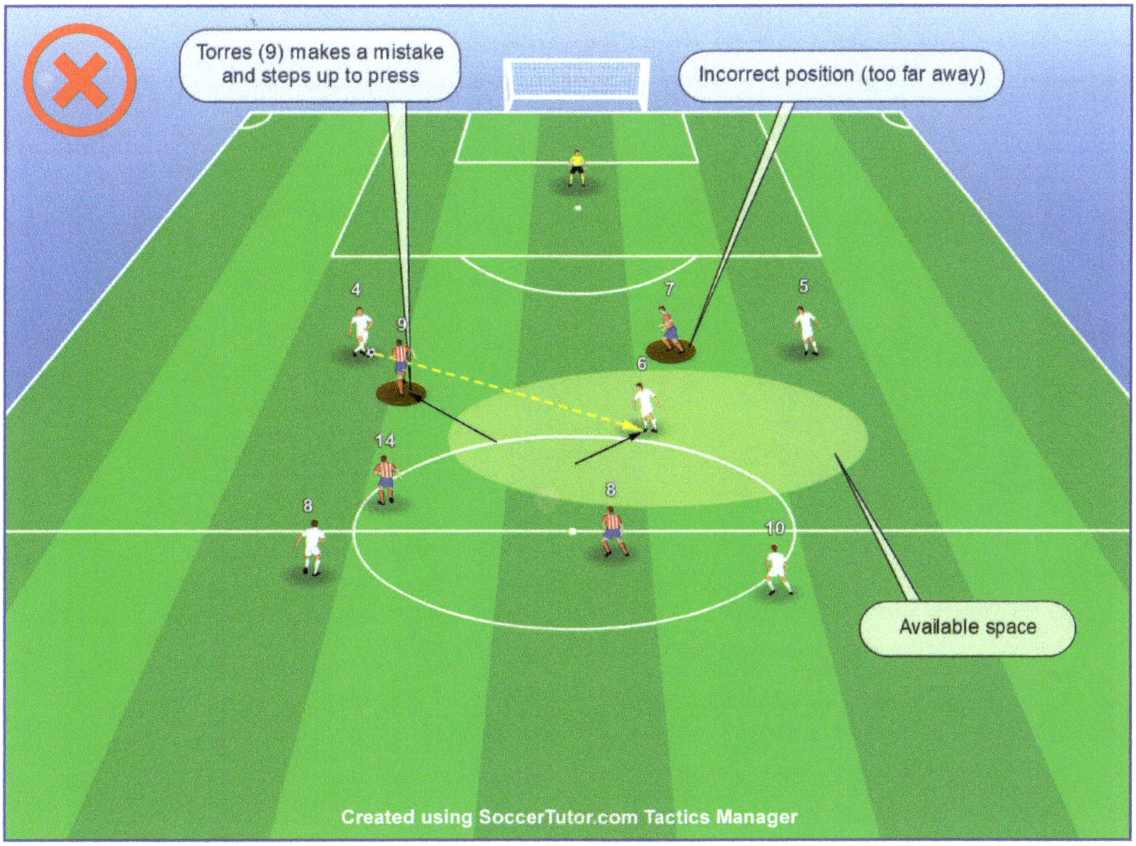

If the opposition have 1 defensive midfielder (No.6) and 2 attacking midfielders (No.8 & No.10), the Atlético forwards should deal with the situation in the same way as they did against 2 central midfielders (**see previous page**), otherwise a problem can arise.

As the most advanced forward **Griezmann (7)** is in an incorrect position and **Torres (9)** moves forward to press the ball (poor decision making), space is created between the lines.

The white defensive midfielder (No.6) moves into the available space, which will enable him to receive free of marking and then make a forward pass.

As **Torres (9)** hasn't taken a balanced position to prevent the pass, the player in possession (white centre back No.4) passes directly to No.6 in the available space.

DIEGO SIMEONE'S DEFENDING TACTICS

Tactical Situation 2 - Defensive Reactions when the Positioning of 1 Forward is Incorrect

2. Forward Blocks the Direct Pass and the Defensive Midfielder Receives After a Pass from a Link Player

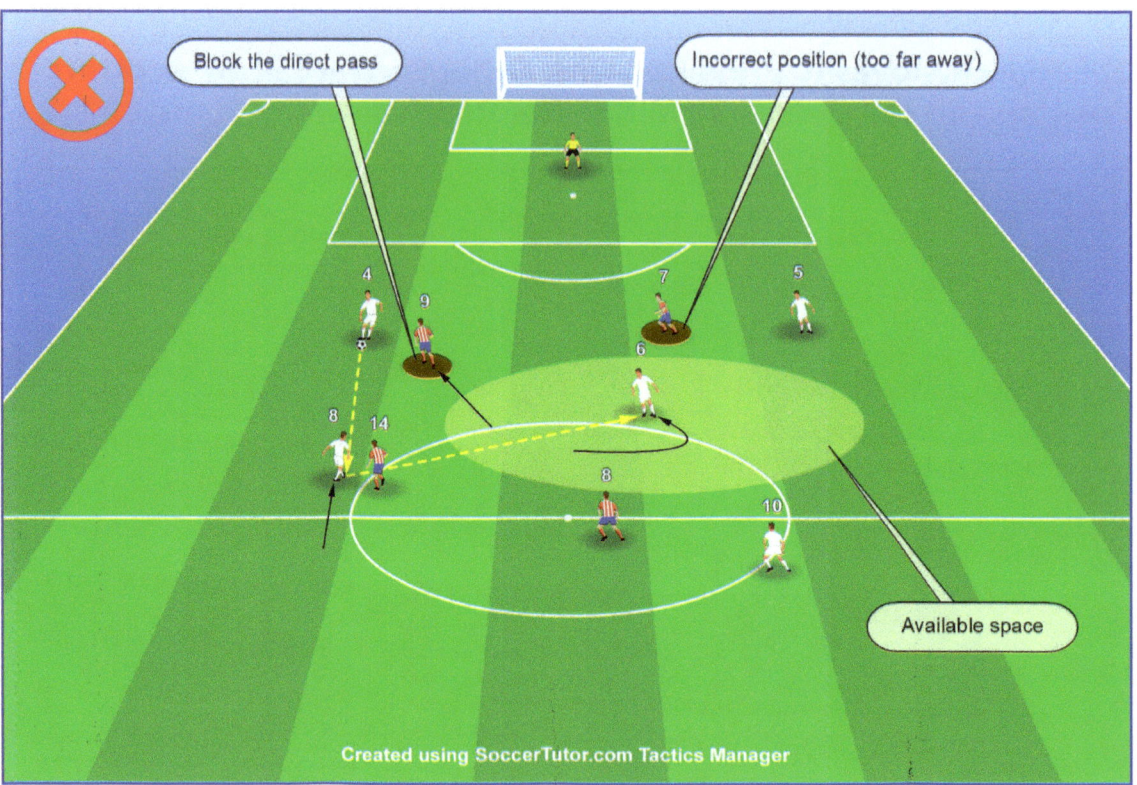

In this variation of the previous example, the forward **Torres (9)** now presses in a way which blocks the direct pass to white No.6.

However, the ball is still played successfully to white No.6 via the attacking midfielder (No.8), who drops back to become a link player.

Both these situations presented lead to the white defensive midfielder (No.6) receiving in the centre with available time on the ball.

This can result in a through pass into a dangerous area for the Atlético defence (which will be analysed later in the book).

Tactical Situation 2 - Defensive Reactions when the Positioning of 1 Forward is Incorrect

ASSESSMENT

1. The appropriate reaction to this tactical situation is very similar to the one shown on page 26. **Torres (9)** does not move forward to press the ball and instead stays close to his midfielders. With this correct decision making, the space between the lines is limited, the pass towards the opposing defensive midfielder (white No.6) is blocked and time is given for the second forward **Griezmann (7)** to recover and drop back into an effective position.

2. The tactical situations displayed in this section highlight the importance of good decision making from the forwards in the defensive phase, and especially the right moment to press the ball.

PRACTICE FOR "DEFENSIVE REACTIONS WHEN THE POSITIONING OF 1 FORWARD IS INCORRECT"

Tactical Situation 2 - Defensive Reactions when the Positioning of 1 Forward is Incorrect

PRACTICE FOR THIS TACTICAL SITUATION
Defensive Reactions when the Positioning of 1 Forward is Incorrect in a Zonal Practice
1/2: Defensive Reactions and Movements

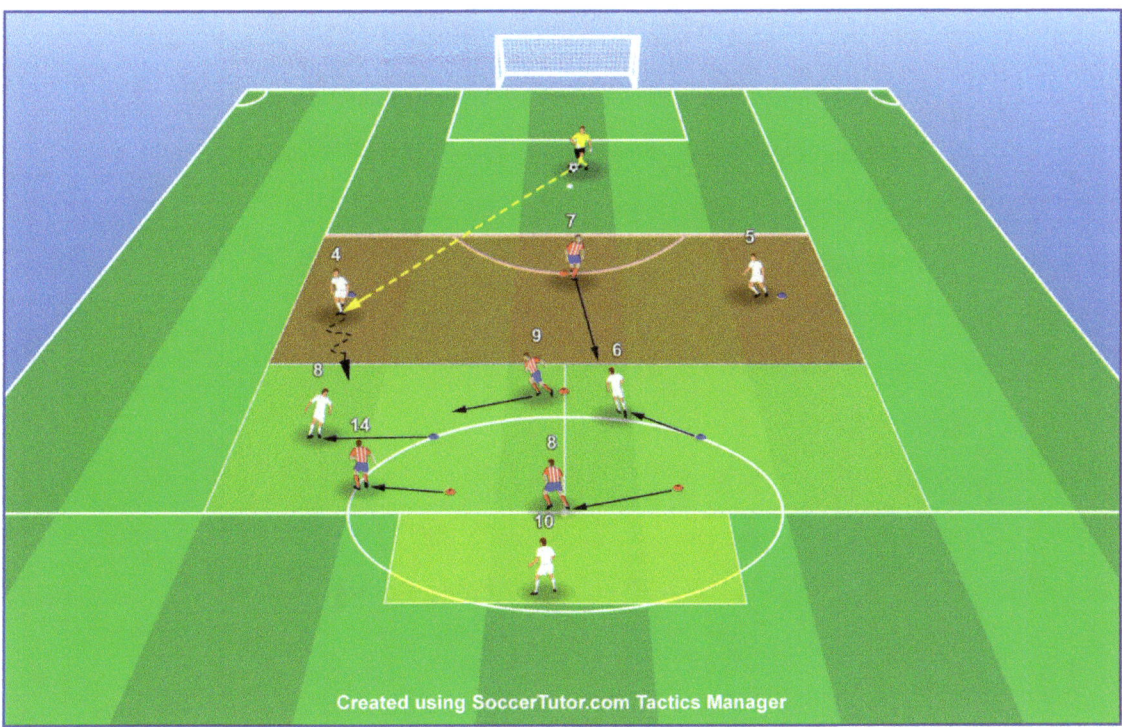

Objective: Prevent a through pass or a switch of play until the advanced forward is able to drop back into an effective position.

Description (1/2)

- Mark out 4 areas as shown. The GK is positioned in the penalty area and the outfield players all start from positions indicated by the cones.
- The GK starts the practice by passing to one of the white centre backs (No.4 or No.5).
- The aim for the white centre backs is to move the ball to No.10 (within the yellow area) either directly or via one of the midfielders.

- The reds try to stop them with the correct defensive reaction of the deepest forward (9), who stays close to his midfielders to block the passing options.
- The aim is to give enough time to the more advanced forward (7) to drop back into an effective position.
- The practice description continues on the following page...

Tactical Situation 2 - Defensive Reactions when the Positioning of 1 Forward is Incorrect

2/2: Win Ball and Counter Attack

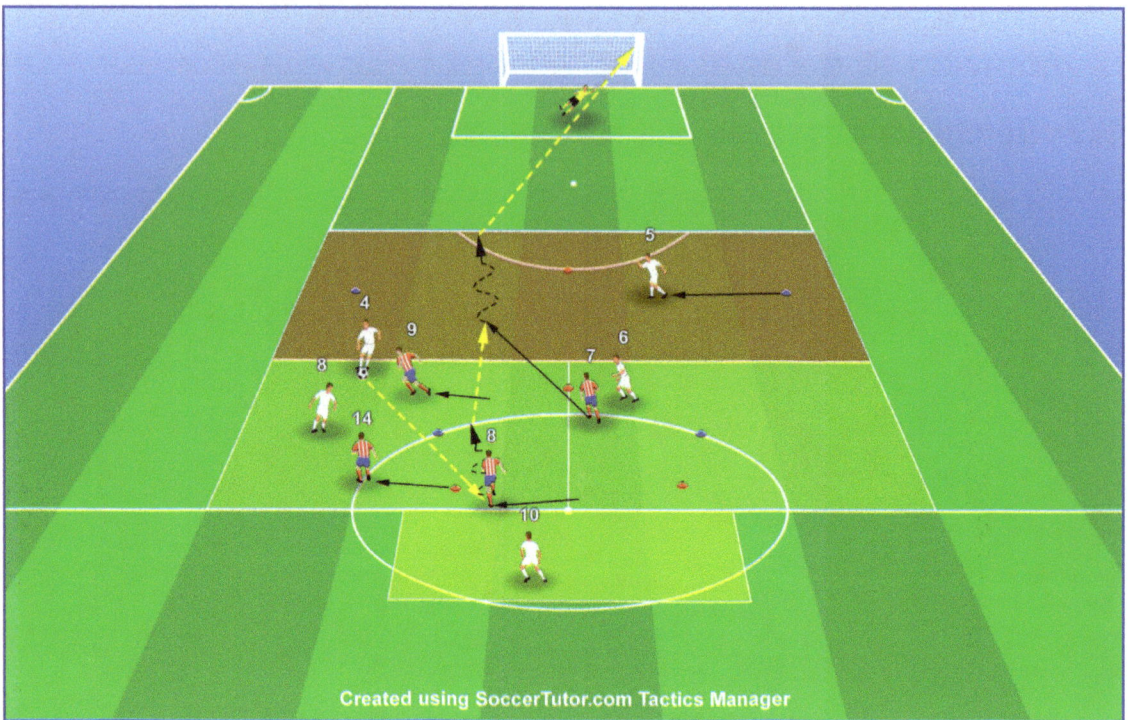

Description (2/2)

- Once the advanced forward **(7)** has dropped back into an effective defensive position, the other forward **(9)** can press the ball.

- The red team are now able to block all passing options and try to win the ball.

- If they win the ball, they launch a very quick direct counter attack, trying to score past the GK in the large goal within 8 seconds.

Coaching Points

1. Use the correct angles and body shape to block through passes.
2. Stop the switch of play with well-timed pressing.
3. Launch a quick counter attack as soon as the ball is won (go direct to goal).

 **ASSESSMENT**

This practice can be easily adjusted to play against the 4-3-3 formation.

©SOCCERTUTOR.COM   DIEGO SIMEONE'S DEFENDING TACTICS

TACTICAL SITUATION 3

Positioning of the Forwards to Prepare for Counter Attacks

The content in this section is from analysis of Diego Simeone's Atlético Madrid teams during the 2017/2018 and 2018/2019 seasons.

The analysis is based on recurring patterns of play observed within the Atlético Madrid team. Once the same phase of play occurred several times (at least 10), the tactics would be seen as a pattern. The analysis on the following pages are examples of the team's tactics being used effectively.

Each action, pass, individual movement with or without the ball, and the positioning of each player on the pitch including their body shape, are presented.

The analysis is then used to create a practice to coach this specific tactical situation.

Tactical Situation 3 - Positioning of the Forwards to Prepare for Counter Attacks

POSITIONING OF THE FORWARDS TO PREPARE FOR COUNTER ATTACKS AGAINST 2 CENTRE BACKS

In order to increase the chances of scoring counter attacks in the 2017-18 season (and after the return of **Diego Costa** from Chelsea FC), Diego Simeone positioned his forwards to be prepared for the counter attack during the defensive phase in several matches.

One of the forwards (usually **Diego Costa**) stayed in an advanced position between the 2 opposing centre backs, while the other forward (**Griezmann**) was in a deeper position to create a formation that looked like a 4-4-1-1.

This positioning looked like the incorrect positioning mentioned in the previous section: Tactical Situation 2 - Defensive Reactions when the Positioning of 1 Forward is Incorrect.

Despite being more effective for a potential counter attack than the usual defensive positioning, it left more available space for the opposition to exploit between the lines.

1. Positioning and Movements of the Central Midfielders and Forwards in Preparation for a Potential Counter Attack

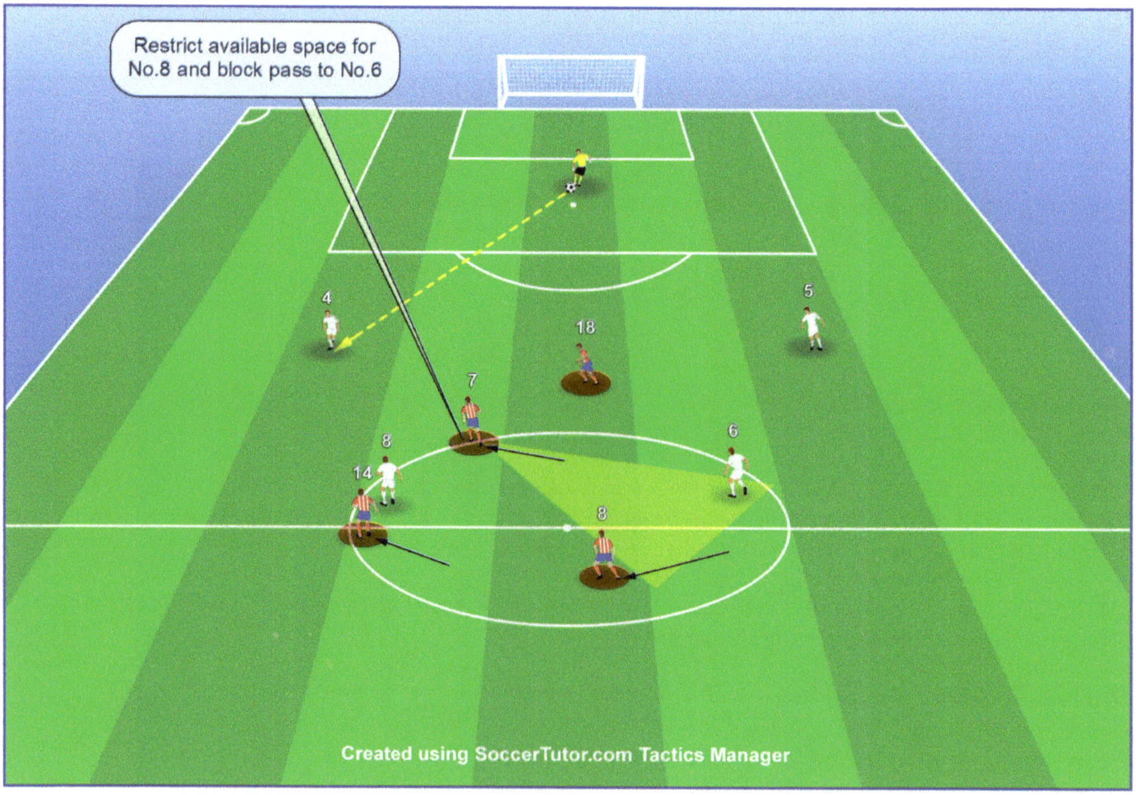

Tactical Situation 3 - Positioning of the Forwards to Prepare for Counter Attacks

As the GK passes to the centre back (No.4), the Atlético players shift towards the strong side, except for **D. Costa (18)** who stays positioned between the 2 centre backs.

The aim of the deepest forward remains the same as in the previous section:
Tactical Situation 2 - Defensive Reactions when the Positioning of 1 Forward is Incorrect.

Griezmann (7) has to:

1. Stay close to the midfielders to restrict the available space for the white central midfielder on the strong side (No.8).
2. Prevent the pass towards the white central midfielder on the weak side (No.6).

The positioning of **D. Costa (18)** in this situation enables Atlético to create a direct attacking threat if they win the ball in a favourable position. This is because **D. Costa (18)** can exploit the space between the 2 white centre backs and potentially receive a pass very close to the goal.

ASSESSMENT

Further analysis about the effectiveness of counter attack-minded positioning of the forwards during the transition from defence to attack is included in the second part of this book set (Diego Simeone's Attacking Tactics: Tactical Analysis and Sessions from Atlético Madrid's 4-4-2).

Tactical Situation 2 - Defensive Reactions when the Positioning of 1 Forward is Incorrect

2. The Advanced Forward Blocks the Inside Pass and the Opposition are Forced to Play Wide

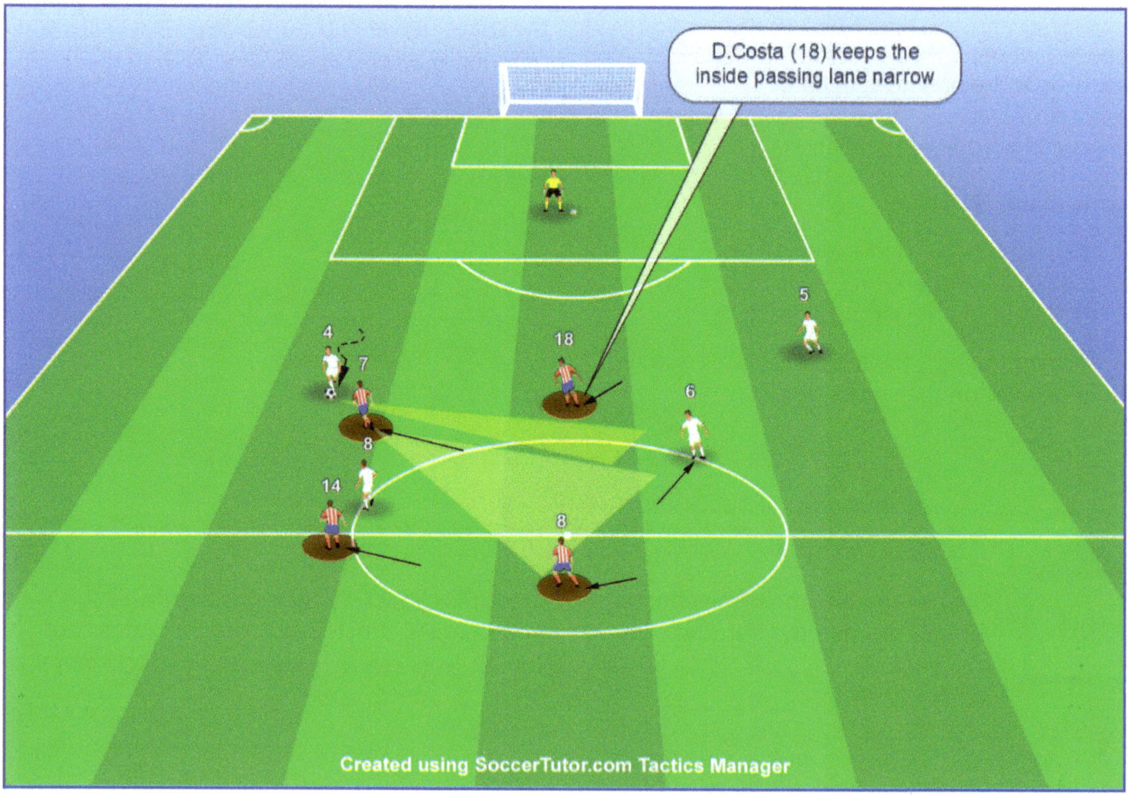

As the centre back No.4 moves forward with the ball, **Griezmann (7)** shifts across to close him down.

D. Costa (18) drops a few yards back to prevent white central midfielder No.6 receiving a pass from No.4, while maintaining a counter attack-minded position at the same time.

The space between the lines is kept limited enough and the opposition's attack becomes predictable, as the ball is forced towards one side.

Tactical Situation 3 - Positioning of the Forwards to Prepare for Counter Attacks

THE FORWARDS CANNOT PREPARE FOR COUNTER ATTACKS AND MUST CONTROL 3 CENTRE BACKS

When the 2 Atlético forwards play against teams with 3 centre backs e.g. 3-5-2, 3-4-3 etc, they take up wider positions in order to control all 3 players.

This means they cannot take up positions focused on preparing for potential counter attacks, as they do when playing against 2 centre backs (**see previous 3 pages**).

If the ball is played to a wide centre back, the forward on that side presses the ball using a curved run to create a strong side and prevent a switch of play. This means that the white No.5 and No.3 are neutralised, and their numerical superiority is eliminated. The deepest forward **Griezmann (7)** shifts diagonally to help create a numerical advantage on the ball side.

DIEGO SIMEONE'S DEFENDING TACTICS

PRACTICE FOR "POSITIONING OF THE FORWARDS TO PREPARE FOR COUNTER ATTACKS"

Tactical Situation 3 - Positioning of the Forwards to Prepare for Counter Attacks

PRACTICE FOR THIS TACTICAL SITUATION

Positioning of the Forwards to Prepare for Counter Attacks in a 4 v 5 (+GK) Functional Practice

1/2: Defensive Reactions and Movements Against 2 Centre Backs

Objective: Prevent a through pass or a switch of play while using the counter attack-minded positioning of the forwards.

Description (1/2)

- We have a 4v4 situation inside the main area, with 2 red forwards **(18 & 7)** and 2 red central midfielders **(14 & 8)** against 2 white centre backs and 2 white central midfielders.

- There is an extra white player (No.10) in the yellow target area.

- The practice starts with the GK's pass and the players start on their respective cones.

- The aim for the white centre backs is to move the ball to No.10 (within the yellow area) either directly or via one of the midfielders. The first aim for the reds is to stop them.

- After a switch of play (from white No.4 to No.5 in diagram), the red forwards take up their counter attack-minded positions shown in the analysis.

- The deepest forward **(7)** stays close to his midfielders to block the passing options and the advanced forward **(18)** is ready to receive close to goal for a potential counter attack.

DIEGO SIMEONE'S DEFENDING TACTICS

Tactical Situation 3 - Positioning of the Forwards to Prepare for Counter Attacks

2/2: Win Ball and Counter Attack Against 2 Centre Backs

Description (2/2)

- With good defensive positioning and collective movements, the red team are now able to block all passing options and try to win the ball.

- If they win the ball, they launch a very quick direct counter attack, trying to score past the GK in the large goal within 8 seconds.

Coaching Points

1. Use the correct angles and body shape to block through passes.
2. Deny space between the lines.
3. Launch a quick counter attack as soon as the ball is won by passing to the advanced forward **(18)**.

 **ASSESSMENT**

This practice can be easily adjusted to play against the 4-3-3 formation.

©SOCCERTUTOR.COM   DIEGO SIMEONE'S DEFENDING TACTICS

TACTICAL SITUATION 4

Positioning and Defensive Movements of the Midfielders

The content in this section is from analysis of Diego Simeone's Atlético Madrid teams during the 2017/2018 and 2018/2019 seasons.

The analysis is based on recurring patterns of play observed within the Atlético Madrid team. Once the same phase of play occurred several times (at least 10), the tactics would be seen as a pattern. The analysis on the following pages are examples of the team's tactics being used effectively.

Each action, pass, individual movement with or without the ball, and the positioning of each player on the pitch including their body shape, are presented.

The analysis is then used to create a practice to coach this specific tactical situation.

Tactical Situation 4 - Positioning and Defensive Movements of the Midfielders

SHAPE, DISTANCE AND DEFENSIVE COHESION OF THE MIDFIELD LINE (BALL IN CENTRE)

1a. Shape and Cohesion of the Midfield Line to Make Sure Passing Lanes are Kept Narrow

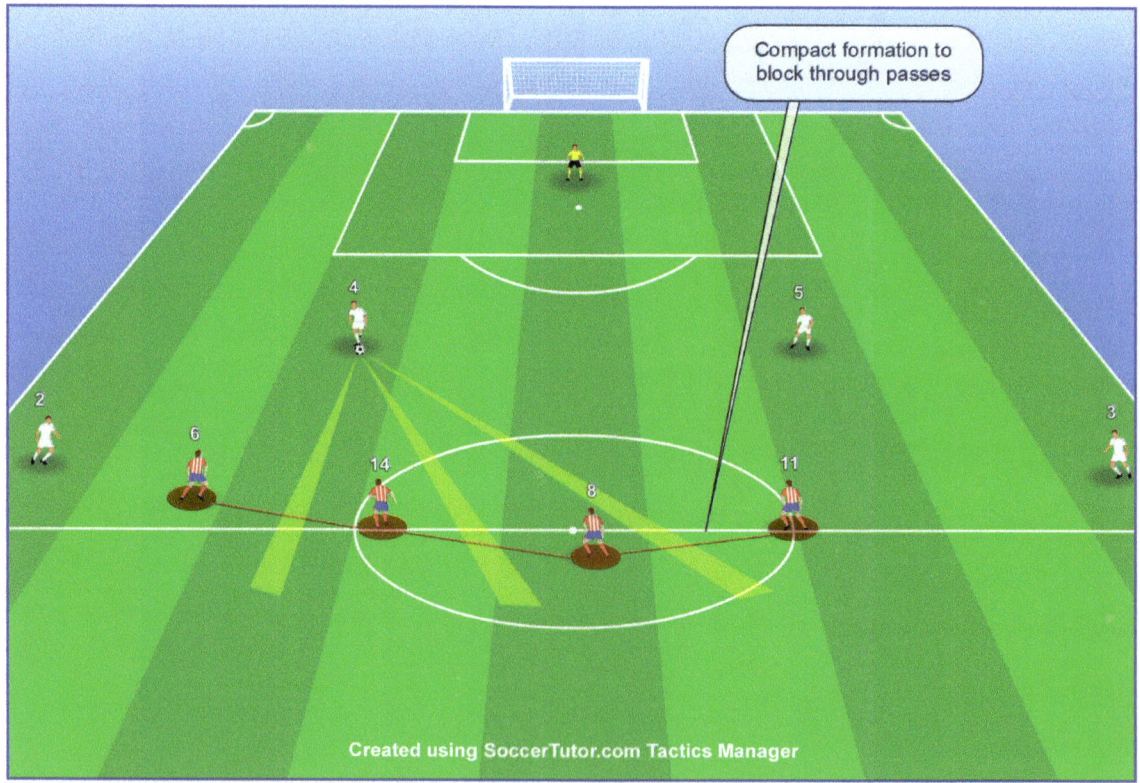

The midfielders shift collectively, according to the position of the ball.

When shifting, their aim is to defend the space and prevent any through passes towards players positioned within the space between the midfield and defensive line.

By blocking through passes, the midfielders are able to protect the **Crucial Central Area**, which is one of the basic aims of Atlético's defensive phase. They retain a compact formation with short distances between each other.

Normally, when the opposing defender is 15 yards away, the distance between each midfielder is approximately 10 yards.

The distance can vary because it is strongly related to the distance from the player in possession.

DIEGO SIMEONE'S DEFENDING TACTICS

Tactical Situation 4 - Positioning and Defensive Movements of the Midfielders

1b. Retain a Safety Distance from the Ball Carrier, React, Shift and Block Attempted Through Passes

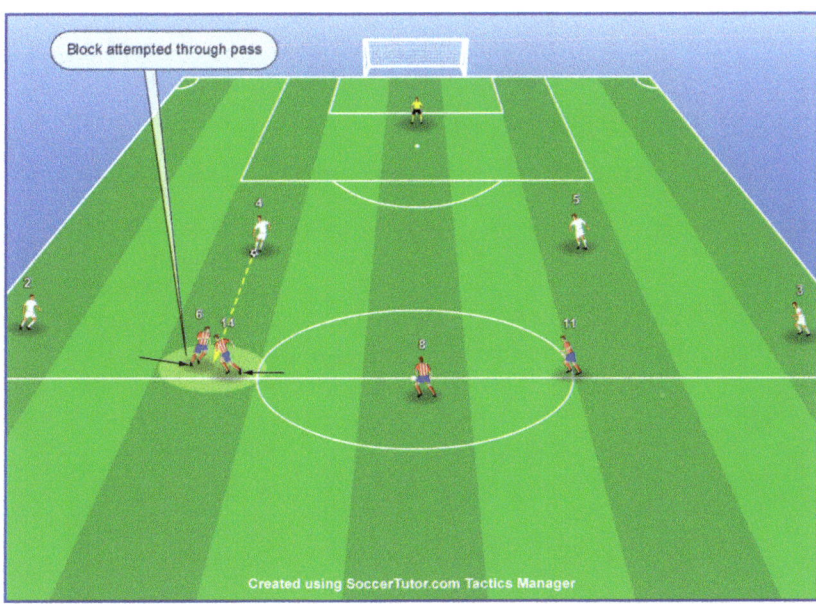

Keeping a safety distance from the player in possession means retaining a distance which enables the midfielders to react, shift and block any potential pass played in between them. Specific attention must be given to the position of the deepest central midfielder on the weak side **Saúl (8)**, who can control the space between the lines and be closer to the defensive line in case he needs to support them.

2. Reducing the Distance Between Players in the Midfield Line when the Ball Carrier is Closer (Compactness)

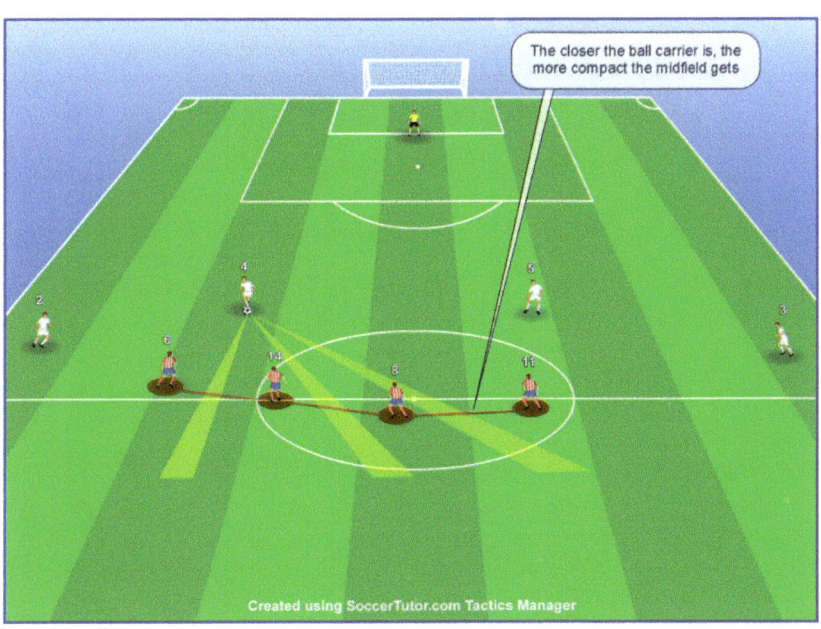

If the distance between the midfielders and the player in possession is shorter than in the previous example, the midfielders keep a shorter distance between each other.

They must still able to block through passes, otherwise they will no longer be at a safety distance.

DIEGO SIMEONE'S DEFENDING TACTICS

Tactical Situation 4 - Positioning and Defensive Movements of the Midfielders

DEFENSIVE REACTIONS OF THE MIDFIELD LINE WHEN THE CENTRE BACK DRIBBLES FORWARD

a. Midfield Line Drop Back to Retain a Safety Distance and Become More Compact to Prevent Through Passes

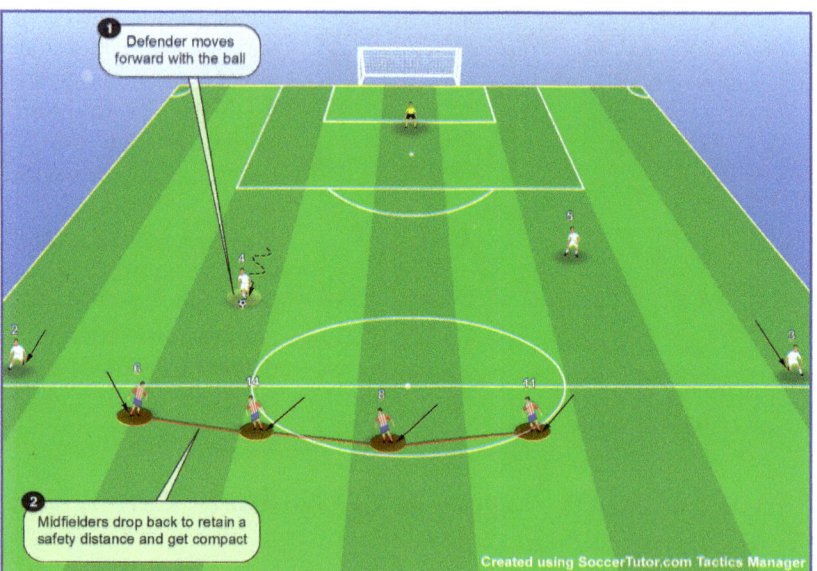

When a centre back moves forward with the ball, the distance between him and the midfielders get shorter. This means that the possibility of playing a successful through pass is increased.

To deal with this situation, the Atlético midfielders drop back to retain a safety distance and converge to become more compact and counter the reduced distance.

b. Midfielders Create an Effective Defensive Triangle

As soon as they get compact enough horizontally, the closest midfielder to the ball carrier, which is central midfielder **Gabi (14)** in this example, moves to press him, while an effective defensive triangle is created.

This defensive reaction narrows the through passing lanes and the ball is forced towards the side-line.

©SOCCERTUTOR.COM DIEGO SIMEONE'S DEFENDING TACTICS

Tactical Situation 4 - Positioning and Defensive Movements of the Midfielders

SHAPE, DISTANCE AND DEFENSIVE COHESION OF THE MIDFIELD LINE (BALL NEAR SIDE-LINE)

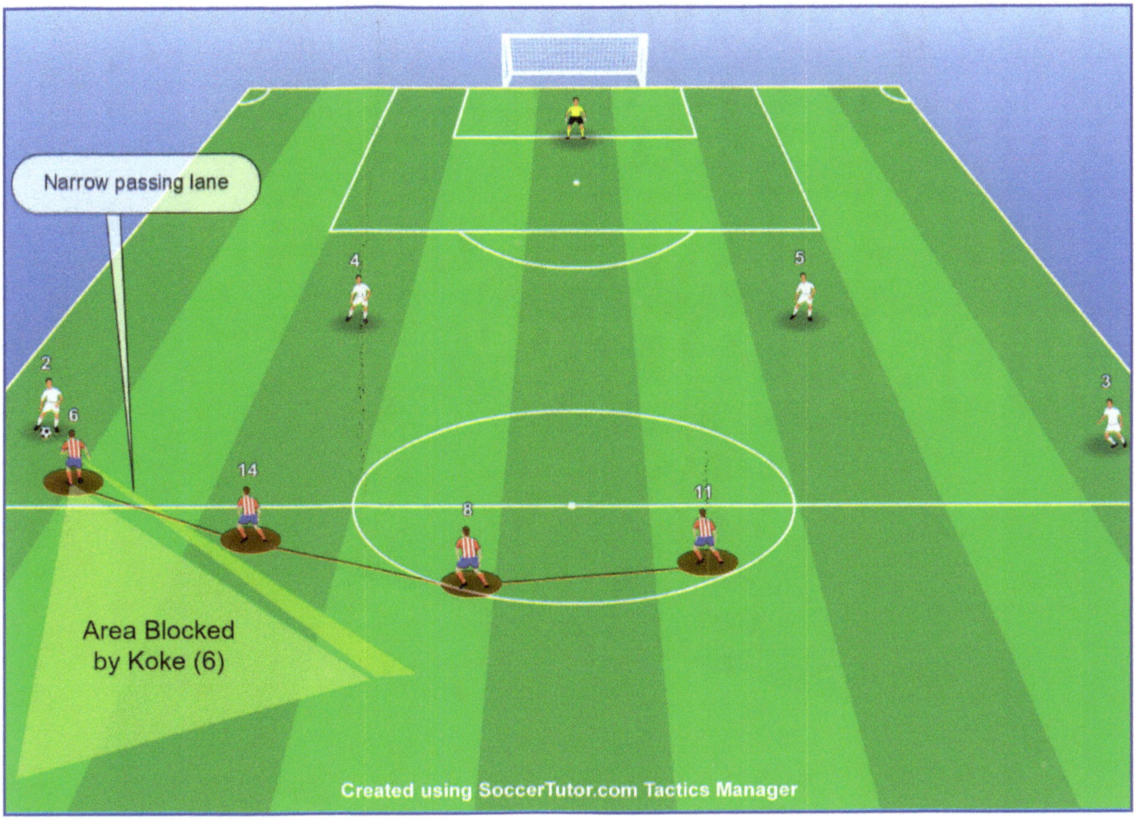

Diagram: Narrow passing lane; Area Blocked by Koke (6)

When the full back is in possession near the side-line, the midfield line is positioned as shown in the diagram. **Koke (6)** presses in a way to prevent the inside pass and blocks a large area behind him. Together with **Gabi (14)**, they make sure there is a narrow through passing lane.

The central midfielder on the weak side **Saúl (8)** is in a deeper position to be close to his centre backs and control the space between the lines.

ASSESSMENT

1. The Atlético midfielders shift according to the ball position. They have a fixed shape when shifting as they want to defend the spaces rather than mark the players within their zone of responsibility. However, their positioning and shape is affected by the positioning of their opponents, which will be analysed in the front block section.

2. The same reactions displayed would be used against a 3 man defence.

DIEGO SIMEONE'S DEFENDING TACTICS

Practice for "Positioning and Defensive Movements of the Midfielders"

Tactical Situation 4 - Positioning and Defensive Movements of the Midfielders

PRACTICE FOR THIS TACTICAL SITUATION
Compact Midfield Line Blocking Through Passes in a Functional Game

Scenario A: Shift to Ball Position, Retain Safety Distance & Block Passes

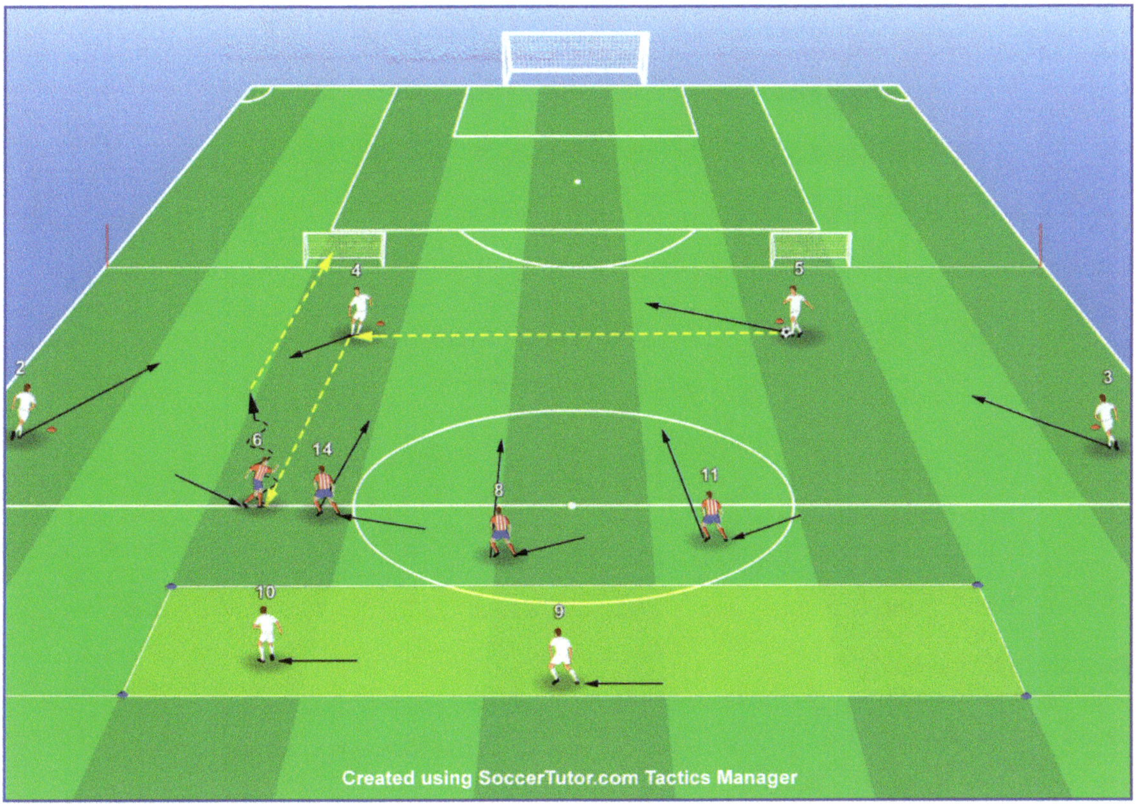

Description (Scenario A)

- We have a 4v4 situation inside the main area, with 4 red midfielders against 2 white centre backs and 2 white full backs.
- The white defenders pass the ball to each other in set positions and try to play a through pass to a white forward inside the yellow area.
- The red midfielders shift according to the position of the ball, try to retain a safety distance at all times and block any potential through passes.

- Please **see pages 46 and 47** for the correct defensive reactions.
- As soon as the reds win the ball, they launch a very quick direct counter attack, trying to score in either mini goal within a set amount of time.

DIEGO SIMEONE'S DEFENDING TACTICS

Tactical Situation 4 - Positioning and Defensive Movements of the Midfielders

Scenario B: Retain Safety Distance as the Centre Back Dribbles Forward

Description (Scenario B)

- In this second scenario, the white defenders can now move forward or backwards with the ball and their distance from the red midfielders can vary.

- The aim for the white team stays the same: Play a through pass to a forward inside the yellow area.

- The red midfielders adapt to the new situation by moving backwards or forward, making sure a safety distance is always retained and through passes are blocked.

- Please **see pages 48 and 49** for the correct defensive reactions, including creating a defensive triangle and what to do when the ball is played out wide to a full back.

Coaching Points

1. Retain a safety distance at all times.
2. Use the correct angles and body shape to block through passes.
3. Launch a quick counter attack as soon as the ball is won.

DIEGO SIMEONE'S DEFENDING TACTICS

TACTICAL SITUATION 5

Positioning and Defensive Movements of the Defenders

The content in this section is from analysis of Diego Simeone's Atlético Madrid teams during the 2017/2018 and 2018/2019 seasons.

The analysis is based on recurring patterns of play observed within the Atlético Madrid team. Once the same phase of play occurred several times (at least 10), the tactics would be seen as a pattern. The analysis on the following pages are examples of the team's tactics being used effectively.

Each action, pass, individual movement with or without the ball, and the positioning of each player on the pitch including their body shape, are presented.

The analysis is then used to create 3 practices to coach this specific tactical situation.

Tactical Situation 5 - Positioning and Defensive Movements of the Defenders

POSITIONING AND DEFENSIVE MOVEMENTS OF THE DEFENDERS

In contrast to the midfielders who are mainly focused on defending space, the defenders mark their opponents within their zone of responsibility.

Diego Simeone's Atlético Madrid players follow these principles for their positioning and defensive movements:

- They shift according to the position of the ball, but their focus is on their direct opponents.

- If a pass is directed to their direct opponent, the Atlético defender's positioning should enable them to reach the ball first or immediately limit the time and space available for the attacker if he receives.

- The defensive positions are taken according to the distance from the player in possession to their direct opponent (centre forward or winger). So, the closer the ball carrier is to the player the defender is marking, the tighter the marking will be.

- However, there is a limitation on how close the full back on the strong side can be to the winger, as it can lead to problems. This will be further analysed in the section about the rear block and the collaboration of the wide midfielder with the full back.

- The focus on the direct opponents is more obvious when the Atlético defenders are playing against 3 forwards.

- Against 2 forwards, the Atlético defenders' positioning is more balanced.

Tactical Situation 5 - Positioning and Defensive Movements of the Defenders

POSITIONING AND DEFENSIVE MOVEMENTS AGAINST 3 FORWARDS (4-3-3)

1. Positioning of the Defenders Against 3 Forwards with the Ball in the Centre

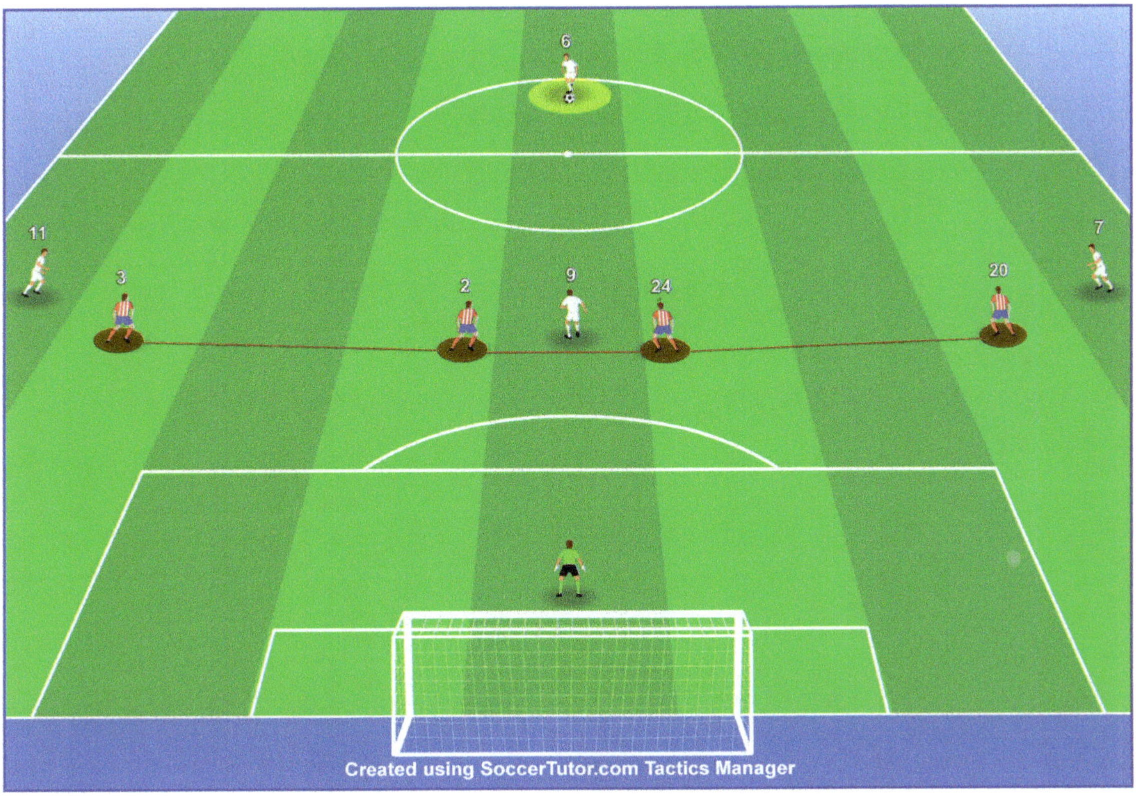

When playing against 3 forwards, the Atlético Madrid defenders take up the positions shown in the diagram above.

The 2 centre backs **Godín (2)** and **Giménez (24)** focus on marking the 1 opposing forward (2v1) and the full backs **F. Luis (3)** and **Juanfran (20)** are in wide positions (1v1).

The positioning of the full backs enables them to be as close as possible to the centre backs while also being in position to intercept a long pass directed towards the opposing wingers, or in the worst case scenario, to immediately limit their available time and space if they receive.

NOTE: This kind of defensive positioning is key when playing top class wingers such as **Ronaldo**, **Bale**, **Neymar**, **Salah**, **Robben**, and **Douglas Costa**, who can be extremely dangerous if they receive facing their opponent's goal and have time and space on the ball. By using Diego Simeone's defensive positioning, this threat can be neutralised.

DIEGO SIMEONE'S DEFENDING TACTICS

Tactical Situation 5 - Positioning and Defensive Movements of the Defenders

2a. Positioning of the Defenders with the Ball Near the Side-line

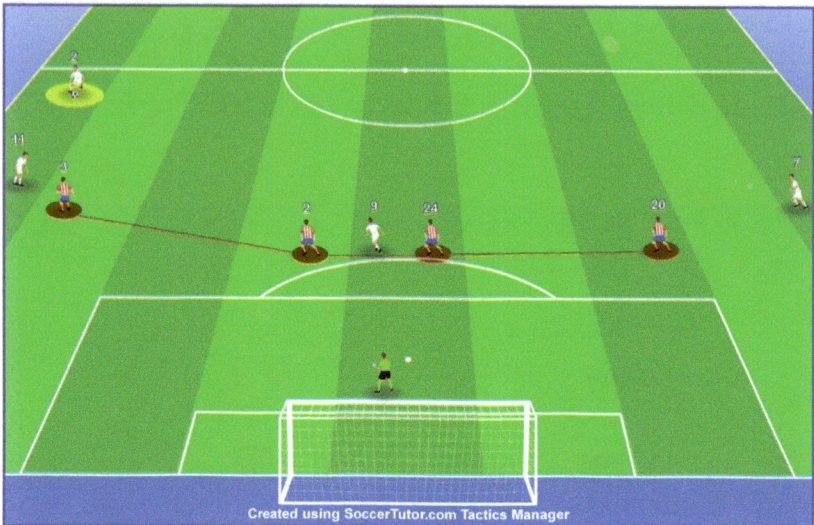

When the ball is near the side-line, the players take up positions in relation to the position of the ball, but also strongly focus on marking the opposing players.

The full back on the strong side **F. Luis (3)** is in a slightly more advanced position, while the other 3 defenders are in the same line.

2b. Defenders Shift Across when the Forward Moves Towards the Side-line

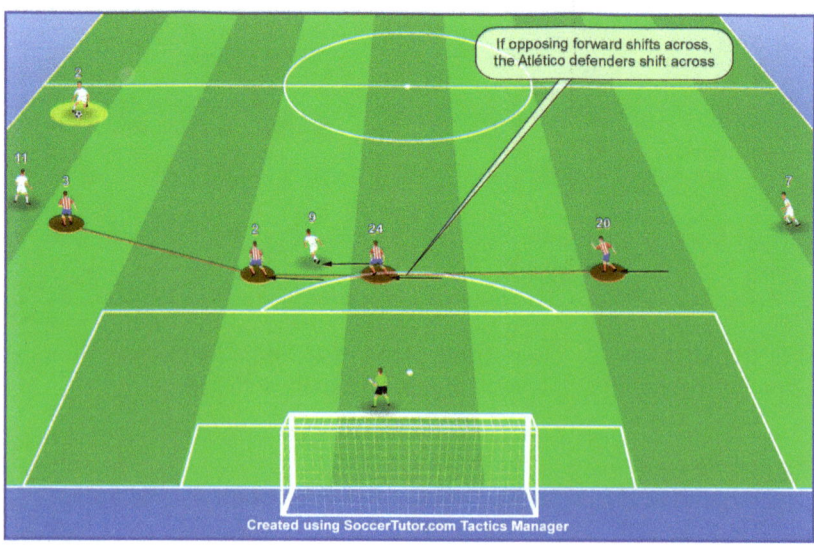

If the opposing centre forward (white No.9) shifts towards the strong side, all the Atlético defenders shift across accordingly.

The right back **Juanfran (20)** also shifts across to be as close as possible to the centre backs but must control the white winger (No.7) at the same time.

ASSESSMENT

The wide positions of the full backs change according to the distance the player in possession is from the goal. Therefore, the closer the player in possession moves towards the goal, the closer the full backs move into the centre to protect their goal.

Tactical Situation 5 - Positioning and Defensive Movements of the Defenders

3. Positioning of the Defenders Against 3 Narrow Forwards with the Ball in the Centre

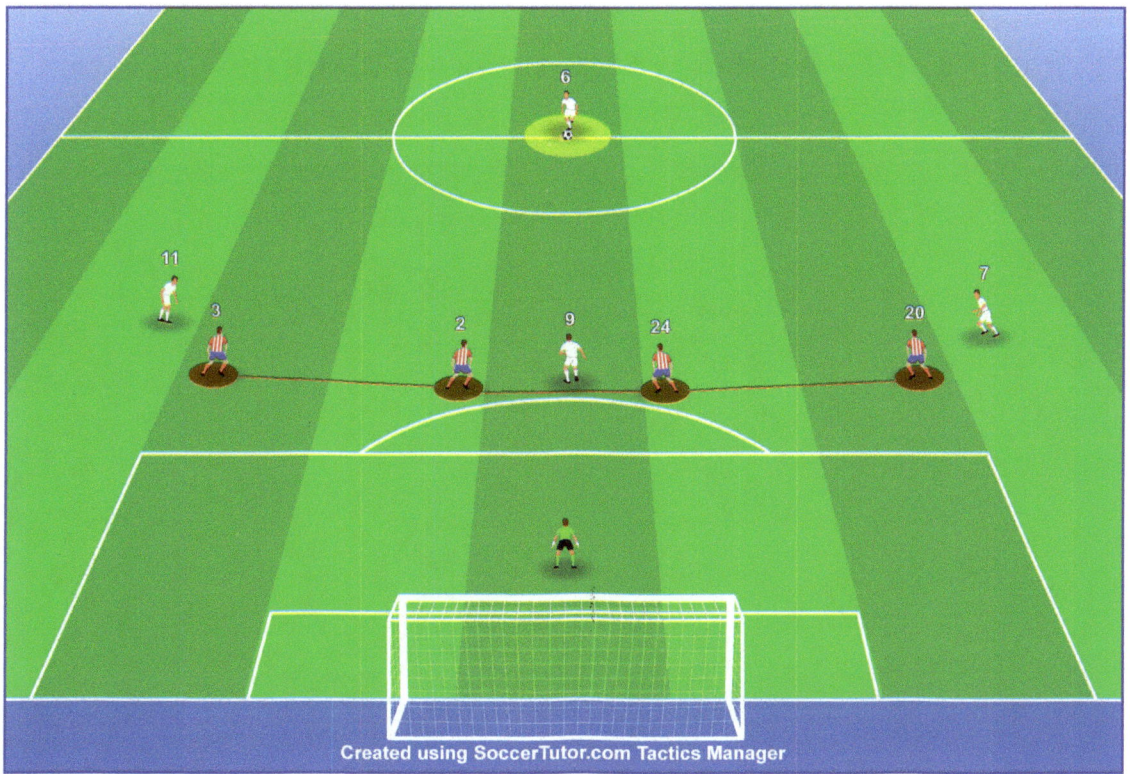

When playing against 3 narrow forwards, the Atlético Madrid defenders take up the positions shown in the diagram above.

The 2 full backs **F. Luis (3)** and **Juanfran (20)** are now in narrower positions and Atlético Madrid have a compact back 4.

The 2 centre backs **Godín (2)** and **Giménez (24)** focus on marking the 1 opposing forward (2v1) and the full backs **F. Luis (3)** and **Juanfran (20)** mark the wingers (1v1).

Tactical Situation 5 - Positioning and Defensive Movements of the Defenders

DEFENSIVE POSITIONING WITH THE BALL IN THE CENTRE AGAINST 2 FORWARDS (4-4-2)

Positioning of the Defenders Against the 4-4-2 with the Ball in the Centre

When playing against 2 forwards (4-4-2 formation), the Atlético Madrid defenders take up the positions shown in the diagram above.

The 2 full backs **F. Luis (3)** and **Juanfran (20)** take up more balanced positions, which enable them both to provide support to the centre backs and to restrict the space of the opposing wingers in the best possible way.

The 2 centre backs **Godín (2)** and **Giménez (24)** stay close to the 2 opposing forwards (No.9 and No.10).

Tactical Situation 5 - Positioning and Defensive Movements of the Defenders

DEFENSIVE POSITIONING WITH THE BALL OUT WIDE AGAINST 2 FORWARDS (4-4-2)

a. Positioning of the 2 Centre Backs with the Ball Near the Side-line

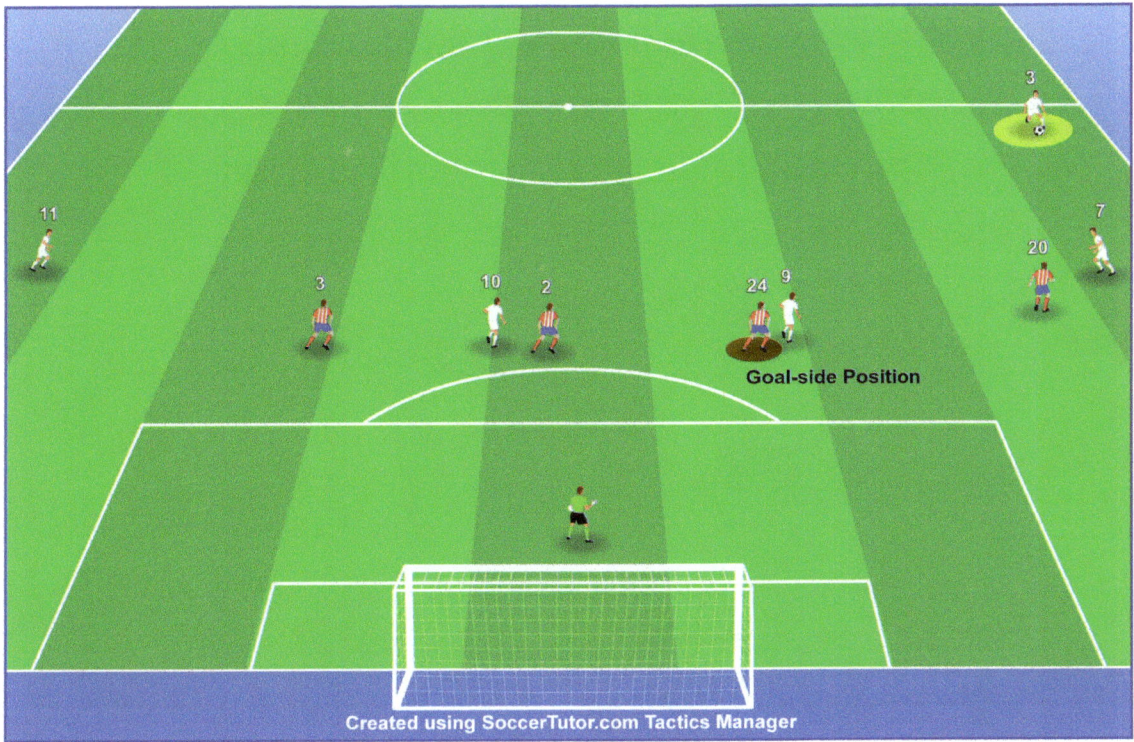

The advantages displayed on the previous 3 pages (against 1 forward) are not applied against 2 forwards, as the centre backs have to control both of them.

The centre back on the strong side **Giménez (24)** has to stay close to his direct opponent (white No.9) in a goal-side position in order to neutralise the most dangerous passes, which are the ones played in behind him.

The goal-side positioning is important, as the other centre back **Godín (2)** is focused on controlling his direct opponent (white No.10). This means moving in front of the forward to clear a potential long pass is not as easy as when playing against just 1 forward, as the other centre back may not be close enough to cover behind his back.

Moving in front of the opposing forward to clear the ball after a long or medium range pass should only occur when the centre back has realised that he has the available time to move in front of the opponent as soon as the pass is made and not in advance.

The full backs are positioned closer to the centre backs in more balanced positions and both are ready to provide support and cover if needed.

DIEGO SIMEONE'S DEFENDING TACTICS

Tactical Situation 5 - Positioning and Defensive Movements of the Defenders

b. Defending a Long Pass from Out Wide by Contesting the Forward from Behind

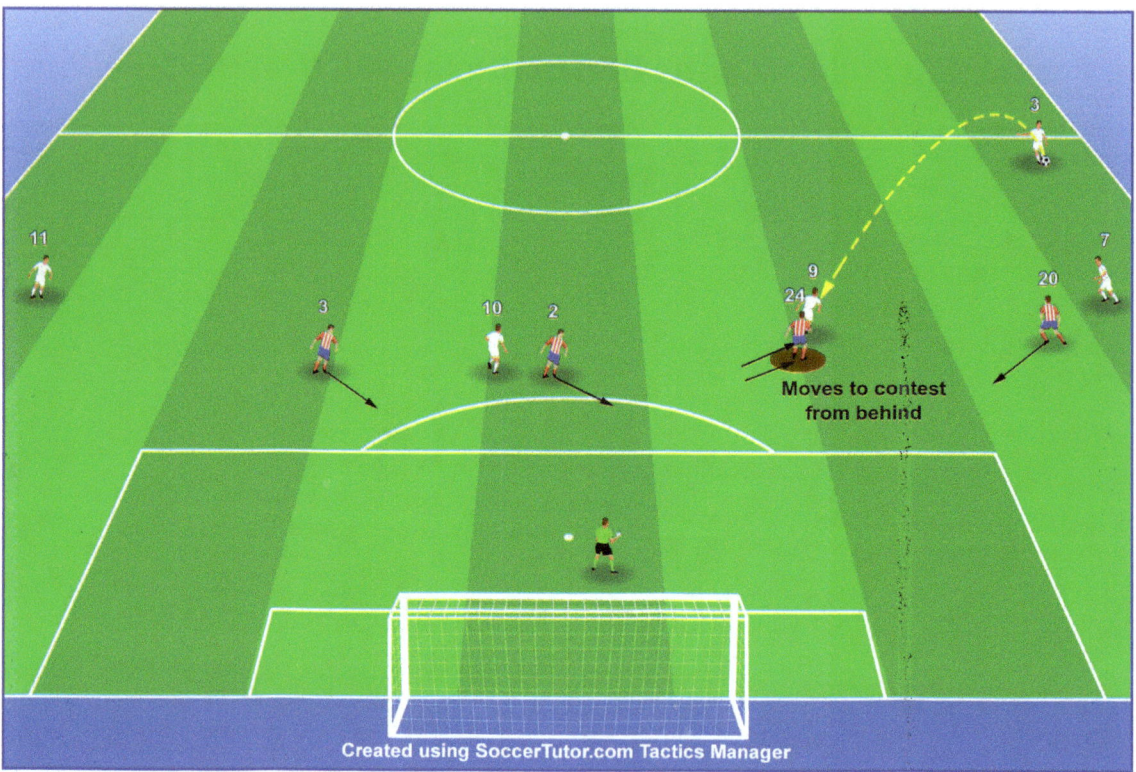

In this tactical situation, a long pass is played from the opposing full back (near the side-line) towards the white forward No.9.

The right centre back **Giménez (24)** realises that moving in front of the forward to win the ball is nearly impossible.

Therefore, **Giménez (24)** applies pressure and contests the white forward No.9 from his goal-side position behind.

The aim is to force a bad first touch and prevent white No.9 from turning.

The other defenders move to create a defensive triangle in order to provide cover.

Tactical Situation 5 - Positioning and Defensive Movements of the Defenders

DEFENSIVE POSITIONING AGAINST 1 FORWARD AND 1 ATTACKING MIDFIELDER (4-2-3-1)

1. Positioning of the Defenders Against the 4-2-3-1 with the No.10 in a Deep Position and the Ball in the Centre

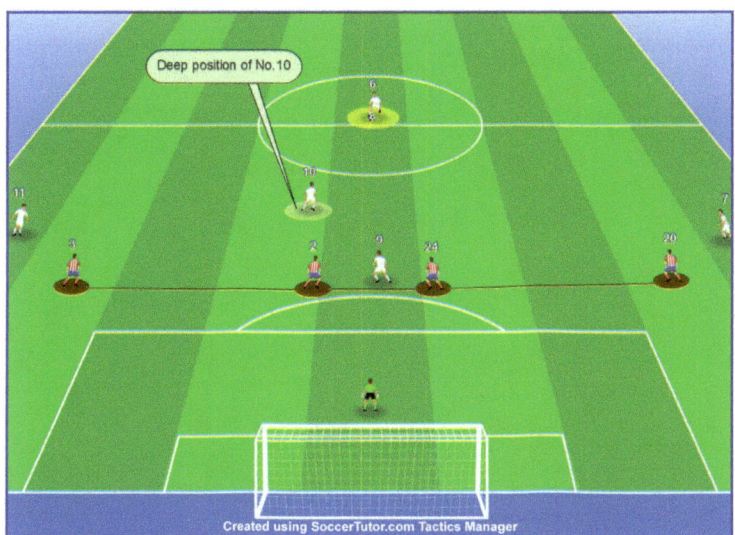

The positioning of the Atlético Madrid defenders against the 4-2-3-1 formation depends on how high up the pitch the opposing attacking midfielder (No.10) is positioned.

If the attacking midfielder is in a deep position, the Atlético defenders are positioned in a similar way as against the 4-3-3 with wide forwards (**see page 55**).

2. Opposing No.10 is in a More Advanced Position

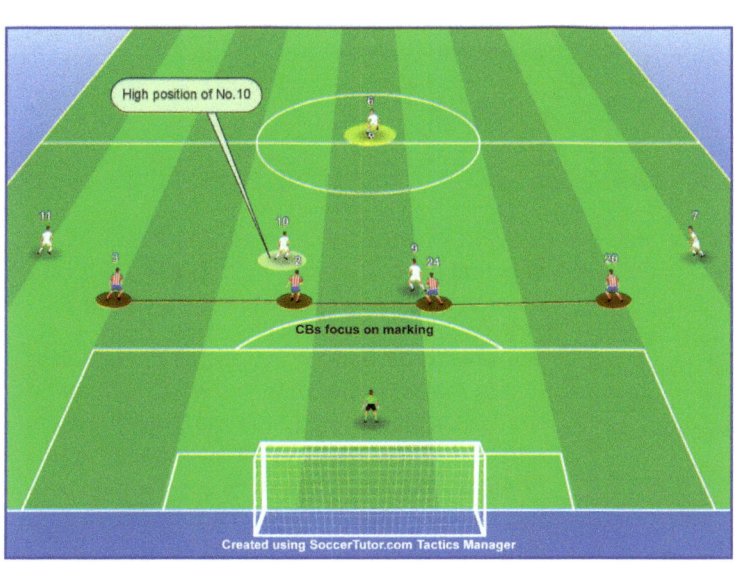

If the No.10 is in a more advanced position, then the Atlético defenders are positioned in a similar way as against the 4-4-2 formation (**see page 58**).

One of the centre backs **Godin (2)** focuses on marking No.10.

The other centre back **Giménez (24)** focuses on marking the centre forward No.9.

The full backs take up more central positions than in the previous situation.

DIEGO SIMEONE'S DEFENDING TACTICS

Tactical Situation 5 - Positioning and Defensive Movements of the Defenders

ADVANTAGES OF 2 CENTRE BACKS AGAINST 1 FORWARD IN THE CENTRE (4-2-3-1)

1a. Positioning of the Centre Backs Against the 4-2-3-1 with the No.10 in a Deep Position and the Ball Near the Side-line

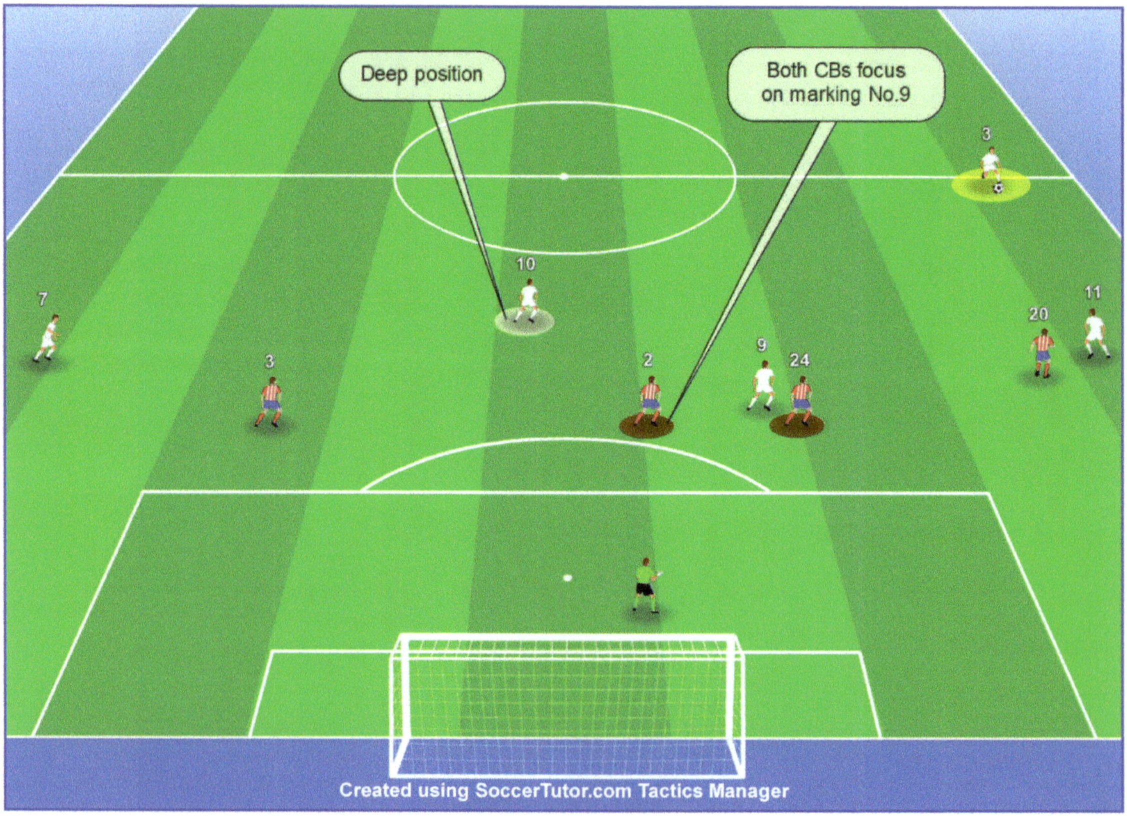

When playing against 1 forward, both Atlético centre backs **Godín (2)** and **Giménez (24)** are focused on marking him. This creates a 2v1 situation and it is difficult for the forward (white No.9 in diagram) to escape, as the available space for him is limited and the Atlético centre backs are able to neutralise almost every possible pass towards him.

As shown in the diagram above, the centre back on the strong side **Giménez (24)** doesn't have to take up a goal-side position against the forward because he can mark white No.9 using anticipation, as his team-mate **Godín (2)** is close enough to neutralise a pass in behind him.

Giménez (24) marking in anticipation enables him to move in front of the forward (as soon as the pass is played) and clear the ball before it is received. This situation is far more effective for Atlético when the opponents use medium or long range passes towards the forward, as there is more time for the centre back to act.

©SOCCERTUTOR.COM

DIEGO SIMEONE'S DEFENDING TACTICS

Tactical Situation 5 - Positioning and Defensive Movements of the Defenders

1b. Defending a Long Pass from Out Wide by Getting in Front of the Forward to Clear the Ball

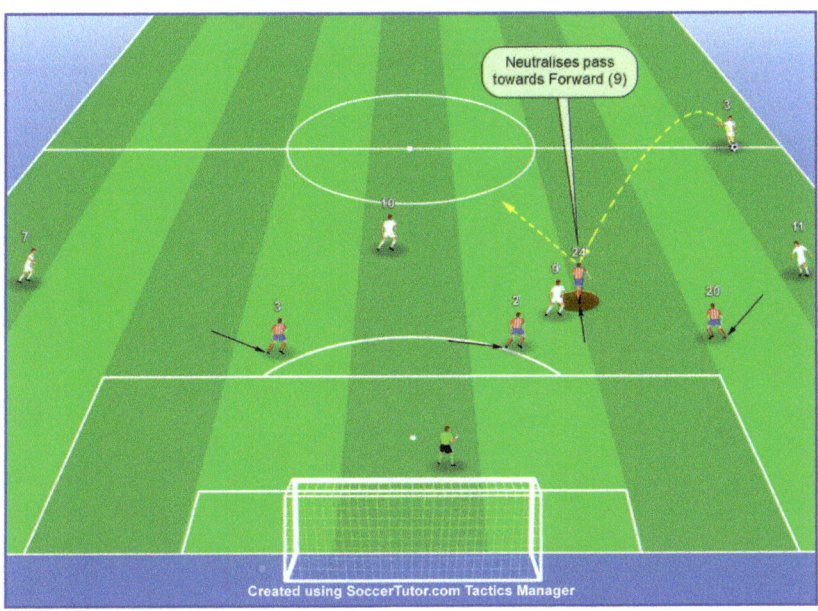

In this tactical situation, a long pass is played from the opposing full back (near the side-line) towards the lone white forward No.9.

The right centre back **Giménez (24)** is able to move in front of white No.9 (due to positioning shown on previous page) and neutralise a potential pass directed to him, while the left centre back **Godín (2)** provides cover.

2. If the Ball is Played Over the Top and in Behind, the Other Centre Back Provides Cover

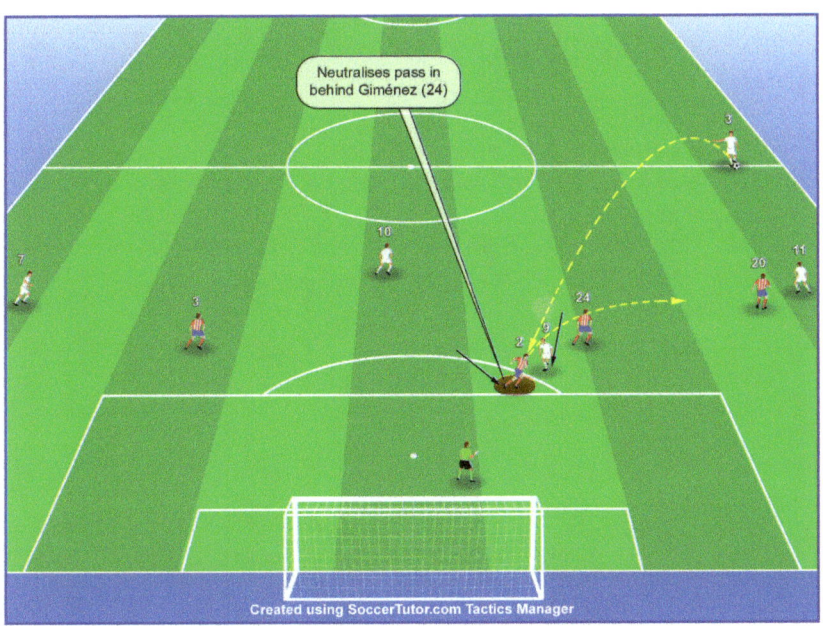

This is a variation of the example above and shows the opposing full back playing a pass over the top of the right centre back **Giménez (24)**.

If this happens, the left centre back **Godín (2)** is in position to easily provide cover and get to the ball first, as shown in the diagram.

©SOCCERTUTOR.COM DIEGO SIMEONE'S DEFENDING TACTICS

Tactical Situation 5 - Positioning and Defensive Movements of the Defenders

3. If the Ball is Passed on the Blind Side of the First Centre Back, the Other Centre Back Provides Cover

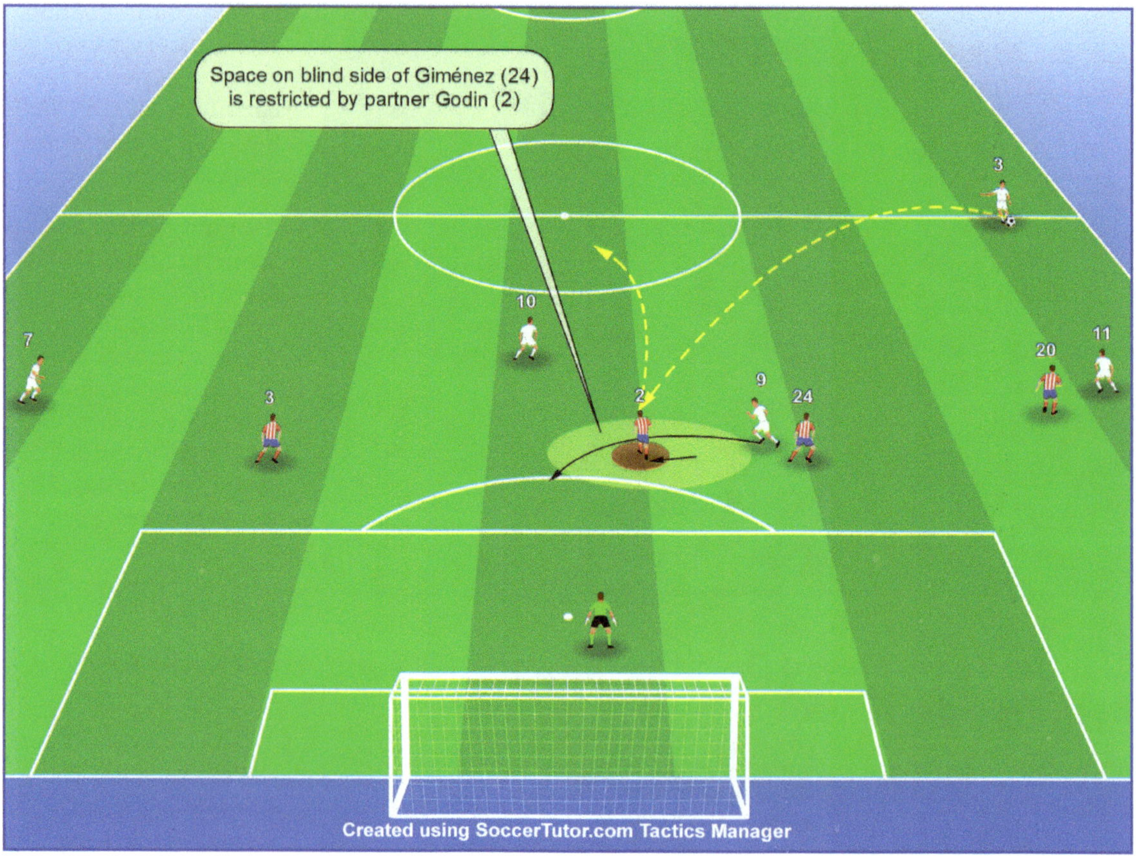

Another important advantage of the positioning of the 2 centre backs against 1 forward is that the left centre back **Godín's (2)** positioning close to the right centre back **Giménez (24)** allows no available space for the white forward to move and receive on the blind side of **Giménez (24)**.

In the diagram example, the white forward No.9 makes a run on the blind side of **Giménez (24)** but it is impossible to receive a pass from his team-mate (white No.3), as **Godín (2)** can easily intercept this kind of pass, as shown.

Tactical Situation 5 - Positioning and Defensive Movements of the Defenders

ASSESSMENT

The examples displayed show passes from wide areas. If the pass was played from a central area, it is more difficult for the centre backs to move in front of the forwards and intercept the passes.

The wide positioning of the full backs and the positioning of the centre backs close to their direct opponents is a tactic that has logic. As the midfielders prevent through passes, the only way of moving the ball to the forwards is by playing long balls. These kinds of passes can be easily neutralised by the Atletico defenders such as Godín, Giménez or Savić who are excellent in aerial duels.

Additionally, turning to play 1v1 is very difficult for opposing forwards after receiving long balls. Thus, the Atlético defenders do not have to be positioned too close to each other when playing against 3 forwards.

When playing against 4 advanced players (2 forwards + 2 wide midfielders) the defenders should be closer to each other as there are more possibilities (with the extra player) of their opponents exploiting the gaps between them or the space behind them. With shorter distances between them, they can immediately limit the space behind a centre back who moves out of position to mark a player and they can also provide immediate cover and support if an opposing forward manages to receive, turn, and play 1v1.

The positioning of the centre backs against 1 forward may be difficult for semi-pro or amateur players to adapt to. As shown in the analysis to follow in this book, they have to be aware of many aspects of the game including the potential gaps and the opposing midfielders' positioning etc).

In contrast, taking up more balanced positions, like against 2 forwards, would be easier for them to control the gaps and they don't have to possess the same high level of awareness.

However, the strategy with 2 centre backs close to the 1 forward can be effective when the opposing forward is a dangerous player who needs extra attention. Additionally, the same strategy can be highly effective when the opposing team use mainly direct play when they build up and their target player is the forward.

In conclusion, the tactics outlined in this book should be adapted to the level of the players. By doing this, the coaches can be at their most effective to win matches.

3 PRACTICES FOR "POSITIONING AND DEFENSIVE MOVEMENTS OF THE DEFENDERS"

Tactical Situation 5 - Positioning and Defensive Movements of the Defenders

PRACTICES FOR THIS TACTICAL SITUATION (3 PRACTICES)
1. Appropriate Positioning and Defending Medium and Long Passes Against 1 Forward (4-3-3)

Scenario A: Anticipate and Get in Front of Forward to Clear the Ball

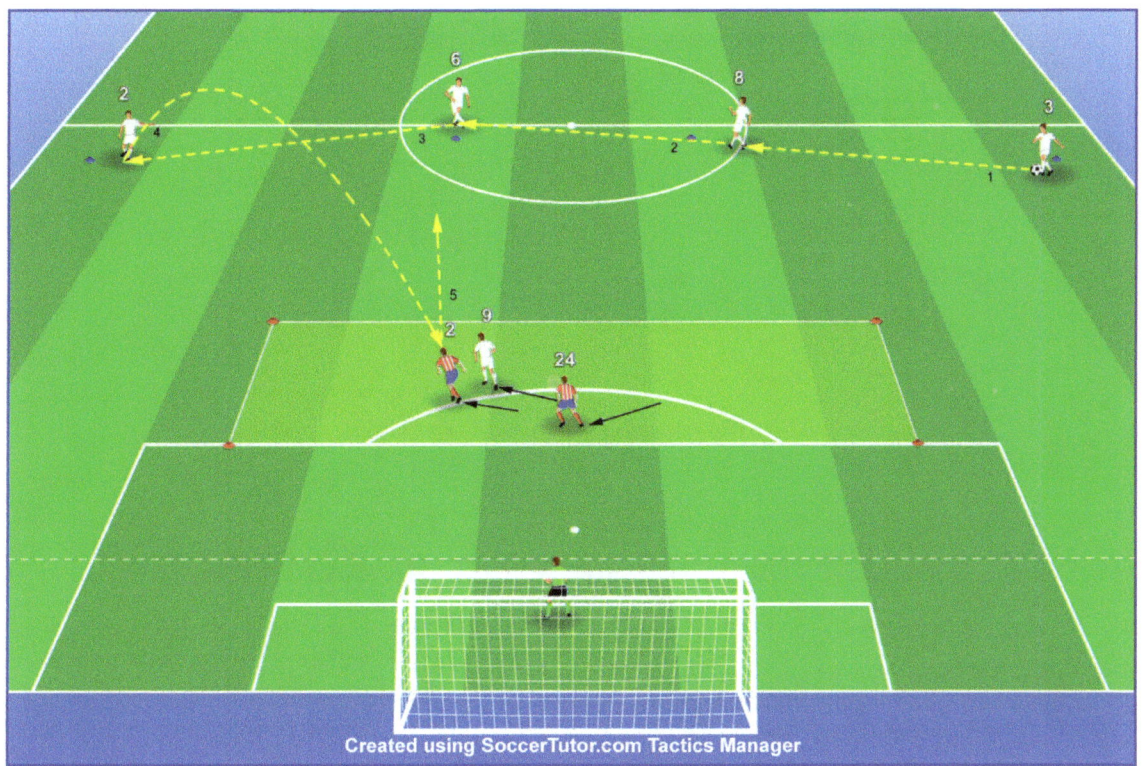

Description (Scenario A)

- The focus is on the 2 red centre backs. There is also a GK defending a large goal.

- The white players pass the ball to each other in set positions and then play a long pass towards the white forward (No.9).

- The red centre backs (**2** and **24**) take up the right positions against the white forward and try to neutralise any potential passes.

- The passes are either aimed at the forward (as shown in the diagram example) or into the space in behind (**see next page**).

- The red centre backs have to deal with a variety of situations (**see analysis pages**).

- If possible, a red centre back uses anticipation and moves forward to clear the ball before it is received (passes coming from wide areas), as shown with red **No.2** in the diagram example.

- If the white forward No.9 receives facing the goal, he tries to score. If he receives with his back to goal (passes coming from central areas), he should be pressed immediately, so he passes the ball back to his team-mates.

Tactical Situation 5 - Positioning and Defensive Movements of the Defenders

Scenario B: Provide Cover for Pass Over the Top and in Behind

Description (Scenario B)

- In this second scenario, we show what happens when a long pass from a wide area is played over the more advanced centre back's **(2)** head.

- The other centre back **(24)** was already in a good position close to his team-mate and is ready to provide cover, track the white forward's movement and clear the ball easily.

Coaching Points

1. In the early stages of the practice, both centre backs need to shift collectively in relation to the position of the ball.

2. The centre back on the strong side focuses on defending with anticipation and trying to get in front of the white forward to clear any passes from wide areas.

3. The centre back on the weak side focuses on providing cover for any passes over his team-mate, making sure to track the white forward very tightly.

Tactical Situation 5 - Positioning and Defensive Movements of the Defenders

VARIATION

2. Appropriate Positioning and Defending Medium and Long Passes Against 2 Forwards (4-4-2)

Scenario A: Defending a Pass from a Central Area

Description (Scenario A)

- This is a variation of the previous practice and now the 2 red centre backs have to defend against 2 white forwards.

- This means the centre back on the strong side should no longer defend with anticipation and look to get in front of his marker. His centre back partner now also has a forward to mark, so is unable to focus on being in a covering position.

- The main aim for the red centre back on the strong side (2) is to prevent the forward from turning, especially towards the inside.

- The second aim is to try to force a bad first touch and force the forward wide.

- In the diagram example, the red centre back on the strong side (2) contests the white forward No.9, who has his back to goal, and forces him wide. The centre back on the weak side (24) drops back and across to provide cover while still controlling his direct opponent No.10.

Restriction: The passes must be played into the marked out area or into the penalty area.

DIEGO SIMEONE'S DEFENDING TACTICS

Tactical Situation 5 - **Positioning and Defensive Movements of the Defenders**

Scenario B: Defending a Pass from a Wide Area

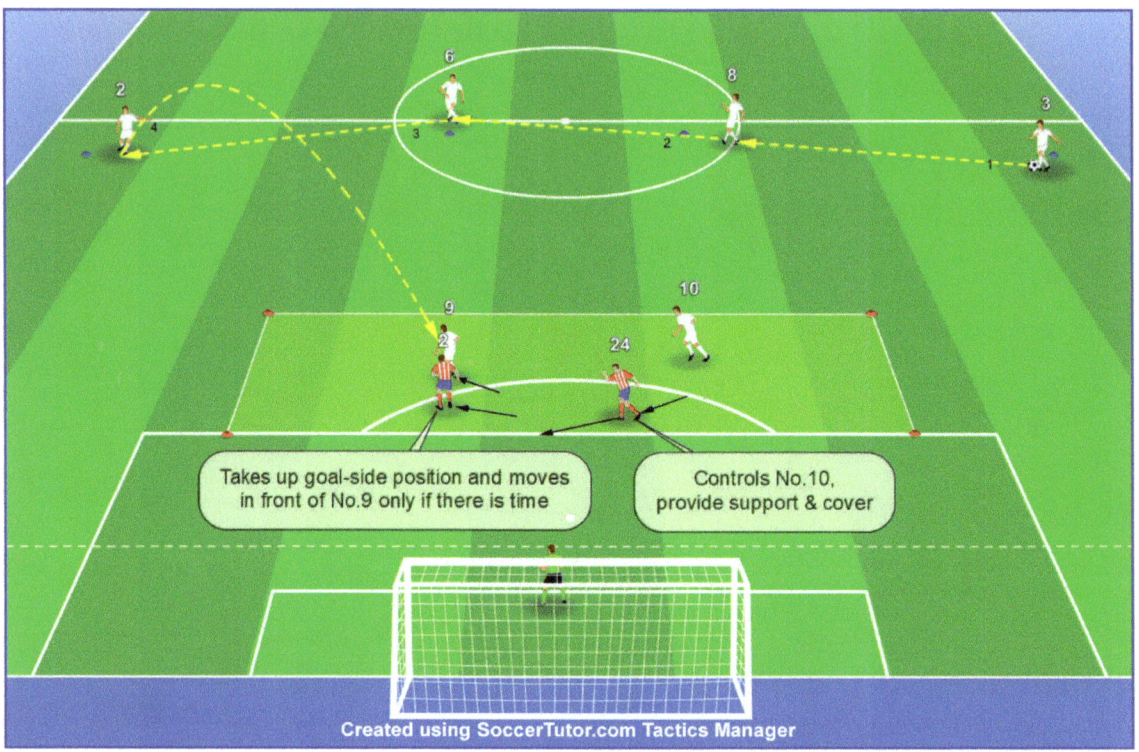

Description (Scenario B)

- In this second scenario, we show how the 2 red centre backs defend against a pass from a wide area.

- When the pass comes from a wide area, the red centre back on the strong side **(2)** is still in a goal-side marking position, but can now anticipate and move in front of the forward (white No.9) to clear the ball if he believes he has enough time.

- In the diagram example, the red centre back on the strong side **(2)** decides not to move forward and contests the white forward No.9 from behind.

- The centre back on the weak side **(24)** drops back and across to provide cover while still controlling his direct opponent No.10.

Variation: The passes can also be played towards the forward on the weak side (No.10) to test the positioning of the other red centre back **(24)** as well.

Coaching Points

1. Shift according to the position of the ball.
2. The centre back on the strong side takes up a goal-side position to the opposing forward.
3. The centre back on the weak side must make sure to focus on 2 aims, which are to support his centre back partner and control his direct opponent.

@SOCCERTUTOR.COM

DIEGO SIMEONE'S DEFENDING TACTICS

Tactical Situation 5 - Positioning and Defensive Movements of the Defenders

VARIATION

3. Appropriate Positioning and Defending Medium and Long Passes Against 2 Forwards (4-2-3-1)

Scenario A: The Opposing No.10 is in a Deep Position

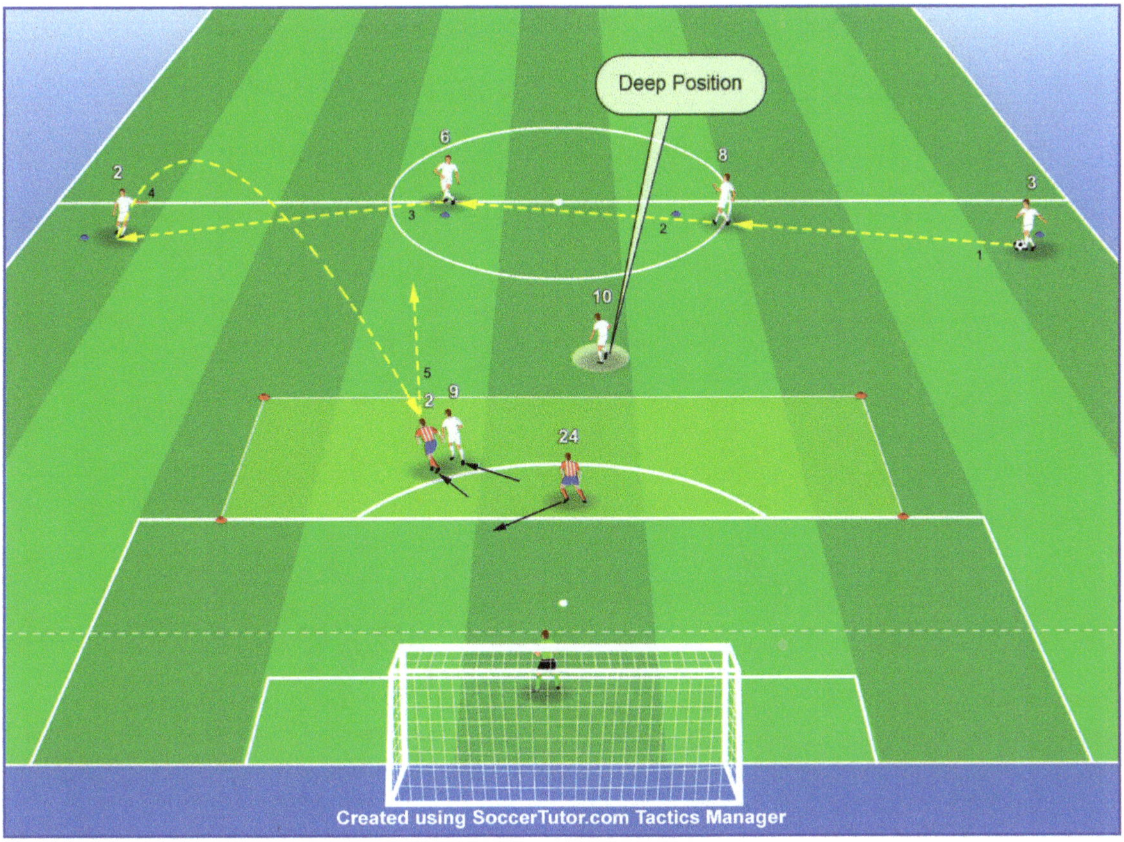

Description (Scenario A)

- This is a variation of the previous practice and now the 2 red centre backs have to defend against 1 white forward and a No.10.

- The important element of this practice is the reading of No.10's position (inside or outside the marked out area).

- In the first part of this practice (Scenario A), the white No.10 is in a deep position.

- Therefore, both red centre backs can focus on defending against the 1 forward No.9.

- If possible, a red centre back uses anticipation and moves forward to clear the ball before it is received (passes coming from wide areas), as shown with red **No.2** in the diagram example.

Restriction: The passes must be played into the marked out area or into the penalty area.

DIEGO SIMEONE'S DEFENDING TACTICS

Tactical Situation 5 - Positioning and Defensive Movements of the Defenders

Scenario B: The Opposing No.10 is in an Advanced Position

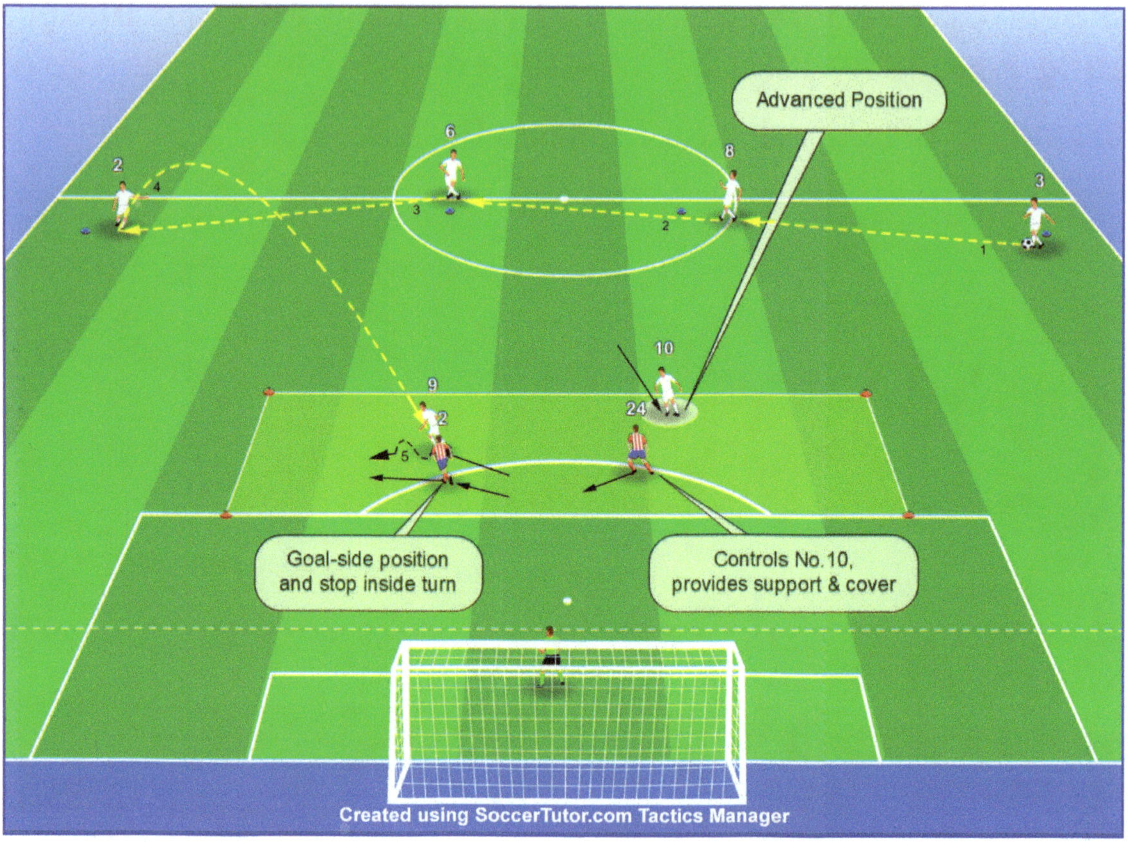

Description (Scenario B)

- In this second scenario, we show how the 2 red centre backs defend when the opposing No.10 is more advanced and positioned within the marked out area.

- The white No.10 now needs to be marked. Both centre backs focus on their direct opponents and the centre back on the strong side **(2)** takes up a goal-side position against the white forward No.9.

- In the diagram example, the red centre back on the strong side **(2)** contests the white forward No.9, prevents him from turning and forces him wide. The centre back on the weak side **(24)** drops back and across to provide cover while still controlling No.10.

Variation: The passes can also be played towards the forward on the weak side (No.10) to test the positioning of the other red centre back **(24)** as well.

Coaching Points

1. The red centre backs shift collectively according to the position of the ball.
2. They must also read the specific tactical situation and react appropriately.

DIEGO SIMEONE'S DEFENDING TACTICS

TACTICAL SITUATION 6

Wide Positioning of the Full Backs to Contest the Opposing Wingers

The content in this section is from analysis of Diego Simeone's Atlético Madrid teams during the 2017/2018 and 2018/2019 seasons.

The analysis is based on recurring patterns of play observed within the Atlético Madrid team. Once the same phase of play occurred several times (at least 10), the tactics would be seen as a pattern. The analysis on the following pages are examples of the team's tactics being used effectively.

Each action, pass, individual movement with or without the ball, and the positioning of each player on the pitch including their body shape, are presented.

The analysis is then used to create 2 practices to coach this specific tactical situation.

Tactical Situation 6 - Wide Positioning of the Full Backs to Contest the Opposing Wingers

ADVANTAGES OF THE WIDE POSITIONING OF THE FULL BACKS

1. Intercepting a Long Pass Towards the Winger from a Central Position Against the 4-3-3

The positioning of the full backs depends on the positioning of the opposing wingers. If there is a possibility of a pass to a winger, the full back has to take up a position which enables him to intercept the ball before it reaches him.

If that is not possible and the winger receives, the Atlético full back immediately restricts his available time and space. It is important to prevent 1v1 situations where the winger can generate speed to help him beat the defender.

In the diagram example, left back **F. Luis (3)** moves aggressively from a central position, to clear the long pass towards the winger No.7.

 **ASSESSMENT**

Intercepting the ball before it reaches the winger can be very effective against fast wingers who possess skills to beat defenders in 1v1 situations like **Ronaldo**, **Neymar**, **Douglas Costa** etc. These players are dangerous if they receive free of marking in available space and move with speed against their direct opponent (full back).

@SOCCERTUTOR.COM   DIEGO SIMEONE'S DEFENDING TACTICS

Tactical Situation 6 - Wide Positioning of the Full Backs to Contest the Opposing Wingers

2. Intercepting a Long Pass Towards the Winger After a Switch of Play Against the 4-3-3

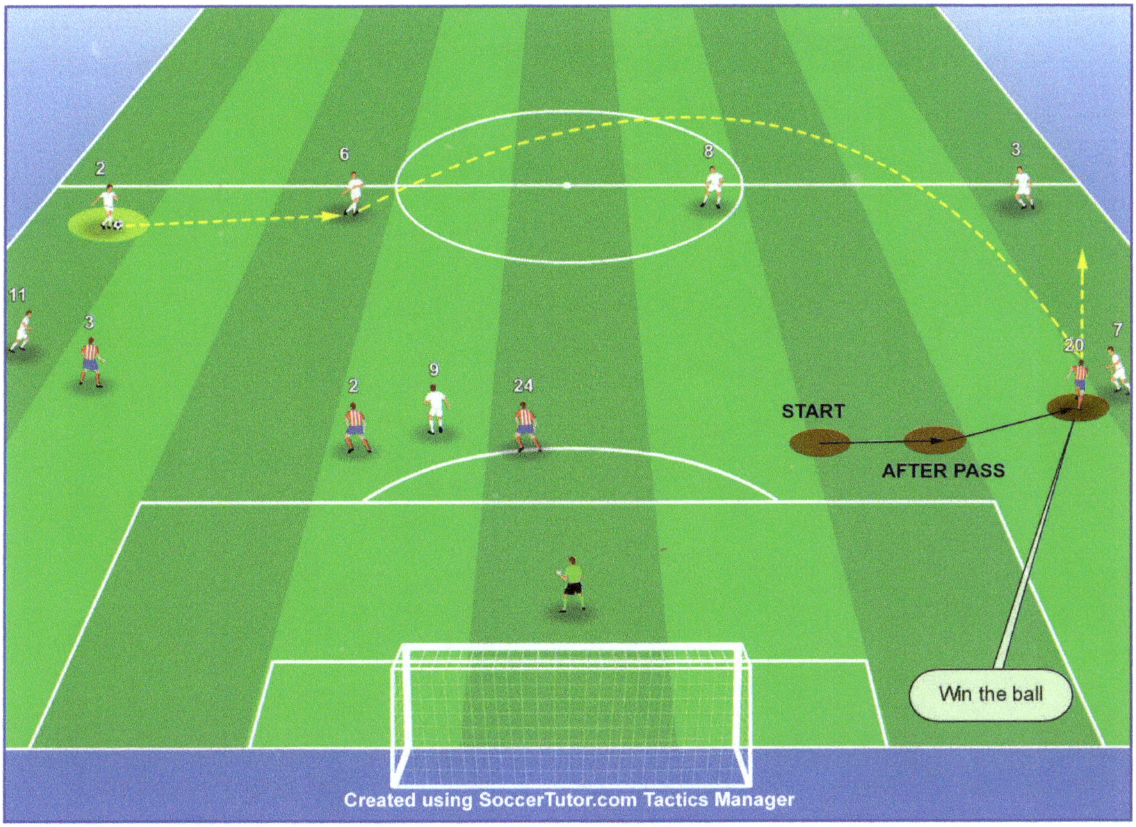

In the diagram example, the full back on the weak side **Juanfran (20)** is initially in a balanced position, as the ball is on the strong side with the opposite full back (white No.2).

After the pass from white No.2 to No.6, **Juanfran (20)** readjusts his position and closes the gap between himself and the winger No.7.

This new position must enable **Juanfran (20)** to either be able to intercept a potential pass towards the winger (white No.7), or at least restrict his available space and time on the ball if he receives.

In the diagram example, **Juanfran (20)** is able to get to the ball ahead of No.7 and head it away.

Tactical Situation 6 - Wide Positioning of the Full Backs to Contest the Opposing Wingers

3. Restrict the Winger's Available Time and Space After a Switch of Play Against the 4-4-2

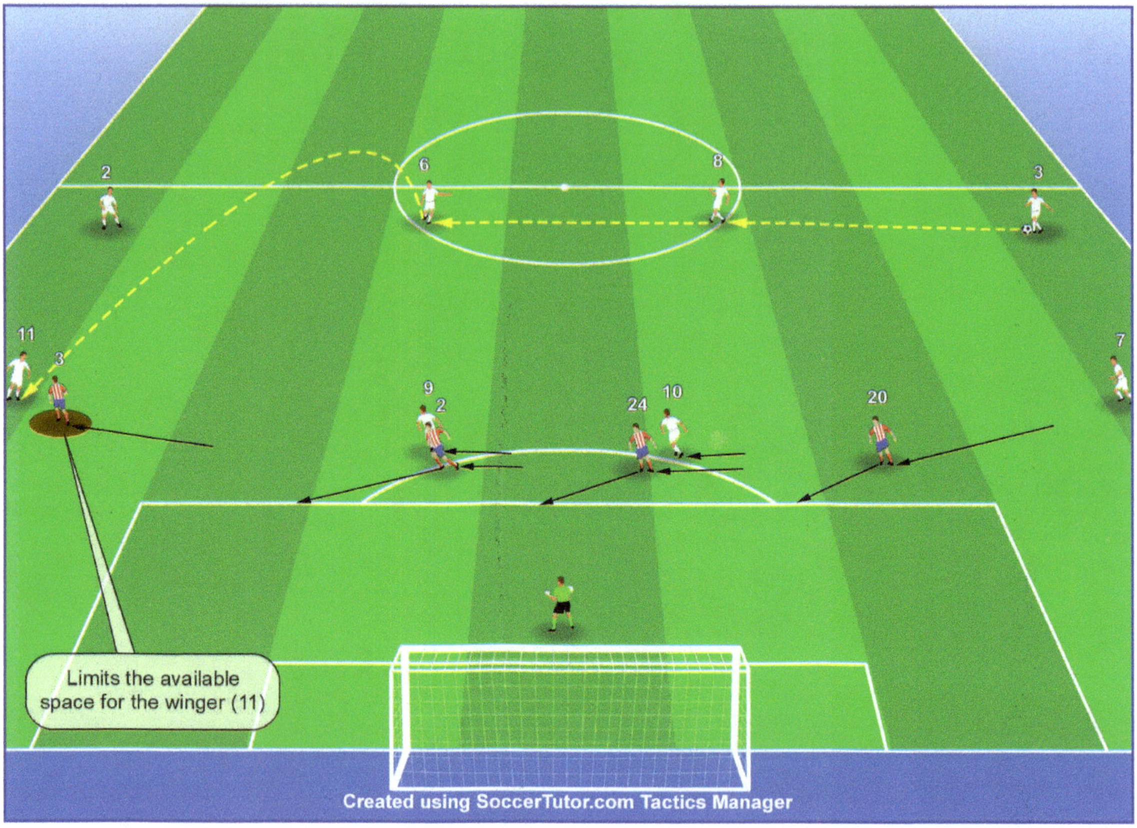

Against the 4-3-3, the Atlético full backs are in wide positions and the 2 centre backs only have 1 forward to mark. However, against the 4-4-2 (and 4-2-3-1), the Atlético full backs retain more balanced positions.

F. Luis (3) and **Juanfran (20)** are positioned as close as possible to the wingers to control them but must also be close enough to their centre backs to provide support if they need it.

In this tactical example, the opposition switch play from one side to the other and all 4 Atlético defenders shift across.

The Atlético left back **F. Luis (3)** is in a more balanced position but it is still his responsibility to defend No.11 in a 1 v 1 situation when the central midfielder No.6 plays the long pass.

Against the 4-4-2, **F. Luis (3)** can move quickly and intercept the pass but it is more likely that the winger (white No.11) receives. Therefore, **F. Luis's (3)** focus is to restrict his available time and space and prevent the winger from creating a 1 v 1 as he has already developed a high level of speed.

The right back **Juanfran (20)** has moved across and back to make sure there is a 3 v 2 numerical advantage in the centre of the pitch against the 2 forwards.

2 PRACTICES FOR "WIDE POSITIONING OF THE FULL BACKS TO CONTEST THE OPPOSING WINGERS"

Tactical Situation 6 - Wide Positioning of the Full Backs to Contest the Opposing Wingers

PRACTICES FOR THIS TACTICAL SITUATION (2 PRACTICES)

1. Wide Positioning and Shifting Across of Full Backs to Contest the Wingers Against the 4-3-3

Scenario A: Intercept the Pass to the Winger from a Central Position

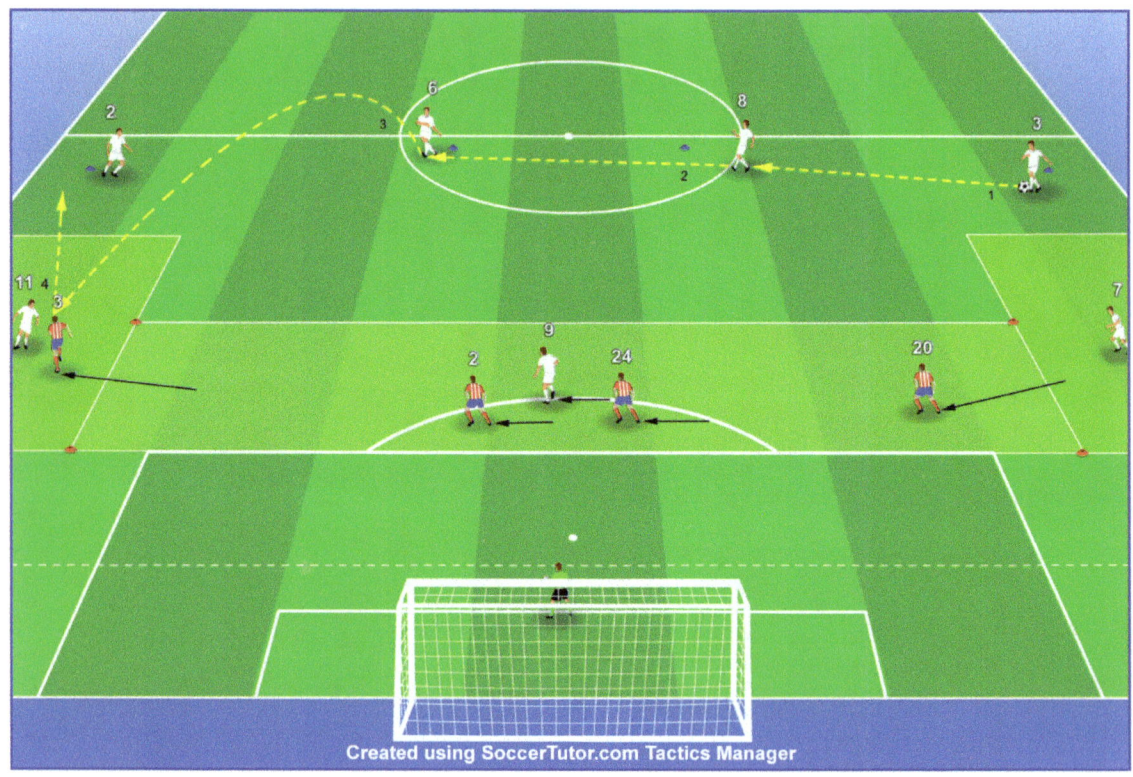

Description (Scenario A)

- The white forward (No.9) and all 4 red defenders start in the central white area and the 2 white wingers (No.11 and No.7) are positioned in the wide yellow areas.

- In this practice, we focus on the positioning of the red full backs (**3** & **20**). The deep white players pass the ball around and the red defenders all shift accordingly.

- The 2 red centre backs (**2** & **24**) take up appropriate positions and the full backs (**3** & **20**) stay close to the opposing wingers.

- The next step is for one of the deep white players to pass to one of the wingers in a wide yellow area. In this first example, the central midfielder No.6 plays the pass.

- The red full back (**No.20** in diagram example) aims to intercept the pass or, if the winger No.11 receives, restrict his available time and space inside the yellow area.

- The aim for the white wingers is to receive, play 1v1 inside the yellow area and cross for the forward No.9 to score past the GK.

©SOCCERTUTOR.COM DIEGO SIMEONE'S DEFENDING TACTICS

Tactical Situation 6 - Wide Positioning of the Full Backs to Contest the Opposing Wingers

Scenario B: Intercept a Long Pass After a Switch of Play

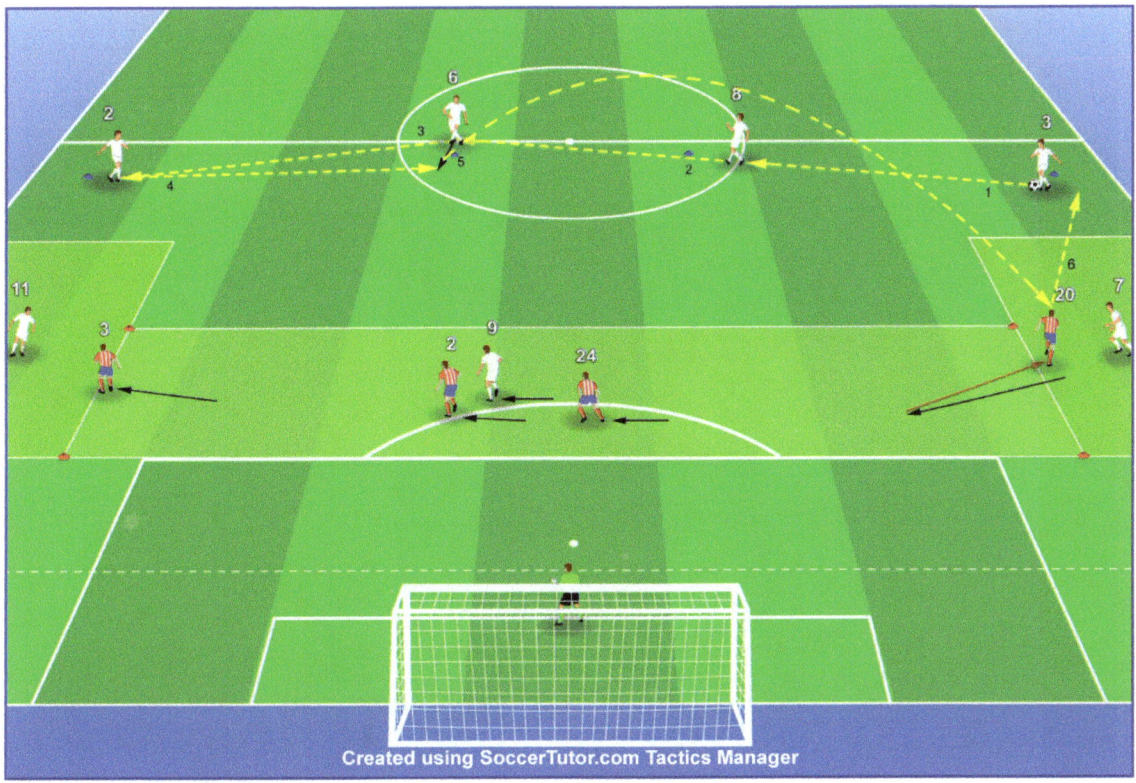

Description (Scenario B)
- In this second scenario, the white central midfielder No.6 passes to the weak side.
- The diagram shows the full back **(20)** has shifted horizontally across during a switch of play.
- After the pass from the white right back No.2 to the white central midfielder No.6, the red right back **(20)** readjusts his position.
- This new position must enable **No.20** to either be able to intercept a potential pass towards the winger (white No.7), or at least restrict his available space and time on the ball if he receives.

Variation
The 4 deep white players can also test the positioning of the centre backs by directing the ball to the centre forward (No.9) occasionally.

Tactical Situation 6 - Wide Positioning of the Full Backs to Contest the Opposing Wingers

VARIATION

2. Positioning and Shifting Across of Full Backs to Contest the Wingers Against the 4-4-2 and 4-2-3-1

Scenario A: Restrict Winger's Time & Space After Switch of Play vs 4-4-2

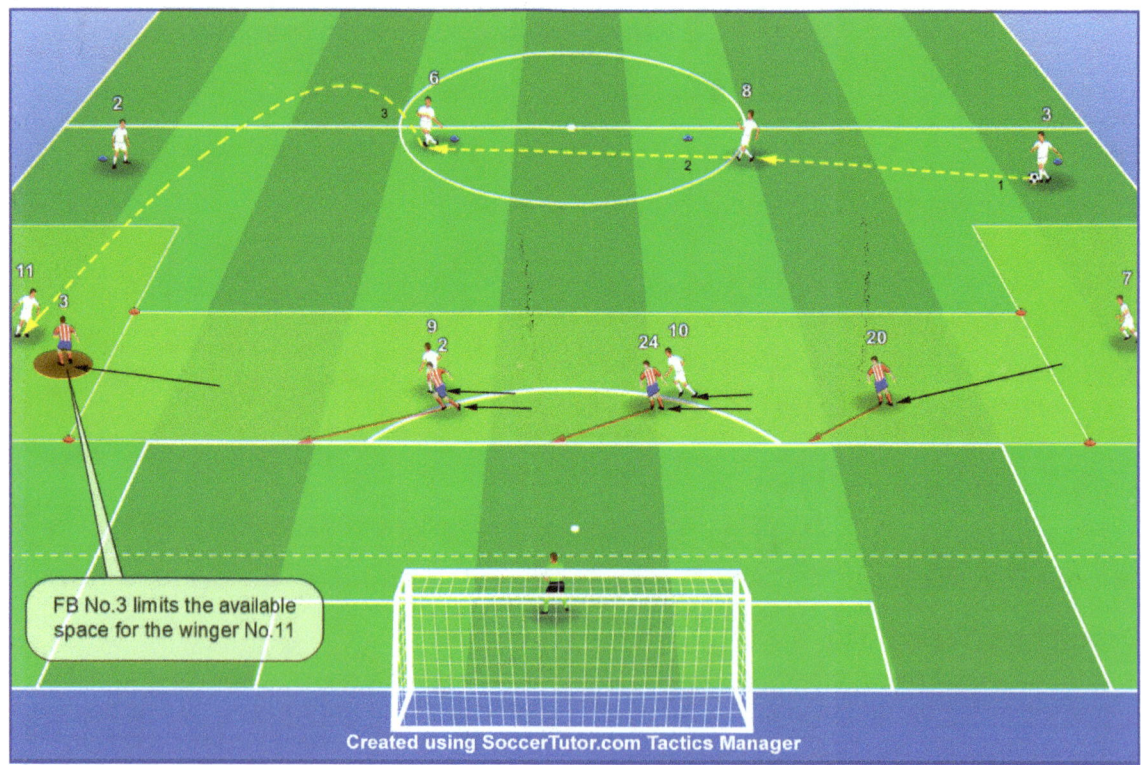

FB No.3 limits the available space for the winger No.11

Description (Scenario A)

- In this variation, the exact same practice is carried out against the 4-4-2 formation.
- The red full backs take up more balanced positions and it is more likely that they will not be able to clear the ball before it is received by the winger.
- The deep white players pass the ball around and the red defenders all shift accordingly.
- The next step is for one of the deep white players to pass to one of the wingers in a wide yellow area (No.6 to No.11 in diagram).

- In this first example, this is part of a conventional switch of play.
- The red full back (20) aims to intercept the pass or, if the winger receives, restrict his available time and space inside the yellow area.
- The aim for the white wingers is to receive, play 1v1 inside the yellow area and cross for the forward to score past the GK.

Tactical Situation 6 - Wide Positioning of the Full Backs to Contest the Opposing Wingers

Scenario B: Intercept Long Pass to Winger After Switch of Play vs 4-2-3-1

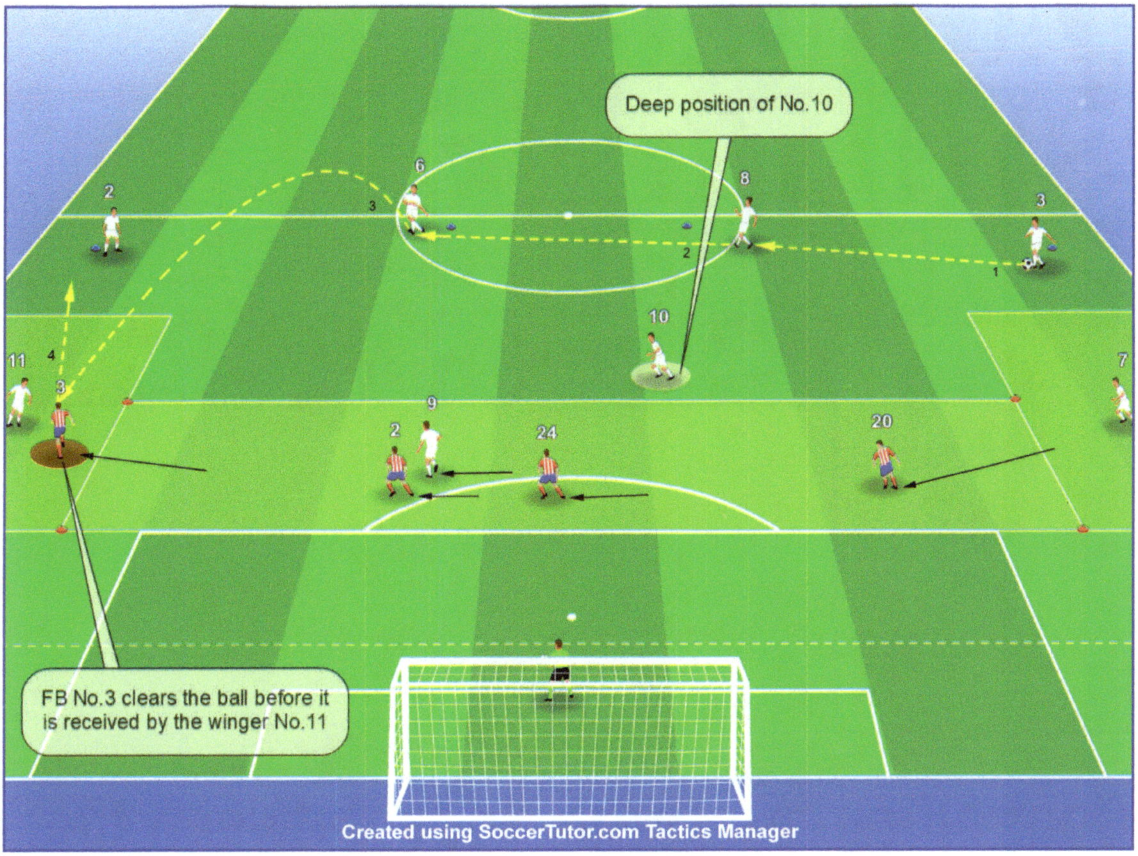

Description (Scenario B)

- In this second scenario, we show a variation against the 4-2-3-1 formation.
- When playing against the 4-2-3-1, the red full backs have to read the positioning of their centre backs, which depends on the positioning of white No.10.
- If the white No.10 is in a deep position, the red full backs take up wide positions and can more easily intercept the ball before the winger receives.
- If the white No.10 is in an advanced position (inside the white area), **the red full backs are positioned closer to the centre backs (just like against the 4-4-2).**
- In the diagram example, the white No.10 is in a deep position, so the red left back **(3)** can be in a wide position.
- After white No.6's pass towards the winger No.11, the red left back **(3)** is close enough to get in front of No.11 and head the ball away.

Coaching Points

1. Shift according to the position of the ball.
2. The focus is on controlling the direct opponent.

DIEGO SIMEONE'S DEFENDING TACTICS

TACTICAL SITUATION 7

Controlling the Large Gaps Between the Centre Backs and Full Backs

The content in this section is from analysis of Diego Simeone's Atlético Madrid teams during the 2017/2018 and 2018/2019 seasons.

The analysis is based on recurring patterns of play observed within the Atlético Madrid team. Once the same phase of play occurred several times (at least 10), the tactics would be seen as a pattern. The analysis on the following pages are examples of the team's tactics being used effectively.

Each action, pass, individual movement with or without the ball, and the positioning of each player on the pitch including their body shape, are presented.

The analysis is then used to create a session to coach this specific tactical situation.

Tactical Situation 7 - Controlling the Large Gaps Between the Centre Backs and Full Backs

DISADVANTAGES OF THE WIDE POSITIONING OF THE ATLÉTICO FULL BACKS

The wide positioning of the full backs against the 4-3-3 and 4-2-3-1 has disadvantages:

1. **The full backs can be isolated in 1 v 1 situations against the opposing wingers**.

In these situations, the central or wide midfielder would provide support - this will be analysed fully in the rear block section of the book.

Additionally, the tactical awareness of the Atlético full backs (**F. Luis**, **Juanfran** and **Lucas Hernandez**) was very good and they can read the game perfectly, knowing when to play for time until support comes. They also have great 1 v 1 defensive qualities to deal with duels. This all made Atlético's defensive play effective, even in these situations.

2. **Gaps are created between the defenders which can be exploited by the opposing midfielders**.

If Atlético play against the 4-4-2, the defenders take up balanced positions. The full backs are positioned towards the centre and close to the centre backs and the positioning of the centre backs is more balanced to control both forwards. Therefore, there are no gaps.

However, when playing against 1 forward and 2 wingers (4-3-3 or 4-2-3-1), gaps are created between the full backs and centre backs, which prevent the centre backs from providing immediate support to the full backs if the opposing wingers receive in a 1 v 1 situation.

In addition, there is a strong possibility that an opposing midfielder can exploit a gap by moving between a full back and centre back.

NOTE: Diego Simeone's Atlético Madrid team have built mechanisms and tactical solutions for this which are shown in this section.

Gaps Between the Centre Backs and Full Backs Against the 4-3-3

If Diego Simeone's Atlético Madrid are playing against the 4-3-3, the gaps between the centre backs and full backs can be exploited by the attacking midfielders.

If they play against the 4-2-3-1, it will be the No.10 who tries to exploit the gaps.

Tactical Situation 7 - Controlling the Large Gaps Between the Centre Backs and Full Backs

CONTROLLING GAPS BETWEEN THE CENTRE BACKS AND FULL BACKS AGAINST THE 4-3-3

1. Shifting Across to Prevent Attacking Midfielders Exploiting the Gaps: Strong Side Attacking Midfielder in an Advanced Position

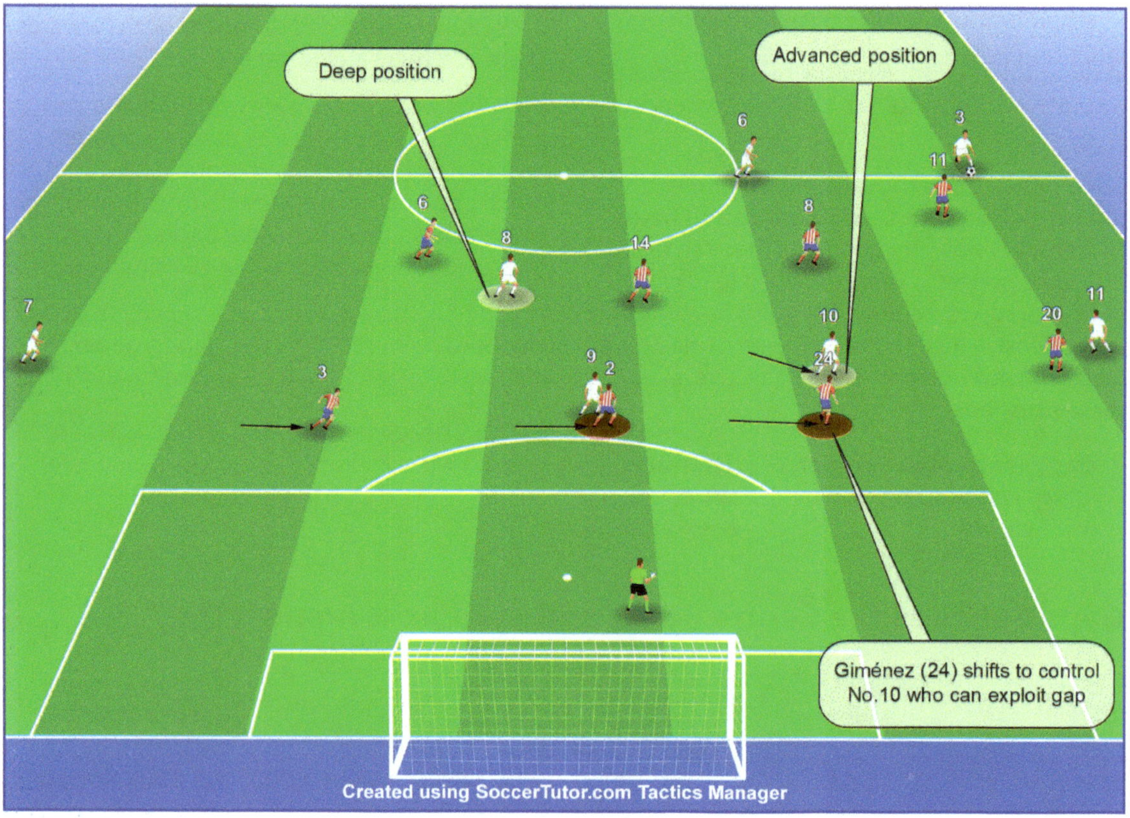

The centre backs **Godín (2)** and **Giménez (24)** have to read the positioning of the most advanced attacking midfielder (No.10) and be ready to control him if he tries to exploit the gap.

The opposing attacking midfielder No.10 is in an advanced position on the strong side, while the other attacking midfielder No.8 is in a deep position.

White No.10 is highly likely to try and exploit the gap between the right back and centre back.

Therefore, the centre back **Giménez (24)** shifts across to control white No.10. At the same time, the other centre back **Godín (2)** shifts across to take over the marking of the forward No.9.

The left back on the weak side **F. Luis (3)** moves towards the centre into a more balanced position, to restrict the available space on the blind side of **Godín (2)**. The positioning of the Atlético defenders now looks similar to when playing against 2 forwards (4-4-2).

DIEGO SIMEONE'S DEFENDING TACTICS

Tactical Situation 7 - Controlling the Large Gaps Between the Centre Backs and Full Backs

2. Shifting Across to Prevent Attacking Midfielders Exploiting the Gaps: Weak Side Attacking Midfielder in an Advanced Position

In this variation, it is now the attacking midfielder on the weak side (white No.8) who is in an advanced position.

In this situation, the centre back on the strong side **Giménez (24)** stays close to the forward (No.9). The other centre back **Godín (2)** controls the attacking midfielder (No.8) and is able to provide support for **Giménez (24)** at the same time. In addition, the left back on the weak side **F. Luis (3)** shifts inside into a more balanced position.

3. Shifting Across to Prevent Attacking Midfielders Exploiting the Gaps: Both Attacking Midfielders in Advanced Positions

In this final variation, both attacking midfielders are in advanced positions, so the left back **F. Luis (3)** shifts towards the strong side to control the most dangerous player.

NOTE: For this tactic to be effective, the awareness of the centre backs is key, as they should not only focus on the ball and their direct opponent, but also frequently scan the positioning of the opposing attacking midfielders too.

DIEGO SIMEONE'S DEFENDING TACTICS

Tactical Situation 7 - Controlling the Large Gaps Between the Centre Backs and Full Backs

CONTROLLING GAPS BETWEEN THE CENTRE BACKS AND FULL BACKS AGAINST THE 4-2-3-1

1. Positioning of the 2 Centre Backs with the Opposing No.10 in a Deep Position on the Weak Side

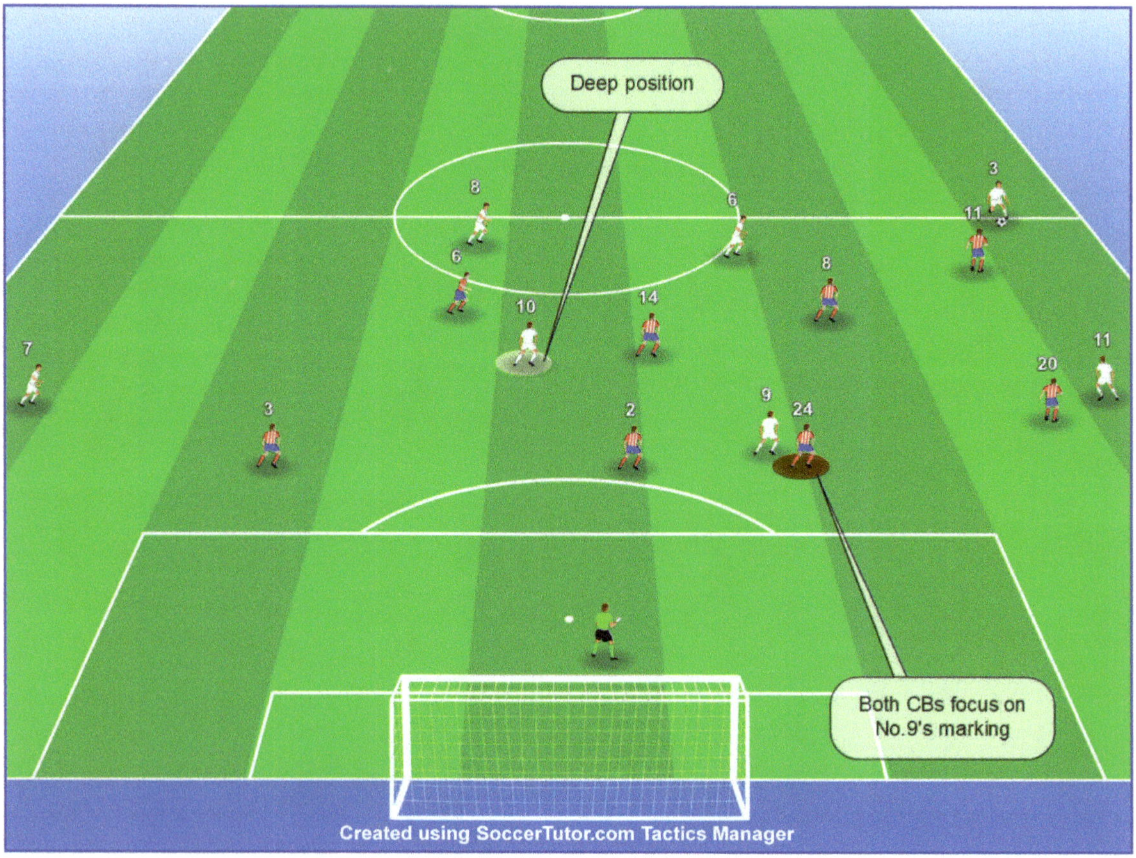

In this tactical example, Diego Simeone's Atlético Madrid team are defending against the 4-2-3-1 formation (1 attacking midfielder).

When the attacking midfielder No.10 is positioned on the weak side and in a relatively deep position, both Atlético centre backs **Godín (2)** and **Giménez (24)** can focus on marking the 1 forward (white No.9).

This is because the white No.10 is too far away to exploit any gaps between the Atlético centre backs and full backs.

DIEGO SIMEONE'S DEFENDING TACTICS

Tactical Situation 7 - Controlling the Large Gaps Between the Centre Backs and Full Backs

2. Positioning of the 2 Centre Backs with the Opposing No.10 in an Advanced Position on the Weak Side

If the opposing attacking midfielder (white No.10) moves into a more advanced position on the weak side, he now becomes a threat to receive a pass in the gap between the left back **F. Luis (3)** and the centre back **Godín (2)**.

Godín (2) therefore readjusts his positioning and shifts a few yards across and towards the weak side in order to control the white No.10.

The left back on the weak side **F. Luis (3)** moves towards the centre to take up a more balanced position, so that he can provide support to **Godín (2)** and also close the gap between the two of them.

In addition, the centre back on the strong side **Giménez (24)** has to readjust his positioning to take up a goal-side position and be ready to neutralise the most dangerous passes (behind his back).

If the centre backs have not adjusted their positioning in time, it is the full back on the weak side who shifts towards the inside to compensate for it and controls the opposing No.10 by filling the gap

DIEGO SIMEONE'S DEFENDING TACTICS

Tactical Situation 7 - Controlling the Large Gaps Between the Centre Backs and Full Backs

3. Positioning of the 2 Centre Backs with the Opposing No.10 in a Deep Position on the Strong Side

If the opposing No.10 is in a deep position on the strong side, the centre backs are focused on marking the forward (white No.9). However, **Giménez (24)** has to keep an eye on No.10 and get ready to readjust his positioning if he moves. It is equally important that **Giménez (24)** checks the positioning of white No.9 frequently. The positioning of both centre backs enables them to neutralise any potential pass directed to No.9 behind or on the blind side of **Giménez (24)**.

4. Positioning of the 2 Centre Backs with the Opposing No.10 in an Advanced Position on the Strong Side

As soon as the opposing No.10 moves into an advanced position, he can potentially exploit the gap between **Giménez (24)** and **Juanfran (20)**.

The centre back on the strong side **Giménez (24)** shifts to control No.10 and **Godín (2)** readjusts his position so he is able to both mark No.9 and provide support to **Giménez (24)**.

The left back **F. Luis (3)** moves across to restrict the available space on the blind side of **Godín (2)**.

©SOCCERTUTOR.COM   DIEGO SIMEONE'S DEFENDING TACTICS

Tactical Situation 7 - Controlling the Large Gaps Between the Centre Backs and Full Backs

FULL BACK'S MOVEMENT TO CONTROL THE GAP BETWEEN THE CENTRE BACK AND FULL BACK

1a. Open Body Shape of the Full Back to Have a Wide View

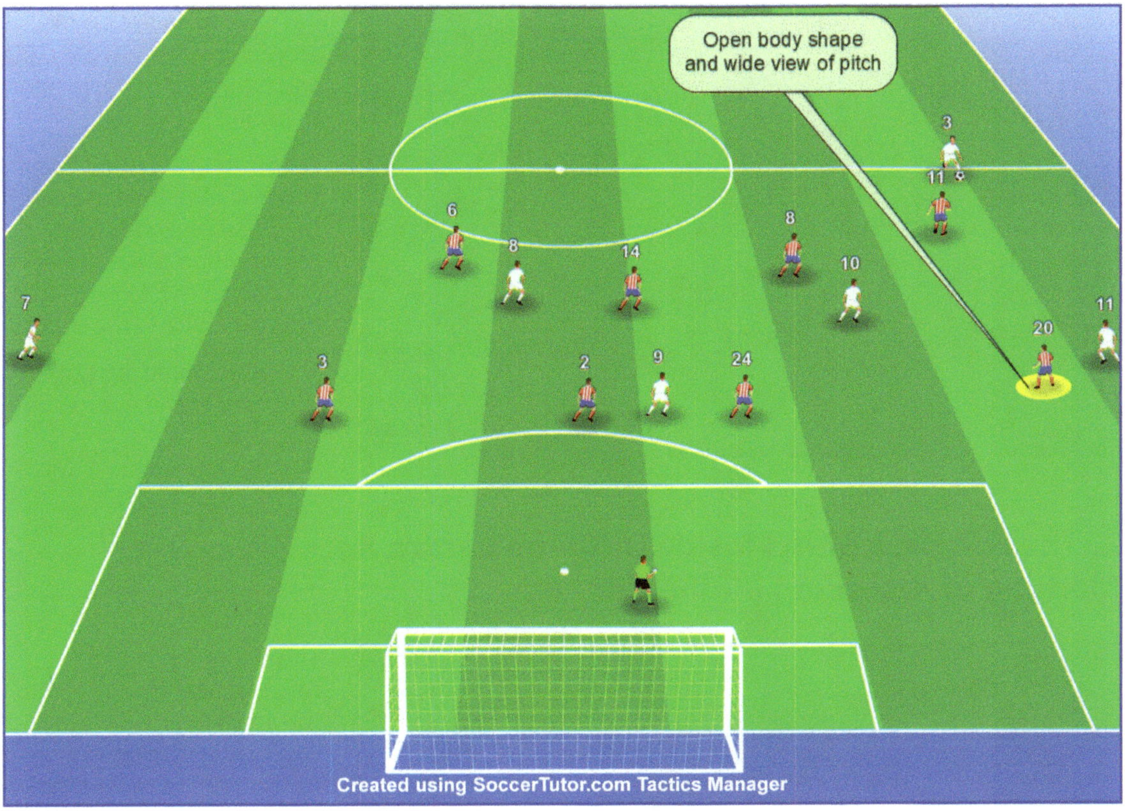

Another option for controlling the potential gaps between the full backs and the centre backs is the horizontal shifting of the full backs.

This strategy can only be effective if the full backs have the appropriate body shape, which enables them to have a wide view of the pitch.

This means that they have a good awareness of the space and know the positions of their opponents and team-mates.

In the diagram example above, the opposing left back (No.3) has possession.

The Atlético Madrid right back **Juanfran (20)** is positioned on the strong side and has an open body shape which enables him to clearly see:

1. The positioning of right centre back **Giménez (24)**, who is the closest team-mate to him.

2. The space between himself and **Giménez (24)**.

3. The positioning of the opposing attacking midfielder (No.10), who could exploit the large gap between himself and **Giménez (24)**.

©SOCCERTUTOR.COM   DIEGO SIMEONE'S DEFENDING TACTICS

Tactical Situation 7 - Controlling the Large Gaps Between the Centre Backs and Full Backs

1b. The Full Back Shifts Inside to Control the Attacking Midfielder Attempting to Exploit the Gap with a Forward Run

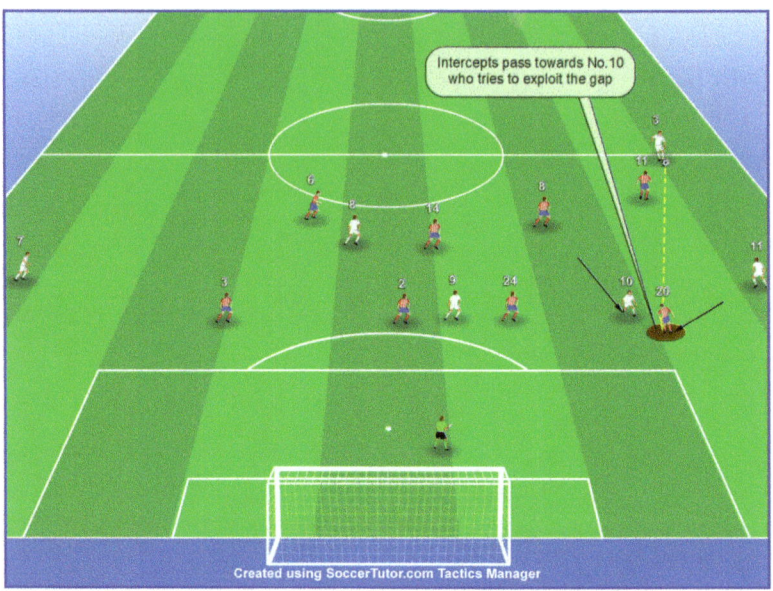

If the full back **Juanfran (20)** notices that the centre back **Giménez (24)** is away from him and there is a gap, he has to keep an eye on the attacking midfielder (No.10) and his potential movement to exploit the gap.

Juanfran's (20) good body shape enables him to read the situation and he sees the intention of the player in possession (white No.3) to pass the ball into the gap.

Therefore, **Juanfran (20)** shifts inside and intercepts the pass.

2. The Full Back Shifts Inside Until the Centre Back Takes Over Marking of Attacking Midfielder

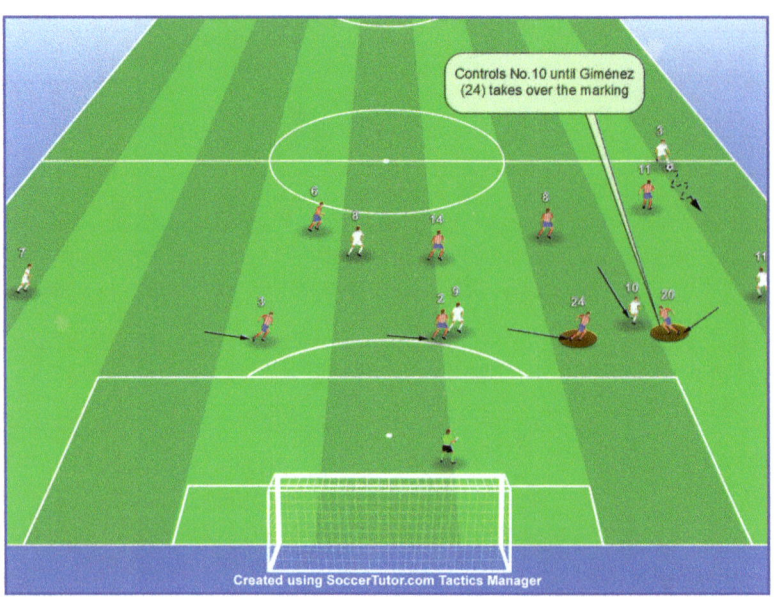

This is a variation of the same tactical situation, with the attacking midfielder (white No.10) making a forward run to exploit the gap again.

Juanfran (20) moves inside to control him again, but this time only until the centre back **Giménez (24)** is able to take over his marking.

Atlético use this reaction as the white No.10 is in a more dangerous position than the winger No.11.

©SOCCERTUTOR.COM   DIEGO SIMEONE'S DEFENDING TACTICS

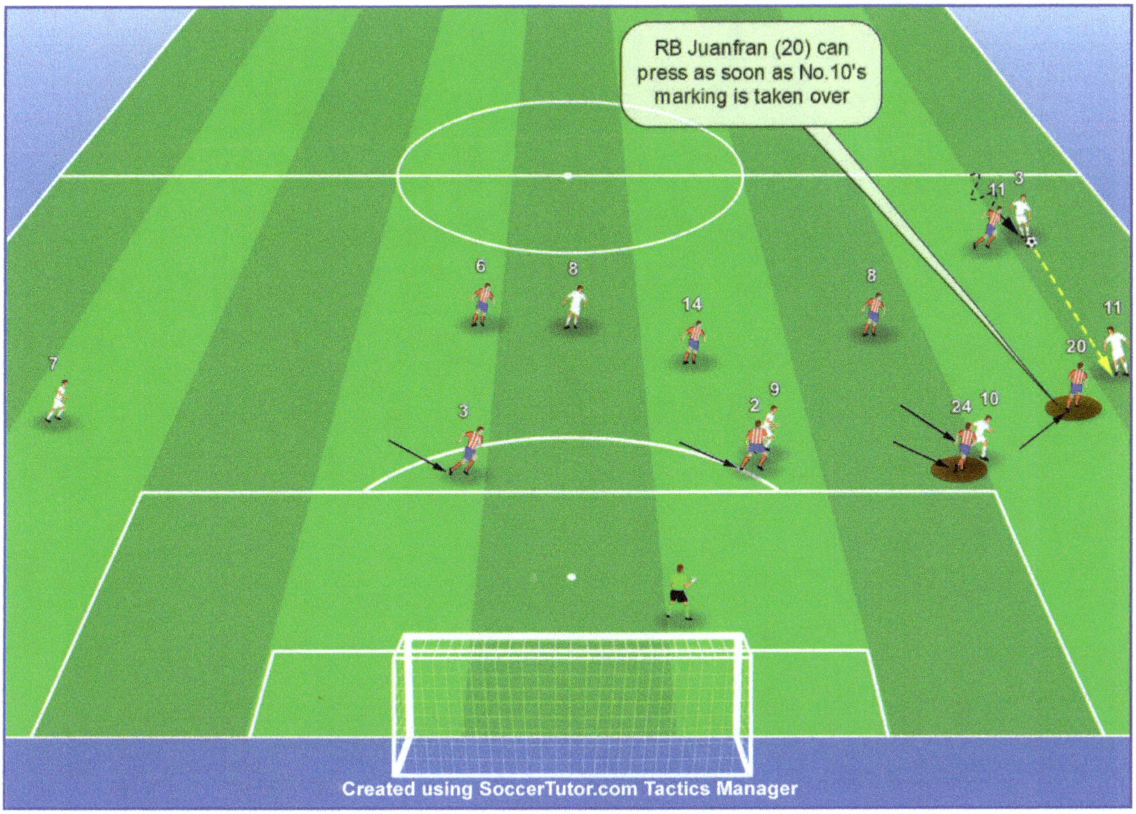

Tactical Situation 7 - Controlling the Large Gaps Between the Centre Backs and Full Backs

RB Juanfran (20) can press as soon as No.10's marking is taken over

As soon as **Giménez (24)** takes over the marking of the white No.10, **Juanfran (20)** can then focus on the winger No.11 when the pass is directed to him from the left back No.3.

The positioning is similar to playing against the 4-4-2, with the weak side left back **F. Luis (3)** close to the weak side centre back **Godín (2)**.

ASSESSMENT

1. The wide positioning of the full backs restricts the available time and space for the opposing forwards/wingers but also creates gaps between the centre backs and full backs. These gaps can be exploited by the opposing attacking midfielders unless the defenders have great tactical awareness, can read the game perfectly, have a wide view (open body shape) and can stay focused during the entire 90 minutes.

2. The open body shape of the full backs should be used against every formation (not only the 4-3-3 and 4-2-3-1), as it ensures a wide view of the pitch and eye contact with the rest of the defenders.

3. Eye contact is a very important element for the coordination and synchronisation of the defensive line. This enables the 4 defenders in the defensive line to not only control the potential gaps, but also carry out synchronised and coordinated defensive movements (forwards and backwards).

©SOCCERTUTOR.COM — DIEGO SIMEONE'S DEFENDING TACTICS

SESSION (3 PRACTICES) FOR "CONTROLLING THE LARGE GAPS BETWEEN THE CENTRE BACKS AND FULL BACKS"

Tactical Situation 7 - Controlling the Large Gaps Between the Centre Backs and Full Backs

SESSION FOR THIS TACTICAL SITUATION (3 PRACTICES)
1. Centre Backs Controlling the Gaps to the Full Backs in a Functional Practice vs 4-3-3
Scenario A: Defend a Pass into the Gap on the Weak Side

Objective: Controlling the gaps between the centre backs and full backs with the horizontal shifting of the centre backs.

Description (Scenario A)
- The focus is on the 2 red centre backs. There is also a GK defending a large goal.
- The 3 deep white players pass the ball to each other in set positions.
- The 2 white attacking midfielders (8 and 10) make forward runs in the gaps, try to receive a pass in behind and then score past the GK.

- The red centre backs (**2** and **24**) try to prevent this by reading the tactical situation and shifting horizontally.
- When an attacking midfielder (white No.8 in diagram example) enters the white area, the respective centre back (**2**) should shift across, control No.8, and neutralise any potential passes towards him.
- In the diagram example, there is a long pass to the weak side and the red centre back (**2**) shifts across to close the gap and clears the ball away.

DIEGO SIMEONE'S DEFENDING TACTICS

Tactical Situation 7 - Controlling the Large Gaps Between the Centre Backs and Full Backs

Scenario B: Defend a Pass into the Gap on the Strong Side

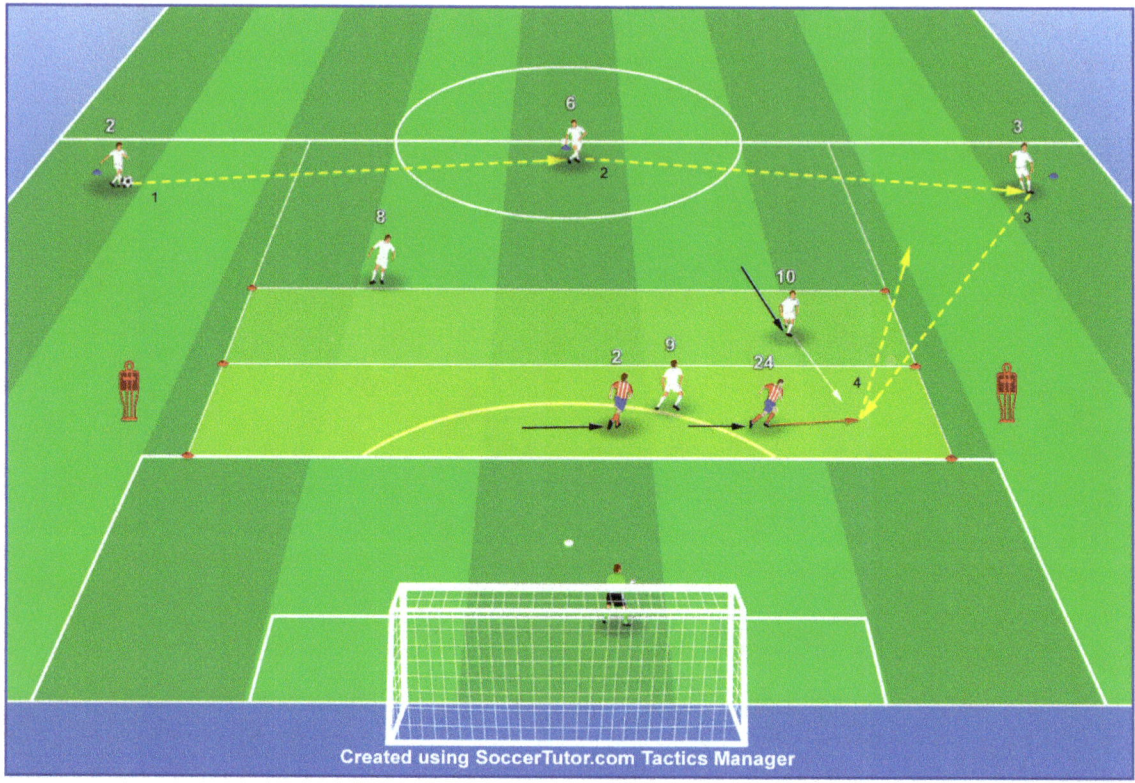

Description (Scenario B)
- In this second scenario, there is a long ground pass on the strong side towards white No.10. Both red centre backs shift across to close the gap and red **No.24** clears the ball away.

Restrictions
1. The passes should be directed into the yellow area or into the penalty area.
2. Only 1 attacking midfielder (at a time) can make a forward run into the white area and then the yellow area.

Variation
This practice can be adapted to play against the 4-2-3-1 with just 1 attacking midfielder (No.10) making forward runs into the potential gaps.

Coaching Points
1. Shift according to the position of the ball.
2. The centre backs must have a wide view of the pitch (open body shape) to control the space and the opposing midfielders.

Tactical Situation 7 - Controlling the Large Gaps Between the Centre Backs and Full Backs

VARIATION
2. Full Backs Controlling the Gaps to the Centre Backs in a Functional Practice vs 4-3-3

Scenario A: Defend a Pass into the Gap on the Weak Side

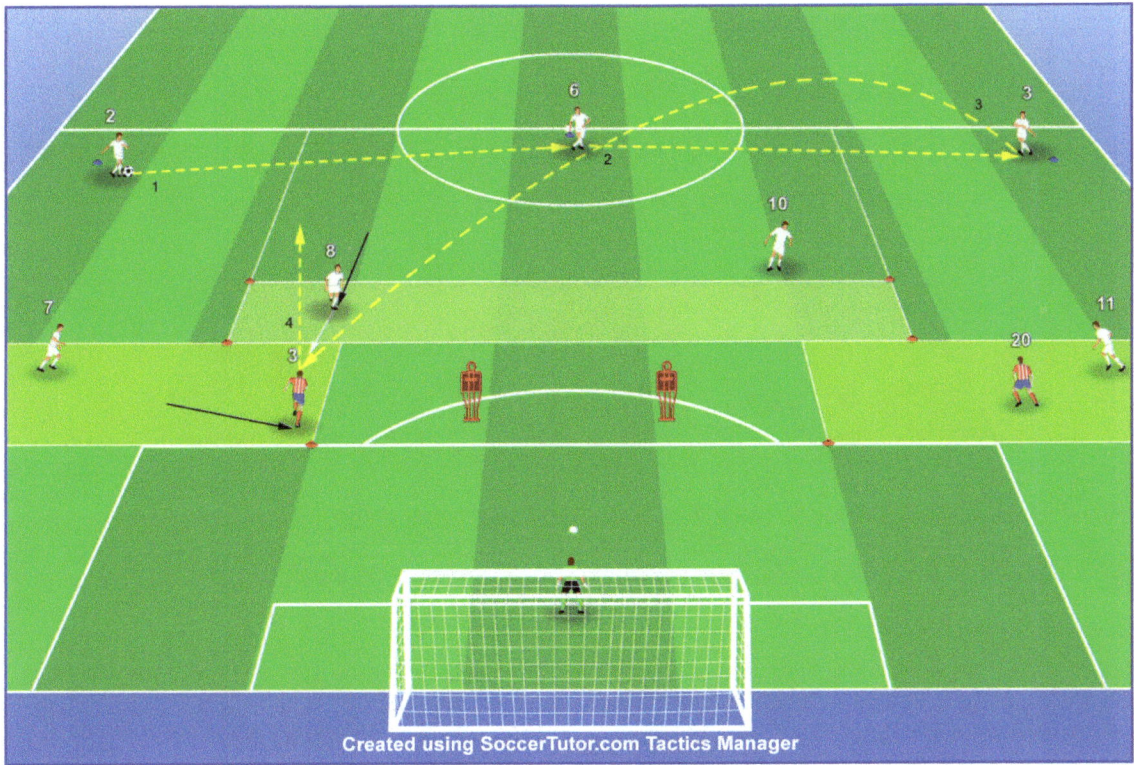

Objective: Controlling the gaps between the centre backs and full backs with the horizontal shifting of the full backs.

Description (Scenario A)

- In this variation, we have 2 yellow wide areas instead of a central area. When a white attacking midfielder enters the white area, a red full back has to control him.

- The red full backs (**3** and **20**) have an open body shape, read the tactical situation, and shift horizontally at the right moment to control the space and block potential passes.

- When an attacking midfielder (white No.8 in diagram) enters the white area, the respective full back (**3**) shifts inside to control him and neutralise any potential passes towards him.

- In this first diagram example, there is a long pass to the weak side and the red left back (**3**) shifts inside to close the gap and clears the ball away.

Tactical Situation 7 - Controlling the Large Gaps Between the Centre Backs and Full Backs

Scenario B: Defend a Pass into the Gap on the Strong Side

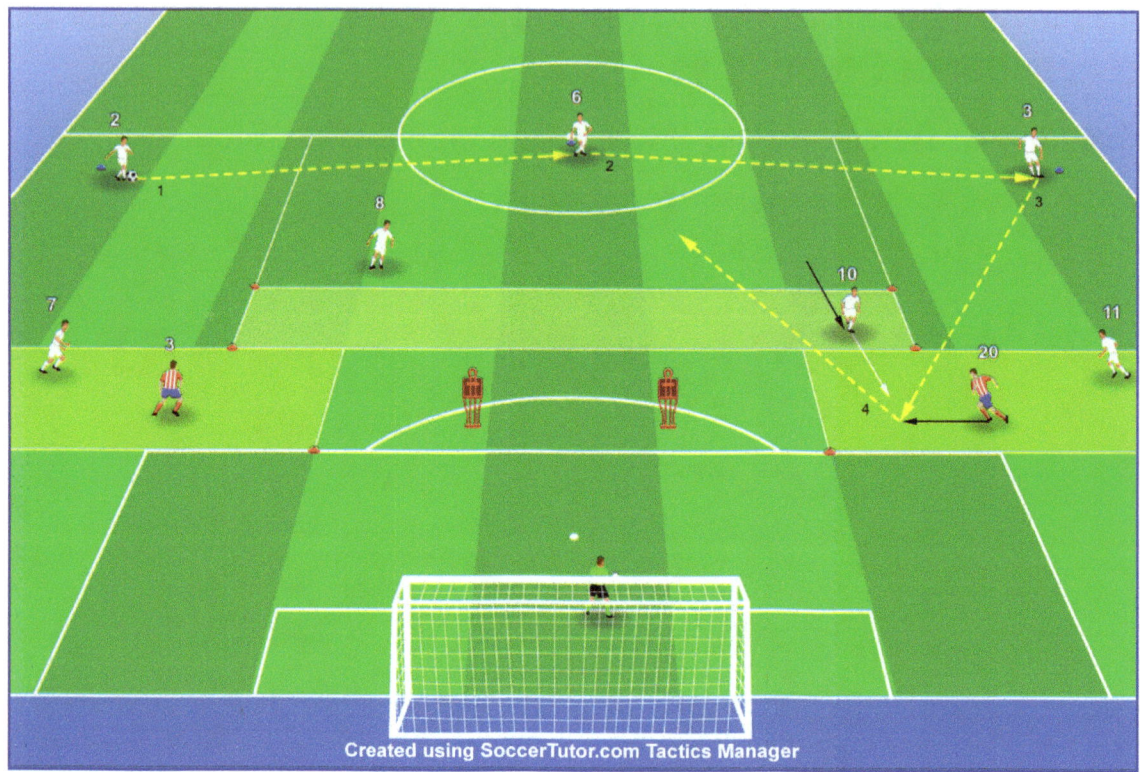

Description (Scenario B)

- In this second scenario, there is a long ground pass on the strong side towards white No.10. The red right back **(20)** shifts inside to close the gap and clears the ball away.

Restrictions

1. The passes should be directed into the yellow areas or into the penalty area.
2. Only 1 attacking midfielder (at a time) can make a forward run into the white area and then the yellow area.

Variation

This practice can be adapted to play against the 4-2-3-1 with just 1 attacking midfielder (No.10) making forward runs into the potential gaps.

Coaching Points

1. Shift according to the position of the ball.
2. The full backs (especially on the strong side) must have a wide view of the pitch (open body shape) to control the space and the opposing midfielders.

Tactical Situation 7 - Controlling the Large Gaps Between the Centre Backs and Full Backs

PROGRESSION
3. Defensive Line Controlling the Gaps Between the Centre Backs and Full Backs in a Functional Practice

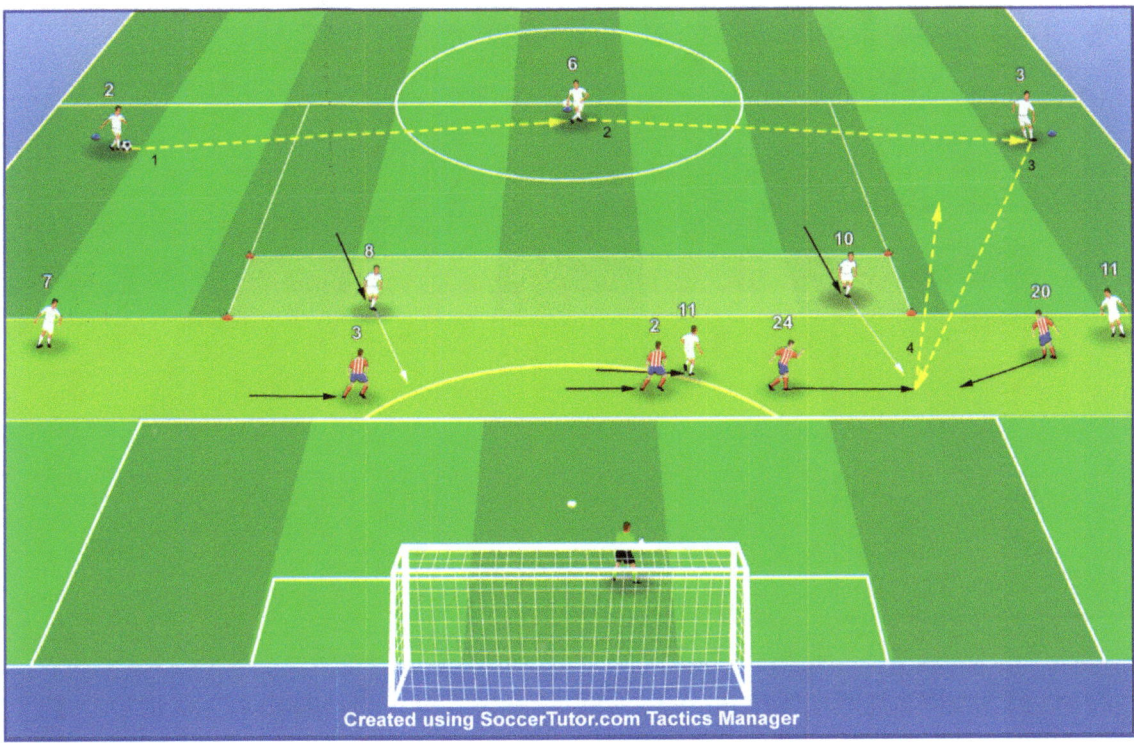

Description
- This is a progression of the previous 2 practices. We now have all 4 defenders who must read the tactical situation and make the correct defensive movements.
- This time, both the white attacking midfielders (white No.8 and No.10) can make forward movements into the potential gaps between the centre backs and full backs.
- The reds defenders use their awareness (open body shape) and horizontal shifting to control these gaps.
- The 3 deep white players can also direct the ball to the wingers (No.7 or No.11) to test the positioning of the red defenders.
- The aim for the white players is to score, while the reds simply try to defend effectively in every possible situation.

Variation
This practice can be adapted to play against the 4-2-3-1 with just 1 attacking midfielder (No.10) making forward runs into the potential gaps.

Coaching Points
1. Shift according to the position of the ball.
2. The defenders must have a wide view of the pitch (open body shape) to control the space and the opposing midfielders.
3. There needs to be clear and constant communication between the defenders.

DIEGO SIMEONE'S DEFENDING TACTICS

TACTICAL SITUATION 8

Positioning and Defensive Movements of the Front Block

The content in this section is from analysis of Diego Simeone's Atlético Madrid teams during the 2017/2018 and 2018/2019 seasons.

The analysis is based on recurring patterns of play observed within the Atlético Madrid team. Once the same phase of play occurred several times (at least 10), the tactics would be seen as a pattern. The analysis on the following pages are examples of the team's tactics being used effectively.

Each action, pass, individual movement with or without the ball, and the positioning of each player on the pitch including their body shape, are presented.

The analysis is then used to create a session to coach this specific tactical situation.

Tactical Situation 8 - Positioning and Defensive Movements of the Front Block

HOW THE OPPOSITION CAN EXPLOIT THE "CRUCIAL CENTRAL AREA"

[Diagram: Crucial Central Area]

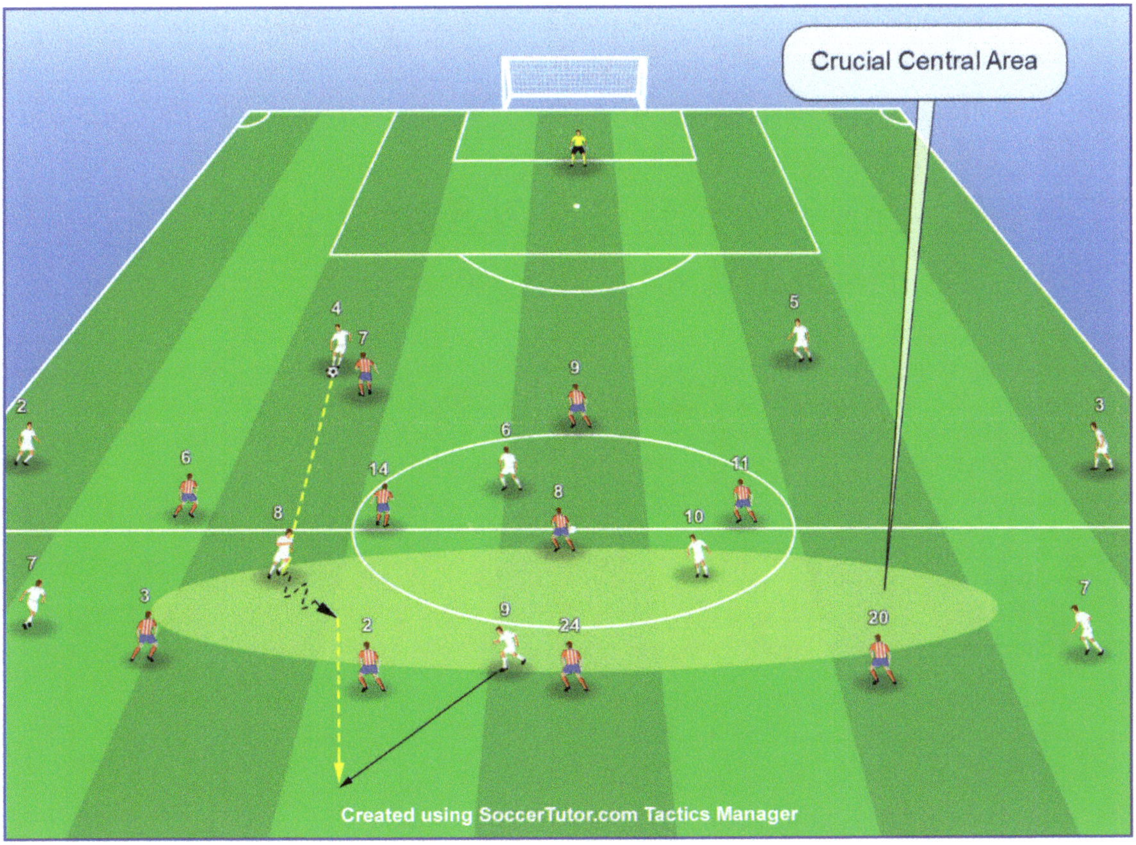

The forwards and the midfielders make the front block of a team.

For Diego Simeone's Atlético Madrid, the players in the front block work in perfect harmony. They shift according to the position of the ball with the aim of defending the crucial central area.

The **Crucial Central Area** is the central area between the midfield and defensive lines of the team (rear block). This area is very important and if the opposing team manages to find space and time on the ball within it, there is a great opportunity for them to then play a final pass or shoot at goal (if in final third).

In the diagram above, Atlético are defending within the middle third. The white opposing team manages to find a way to move the ball to a player within the crucial central area and that player (No.8) has space and time on the ball.

In this situation, it is easy for the white central midfielder No.8 to pass in behind the defensive line (final pass) for one of his team-mates (forward No.9 in diagram), who makes a diagonal run.

If this situation takes place closer to Atlético's goal, No.8 can also shoot instead of passing.

DIEGO SIMEONE'S DEFENDING TACTICS

Tactical Situation 8 - Positioning and Defensive Movements of the Front Block

MAIN AIM OF THE FRONT BLOCK

The main aim of Atlético Madrid's front block is to protect the **"Crucial Central Area."**

To succeed in this main aim, the Atlético players have to succeed in other smaller aims, which are fully analysed on the following pages...

1ST AIM: NARROWING THE PASSING LANES TO PREVENT THROUGH PASSES

There are many small aims which all add up to being successful in main aims as a team. For the 1st aim of "Narrowing the Passing Lanes to Prevent Through Passes," the following smaller aims are very important:

- As the players in the front block (forwards and midfielders) shift according to the position of the ball, they have to make sure that the through passing lanes are kept narrow.

- Narrowing the passing lanes can be achieved by retaining a safety distance from the player in possession.

- The horizontal cohesion (compactness) of the midfielders enables them to react, shift and block any possible through passes attempted.

- The further away the player in possession is from the midfielders, the larger the distances can be between each midfielder.

- A very important element in succeeding with this aim is controlling both centre backs, which limits their available space when they receive the ball. This means that they will have to pass the ball forward from a relatively long distance, which gives the Atlético Madrid midfielders more time to react to potential through passes.

- If the forwards allow the opposing centre backs more space than they should, they can move forward with the ball, reduce their distance from the Atlético midfielders and make a pass from a shorter distance which increases their chances of success.

©SOCCERTUTOR.COM — DIEGO SIMEONE'S DEFENDING TACTICS

Tactical Situation 8 - Positioning and Defensive Movements of the Front Block

1. Positioning of the Front Block to Prevent Through Passes with the Ball in the Centre

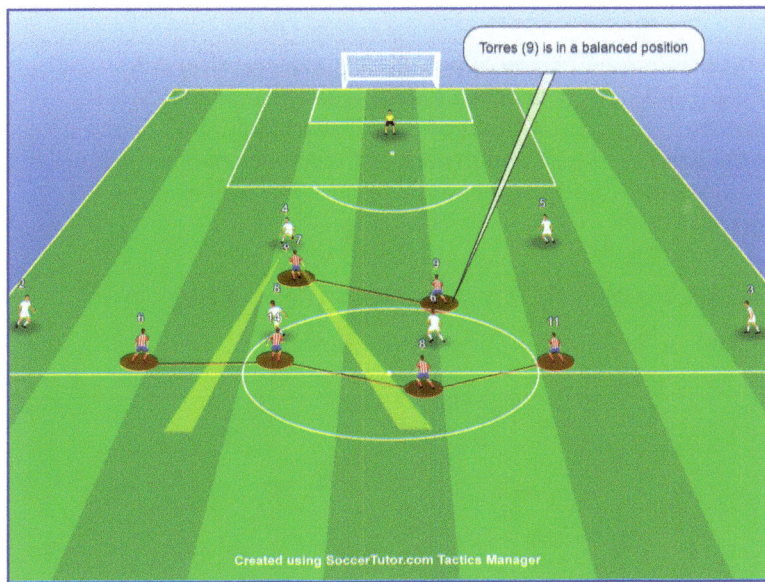

The white centre back No.4 is pressed by **Griezmann (7)**, while the other forward **Torres (9)** is in a balanced position to control both the potential through pass and the other centre back No.5.

The Atlético midfielders retain the appropriate compactness according to the distance they are from the player in possession.

This enables them to keep the passing lanes narrow and make a successful through pass almost impossible.

2. Positioning of the Front Block to Prevent Through Passes with the Ball Near the Side-line

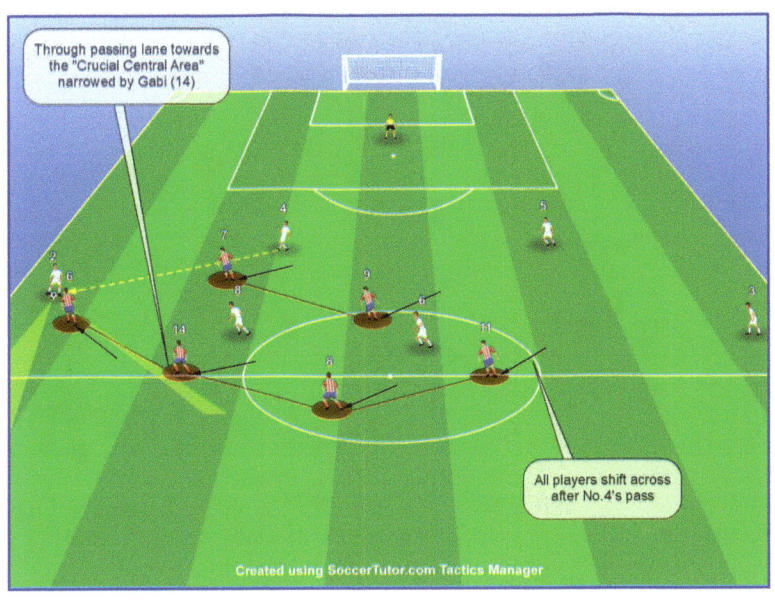

When the pass is played towards the full back No.2 near the side-line, the players shift towards the ball. The through passing lane is narrowed by the central midfielder **Gabi (14)**, so the ball cannot be passed to an opponent within the **Crucial Central Area**.

However, the forward pass to a player down the line is left open. This option is neutralised by mechanisms activated by Atlético's rear block, which will be analysed fully later in the book.

Tactical Situation 8 - Positioning and Defensive Movements of the Front Block

2ND AIM: LIMITING THE AVAILABLE SPACE BETWEEN THE FORWARD AND MIDFIELD LINES

The second aim of Atlético's front block is to keep the space between the forward and midfield lines limited, so the opponents positioned within the **Crucial Central Area** can be immediately put under pressure and prevented from turning if they receive.

If an opposing midfielder receives within the **Crucial Central Area** and manages to turn without pressure, he is highly likely to play a through pass, as the Atlético midfield line will no longer be at a good safety distance.

1. How the Opposition Can Receive, Turn Between the Lines and Play a Final Pass in Behind

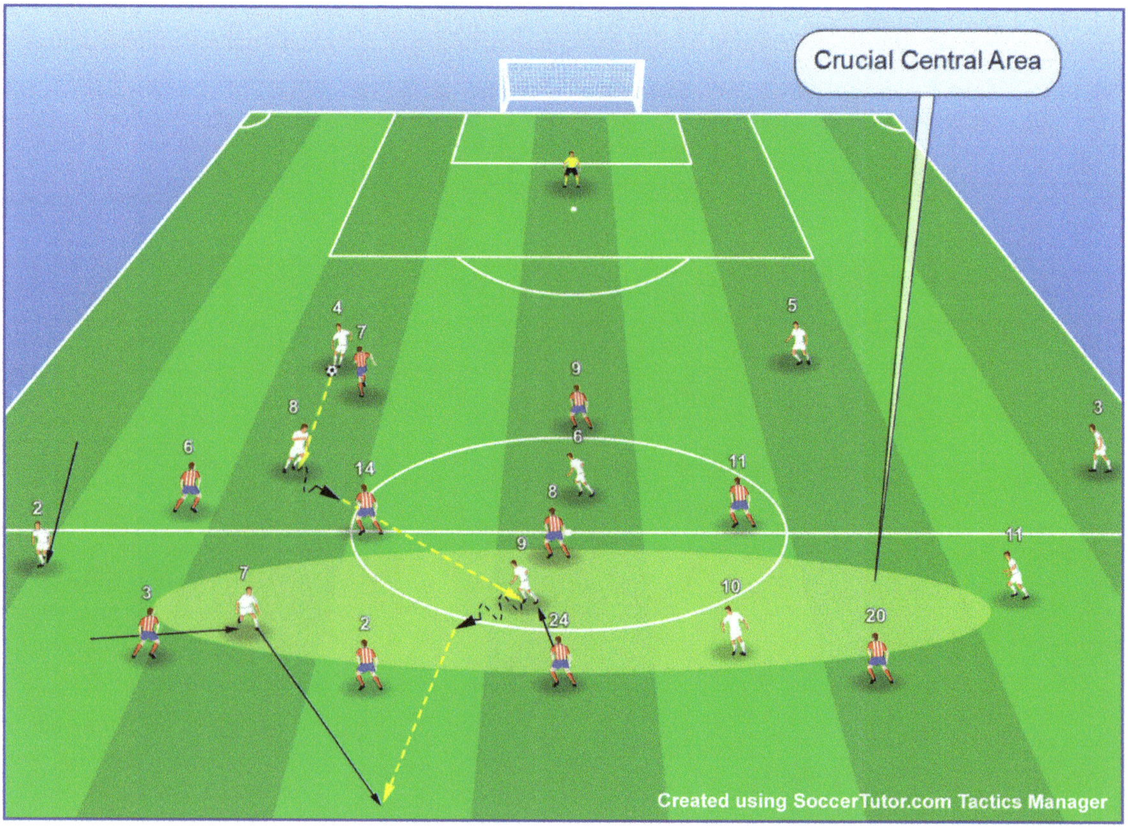

In the diagram above, the opposing central midfielder (white No.8) receives, turns, and passes forward to a team-mate (No.9) positioned inside the **Crucial Central Area**.

It is easy for the white forward No.9 to play a final pass for one of his team-mates (winger No.7 in diagram), who makes a diagonal run.

@SOCCERTUTOR.COM

DIEGO SIMEONE'S DEFENDING TACTICS

Tactical Situation 8 - Positioning and Defensive Movements of the Front Block

2. Adjusting the Positioning of the Front Block to Limit the Available Space Between the Lines

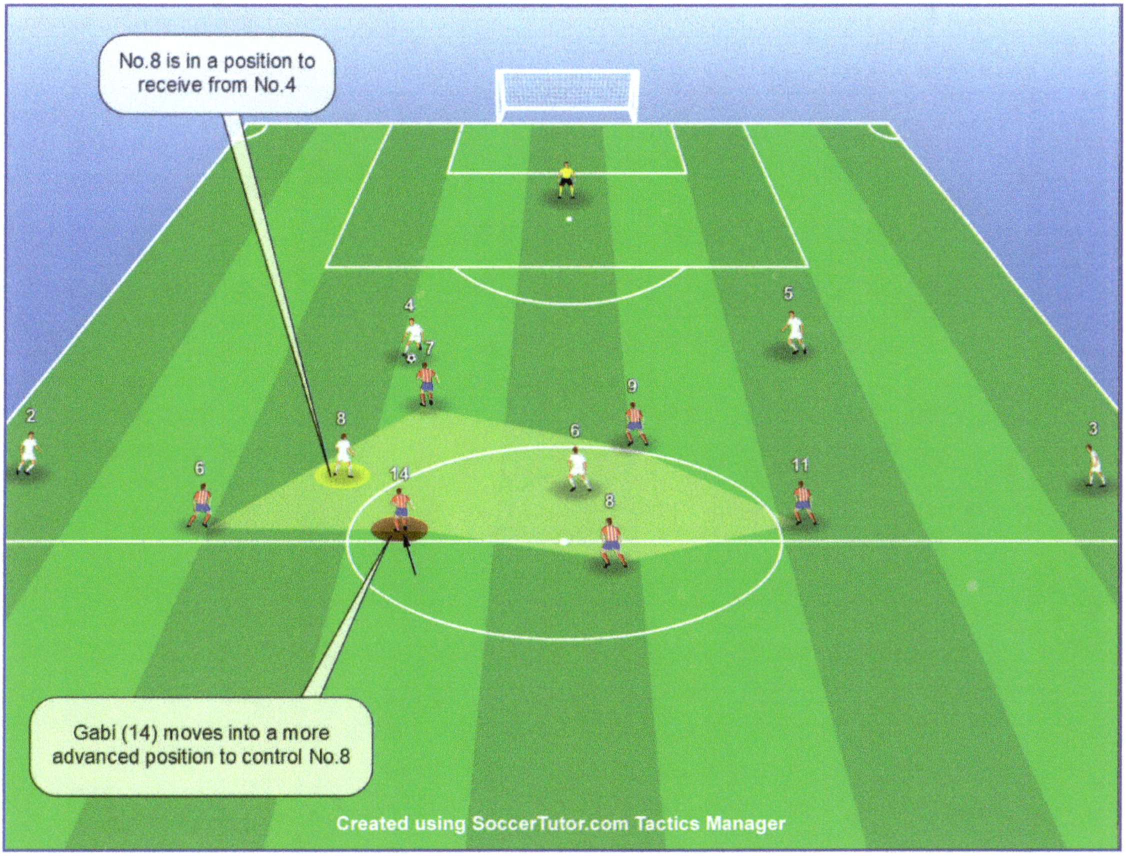

No.8 is in a position to receive from No.4

Gabi (14) moves into a more advanced position to control No.8

In the section "Tactical Situation 4 - Positioning and Defensive Movements of the Midfielders," we showed the shape of the Atlético midfielders during the defensive phase. However, this shape is sometimes affected.

For example, when the distance between the Atlético forwards and midfielders is too large to prevent an opposing midfielder from receiving and turning in between the 2 lines, the Atlético midfielders have to move forward a few yards to control the opposing central midfielders within the space in front of them.

In this example, the white central midfielder No.8 is in position to receive from centre back No.4.

The distance between white No.8 and the Atlético central midfielder **Gabi (14)** is large enough for No.8 to receive from his team-mate and turn.

Therefore, **Gabi (14)** has to adjust his positioning. He steps a few yards forward to make sure his is able to prevent white No.8 from receiving and turning if a pass is directed to him.

Tactical Situation 8 - Positioning and Defensive Movements of the Front Block

3. Preventing the Opposing Midfielders from Receiving and Turning in their Half

As soon as the pass is directed to the white central midfielder No.8, **Gabi (14)** moves to press him and prevent him from turning.

The 2 forwards **Griezmann (7)** and **Torres (9)** move towards the ball area, limit the available space for No.8 and get ready to intercept the ball if he takes a bad first touch under heavy pressure from **Gabi (14)**.

In a very similar situation, the Atlético right central midfielder **Saúl (8)** moves to press the other opposing central midfielder No.6 as soon as he receives a pass from the centre back No.4.

The 2 forwards **Griezmann (7)** and **Torres (9)** move towards the ball area again and get ready to intercept the ball if he takes a bad first touch under heavy pressure from **Saúl (8)**.

DIEGO SIMEONE'S DEFENDING TACTICS

Tactical Situation 8 - Positioning and Defensive Movements of the Front Block

4. Adjusting the Positioning of the Front Block to Limit Space Between the Lines with the Ball in the Centre

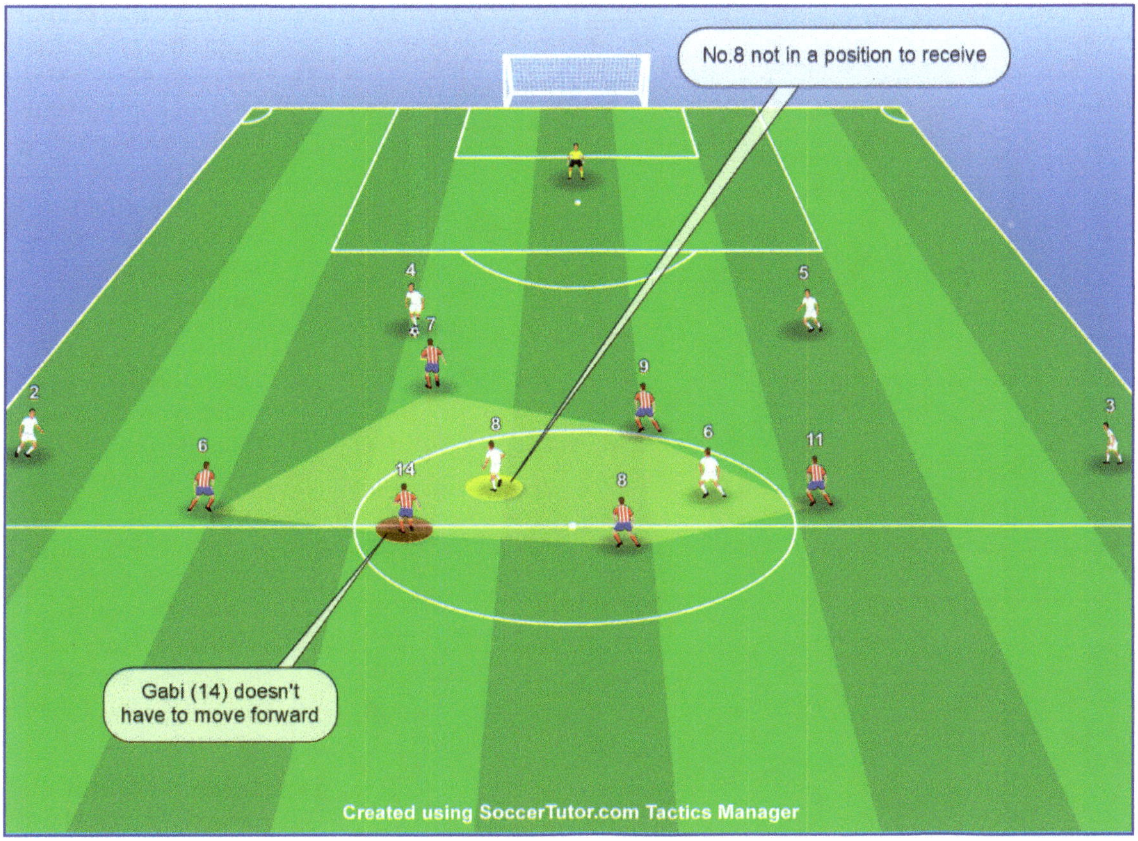

[Diagram showing Atlético defensive positioning with Gabi (14) and annotations: "No.8 not in a position to receive" and "Gabi (14) doesn't have to move forward"]

If the opposing midfielders are not in a position to receive a potential pass from their defenders, or the distance between them and the Atlético midfielders is short enough to prevent them from turning, the Atlético midfielders don't have to step forward like they did in the previous examples.

ASSESSMENT

1. The reaction of the Atlético midfielders is the same if the opposing team plays with the 4-4-2, the 4-2-3-1 or the 4-3-3.

2. The most important aspect in this situation is whether the positioning of the opposing midfielder enables him to receive and turn.

Tactical Situation 8 - Positioning and Defensive Movements of the Front Block

5. The Opposing Central Midfielder Drops Back into the Forwards' Zone of Responsibility

If an opposing central midfielder drops back between Atlético's forward and midfield lines to avoid being closed down by the midfielders, then he enters the zone of responsibility of the forwards.

In this example, white No.6 drops back to move away from **Saúl (8)** and would be able to receive unmarked.

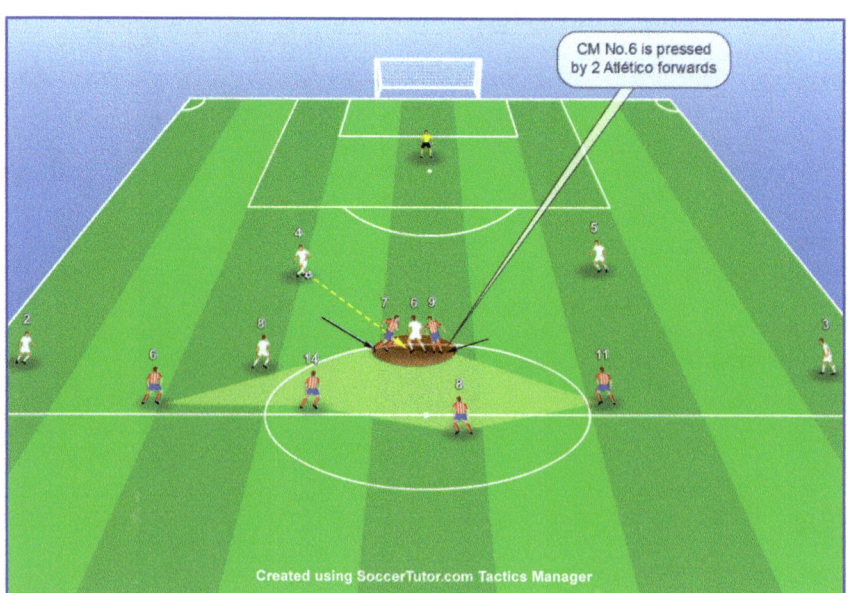

The white central midfielder No.6 enters the zone of responsibility of the forwards.

Before the pass is played, **Torres (9)** was keeping an eye on No.6.

So, as soon as the pass is directed to No.6, the forwards take over the role of closing him down, as shown.

 **ASSESSMENT**

To be effective in this situation, the forwards should scan the positioning of the players around them frequently and not only focus on the player in possession.

@SOCCERTUTOR.COM   DIEGO SIMEONE'S DEFENDING TACTICS

Tactical Situation 8 - Positioning and Defensive Movements of the Front Block

6. Adjusting the Positioning of the Front Block to Limit Space Between the Lines with the Ball Near the Side-line

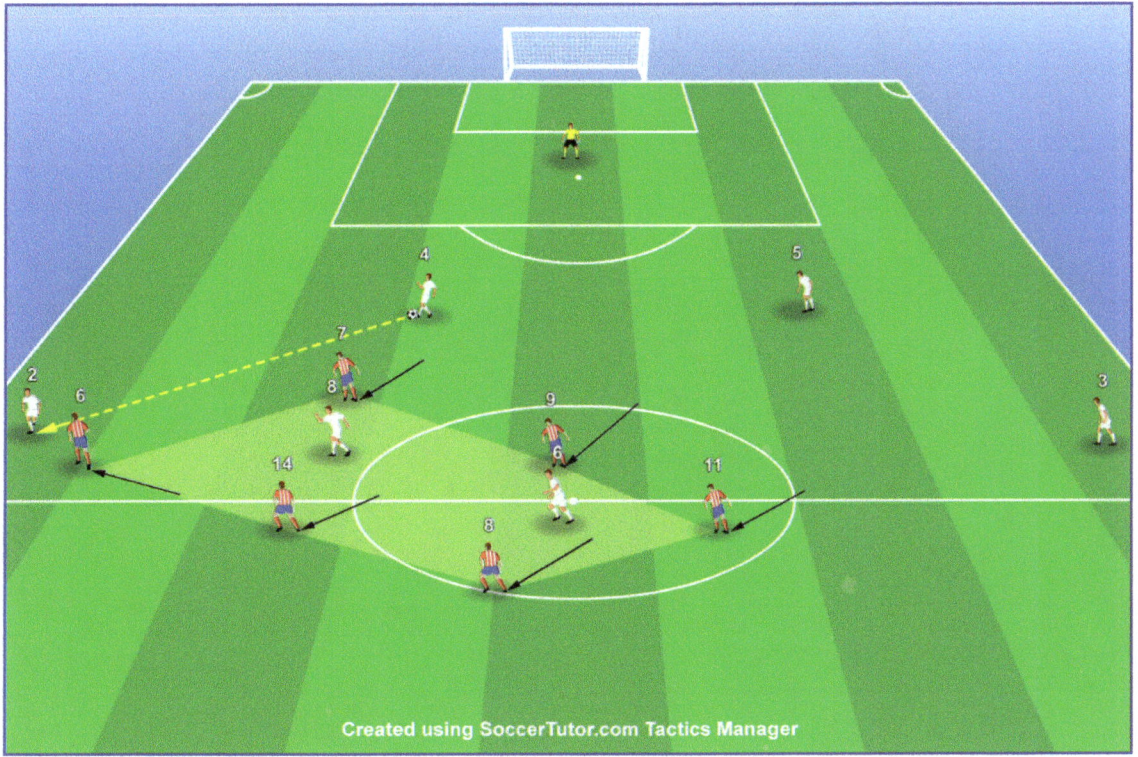

If the ball is directed to the full back (white No.2 in diagram example) **near the side-line**, the Atlético players readjust their positions with the aim of keeping the space between the forward and midfield lines limited. At the same time, the wide midfielder **Koke (6)** presses the ball and tries to block the path to the space inside the **Crucial Central Area**.

The most important element in this situation is the positioning of the forward **Griezmann (7)** on the strong side, who drops back and across to control a potential inside pass towards the white central midfielder No.8.

Without **Griezmann's (7)** defensive movement, white No.8 would be able to receive in between the lines and then play a forward through pass towards the **Crucial Central Area**.

If the ball is passed back to the centre back No.4, there is no possibility of playing a forward through pass towards the crucial central area.

Therefore, between white No.4 and No.8, the white central midfielder is the most dangerous receiver for Atlético, which is why he is controlled.

This tactical situation continues on the next page...

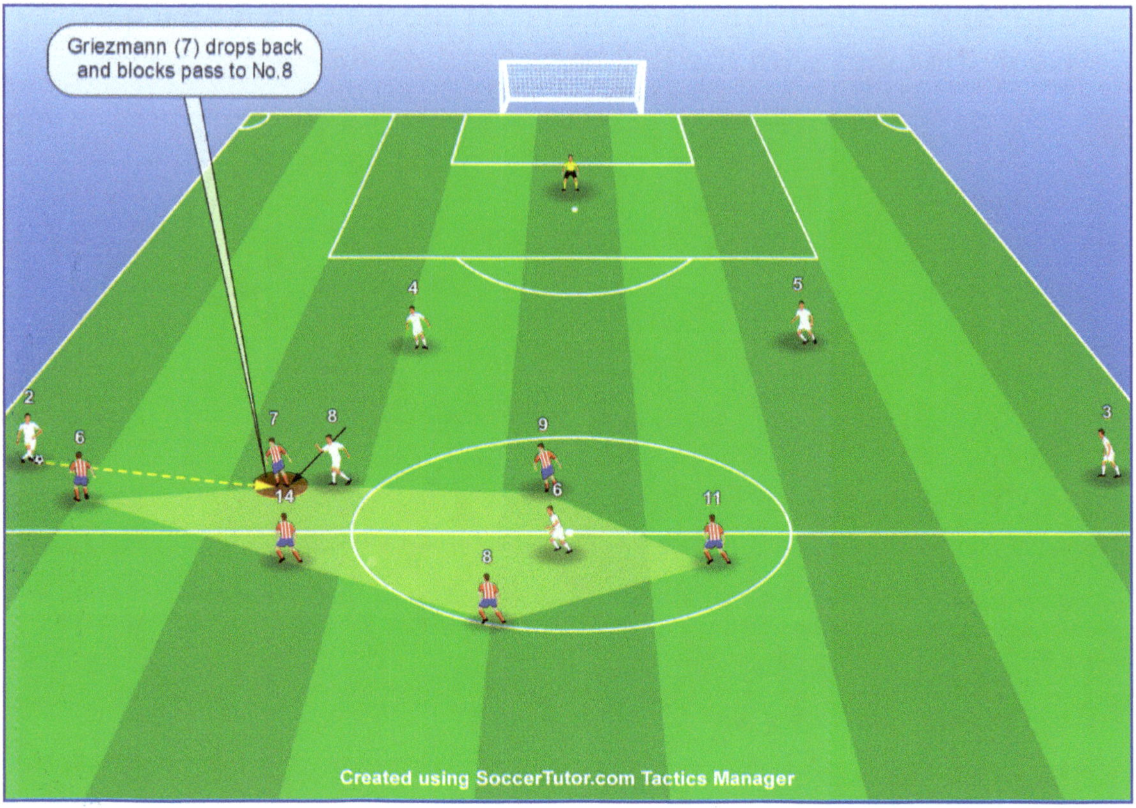

Tactical Situation 8 - Positioning and Defensive Movements of the Front Block

Griezmann (7) drops back and blocks pass to No.8

This tactical example follows on from the diagram on the previous page...

We show what happens when the opposing full back No.3 attempts to pass inside to the central midfielder No.8.

The forward **Griezmann (7)** is in a suitable position to intercept the pass, or at the very least apply immediate pressure to white No.8.

In the diagram example, the Atlético forward **Griezmann (7)** reads the situation and the attempted pass, which enables him to get in front of white No.8 and win the ball.

Tactical Situation 8 - Positioning and Defensive Movements of the Front Block

7. Tactical Solution when the Opposing Central Midfielder Moves Forward to Avoid Being Closed Down by the Forward

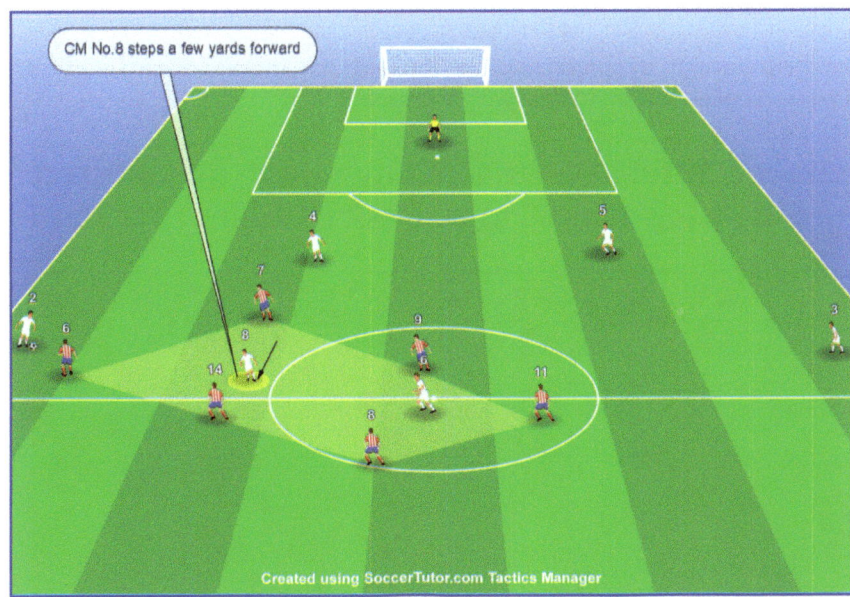

In a variation of the tactical example on the previous page, we show the only option for the white central midfielder No.8 to receive in this situation.

He adjusts his positioning by moving forward a few yards, so the distance between him and the Atlético forward **Griezmann (7)** is much larger.

However, Atlético have a solution for No.8's movement.

Although he has moved away from **Griezmann (7)**, white No.8 moves closer to **Gabi (14)** who closes him down as soon as the pass is played.

These examples prove that if the space between the lines is kept limited, there is no way for the opposing midfielders to receive free of marking in there.

Tactical Situation 8 - Positioning and Defensive Movements of the Front Block

DEFENSIVE REACTIONS OF THE FRONT BLOCK WHEN THE OPPOSITION BREAK THROUGH PRESSURE

If the opposing centre back breaks through the pressure of the forwards and moves forward with the ball, the front block should work in collaboration to deal with the situation.

1a. Drop Back to Retain a Safety Distance, Converge to Be Compact and Create a Strong Side (Opposing Centre Back Dribbling Forward)

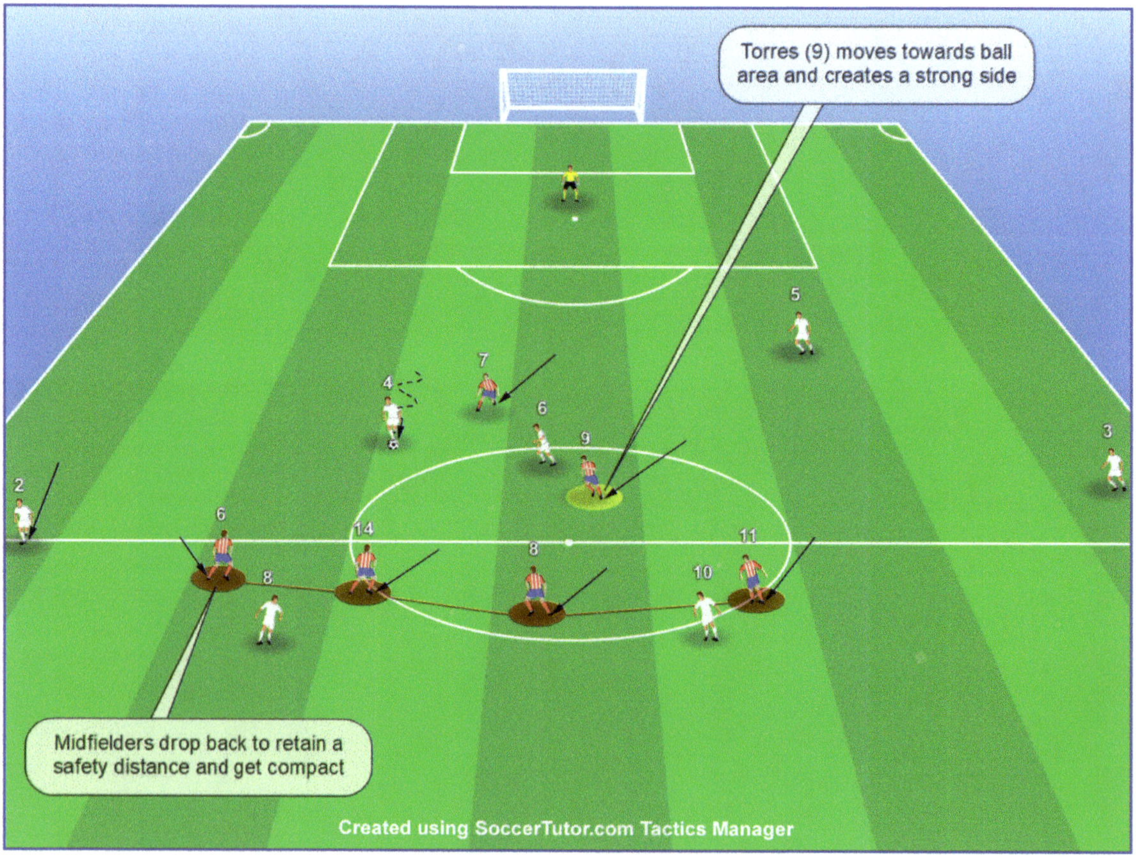

In this tactical example, the opposing white centre back No.4 breaks through the pressure of **Griezmann (7)** and moves forward with the ball.

The reaction of the Atlético midfielders is to drop back collectively and reduce the distance between one another, retain a safety distance from the ball carrier and become more compact.

The second forward **Torres (9)** drops back and across towards the ball area. This action creates a strong side for Atlético Madrid and makes the opposition's attacking play predictable.

©SOCCERTUTOR.COM   DIEGO SIMEONE'S DEFENDING TACTICS

Tactical Situation 8 - Positioning and Defensive Movements of the Front Block

1b. The Compact Atlético Midfield with a Good Safety Distance is Able to Intercept Attempted Through Passes

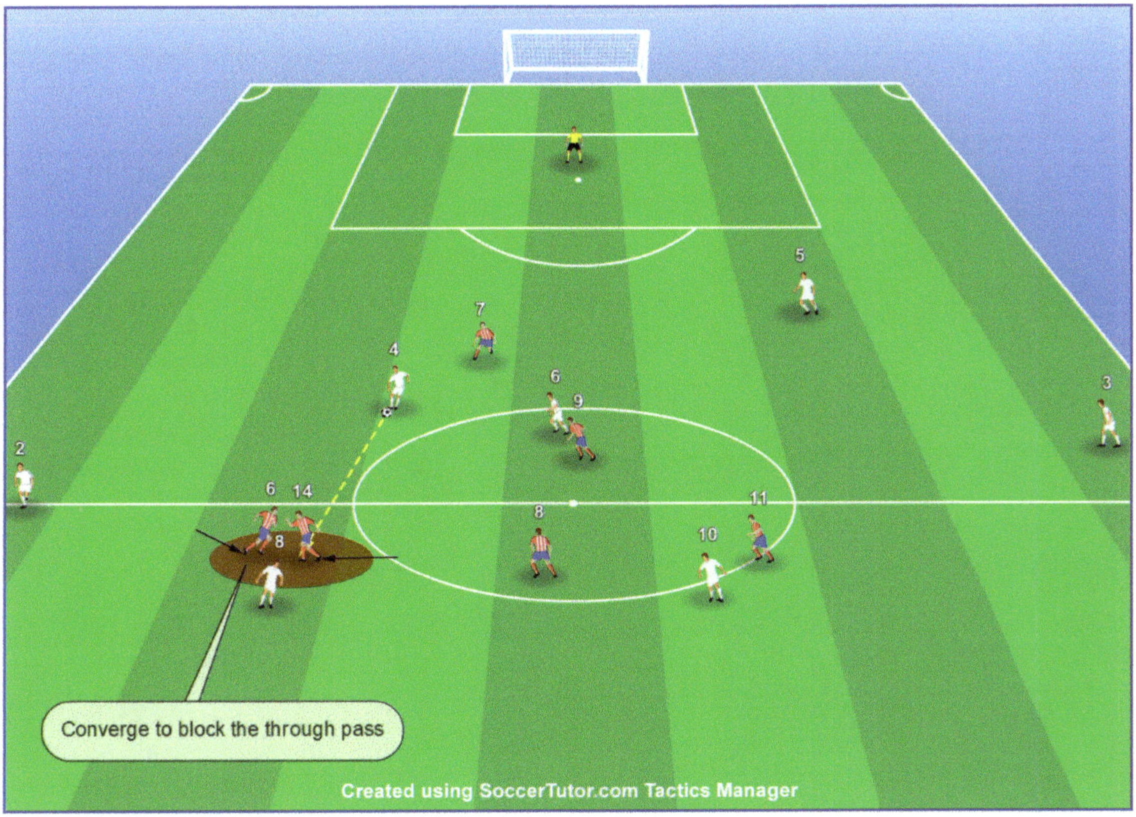

Converge to block the through pass

This tactical example follows on from the previous page, with the Atlético front block having dropped back (safety distance), converged to be compact and having created a strong side.

If a through pass is attempted, the Atlético midfielders have a very good chance of intercepting the ball, as they have more time to react.

In the diagram example, the right midfielder **Koke (6)** and the central midfielder **Gabi (14)** both have time to converge and close the gap between them and block the pass towards white No.8.

Gabi (14) easily intercepts white No.4's pass.

Tactical Situation 8 - Positioning and Defensive Movements of the Front Block

2. Creating a Defensive Triangle in the Centre of the Pitch to Force the Play Wide and then Shift Across

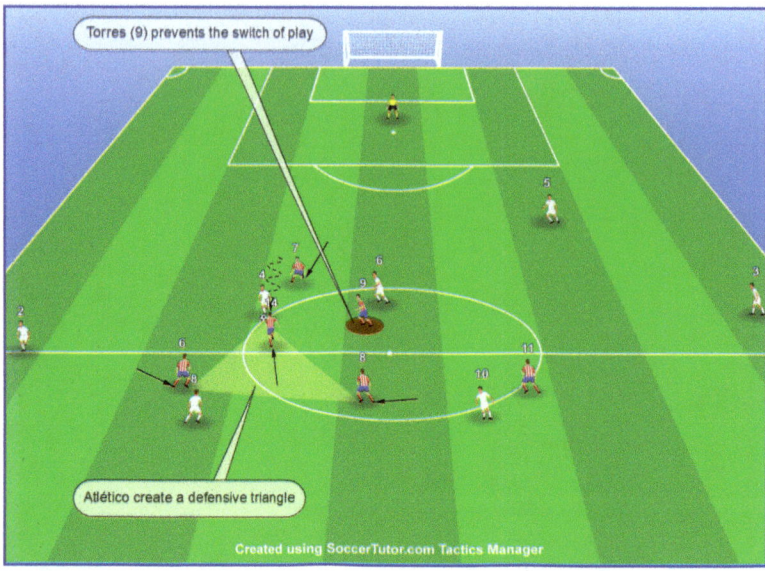

In this variation, the white centre back No.4 moves further forward, so the closest Atlético central midfielder **Gabi (14)** moves to close him down.

This action takes place as soon as the midfielders have obtained the appropriate compactness, so that an effective defensive triangle can be created.

Torres (9) positions himself to prevent a switch of play, so the only passing option is the right back No.2.

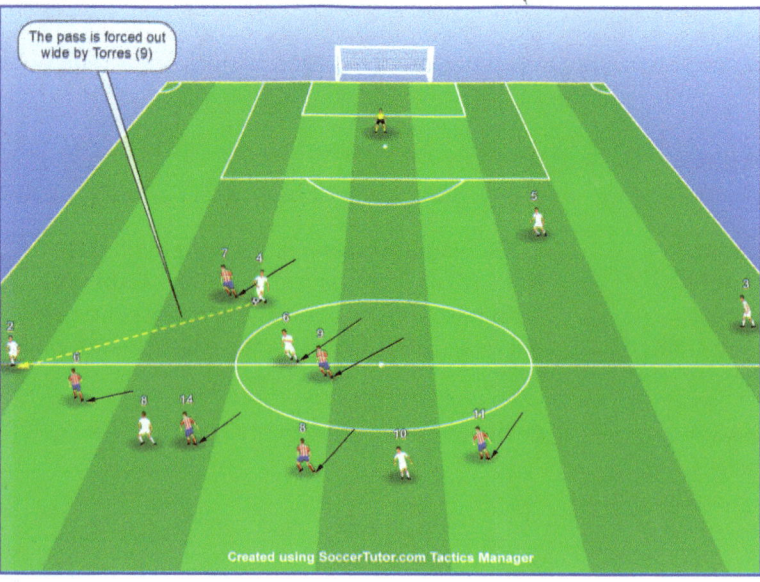

As soon as the pass is directed out wide and towards the side-line, the entire Atlético front block shift across to that side.

ASSESSMENT

Forcing the ball towards the side-line gives time for the Atlético players to readjust their positioning and get well organised.

©SOCCERTUTOR.COM   DIEGO SIMEONE'S DEFENDING TACTICS

SESSION (3 PRACTICES) FOR "POSITIONING AND DEFENSIVE MOVEMENTS OF THE FRONT BLOCK"

Tactical Situation 8 - Positioning and Defensive Movements of the Front Block

SESSION FOR THIS TACTICAL SITUATION (3 PRACTICES)
1. Block Through Passes with the Front Block in a Functional Practice (6 v 6 +GK)

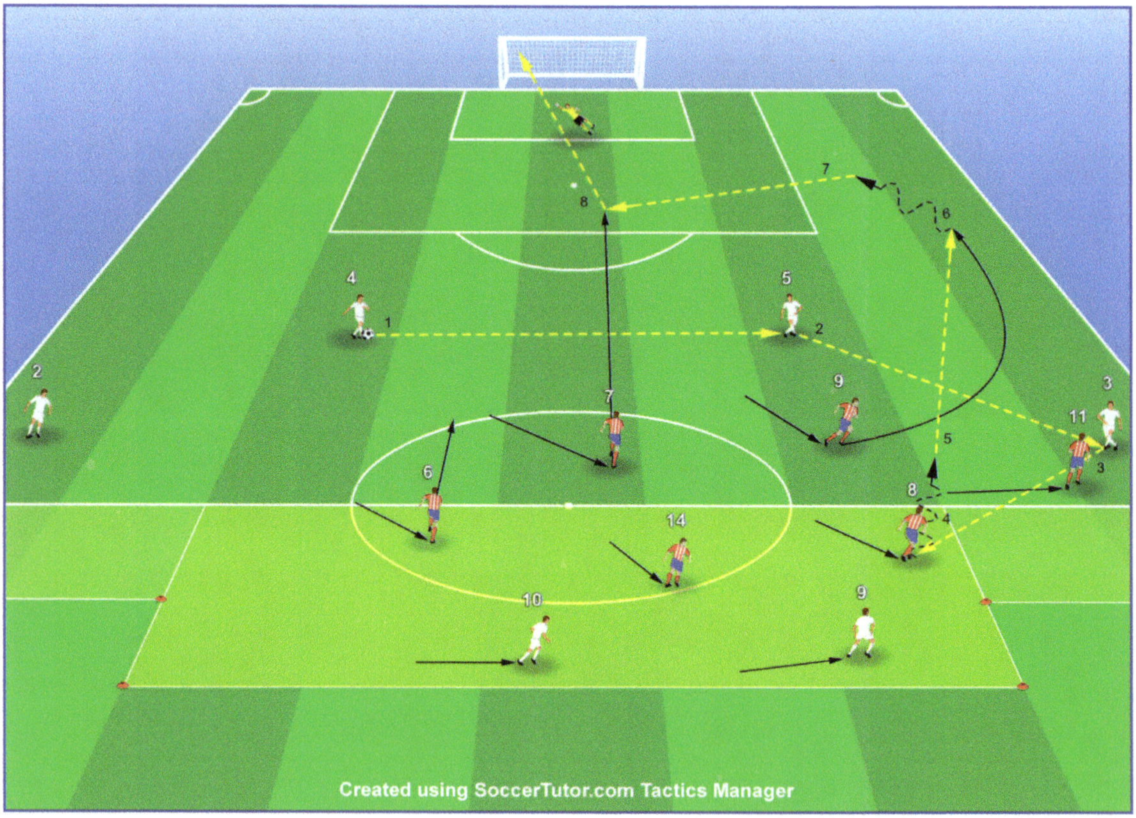

Description
- The white defenders pass the ball to each other in set positions and try to play a through pass to a white forward inside the yellow area.
- The red forwards and midfielders (front block) shift according to the position of the ball, try to retain a safety distance at all times and block any potential through passes by being compact (close to each other).
- The red team aim is to keep the passing lanes towards the yellow area narrow and block the through passes.

- Please **see the analysis pages** in this section for the correct defensive reactions.
- As soon as the reds win the ball, they launch a quick direct counter attack, trying to score past the GK within 8-10 seconds.

Coaching Points
1. Shift according to the position of the ball.
2. Retain the correct horizontal distances (between the players in the midfield line).
3. Retain the correct vertical distances (between the forward and midfield lines).

DIEGO SIMEONE'S DEFENDING TACTICS

Tactical Situation 8 - Positioning and Defensive Movements of the Front Block

PROGRESSION

2. Block Through Passes with the Front Block in a Functional Practice (6 v 8 +GK)

Scenario A: Narrow Passing Lanes and Limit Space Between Lines

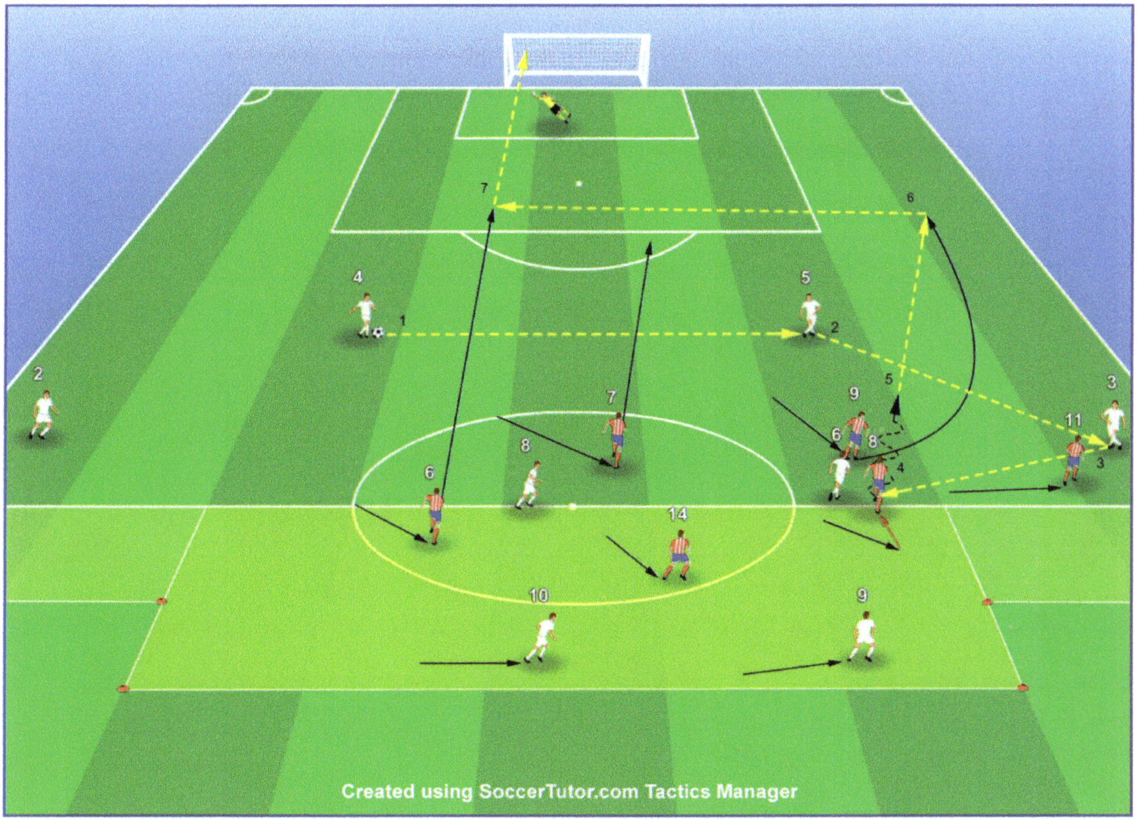

Description (Scenario A)

- This is a progression of the previous practice with 2 white central midfielders (6 and 8) added, who can be used as link players to move the ball to the 2 forwards inside the yellow area.

- The red forwards and midfielders (front block) shift collectively according to the position of the ball and retain narrow passing lanes to block any potential through passes.

- They must also keep the space between the lines limited and prevent the white midfielders from turning if they receive.

- Please **see analysis pages 100-109** for the correct defensive reactions in the different tactical situations.

- As soon as the reds win the ball, they launch a quick direct counter attack, trying to score past the GK within 8-10 seconds.

DIEGO SIMEONE'S DEFENDING TACTICS

Tactical Situation 8 - Positioning and Defensive Movements of the Front Block

Scenario B: Centre Back Dribbling Forward (Breaks Through Pressure)

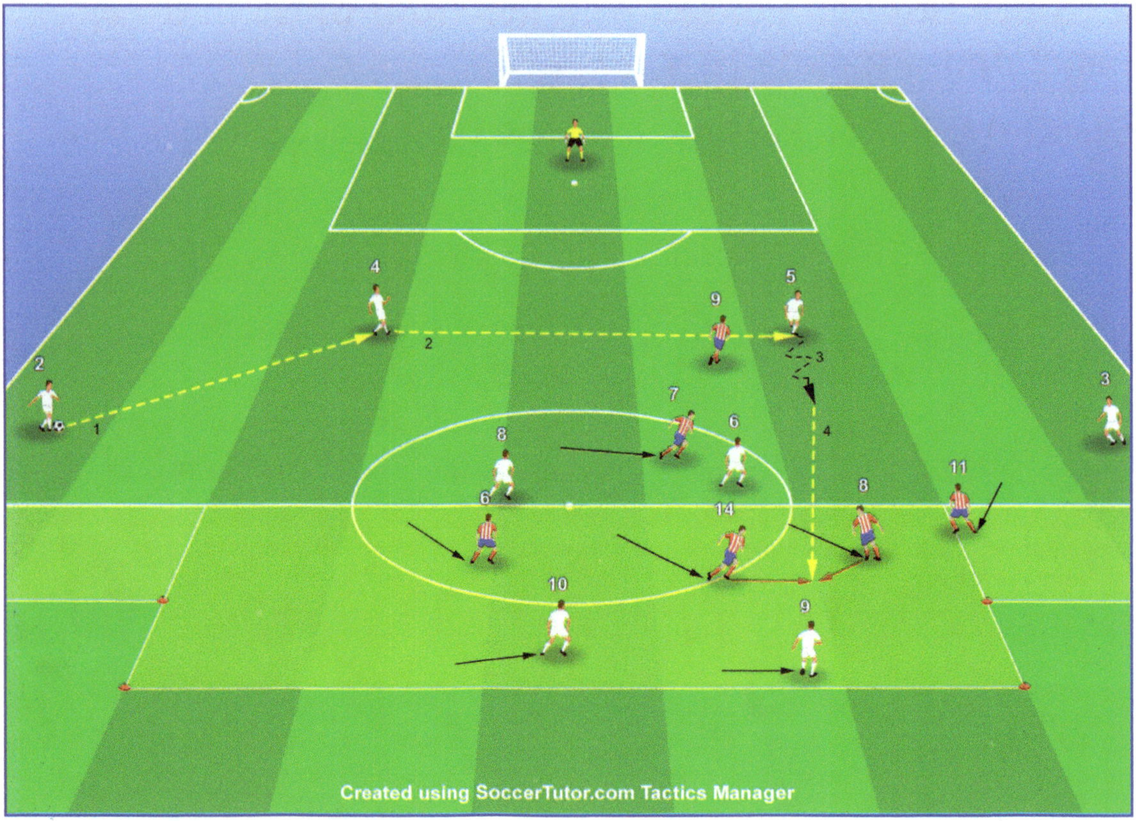

Description (Scenario B)

- In this second scenario, we practice what happens when the opposing centre back breaks through the forward's pressure and moves forward with the ball.

- For this practice, the Coach tells the forwards to let the white centre back (No.5 in diagram) dribble forward without pressure so this situation can be replicated.

- The red forwards and midfielders (front block) have to adapt to the situation.

- As shown in this example, the red midfielders drop back to retain a good safety distance from the ball carrier, so they will still have time to react and block any attempted through passes.

- Please **see the analysis on pages 110-112** for the correct defensive reactions in this tactical situation.

Coaching Points

1. Shift according to the position of the ball.
2. Read the tactical situation.
3. Retain the correct horizontal distances (between the players in the midfield line).
4. Retain the correct vertical distances (between the forward and midfield lines).

Tactical Situation 8 - Positioning and Defensive Movements of the Front Block

PROGRESSION
3. Block Through Passes and Defend the Crucial Central Area with the Front Block in a Tactical 11 v 11 Game

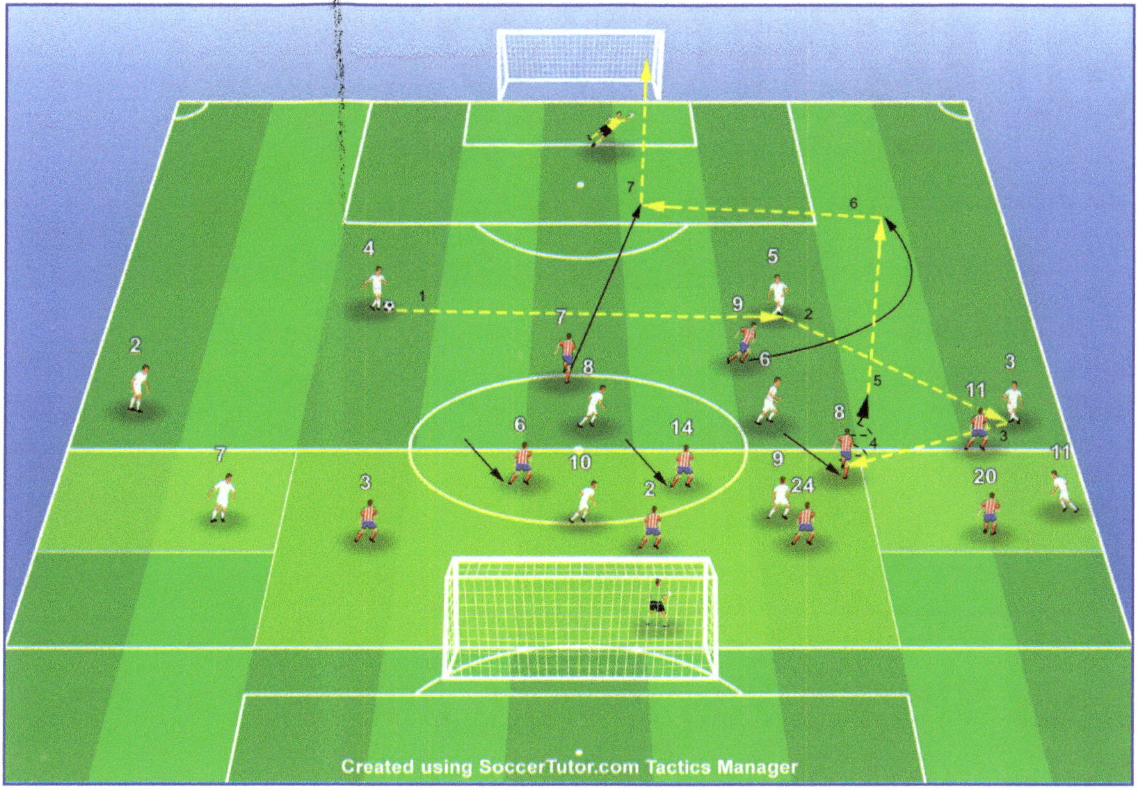

Description
- In this final practice of the session, the 2 teams now play an 11 v 11 game.
- The practice starts with the white team's GK and they try to score
- If the white team score after playing a pass to a forward (9 or 10) within the central yellow area, they score 3 goals.
- The reds defend and try to stop the whites.
- Please **see the analysis pages** for the correct defensive reactions in the different tactical situations.

- As soon as the reds win the ball, they launch a quick direct counter attack, trying to score past the GK within 8-15 seconds.

Coaching Points
1. Shift according to the position of the ball.
2. Read the tactical situation.
3. Retain the correct horizontal distances (between the players in the midfield line).
4. Retain the correct vertical distances (between the forward and midfield lines).

DIEGO SIMEONE'S DEFENDING TACTICS

TACTICAL SITUATION 9

Rear Block's Positioning and Movements to Control Wide Areas

The content in this section is from analysis of Diego Simeone's Atlético Madrid teams during the 2017/2018 and 2018/2019 seasons.

The analysis is based on recurring patterns of play observed within the Atlético Madrid team. Once the same phase of play occurred several times (at least 10), the tactics would be seen as a pattern. The analysis on the following pages are examples of the team's tactics being used effectively.

Each action, pass, individual movement with or without the ball, and the positioning of each player on the pitch including their body shape, are presented.

The analysis is then used to create a practice to coach this specific tactical situation.

Tactical Situation 9 - Rear Block's Positioning and Movements to Control Wide Areas

SPACE CREATED OUT WIDE DUE TO ATLÉTICO'S COMPACT MIDFIELD LINE

1. Available Space Created Out Wide Due to the Compactness of Atlético's Madrid's Midfield Line

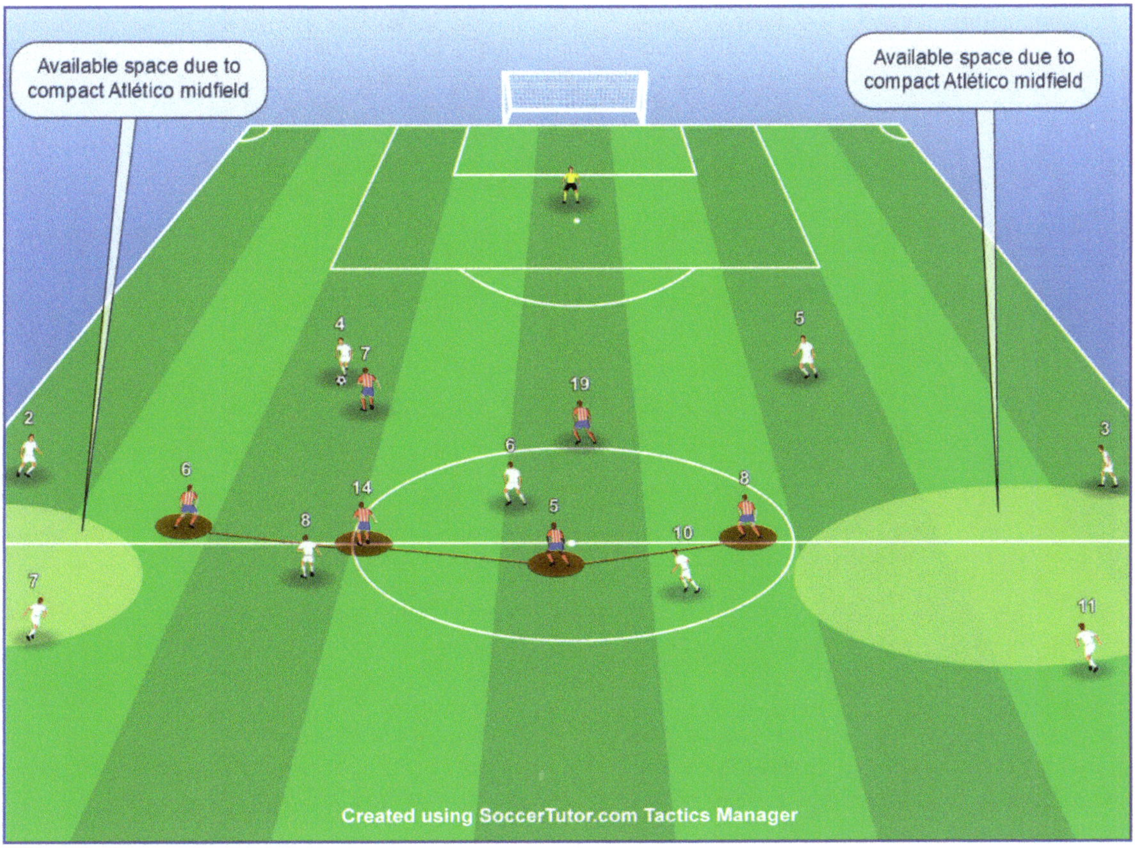

As already mentioned, the aim of the front block is to prevent through passes towards the **Crucial Central Area**.

To succeed in this aim, the front block has to work in coordination with each other.

The forwards **Griezmann (7)** and **D. Costa (19)** control the centre backs, while the midfielders (with forwards) keep the space between the lines limited and the through passing lanes narrow.

This is achieved as there are short distances between the midfielders (compactness).

This creates a problem that Diego Simeone's Atlético Madrid team must deal with, as the good horizontal cohesion leaves available space out wide near the side-lines.

Tactical Situation 9 - Rear Block's Positioning and Movements to Control Wide Areas

2. Forward Passing Options Left Open for the Opposition with the Centre Back in Possession

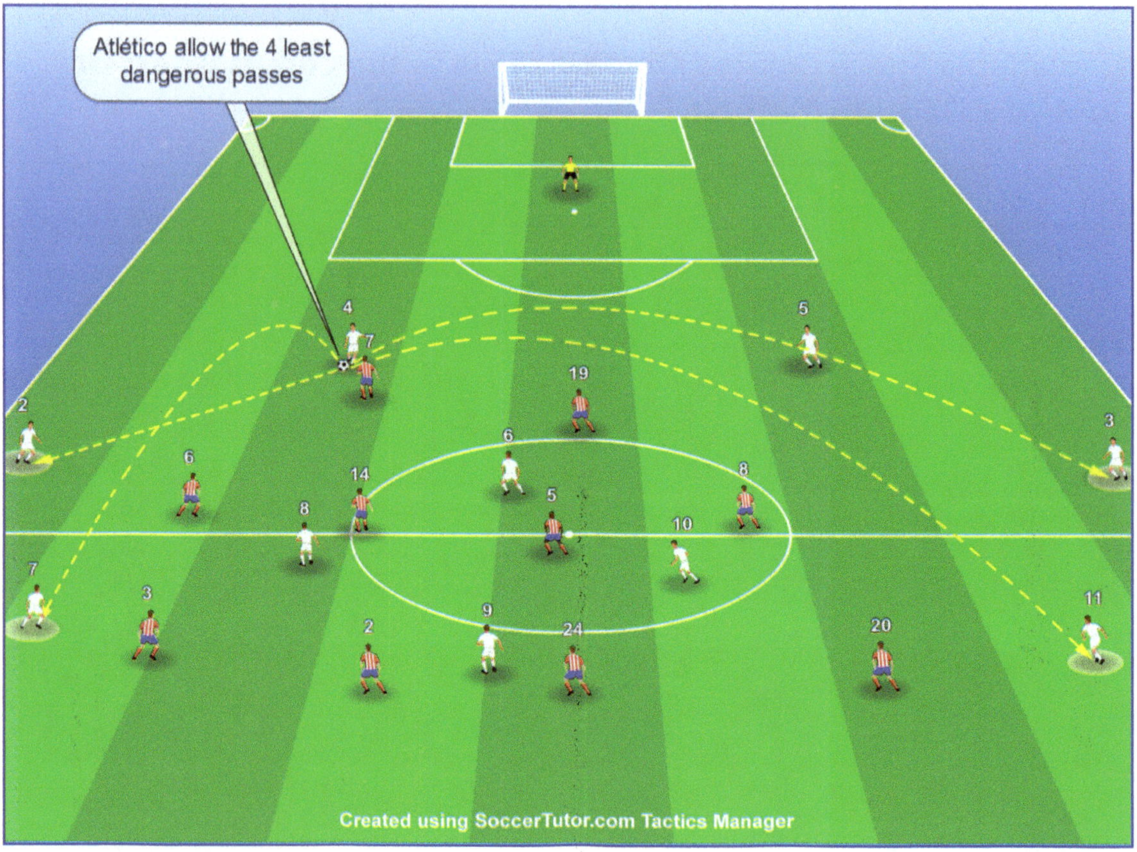

The front block is focused on preventing through passes towards the **Crucial Central Area** but when focusing on this aim, some types of passes are impossible to block.

Therefore, Diego Simeone's Atlético Madrid team allow the least dangerous passes to be played, as the players who receive in wide areas have more limited options to pass the ball compared to those who receive in a central area.

The passes allowed include square passes between the 2 opposing centre backs, as well as the forward passes towards the full backs (No.2 and No.3) and the wingers (No.7 and No.11).

The diagram above shows what forward passing options are left open with the opposing centre back (No.4) in possession.

Tactical Situation 9 - Rear Block's Positioning and Movements to Control Wide Areas

3. Forward Passing Options Left Open for the Opposition with the Full Back in Possession

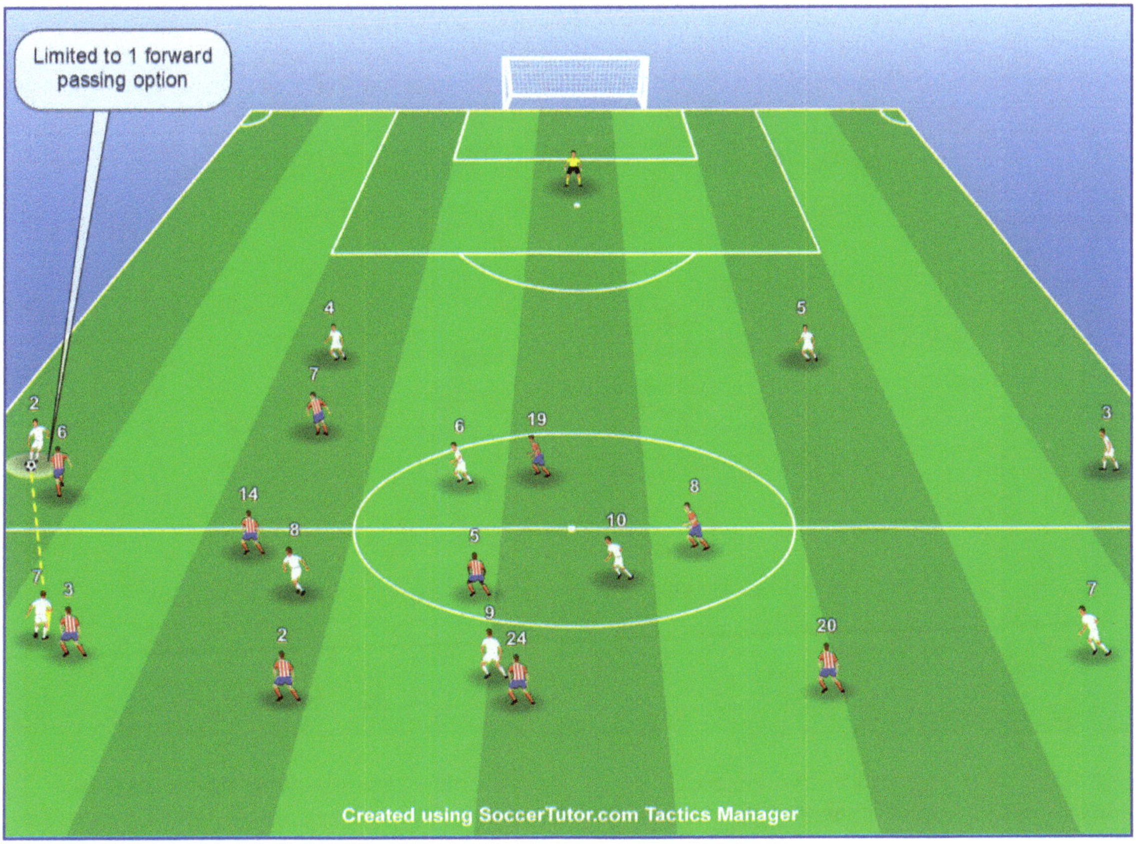

This diagram follows on from the previous page and the white centre back No.4 has passed out wide to the right back No.2 near the side-line. The Atlético players have all shifted across slightly.

In this situation, Simeone's Atlético Madrid team leave 1 forward passing option open, which is the pass to the winger (No.7) up the line.

ASSESSMENT

All these forward passes are directed towards players who are positioned within spaces (according to the defensive positioning of the players) that can easily be controlled.

As nothing is left to chance in Diego Simeone's Atlético tactics, the team has developed mechanisms to deal with these forward passes (which they leave open) successfully.

Tactical Situation 9 - Rear Block's Positioning and Movements to Control Wide Areas

POSITIONING OF THE REAR BLOCK

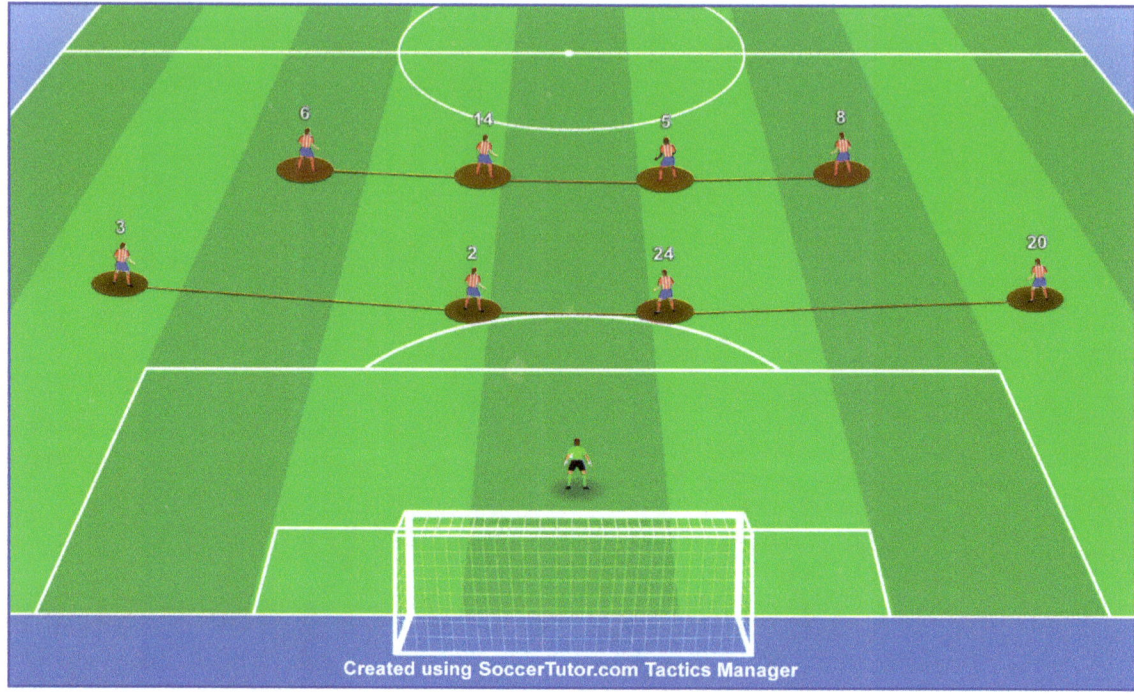

In Atlético's 4-4-2 formation, the rear block consists of all the midfielders and defenders.

The Atlético midfielders are very compact as their main aim is to prevent through passes towards the **Crucial Central Area**.

The defenders are more focused on marking the players within their zone of responsibility, so the full backs are positioned wider.

As long as the through passes are blocked by the midfielders, the only way of moving the ball to the opposing forwards is with long balls, which are more difficult for the forwards to control and easier for the defenders to neutralise.

From what we have already analysed, medium and long range passes (especially from wide positions) can be very easily neutralised.

Additionally, providing immediate cover to a defender who is very good in aerial duels and is about to contest an opponent in the air is not as important as it would have been if the pass was directed to the forward's feet and he managed to turn towards goal.

Furthermore, as the through passes towards the crucial central area are prevented, the ball is usually directed into wide areas. The wide positioning of the full backs enables Atlético to control these areas easily, especially if the ball is directed to the opposing wingers.

After the opposition play a pass into a wide area, the collaboration of the rear block is crucial to deal with this tactical situation.

MAIN AIMS OF THE REAR BLOCK

During the defensive phase, the main aims for the **Rear Block** are:

1. **Controlling the Wide Areas**
2. **Controlling Long Passes Out Wide to the Wingers**
3. **Controlling Short Passes in Wide Positions** (see "Tactical Situation 10" from page 135)

Tactical Situation 9 - Rear Block's Positioning and Movements to Control Wide Areas

1ST AIM: CONTROLLING THE WIDE AREAS

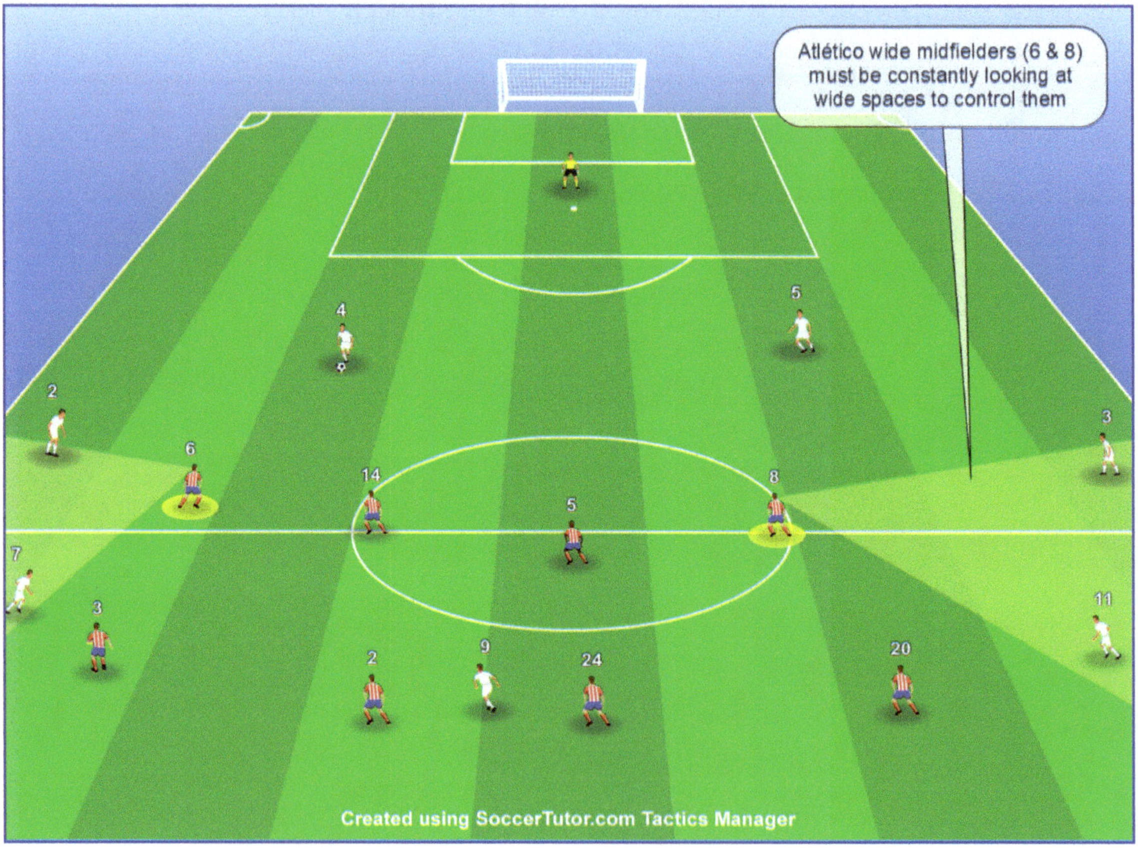

Atlético wide midfielders (6 & 8) must be constantly looking at wide spaces to control them

When the opposing centre back (or deep and wide central midfielder) is in possession, it is likely the full back will move into an advanced position.

During the defensive phase, Simeone's Atlético team are compact and aim to force the ball towards the side-line. This is done in order to protect the **Crucial Central Area**. For this reason, Simeone has successfully developed mechanisms to defend potential passes towards opponents near the side-lines.

Controlling the space near the side-line is the job of the full back and the wide midfielder. These 2 players have to work in collaboration with each other, making sure to have good synchronisation and communication.

The most important thing Atlético Madrid's wide midfielders must do to control the space near the side-lines is to constantly be looking at this area of the pitch, making sure to be aware of the size of the space and all player movements.

CONTROLLING THE MOVEMENTS OF THE OPPOSING FULL BACKS AND WINGERS

As the wide midfielders check the space near the side-lines frequently, they can either control the forward movements of the full backs or the dropping back movements of the wingers.

First of all, the distance between the 2 lines (midfielders and defenders) should be about 12 yards (good cohesion).

For the best possible cooperation between the wide midfielder and full back, the space near the side-line is divided into 2 parts (6 yards each) - **please see the diagram on the next page**.

The wide players have to quickly analyse the situation and the positioning of their opponents to decide which player each of them is going to control or mark.

Tactical Situation 9 - Rear Block's Positioning and Movements to Control Wide Areas

1a. Opposing Full Back Moves Forward and the Winger Moves Inside with the Centre Back in Possession

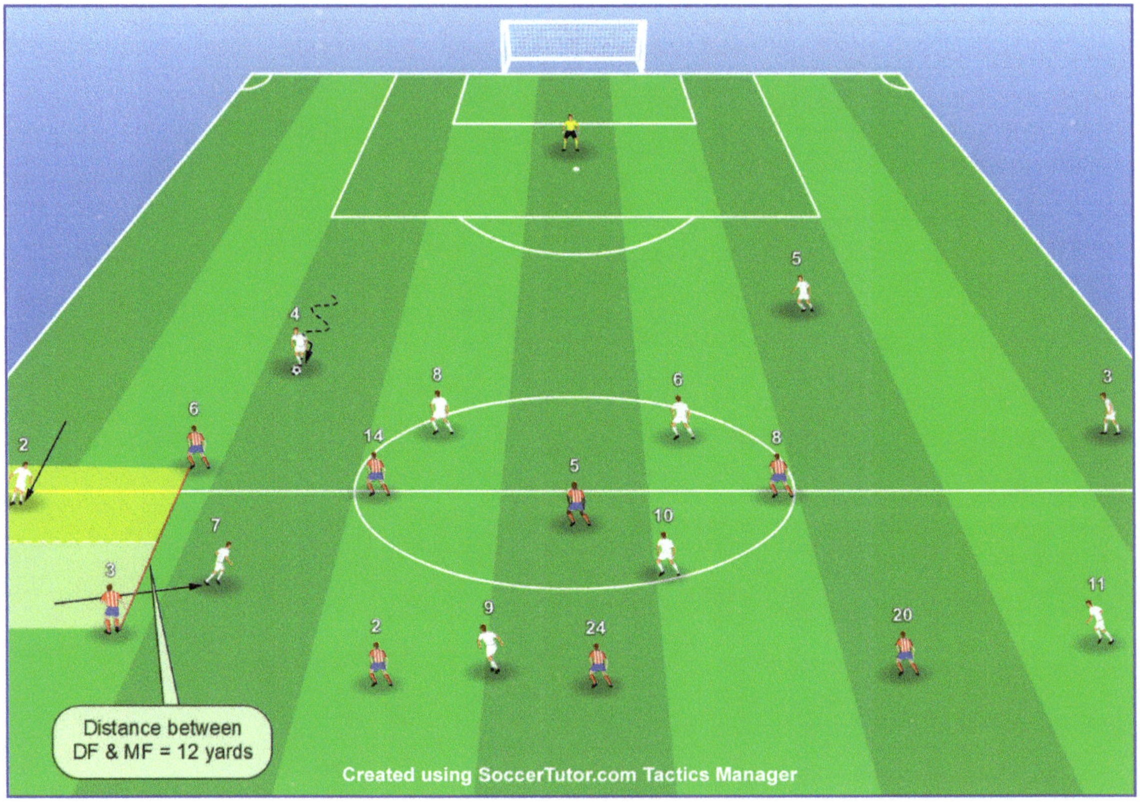

In this example, the white centre back No.4 moves forward with the ball, while the full back No.2 moves forward, and the winger No.7 moves inside to offer an extra passing option in the centre.

In this situation, the Atlético left back **F. Luis (3)** stays in his zone of responsibility and doesn't move inside to follow the winger.

This reaction is due to the compactness of the midfielders who, as analysed, block through passes towards the **Crucial Central Area**, so it would be difficult for white No.7 to receive.

Despite this, the left midfielder **Koke (6)** has to frequently check the space near the side-line, as well as the movements of white No.2 and No.7.

For as long as the white No.2 is within the high yellow area, **Koke (6)** is responsible to control him.

If the white No.2 moves into the low white area, then the left back **F. Luis (3)** is responsible for his marking.

DIEGO SIMEONE'S DEFENDING TACTICS

Tactical Situation 9 - Rear Block's Positioning and Movements to Control Wide Areas

1b. The Opposing Full Back Receives and the Wide Midfielder Moves to Close Him Down

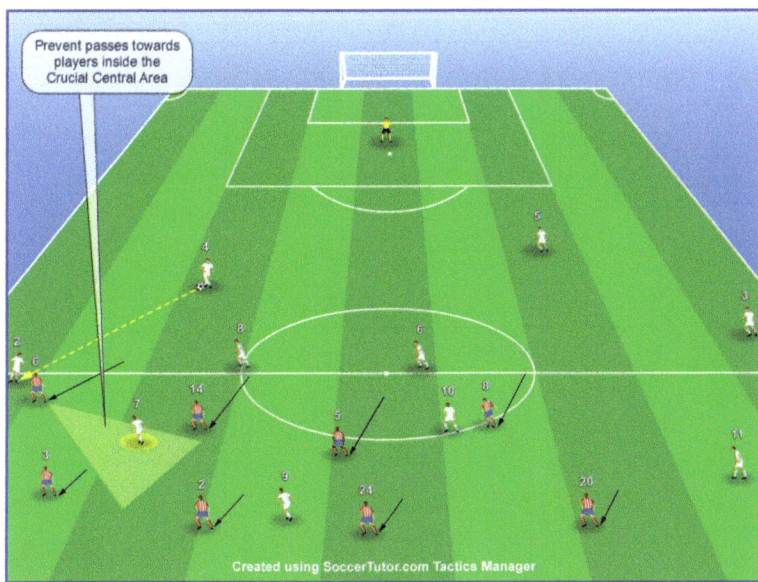

If the ball is directed to the white right back No.2 positioned inside the high area (**see yellow area on previous page**), the left midfielder **Koke (6)** moves to close him down.

The rest of the Atlético midfielders and the defenders drop back a few yards and across, as shown.

The aim for **Koke (6)** is to get in position to prevent a through pass towards the **Crucial Central Area**.

2. The Opposing Full Back Receives in an Advanced Position and the Full Back Closes Him Down

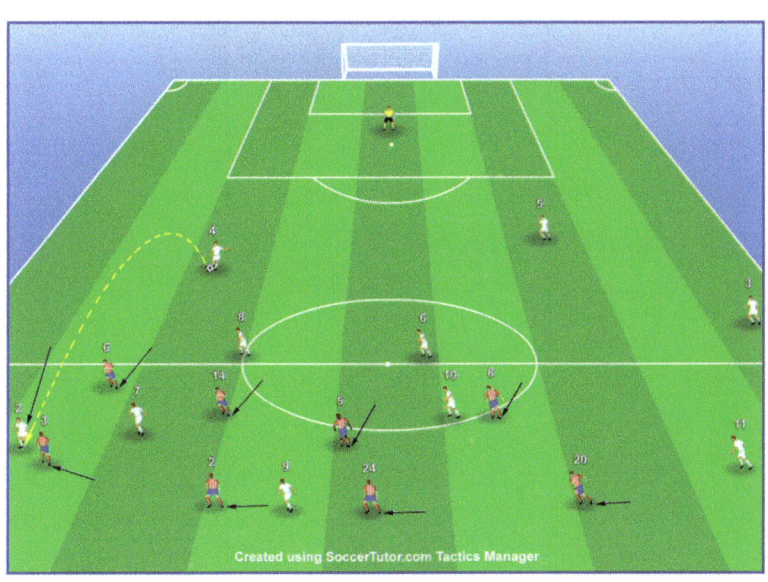

If the white full back No.2 moves further forward and the ball is played to him, it is likely that the pass will be intercepted by the Atlético left back **F. Luis (3)**.

However, if white No.2 does receive, **F. Luis (3)** immediately closes him down and the rest of the Atlético players shift across.

It is likely that white No.2 won't have much time and space to search for his next forward pass, so will have to simply protect the ball and pass backwards.

Tactical Situation 9 - Rear Block's Positioning and Movements to Control Wide Areas

2ND AIM: CONTROLLING LONG PASSES OUT WIDE TO THE WINGERS

1. Positioning of the Rear Block and Wide Positioning of the Full Backs Against the 4-3-3

Opposing wingers have to drop back to receive in the available spaces

As already shown, the passes towards the players near the side-lines are left free (**see page 119**).

As shown in the analysis in the section "Tactical Situation 5 - Positioning and Defensive Movements of the Defenders," **the Atlético full backs take up very wide positions.**

These wide positions enable them to better control the opposing wingers and the available space near the side-lines.

In the diagram above, the highlighted areas show the available space. As you can see, it is not in front of the opposing wingers but behind them. It is therefore hard for them to receive in their starting positions or in front of them.

The opposing wingers (No.7 and No.11) can receive much more easily if they drop back.

Tactical Situation 9 - Rear Block's Positioning and Movements to Control Wide Areas

2. Positioning of the Rear Block and Wide Positioning of the Full Backs Against the 4-4-2

F.Luis (3) is closer to opponent as the ball is on his side of the pitch

The positioning of the Atlético full backs is taken according to the position of the player in possession (white centre back No.4 in diagram), their team-mates and the opponents.

For example, the left back **F. Luis (3)** is closer to his direct opponent (white No.7) than the right back **Juanfran (20)** is to No.11.

This is because **F. Luis (3)** is closer to the player in possession (white No.4) and would have less available time to react to a potential long pass towards No.7.

When playing against the 4-4-2, the 2 Atlético centre backs **Godín (2)** and **Giménez (24)** would be positioned a little bit wider to control the 2 forwards.

Both full backs **F. Luis (3)** and **Juanfran (20)** would be in narrower (more balanced) positions. However, **F. Luis (3)** would still be closer to white No.7 than **Juanfran (20)** would be to No.11.

DIEGO SIMEONE'S DEFENDING TACTICS

Tactical Situation 9 - Rear Block's Positioning and Movements to Control Wide Areas

3. The Full back Controls the Long Pass to the Opposing Winger and Intercepts

With this positioning, the full backs can intercept long passes directed to the wingers or at least immediately press the winger to limit their available time and space.

The white centre back No.4 plays a long pass to the left winger No.11.

The right back **Juanfran (20)** has a position which enables him to intercept the pass before it reaches No.11, while the rest of the Atlético players adjust their positions as shown.

4. The Full back Controls the Long Pass to the Opposing Winger and Restricts the Space and Time Available

In this variation, **Juanfran (20)** is unable to intercept the pass and instead restricts white No.11's available time and space, so the new ball carrier can't easily lift his head up to choose the best passing option.

At the same time, Atlético's right midfielder **Saúl (8)** drops back to narrow the inside passing lane towards the attacking midfielder No.10, who is positioned within the **Crucial Central Area**.

Tactical Situation 9 - Rear Block's Positioning and Movements to Control Wide Areas

5. The Opposing Winger Drops Back to Receive in Space and the Wide Midfielder Moves to Close Him Down

The only way for the opposing winger No.11 to find space and time on the ball is to drop back. The right midfielder **Saúl (8)** moves to close him down.

Juanfran (20) stays close to his team-mates to defend his zone of responsibility, while the inside passing lane towards white No.10 remains blocked. Additionally, **Juanfran's (20)** open body shape enables him to see the positions of the other Atlético defenders and the position of the white No.10.

The attacking play is now predictable as white No.11 can only pass the ball down the line or backwards.

If the attacking midfielder No.10 makes a movement in behind **Juanfran (20)**, his body shape enables him to notice the run and react accordingly.

Therefore, **Juanfran (20)** drops back to block a potential through pass between him and the centre back **Giménez (24)** or behind his back.

PRACTICE FOR "REAR BLOCK'S POSITIONING AND MOVEMENTS TO CONTROL WIDE AREAS"

Tactical Situation 9 - Rear Block's Positioning and Movements to Control Wide Areas

PRACTICE FOR THIS TACTICAL SITUATION
Controlling Wide Areas with the Rear Block in a Functional Practice
Scenario A: Pass Towards the Opposing Full Back on the Strong Side

Description (Scenario A)

- Mark out an area on each side (12 yards long) and divide it into 2 equal areas, which indicate the zones of responsibility for the wide midfielder (yellow area) and the full back (white area).

- The 3 deep white players (No.4, No.5 and No.6) start by passing the ball around, while the red players shift accordingly and retain a good safety distance.

- As soon as a white centre back) receives and moves forward (No.4 in diagram), the red players drop back to retain a safety distance.

- At the same time, the white winger on the strong side moves towards the centre and the full back moves forward into the white area.

- The centre back passes to the advanced full back on the strong side (No.2) in this first scenario and the whites try to score.

- Please see the **analysis on pages 126-127** for how the red players should react.

- The red players (rear block) try to defend effectively, win the ball, and then launch a quick counter attack to score in either of the 2 mini goals within 8-10 seconds.

DIEGO SIMEONE'S DEFENDING TACTICS

Tactical Situation 9 - Rear Block's Positioning and Movements to Control Wide Areas

Scenario B: Pass Towards the Opposing Winger on the Weak Side

Description (Scenario B)

- In this second scenario, the white centre back No.4 now plays a long pass to the winger on the weak side (No.11).
- Please see the **analysis on pages 130-131** for how the red players should react.

Variations

1. The full backs allow the opposing wide players to receive in the first stages of the practice, but after a few minutes they can start to intercept the passes before they reach the white wingers or full backs.
2. This practice can be adjusted to play against any formation.

Coaching Points

1. Shift according to the position of the ball.
2. Read the tactical situation.
3. Frequently check the wide areas.
4. Make the correct decision based on the specific tactical situation and movements of the opponents.

TACTICAL SITUATION 10

Rear Block Controlling Passes within Wide Areas

The content in this section is from analysis of Diego Simeone's Atlético Madrid teams during the 2017/2018 and 2018/2019 seasons.

The analysis is based on recurring patterns of play observed within the Atlético Madrid team. Once the same phase of play occurred several times (at least 10), the tactics would be seen as a pattern. The analysis on the following pages are examples of the team's tactics being used effectively.

Each action, pass, individual movement with or without the ball, and the positioning of each player on the pitch including their body shape, are presented.

The analysis is then used to create a session to coach this specific tactical situation.

Tactical Situation 10 - Rear Block Controlling Passes within Wide Areas

ZONES OF RESPONSIBILITY IN WIDE AREAS (FULL BACKS AND WIDE MIDFIELDERS)

During the attacking phase, the width can be created by the winger, the full back or both if they are both in wide positions. When the ball is in the opposing full back's possession, Simeone's Atlético Madrid team allow only back passes or the pass down the line for the winger to receive.

Atlético have developed specific reactions and mechanisms to deal with this situation effectively, so that every possible threat is neutralised.

As long as the distance between the Atlético wide midfielder and full back is short enough (12 yards or shorter), dealing with the opposing winger is relatively easy.

The same rule we showed in the previous section "Tactical Situation 9 - Rear Block's Positioning and Movements to Control Wide Areas" about the responsibility of the marking in wide areas still applies.

Maintaining the Correct Distancing Between the Full Back and Wide Midfielder to Deal with the Opposing Winger

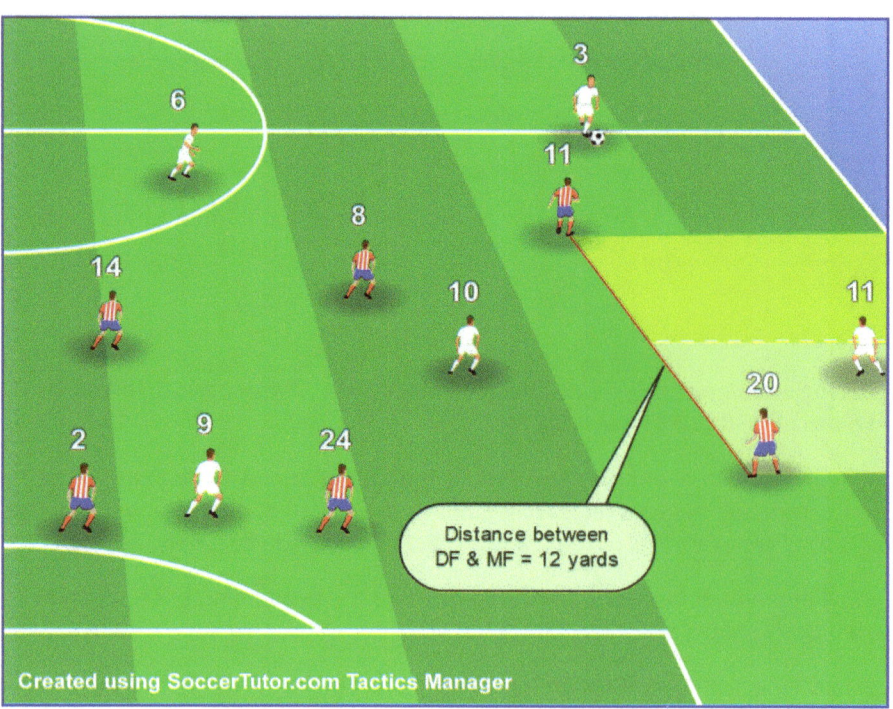

If the opposing winger (white No.11 in diagram below) is high inside the white area as shown in the diagram, the Atlético full back **Juanfran (20)** is responsible for closing him down.

If the winger is positioned deeper inside the yellow area, the wide midfielder **Correa (11)** takes over his marking.

DIEGO SIMEONE'S DEFENDING TACTICS

Tactical Situation 10 - Rear Block Controlling Passes within Wide Areas

IMPORTANCE AND BENEFITS OF THE FULL BACK'S GOOD STARTING POSITION

1a. Balanced Starting Position of the Full Back on the Strong Side in His Zone of Responsibility

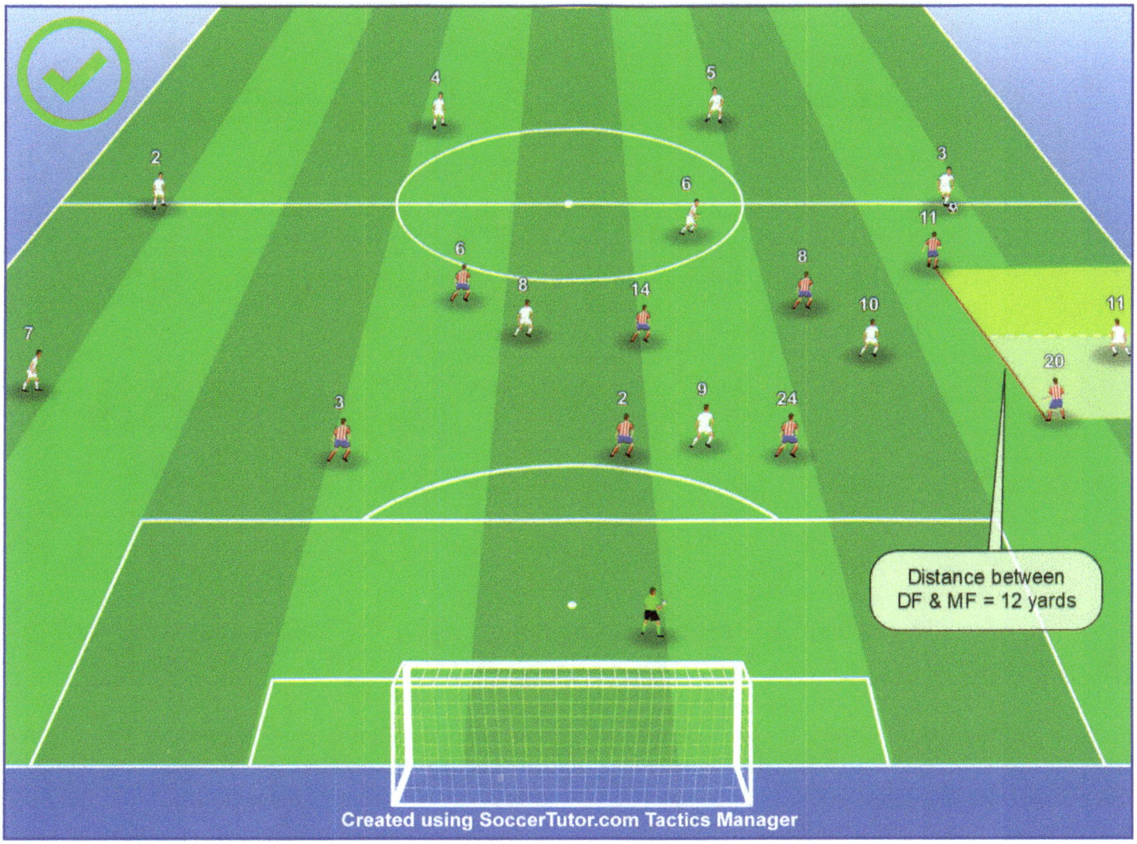

Atlético's right midfielder **Correa (11)** has to be aware of the white winger No.11's positioning by frequently checking the space near the side-line.

As already mentioned in the section "Tactical Situation 5 - Positioning and Defensive Movements of the Defenders," when the opposing full back is in possession near the side-line, the starting position of the Atlético full back on the strong side is slightly advanced compared to the rest of the defenders. The other 3 defenders are together in the same line. With this positioning, the full back (**Juanfran 20** in diagram example) is capable of the following:

- Provide support to the other defenders, as he is close enough to them
- Control the opposing winger (white No.11) who is within **Juanfran's (20)** zone of responsibility (white highlighted area).
- Defend the space behind his back.

DIEGO SIMEONE'S DEFENDING TACTICS

Tactical Situation 10 - Rear Block Controlling Passes within Wide Areas

1b. The Full Back Applies Pressure at the Right Time to Prevent the Winger from Turning

Juanfran (20) presses with the aim of stopping No.11 turning

As soon as the opposing full back No.3 passes the ball to the winger No.11, the Atlético right back **Juanfran (20)** takes advantage of the transmission phase (the time the ball takes to travel) and puts him under pressure.

The aim for **Juanfran (20)** is to prevent the winger No.11 from turning.

As long as the distance between **Juanfran (20)** and the white left winger No.11 is a maximum of 6 yards, **Juanfran (20)** can move the moment the pass is played, and the reaction will be successful.

If **Juanfran (20)** is unable to prevent No.11 from turning, he still makes sure to close him down quickly so he can't lift his head up to see the available forward passing options, thus forcing him to pass backwards.

Tactical Situation 10 - Rear Block Controlling Passes within Wide Areas

2. The Full Back Drops Back and Intercepts a Long Pass for the Forward Run of the Attacking Midfielder

Juanfran (20) intercepts a pass directed in behind him

Another benefit of the full back's good starting position and open body shape is that he can notice the potential forward movement of the attacking midfielder (No.10) behind his back.

Additionally, as **Juanfran (20)** stays close to his defenders, this enables him to deny space and intercept potential passes directed in behind him.

In this tactical example, the opposing left back No.3 plays a long pass into the available space behind **Juanfran (20)** for the run of the attacking midfielder No.10.

Juanfran (20) has a good starting position close to his team-mates, which enables him to drop back and intercept the ball before it reaches the white No.10.

Tactical Situation 10 - Rear Block Controlling Passes within Wide Areas

3. The Full Back Provides Cover in Defence if the Long Pass to the Attacking Midfielder is Successful

This variation of the previous example shows what happens if the white left back No.3's pass is successful.

The good starting position of the Atlético right back **Juanfran (20)** enables him to recover immediately into an effective defensive position and provide support to the centre back **Giménez (24)**, who tracks the run of the white attacking midfielder No.10.

With this reaction, Atlético's defensive line retains a numerical advantage, as 4 players are ready to defend against the 3 white attackers.

The other Atlético centre back **Godín (2)** and the left back **F. Luis (3)** drop back to defend the goal and track runners.

Tactical Situation 10 - Rear Block Controlling Passes within Wide Areas

PROBLEMS THAT OCCUR IF THE FULL BACK HAS A BAD STARTING POSITION

1. The Full Back Leaves Space in Behind to Exploit when Positioned Too High Up the Pitch (Against the 4-3-3)

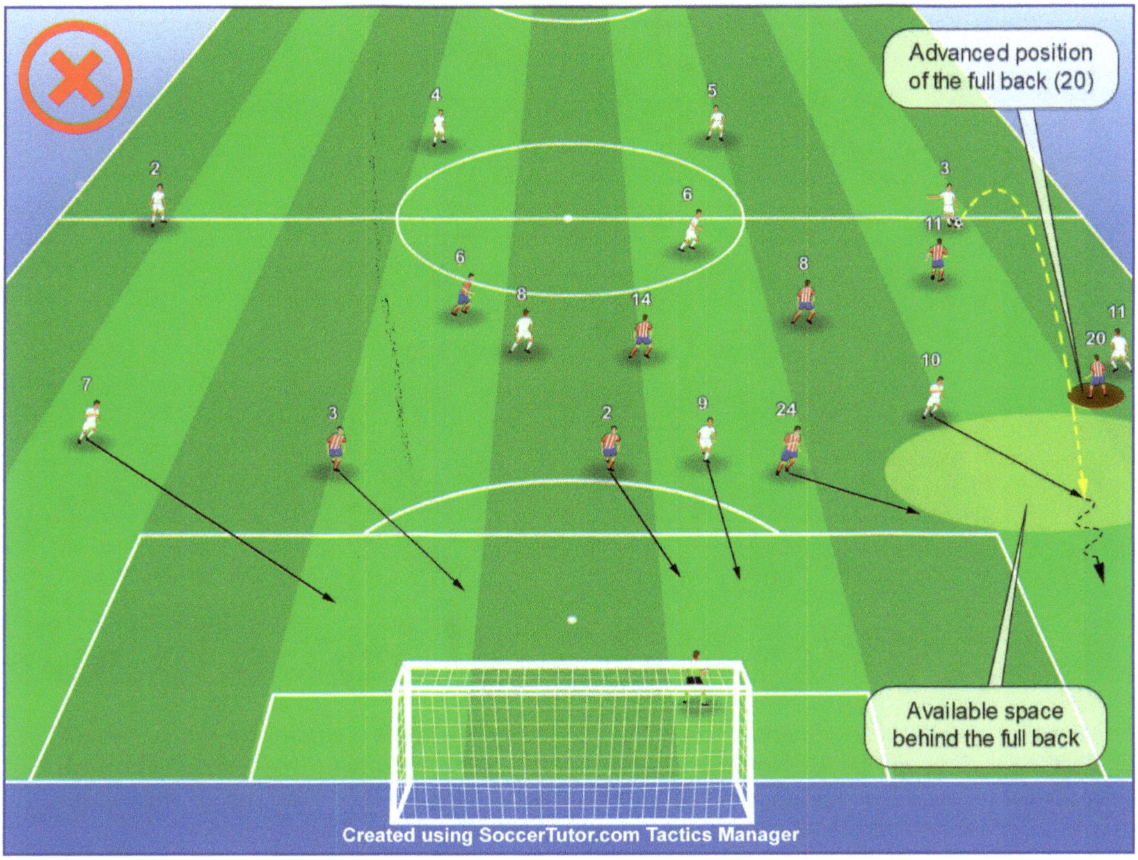

If the full back is in a more advanced position to be closer to the opposing winger, available space is created behind him. This space can be exploited by the opposition and the distance between the full back and the rest of the defenders gets larger at the same time.

In this example, right back **Juanfran (20)** is in an advanced position to deny space to the white winger No.11 before the pass is played by No.3.

Due to **Juanfran's (20)** high positioning, space is created behind his back.

As the centre back **Giménez (24)** is far from the strong side, white No.10 exploits this space and receives unmarked from the long pass by No.3.

Atlético can now only defend with 3 players, as **Juanfran (20)** is too far away to recover and there is a dangerous 3v3 situation at the back.

DIEGO SIMEONE'S DEFENDING TACTICS

Tactical Situation 10 - Rear Block Controlling Passes within Wide Areas

2. The Full Back Leaves Space in Behind to Exploit when Positioned Too High Up the Pitch (Against the 4-2-3-1)

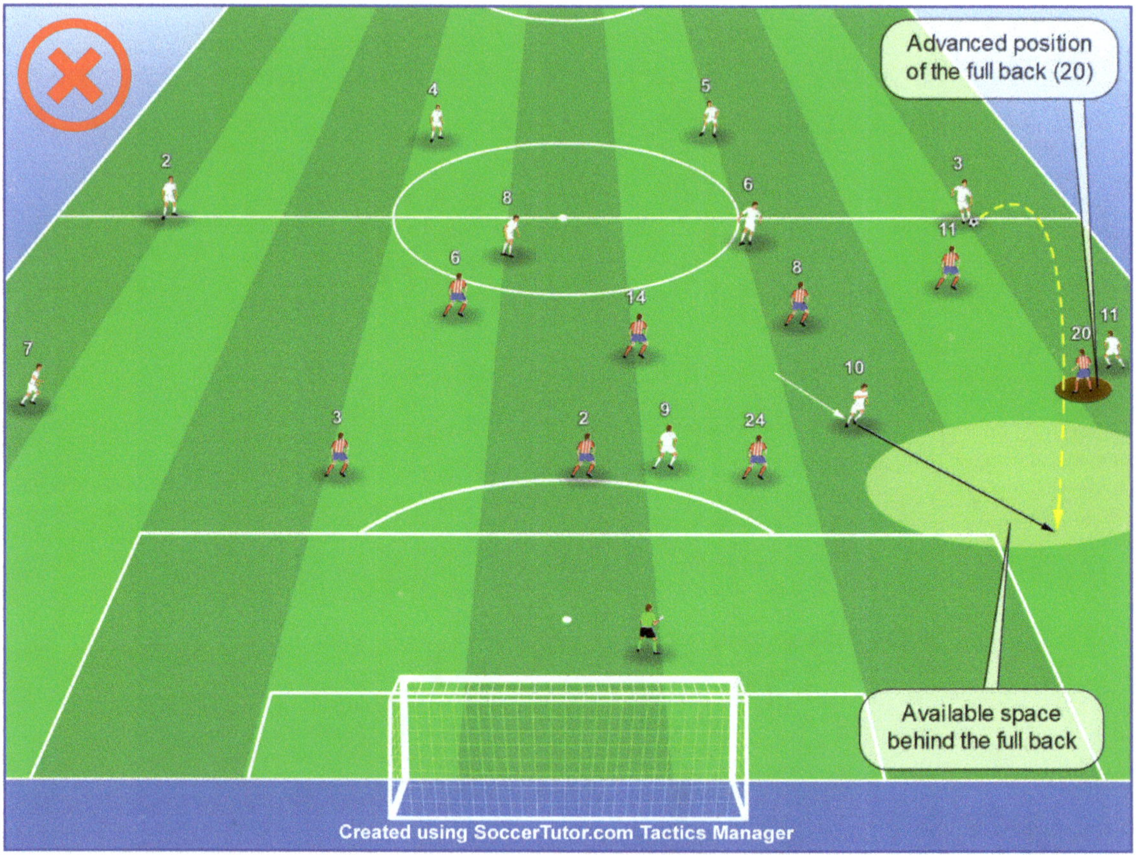

Despite the 4-3-3 providing the best possibilities against Diego Simeone's 4-4-2 formation in this situation, as the attacking midfielders can easily attack the space behind the full back, a similar situation can be created against the 4-2-3-1.

As shown in the diagram, the No.10 is able to attack the available space to receive and the same dangerous 3v3 situation is created for Atlético at the back.

Tactical Situation 10 - Rear Block Controlling Passes within Wide Areas

3. The Opposing Winger Receives and Turns when the Full Back Does Not Immediately Move to Close Him Down (Against the 4-3-3)

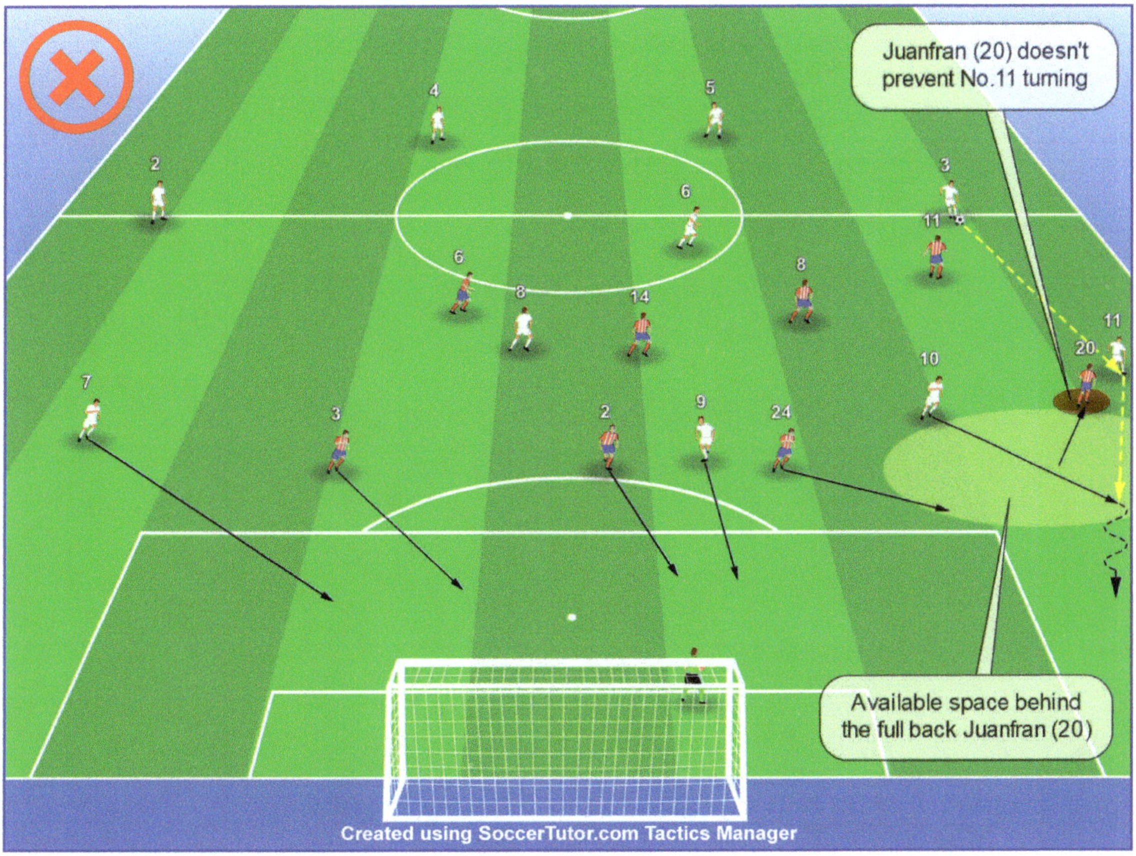

Juanfran (20) doesn't prevent No.11 turning

Available space behind the full back Juanfran (20)

An important element of this situation is the Atlético full back preventing the opposing winger from turning, or at least restricting his time on the ball so he is unable to lift his head up to view the forward passing options. This is why the pressure needs to be applied immediately and without delay.

A similar situation to the previous one can be created If the opposing winger No.11 has available time on the ball before **Juanfran (20)** presses him.

This means that No.11 can turn and see the available forward passing options before he is closed down by **Juanfran (20)**.

In this situation, free space is created behind the back of **Juanfran (20)** and exploited by the run of white No.10.

The white attacking midfielder No.10 moves quickly into the available space in behind **Juanfran (20)** as soon as the white winger No.11 receives and turns.

From this point, white No.11 plays a simple forward pass, which again leads to a dangerous 3v3 situation (numerical equality) at the back for Atlético.

DIEGO SIMEONE'S DEFENDING TACTICS

Tactical Situation 10 - Rear Block Controlling Passes within Wide Areas

REACTION OF THE FULL BACK WHEN THE OPPOSING WINGER DROPS BACK

a. The Opposing Winger Drops Back to Receive and Enters the Wide Midfielder's Zone of Responsibility

No.11 drops back to get free of marking

If the opposing winger drops into a deeper position (more than 6 yards away from the full back) inside the **yellow area shown on page 136**, it is difficult for the Atlético full back to prevent him from turning if he receives.

That is why the responsibility of controlling the white winger is passed to the wide midfielder. There is no need for the full back to move away from his zone of responsibility, which would create space in behind him and take him too far away to offer support to his defenders if needed.

In this example, the opposing left winger No.11 drops back to get free of marking. This action should be seen by the Atlético right midfielder **Correa (11)** so he can prepare his reaction.

The right back **Juanfran (20)** stays within his zone of responsibility to deny space for No.10.

©SOCCERTUTOR.COM

DIEGO SIMEONE'S DEFENDING TACTICS

Tactical Situation 10 - Rear Block Controlling Passes within Wide Areas

b. The Wide Midfielder Takes Over the Marking of the Opposing Winger and the Full Back Retains a Deep Position

As soon as the pass from the white left back No.3 is played towards the winger (No.11), the right midfielder **Correa (11)** takes over the role of closing him down as he has entered his zone of responsibility.

In this situation, the white winger No.11 may have time on the ball to turn, but the space behind **Juanfran (20)** is restricted due to the deep position of the Atlético right back.

The aim of the right midfielder **Correa (11)** is to press with the correct body shape to prevent an inside pass towards the **Crucial Central Area**.

As shown in the diagram, **Correa (11)** is able to block the passing lanes to white No.10 and No.9.

The aim of the right back **Juanfran (20)** is to control a potential pass behind his back (towards No.10).

Tactical Situation 10 - Rear Block Controlling Passes within Wide Areas

COLLECTIVE REACTIONS OF THE 2 WIDE PLAYERS TO WIN THE BALL

As already shown, Diego Simeone's Atlético Madrid team always try to force their opponents to play out wide towards the side-lines.

These passes are either long (switches of play) or shorter passes, such as a pass from the full back to the winger on the same side.

Atlético have developed mechanisms to deal with short passes out wide. In addition to the individual responses of the full backs or wide midfielders, the 2 wide players often work in collaboration with each other to win the ball and not only to close down their opponents.

a. Maintaining the Correct Distance Between the 2 Wide Players

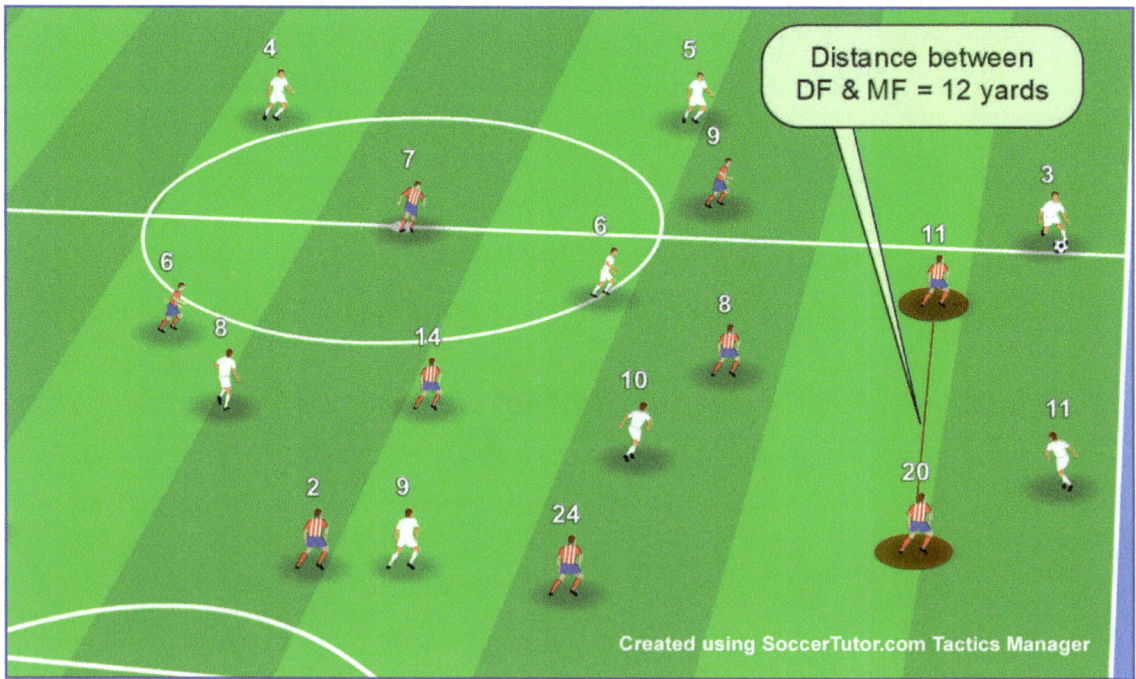

One of the trade-marks of Diego Simeone's Atlético side is the application of double marking near the side-lines. For this double marking to be successful, there should be 3 basic elements:

1. **Appropriate distance between the wide midfielder and full back:** Keep the distance within 12 yards and the available space for the winger or advanced full back will be restricted.

2. **Appropriate timing of both wide players to press the target player:** If the full back and wide midfielder move immediately after the short pass is played, the receiver will have no available time on the ball.

3. **Rear block retains a 12 yard distance between the defensive and midfield lines.**

Tactical Situation 10 - Rear Block Controlling Passes within Wide Areas

b. Applying Double or Triple Marking Near the Side-line

Double or triple marking

This tactical example follows on from the diagram on the previous page...

As soon as the short pass is played, both the right back **Juanfran (20)** and the right midfielder **Correa (11)** move towards the receiver (white No.11) and restrict his available time and space on the ball.

At the same time, the central midfielder on the strong side **Saúl (8)** moves into a supporting position to block the potential pass towards the **Crucial Central Area** and white No.10.

Saúl (8) is also ready to intervene if white No.11 overcomes the press and dribbles the ball inside.

ASSESSMENT

In this section, we show Diego Simeone's wide players' defensive reactions against the 4-3-3, but they can easily be adapted to play against the 4-2-3-1 and 4-4-2.

Against the 4-2-3-1, it will always be the No.10 trying to exploit the space behind the Atlético full back. Against the 4-4-2, it would be one of the 2 forwards.

DIEGO SIMEONE'S DEFENDING TACTICS

SESSION (3 PRACTICES) FOR "REAR BLOCK CONTROLLING PASSES WITHIN WIDE AREAS"

Tactical Situation 10 - Rear Block Controlling Passes within Wide Areas

SESSION FOR THIS TACTICAL SITUATION (3 PRACTICES)
1. Rear Block Controlling Passes within Wide Areas in a Functional Practice

Description

- The 3 white defenders start by passing the ball between each other, until a full back passes to a winger.

- The red players (especially the wide midfielders) check the wide areas frequently to see the positioning of the opposing winger and read the tactical situation.

- As soon as a white full back receives (No.2 in diagram), the red players must react accordingly to the situation.

- If the white winger No.7 is inside the white area, the red full back (3) should immediately press him and prevent him from turning, or at least restrict his available time and space and force him backwards if he does receive.

- The red left midfielder (6) should drop back to apply double marking and both of them prevent white No.7 from dribbling the ball through the red lines or passing to No.9.

- If the white winger receives within the yellow area, the red left midfielder (6) takes over his marking and the left back (3) stays in his position to retain balance at the back. The left midfielder (6) should press with the correct body shape to block the pass to No.9.

DIEGO SIMEONE'S DEFENDING TACTICS

Tactical Situation 10 - Rear Block Controlling Passes within Wide Areas

PROGRESSION
2. Rear Block Controlling Passes within Wide Areas in a Functional Zonal Small Sided Game

Scenario A: Applying Double Marking with the 2 Wide Players

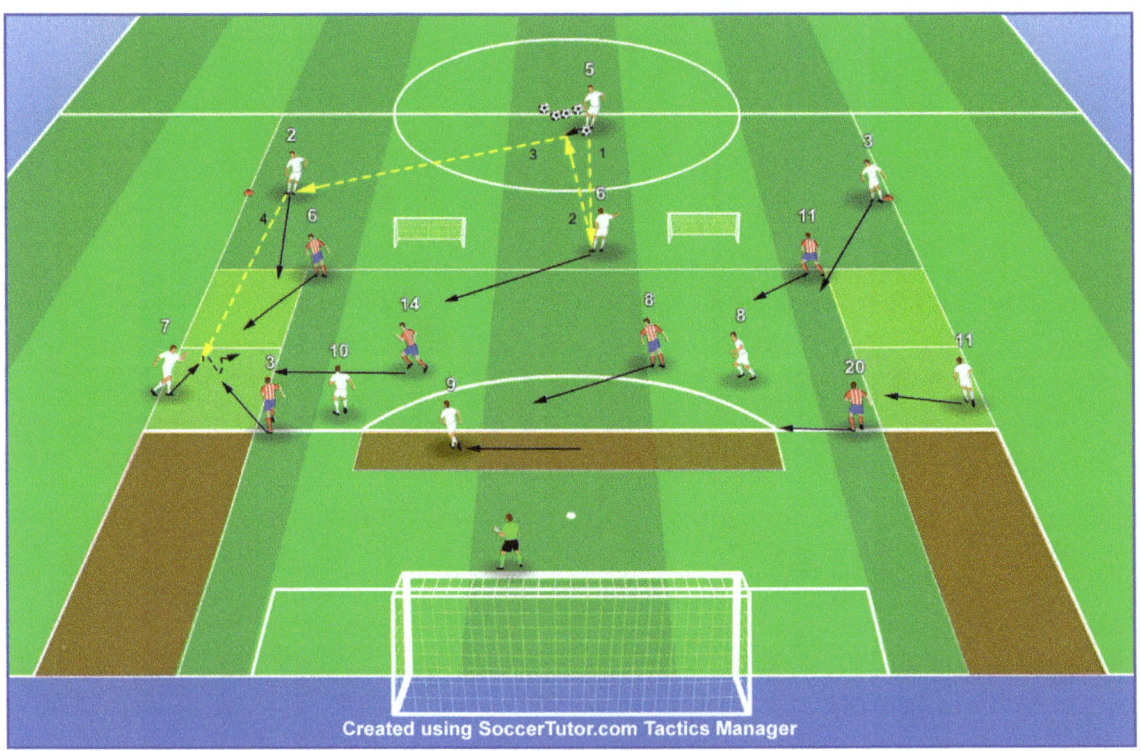

Description (Scenario A)
- In this progression, we add 2 red central midfielders, 3 white central midfielders, 2 mini goals and a large goal with a GK.
- The white team aim to either move the ball to the forward No.9 within the central red area, who can then shoot, or move the ball to an attacking midfielder (No.8 or No.10) in a wide red area, who can cross for No.9.
- The red full back on the strong side has to react according to the situation and control the attacking midfielder who can move to receive behind his back (wide red area).
- The red wide players (**3 and 6**) read the tactical situation and react according to the positioning of the opposing winger (white or yellow area), win the ball and then counter attack quickly to score in the 2 mini goals. This example is the same as the previous page, as both wide players apply double marking.

Restrictions
1. As soon as the white winger (No.7) receives, he is not allowed to pass the ball back.
2. The white full backs (No.2 and No.3) and the defensive midfielder (No.6) can only enter the playing area after the reds win possession.

©SOCCERTUTOR.COM DIEGO SIMEONE'S DEFENDING TACTICS

Tactical Situation 10 - Rear Block Controlling Passes within Wide Areas

Scenario B: Wide Midfielder Presses and Full Back Drops Off to Cover

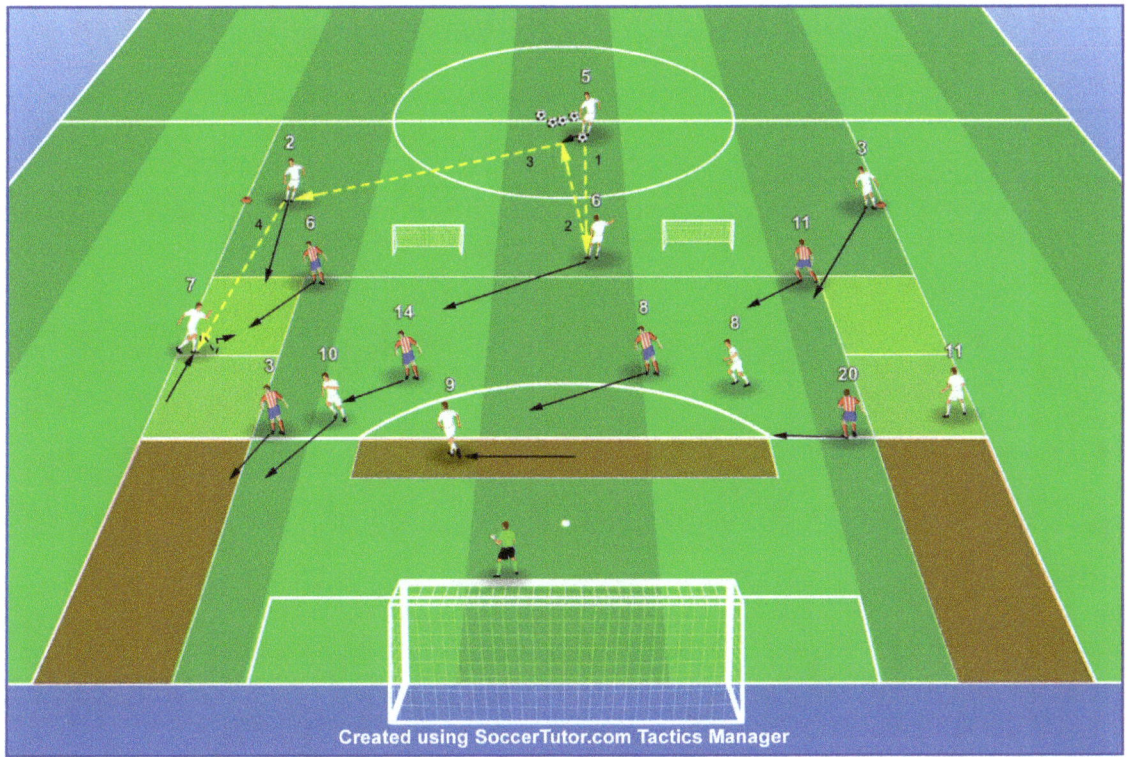

Description (Scenario B)

- In this second scenario, the white winger No.7 drops into a deeper position away from the red full back to receive in the yellow area.

- In this situation, the red wide midfielder **(6)** moves to close him down.

- The red full back **(3)** stays in a deep position and controls the movement of the white No.10, to make sure he doesn't receive in behind him.

- The closest red central midfielder **(14)** shifts across towards the strong side and blocks the passing lane towards the white No.9.

- The other red players also shift across.

Coaching Points

1. Read the tactical situation.
2. There needs to be good communication between the 2 wide players about the positioning of the opposing winger.
3. Check the wide areas and positioning of the opposing winger often.
4. Use the correct decision making for the specific tactical situation.

Tactical Situation 10 - Rear Block Controlling Passes within Wide Areas

PROGRESSION

3. Rear Block Controlling Passes within Wide Areas in a Functional 9v9 Game

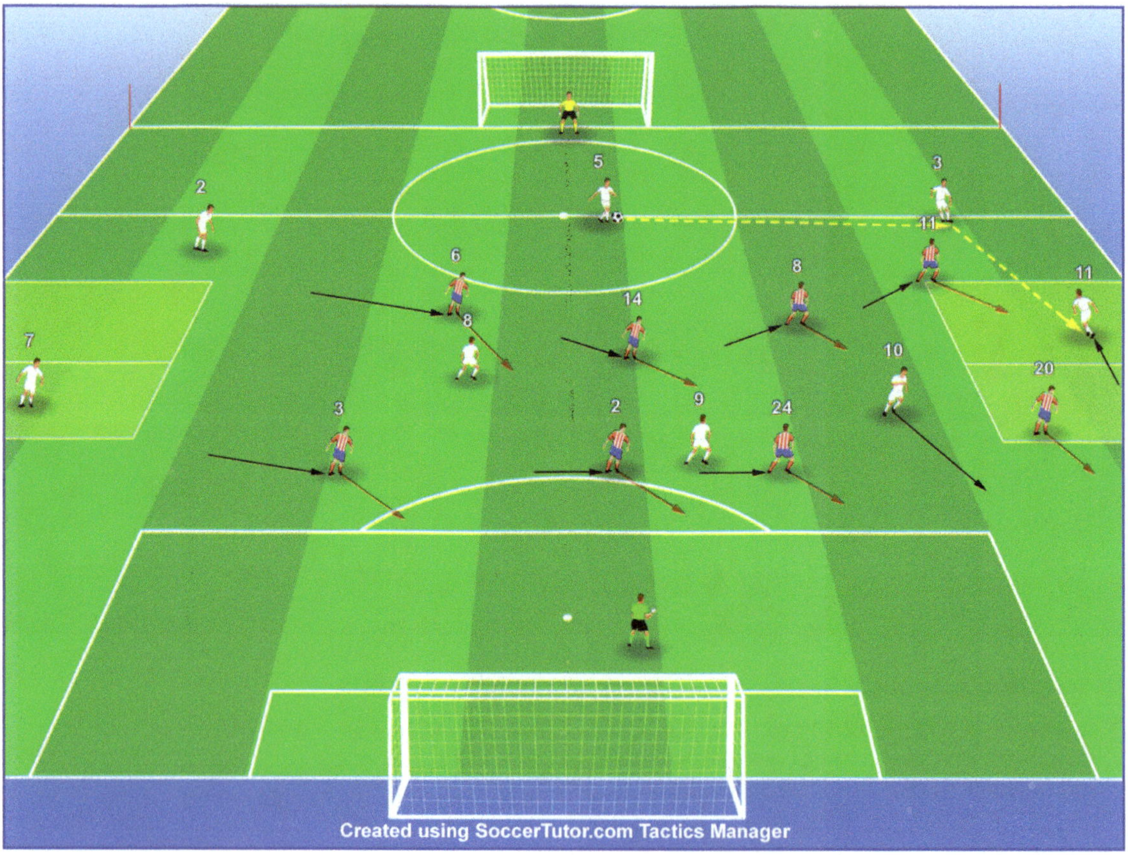

Description

- In the final practice of this session, the 2 teams play a 9v9 game.
- The practice starts with the white team's GK and the white team try to score.
- The red players aim to force the ball wide and then defend a potential short pass towards the winger (No.11 in diagram).
- The wide areas (white and yellow) can be used to help the red wide players identify zones of responsibility or they can be removed.
- The red players must react according to the position of the white winger (No.11) - **see previous practices and analysis pages**.
- The red players try to win the ball and then counter attack to score.

Progression: 11v11 game using 2/3 of pitch. The whites can score in any way but if they do it after a short pass in a wide area, they score 3 goals. The reds try to win the ball and score with a counter attack within a set amount of time.

TACTICAL SITUATION 11

Rear Block's Reaction After the Extensive Shift of the Centre Back

The content in this section is from analysis of Diego Simeone's Atlético Madrid teams during the 2017/2018 and 2018/2019 seasons.

The analysis is based on recurring patterns of play observed within the Atlético Madrid team. Once the same phase of play occurred several times (at least 10), the tactics would be seen as a pattern. The analysis on the following pages are examples of the team's tactics being used effectively.

Each action, pass, individual movement with or without the ball, and the positioning of each player on the pitch including their body shape, are presented.

The analysis is then used to create a session to coach this specific tactical situation.

Tactical Situation 11 - Rear Block's Reactions After the Extensive Shift of the Centre Back

REAR BLOCK'S REACTION AFTER THE EXTENSIVE SHIFT OF THE CENTRE BACK

1a. The Centre Back Shifts Towards the Side-line to Control the Opposing Attacking Midfielder Against the 4-3-3

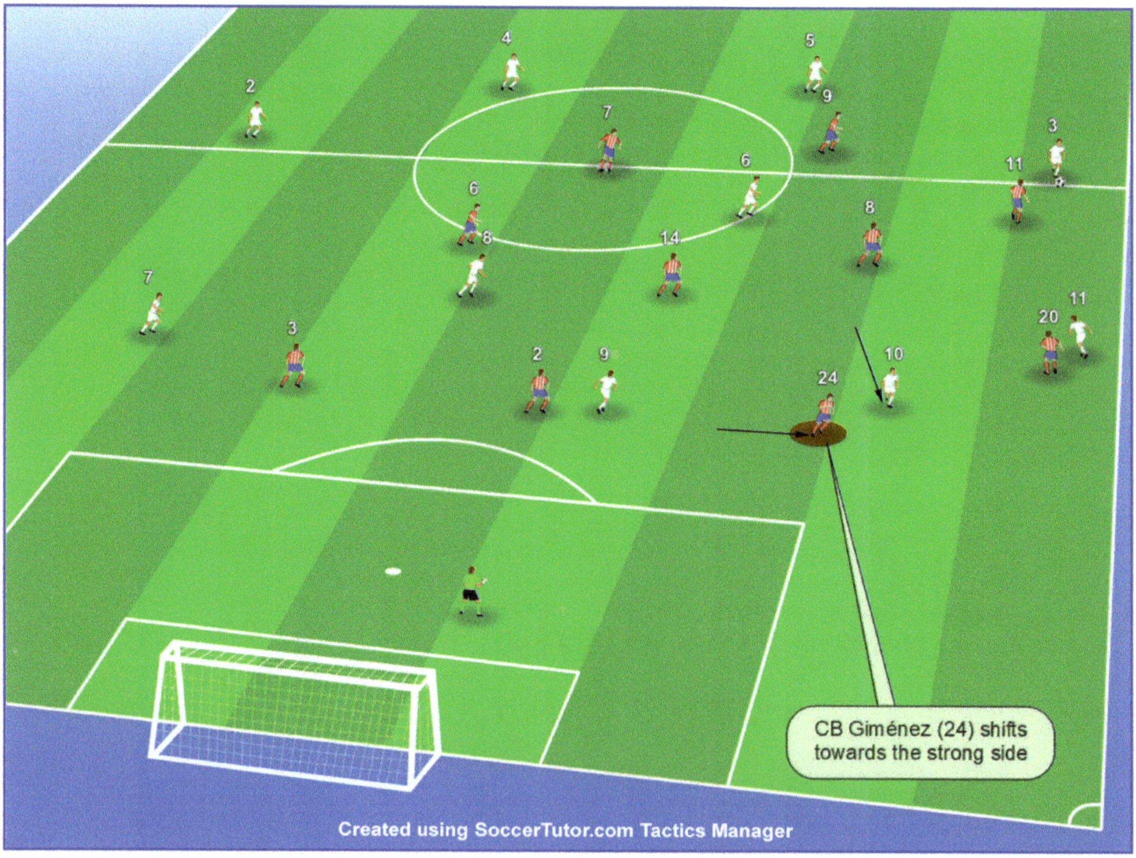

![Tactical diagram]

CB Giménez (24) shifts towards the strong side

Created using SoccerTutor.com Tactics Manager

In this tactical situation, the Atlético wide midfielder **Correa (11)** has to be aware of the white winger No.11's positioning by frequently checking the space near the side-line.

When the opposing full back is in possession near the side-line, the starting position of the Atlético full back on the strong side is slightly advanced compared to the rest of the defenders. The other 3 defenders are in the same line.

With this positioning, the full back **Juanfran (20)** is able to provide support to the other defenders and also control the space behind his back.

In this specific situation, the white winger No.11 is within **Juanfran's (20)** zone of responsibility, so he marks him. The attacking midfielder No.10 makes a run into the space behind **Juanfran (20)**, so the centre back **Giménez (24)** has to shift across towards the strong side to track him.

©SOCCERTUTOR.COM

DIEGO SIMEONE'S DEFENDING TACTICS

Tactical Situation 11 - Rear Block's Reactions After the Extensive Shift of the Centre Back

1b. The Central Midfielder Fills the Gap Created in the Defensive Line by the Extensive Shift of the Centre Back Against the 4-3-3

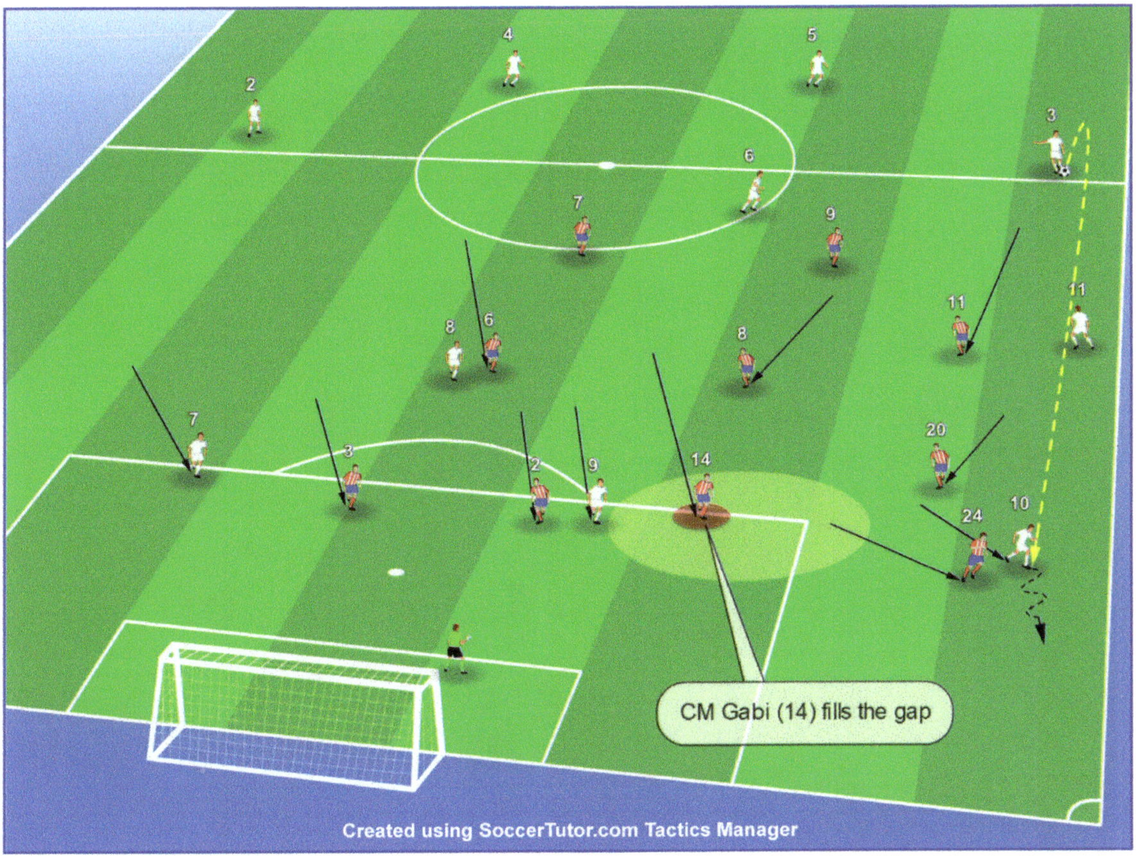

CM Gabi (14) fills the gap

This tactical example follows on from the diagram on the previous page...

As soon as the pass is played in behind the Atlético right back **Juanfran (20)**, the centre back **Giménez (24)** tracks the run of the white attacking midfielder No.10 towards the side-line.

This extensive shift of the Atlético centre back creates a gap in the defensive line which could lead to a potentially dangerous 2v2 situation inside the box If No.10 is able to cross.

However, the deepest positioned Atlético central midfielder provides safety in situations like this by dropping back in time to provide cover.

In this example, it is **Gabi (14)** who drops back to fill the gap.

This reaction enables Atlético to retain 3 players inside the box and a numerical superiority.

The other central midfielder **Saúl (8)** and left midfielder **Koke (6)** drop back and inside to collect any second balls in the central area after a potential clearance by the defenders.

Tactical Situation 11 - Rear Block's Reactions After the Extensive Shift of the Centre Back

2. The Centre Back Shifts Towards the Side-line to Control the Opposing Attacking Midfielder Against the 4-4-2

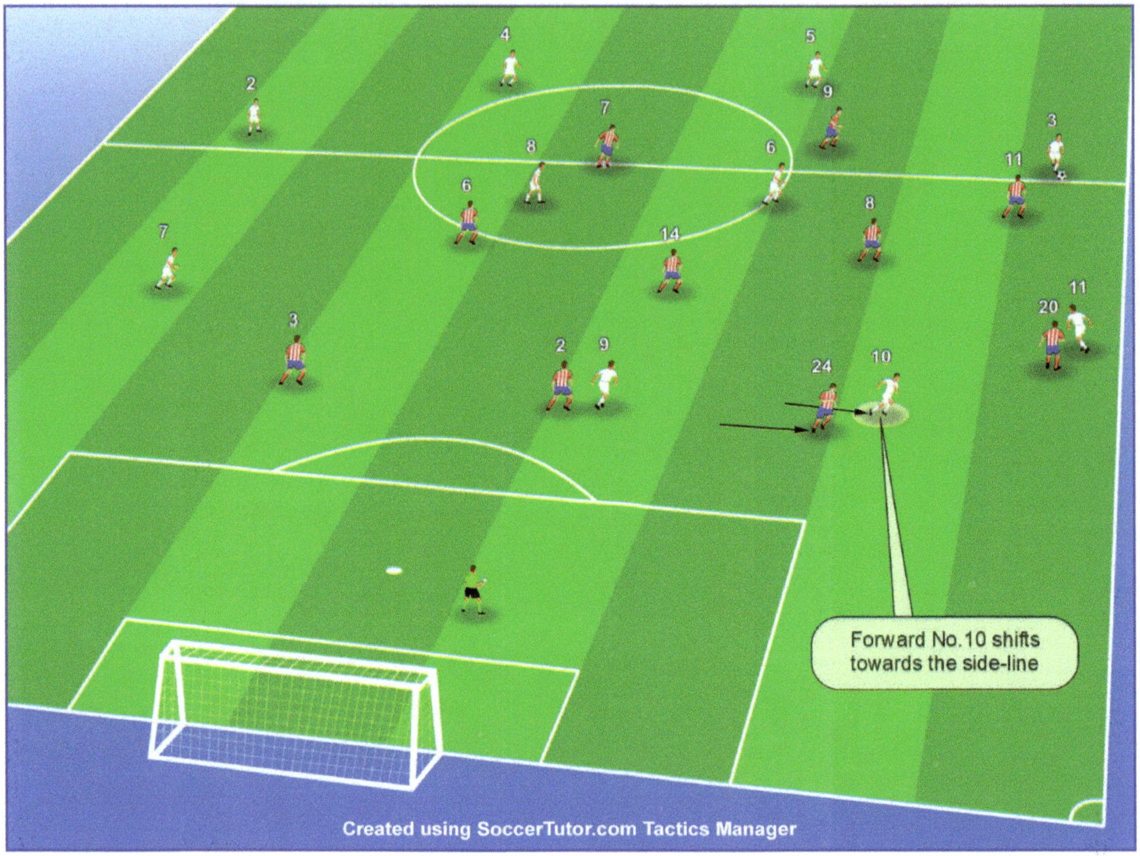

Forward No.10 shifts towards the side-line

This diagram shows what happens when playing against the 4-4-2.

The extensive shift of the centre back can be caused by the movement of one of the forwards behind the back of the full back.

If the ball is directed in behind **Juanfran (20)**, the white forward No.10 will move to receive and the centre back **Giménez (24)** will track his run.

The gap created should again be filled by the deepest central midfielder **Gabi (14)**.

DIEGO SIMEONE'S DEFENDING TACTICS

Tactical Situation 11 - Rear Block's Reactions After the Extensive Shift of the Centre Back

ASSESSMENT

1. The central midfielders must be alert to fill every potential gap created. It is possible for a gap to be created between the full back and centre back on the weak side. In this situation, the deepest positioned central midfielder again moves between these 2 players to fill the gap and retain a numerical advantage at the back.

2. In many cases, the full back moved to provide support to the centre back and the central midfielder moved to fill the gap that was temporarily created. This reaction provided extra safety for Diego Simeone's Atlético Madrid.

3. The same situation can be created by a team using the 4-2-3-1 formation, with the attacking midfielder No.10 being the player who moves towards the side-line and forcing the extensive shift of the centre back.

SESSION (3 PRACTICES) FOR "REAR BLOCK'S REACTION AFTER THE EXTENSIVE SHIFT OF THE CENTRE BACK"

Tactical Situation 11 - Rear Block's Reactions After the Extensive Shift of the Centre Back

SESSION FOR THIS TACTICAL SITUATION (3 PRACTICES)

1. Rear Block's Reaction After the Extensive Shift of the Centre Back in a 4v6 Functional Practice

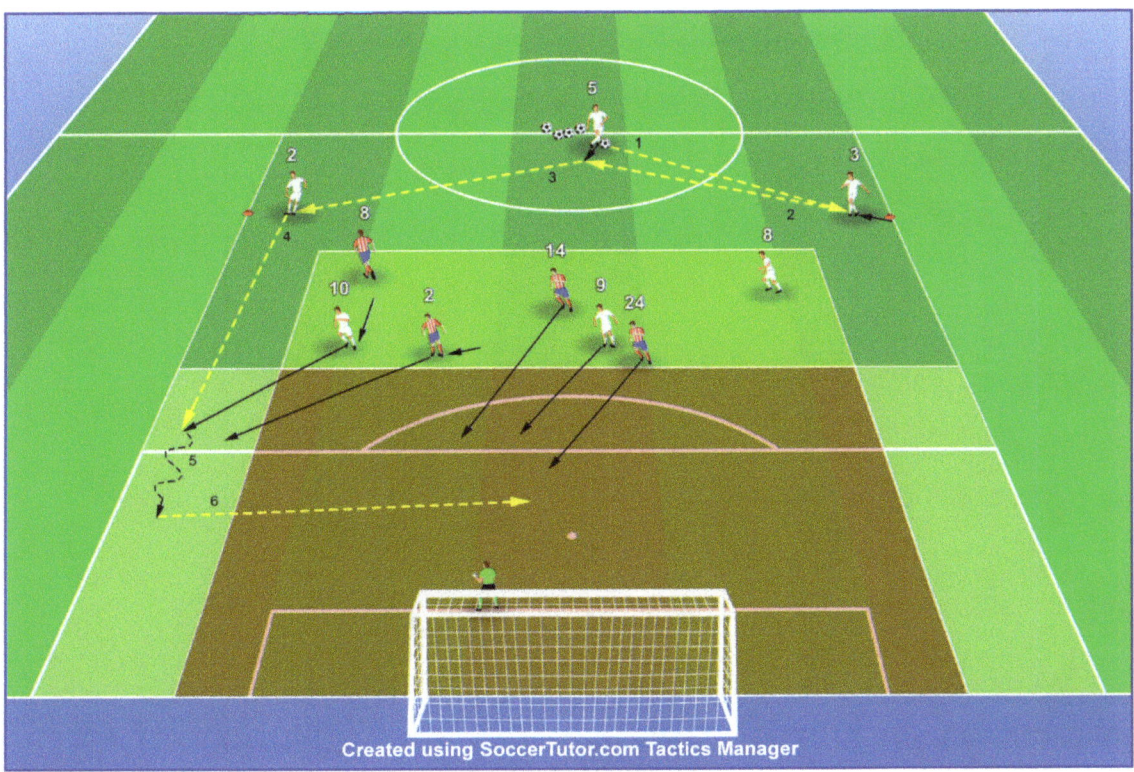

Description

- The 3 white defenders start by passing the ball between each other and the red players shift according to the position of the ball.

- As soon as the white full back (No.2 in diagram) receives, the attacking midfielder (No.10) makes a run towards the wide area, receives, and then tries to cross for the forward (No.9) to score.

- This movement forces the red centre back (**2**) to shift extensively towards the side-line.

- The deepest central midfielder (**14**) runs back to fill the gap and create a 2v1 numerical advantage inside the red central area.

- The reds should defend effectively by stopping or defending the cross. They then return to their starting positions.

Coaching Point: The movements of the centre back and central midfielder need to be synchronised.

DIEGO SIMEONE'S DEFENDING TACTICS

Tactical Situation 11 - Rear Block's Reactions After the Extensive Shift of the Centre Back

PROGRESSION
2. Rear Block's Reaction After the Extensive Shift of the Centre Back in a 6v8 Functional Practice
Scenario A: Central Midfielder Drops Back to Fill the Gap

Description (Scenario A)

- In this progression, we add extra 5 x 8 yard blue wide areas for the 2 red full backs and 2 white wingers. The white full backs can now pass to the wingers (No.2 to No.7 in diagram), as well as the attacking midfielders.

- The aim for the white full back (No.2) is to play a long pass for the run of the attacking midfielder (No.10), as shown in the diagram.

The extensive shift of the red centre back (2) can be dealt with in 3 different ways:

1. When the full back (3) is marking the winger (No.7), the deepest central midfielder (14) drops back to fill the gap in the defensive line (**see diagram above**).

2. When the full back (3) is in a deeper position, he is able to cover the extensive shift of the centre back (**see diagram on next page**).

3. Both the full back (3) and central midfielder (14) drop back to create extra safety.

Tactical Situation 11 - Rear Block's Reactions After the Extensive Shift of the Centre Back

Scenario B: The Full Back is Deep Enough to Provide Cover

Description (Scenario B)

- In this second scenario, the full back (3) is not marking the white winger No.7, so he is in a deeper position.

- This enables him to immediately cover the extensive shift of the centre back (2) and make sure there is a numerical advantage in the red central area.

- This means that there is no need for the central midfielder (14) to drop back.

- The reds should defend effectively by stopping or defending the cross. They then return to their starting positions.

Coaching Points

1. Read the tactical situation.
2. There needs to be good communication between the players about positioning and who needs to provide cover.
3. The movements of the centre back and central midfielder need to be synchronised.
4. The full back reacts according to the specific tactical situation.

DIEGO SIMEONE'S DEFENDING TACTICS

Tactical Situation 11 - Rear Block's Reactions After the Extensive Shift of the Centre Back

PROGRESSION
3. Rear Block's Reaction After the Extensive Shift of the Centre Back in a Functional Game

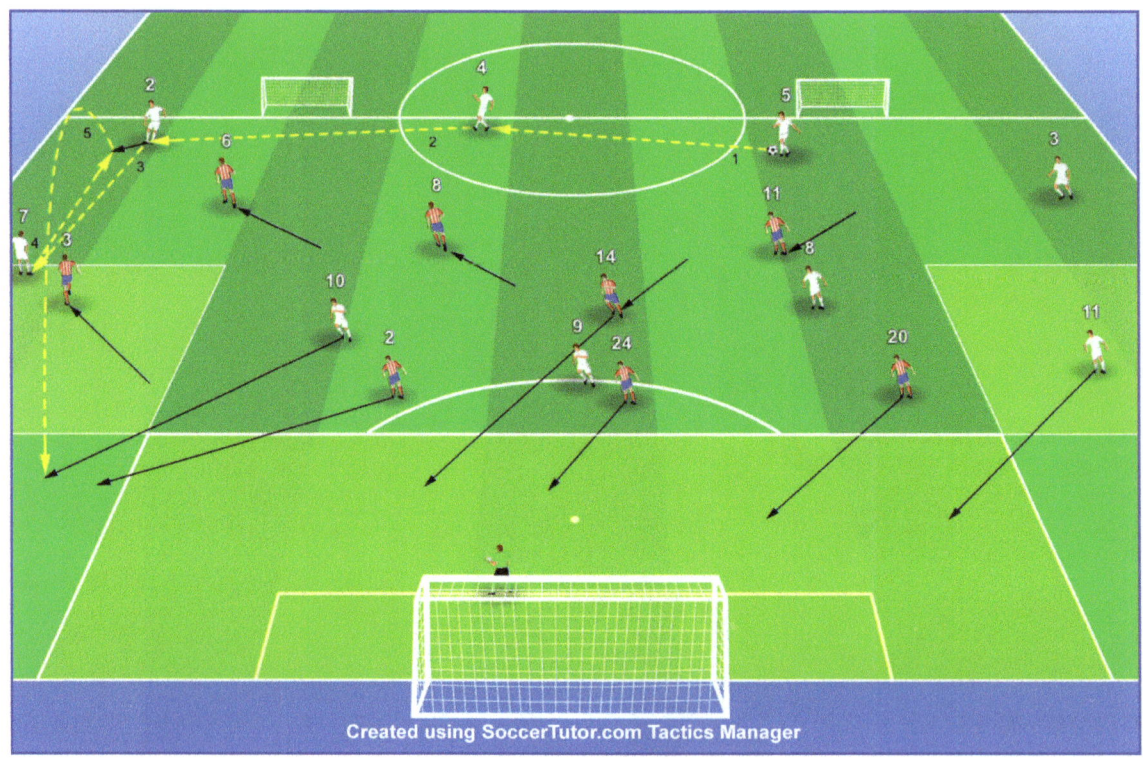

Description
- In the final practice of this session, the 2 teams play an 8 (+GK) v 9 game. The practice starts with the white team trying to score. If they score from a cross after receiving in the wide areas, the goal counts double.
- The red players must react according to the tactical situation - **see previous practices and analysis pages**.
- If the red team win the ball, they then try to score in the 2 mini goals (counter attack).

Progression
The 2 teams play 11 v 11 in 2/3 of the pitch. The whites try to score in any possible way but if they do it from a cross after a pass behind the full back, they score 3 goals. The reds try to win the ball and counter within a set amount of time.

ASSESSMENT
All the practices in this session are against the 4-3-3 but can be easily adapted to play against the 4-2-3-1 and 4-4-2. When playing against the 4-4-2, one of the 2 forwards moves towards the side-line to receive within the wide area and cross.

@SOCCERTUTOR.COM   DIEGO SIMEONE'S DEFENDING TACTICS

TACTICAL SITUATION 12

Rear Block's Defensive Reactions After Wide Players Receive

The content in this section is from analysis of Diego Simeone's Atlético Madrid teams during the 2017/2018 and 2018/2019 seasons.

The analysis is based on recurring patterns of play observed within the Atlético Madrid team. Once the same phase of play occurred several times (at least 10), the tactics would be seen as a pattern. The analysis on the following pages are examples of the team's tactics being used effectively.

Each action, pass, individual movement with or without the ball, and the positioning of each player on the pitch including their body shape, are presented.

The analysis is then used to create a session to coach this specific tactical situation.

Tactical Situation 12 - Rear Block's Defensive Reactions After Wide Players Receive

THE CENTRAL MIDFIELDER COVERS THE SPACE BEHIND THE FULL BACK AGAINST THE 4-3-3

As already mentioned, the aim of the Atlético full backs is to immediately press opponents who received in advanced positions near the side-line and prevent them from turning.

However, this was not always possible and there were situations when either the winger or the full back found time on the ball to turn and search for the next pass. So Atlético had to develop mechanisms to deal with all kinds of situations in wide areas.

In this example against the 4-3-3, we show a situation where the opposing winger receives and turns near the side-line, while the attacking midfielder makes a forward run from a low position to exploit the gap between the Atlético full back and centre back.

a. Central Midfielder Controls the Opposing Attacking Midfielder in a Deep Position

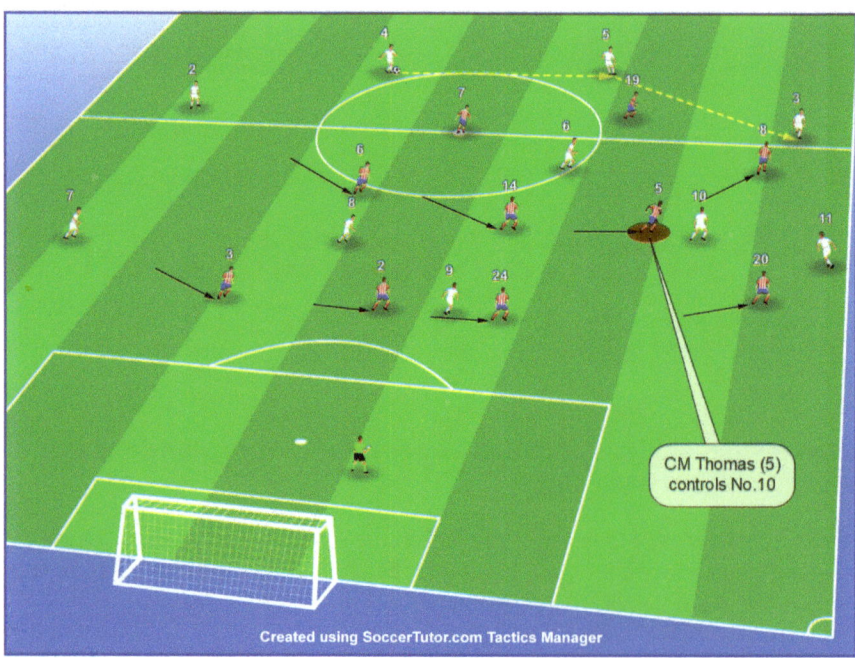

The opposing attacking midfielder No.10 is in a deep position and within the zone of responsibility of central midfielder **Thomas (5)**.

If white No.10 moves forward quickly, he is likely to find space between the full back and centre back to exploit.

Both Atlético centre backs are focused on the forward No.9, so the distance between **Giménez (24)** and **Juanfran (20)** is large.

The description continues on the next page...

DIEGO SIMEONE'S DEFENDING TACTICS

Tactical Situation 12 - Rear Block's Defensive Reactions After Wide Players Receive

b. Central Midfielder Tracks the Run of the Attacking Midfielder and Covers the Space Behind the Full Back

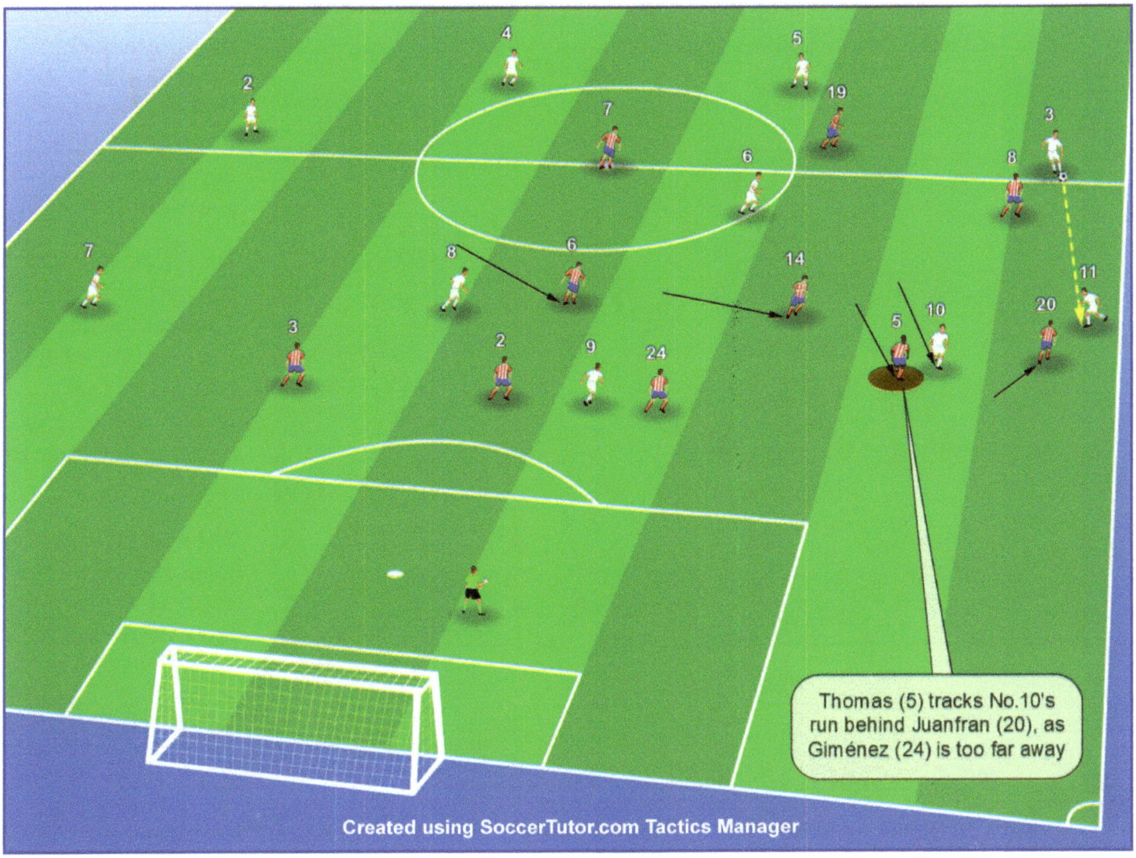

Thomas (5) tracks No.10's run behind Juanfran (20), as Giménez (24) is too far away

This tactical example follows on from the diagram on the previous page...

In order for the Atlético central midfielder **Thomas (5)** to prevent his team being caught by surprise, as soon as the pass from No.3 is directed to No.11, he tracks the forward run of No.10. The white winger No.11 has time to receive on the half-turn or receive and then turn.

When tracking No.10, **Thomas (5)** must be aware of the centre back **Giménez's (24)** positioning.

If **Giménez (24)** has already shifted across and is able to take over No.10's marking, **Thomas (5)** passes over the responsibility (**see next page**).

If **Giménez (24)** has not shifted across, **Thomas (5)** continues to track white No.10's run.

The other centre midfielder **Rodri (14)** and left midfielder **Koke (6)** shift towards the strong side to keep the team balanced.

Rodri (14) moves to provide support to the right back **Juanfran (20)** from the inside and create a 2v1 advantage around the ball area.

Tactical Situation 12 - Rear Block's Defensive Reactions After Wide Players Receive

Variation: Central Midfielder Tracks the Run of the Attacking Midfielder Until the Centre Back Takes Over the Marking

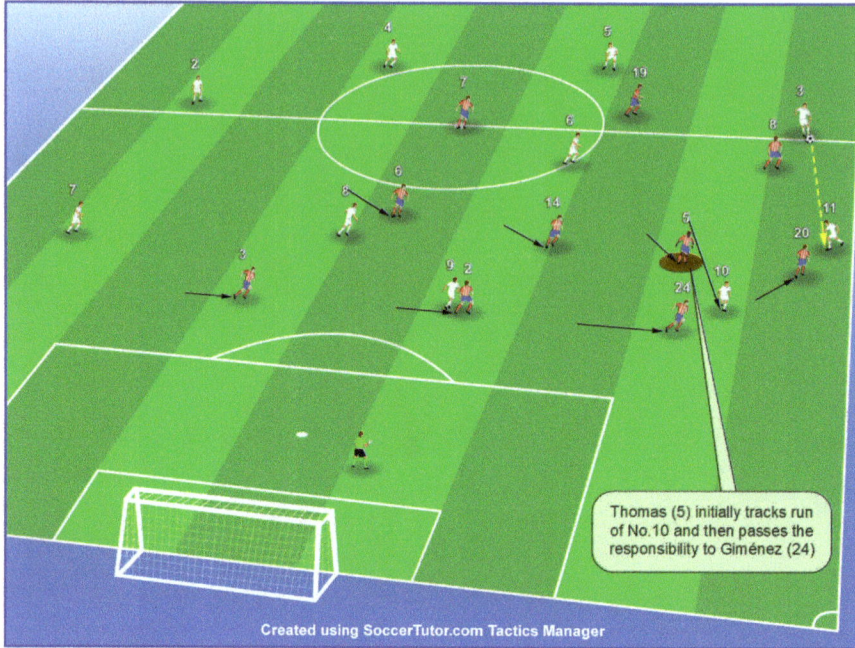

Thomas (5) initially tracks run of No.10 and then passes the responsibility to Giménez (24)

In this variation, the centre back **Giménez (24)** has shifted across in time to close the gap to the right back **Juanfran (20)**.

Therefore, the right central midfielder **Thomas (5)** stops tracking white No.10 and passes the responsibility of his marking to **Giménez (24)**.

Thomas (5) now focuses on providing support to the right back **Juanfran (20)**.

ASSESSMENT

1. If the white winger No.11 is immediately pressed by the full back **Juanfran (20)** and his turn or half turn is prevented, then even if the attacking midfielder No.10 makes a forward run, there is no need for **Thomas (5)** to track his run. His aim in this situation is to provide support from the inside to the full back **Juanfran (20)**, as a forward pass cannot be played.

2. In the last example (above), the central midfielder on the weak side **Rodri (14)** has to be ready to drop back and fill any potential gap created by the extensive shift of the centre back **Giménez (24)**.

3. These examples analysed were mainly used against the 4-3-3 formation. When a team plays against Atlético with the 4-2-3-1, the opposing central midfielders rarely try to make forward runs to exploit the space between the defenders.

Tactical Situation 12 - Rear Block's Defensive Reactions After Wide Players Receive

COMPACT LINES PREVENT INSIDE PASSES FROM WIDE AREAS AGAINST THE 4-2-3-1 OR 4-4-2

a. Intelligent Positioning of the Opposing Full Back to Receive Near the Side-line

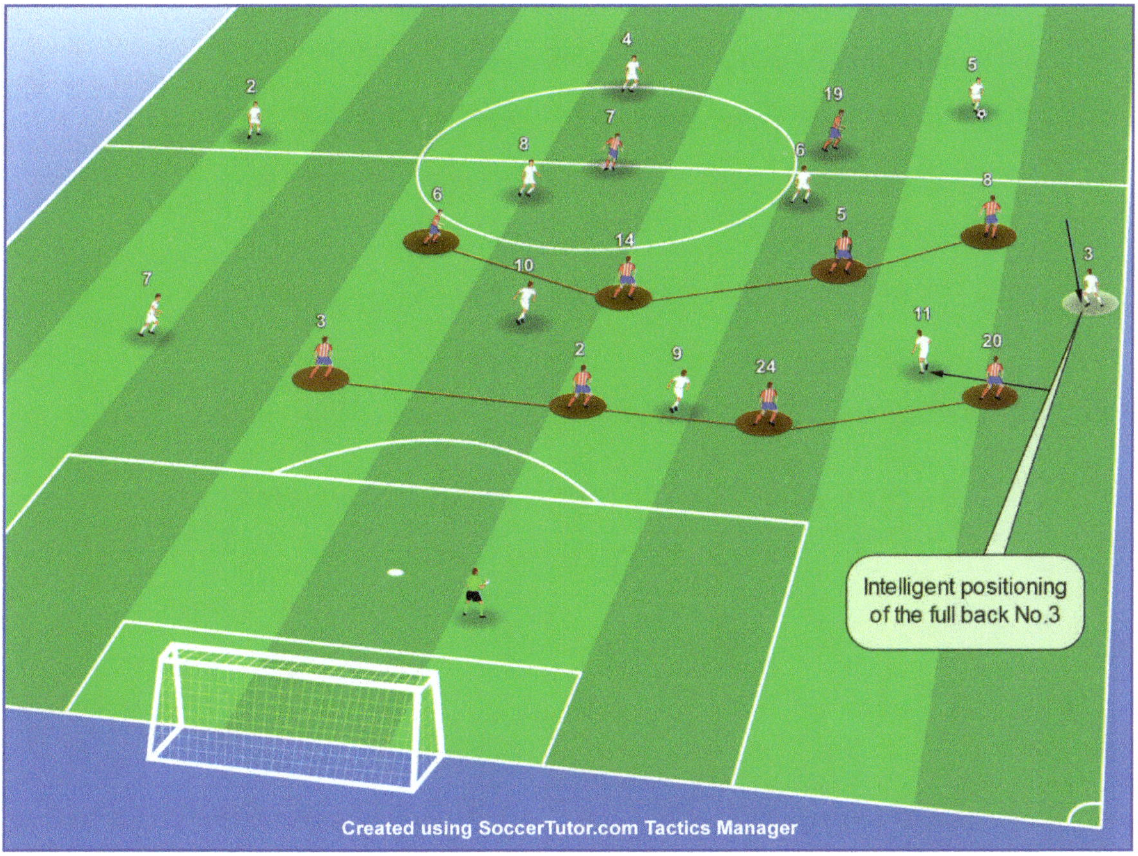

If the opposing full back takes up an intelligent positioning in between the Atlético full back and wide midfielder, there is a possibility that he will find available time on the ball, turn and then be able search for the next forward pass.

However, even in this situation, Atlético's compact rear block can make it very difficult for their opponents to play a successful inside pass towards the **Crucial Central Area**.

In this tactical example, the white left back No.3 has taken up an intelligent position, which is 6 yards away from both of Atlético's wide players.

This means that the white left back No.3 is in an ideal position to receive from No.5 in space.

Tactical Situation 12 - Rear Block's Defensive Reactions After Wide Players Receive

b. Compact Lines to Block Inside Passes with the Opposing Full Back in Possession

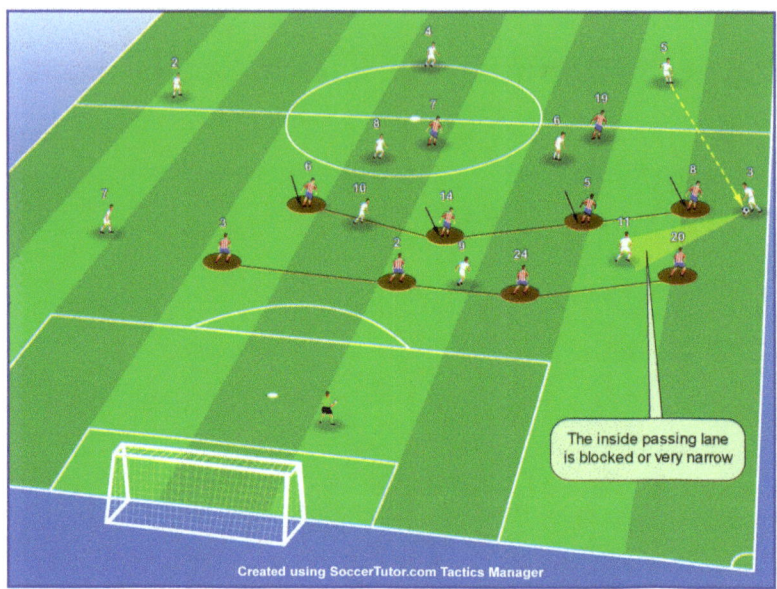

As soon as No.5 plays the pass, the Atlético right back **Juanfran (20)** realises that if he moves forward, even at the right time, he won't be able to prevent No.3 turning. So, his marking is passed to the right midfielder **Saúl (8)** and **Juanfran (20)** stays to control his zone. White No.3 receives and turns, looking for the next pass.

The Atlético midfielders drop back collectively and the close distance between the 2 lines means the inside passing lane is blocked or very narrow.

c. The Full Back and Central Midfielder Move to Intercept the Attempted Inside Pass

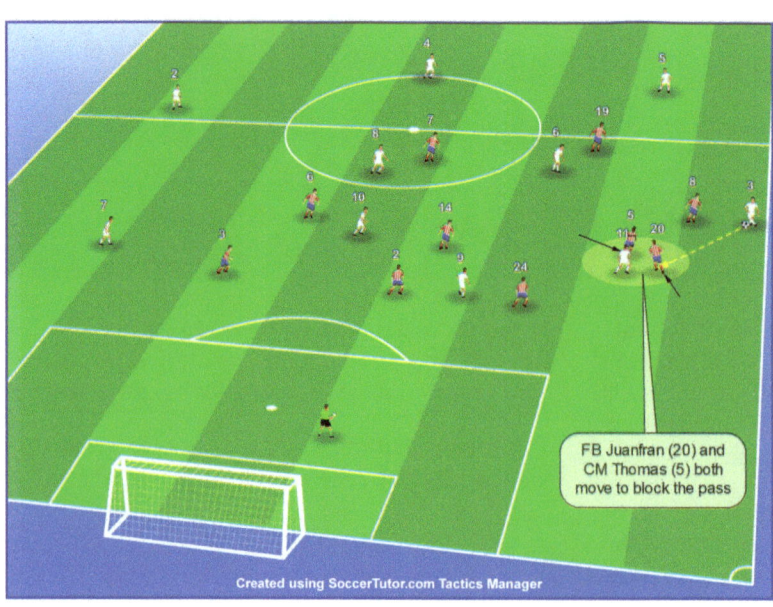

If a pass towards the inside is attempted, both the right back **Juanfran (20)** and the right central midfielder **Thomas (5)** can move to block it.

Even if the white winger No.11 manages to receive the pass, he will immediately be under double marking and turning between the lines will be impossible for him.

NOTE: A similar defensive reaction is applied against the 4-4-2.

Tactical Situation 12 - Rear Block's Defensive Reactions After Wide Players Receive

COMPACT LINES PREVENT INSIDE PASSES FROM WIDE AREAS AGAINST THE 4-3-3

Intelligent Positioning of the Opposing Full Back to Receive Near the Side-line

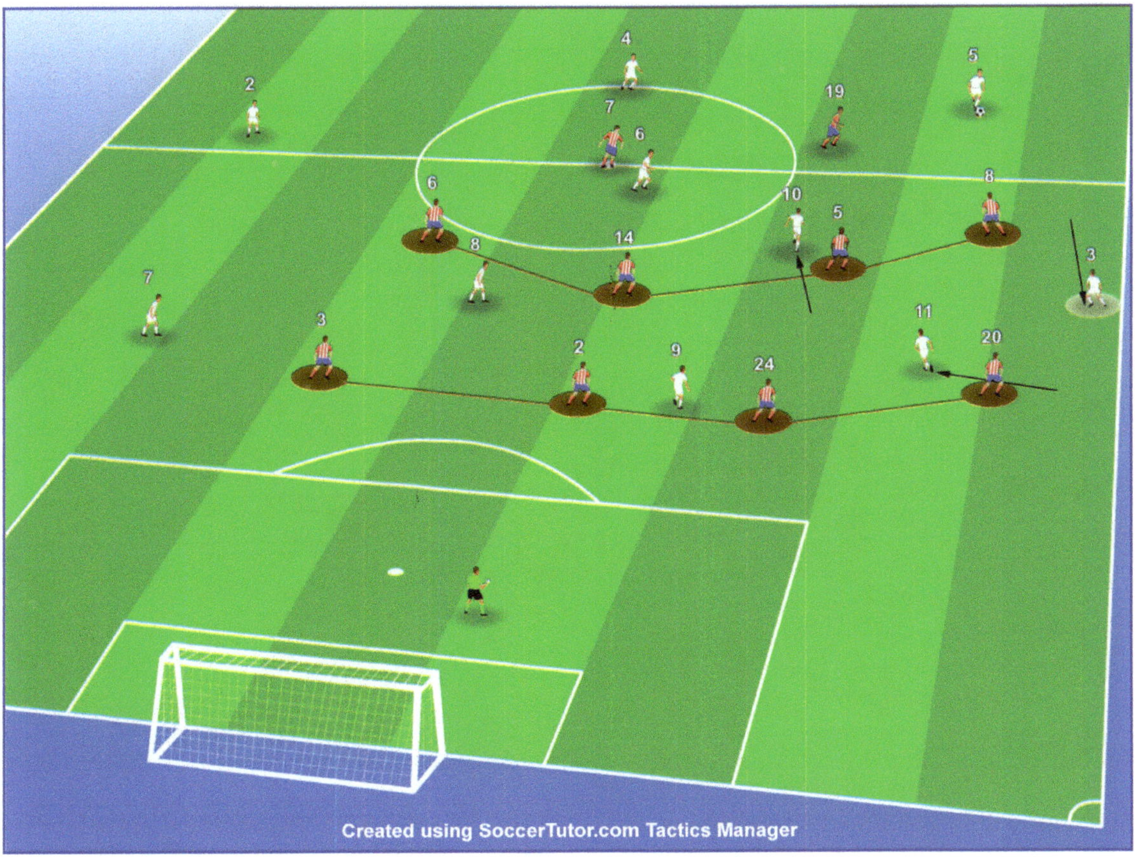

This tactical example is a variation of the example shown on the previous 2 pages...

A similar situation can be created against teams using the 4-3-3 formation.

As the white defensive midfielder No.6 is away from the strong side, the attacking midfielder No.10 drops back, and the winger No.11 moves towards the inside to provide a passing option for a through pass.

The white left back No.3 moves into an advanced and intelligent position.

As soon as the pass is directed to the No.3, the reaction of the Atlético players is similar to when playing against the 4-2-3-1 formation, which is fully described on the previous page.

DIEGO SIMEONE'S DEFENDING TACTICS

Tactical Situation 12 - Rear Block's Defensive Reactions After Wide Players Receive

THE OPPOSING FULL BACK RECEIVES IN AN ADVANCED POSITION AGAINST THE 4-2-3-1

a. Key Positioning of the Atlético Defenders on the Strong Side when the Opposing Wide Players Make Collaborating Movements

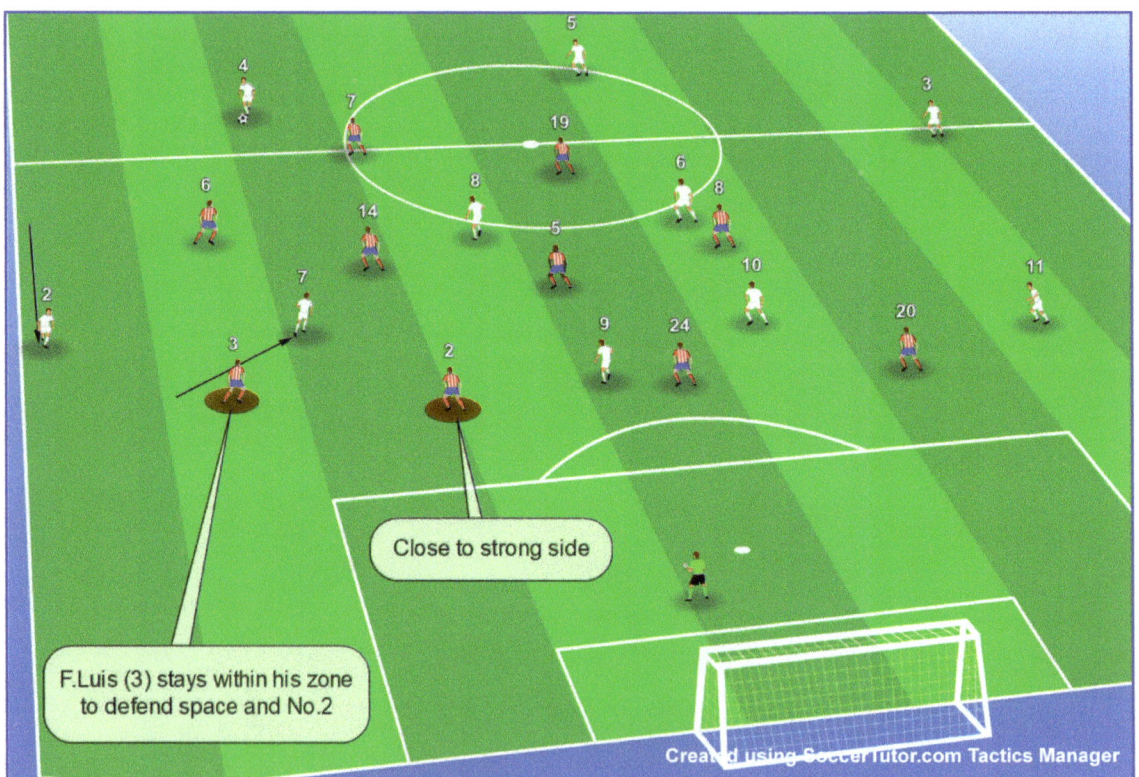

In this example, the opposing winger No.7 moves towards the centre to provide an option for a through pass. At the same time, the full back No.2 moves forward.

As mentioned previously, the distance between the defenders and midfielders is kept short (no more than 12 yards). Within this space, Atlético create 2 areas. When the opposing full back was within the low area, he was controlled by Atlético's wide midfielder. If he was within the high area, it was the full back who took over.

White No.2 enters the high area, so the left back **F. Luis (3)** takes over his marking. The compactness of the Atlético rear block prevents the through pass to white No.7, which enables the left back **F. Luis (3)** to focus on controlling white No.2, rather than No.7.

A very important element is the positioning of the centre back on the strong side **Godín (2)**. If he is close enough to the full back **F. Luis (3)**, as is shown on the diagram above, the Atlético defence can use a chain reaction.

Tactical Situation 12 - Rear Block's Defensive Reactions After Wide Players Receive

b. The Atlético Defenders Use a Chain Reaction to Apply Double Marking and Create a Numerical Advantage Around the Ball

CB Godín (2) is close enough to take over marking of No.7

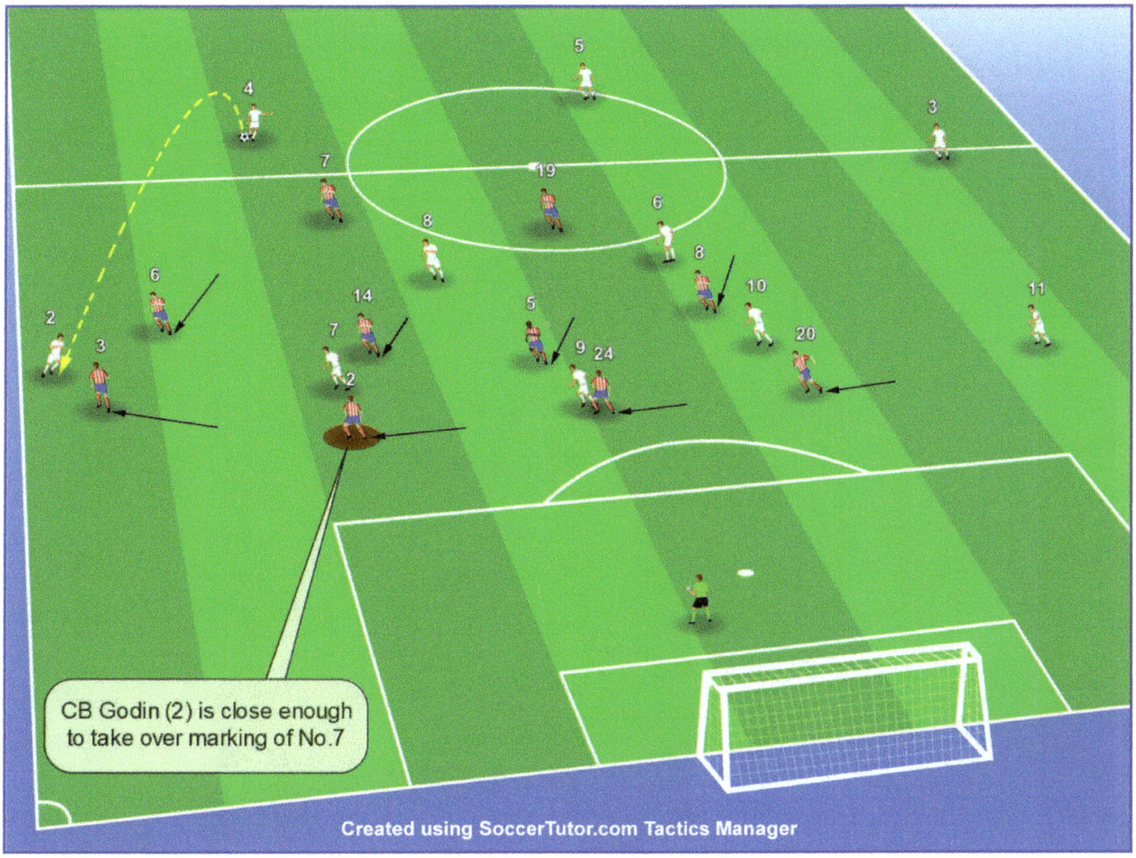

This tactical example follows on from the diagram on the previous page...

As soon as the pass is played towards No.2, **F. Luis (3)** presses him immediately, while left midfielder **Koke (6)** drops back to apply double marking. At the same time, the centre back **Godín (2)** takes over the marking of the winger No.7.

The central midfielder on the weak side **Thomas (5)** drops back and is ready to provide cover if the centre back **Godín (2)** shifts extensively towards the side-line.

Atlético successfully apply double marking, mark all the players near the ball area tightly and have a numerical advantage around the ball.

The inside passing lane is kept narrow and even if there is a successful pass towards No.7, he will be immediately put under double marking by **Godín (2)** and **Rodri (14)**.

DIEGO SIMEONE'S DEFENDING TACTICS

Tactical Situation 12 - Rear Block's Defensive Reactions After Wide Players Receive

Variation: The Opposing Winger Makes a Run into the Space Behind the Full Back

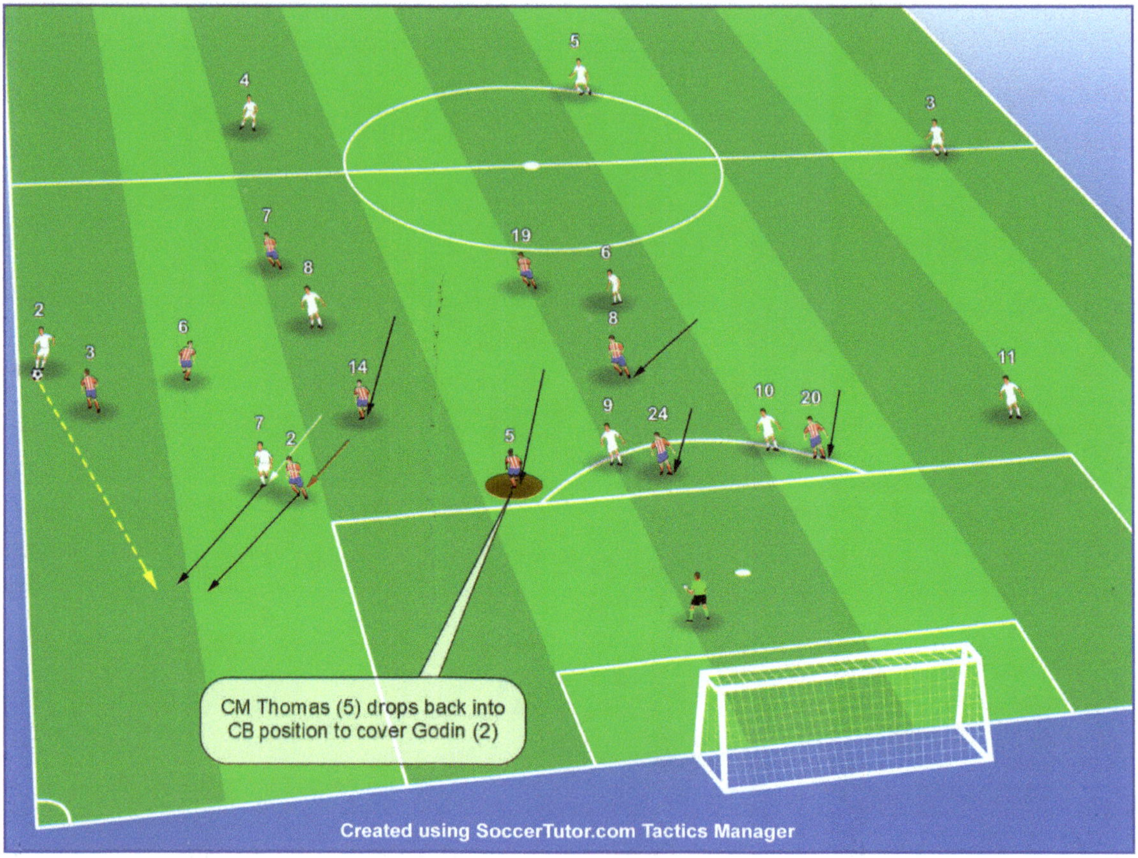

CM Thomas (5) drops back into CB position to cover Godín (2)

In this tactical example, the opposing right winger No.7 makes a run in behind the Atlético left back **F. Luis (3)**.

In this situation, it is the centre back **Godín (2)** who tracks No.7's run.

This shifting towards the side-line is followed by a dropping back movement of the central midfielder on the weak side **Thomas (5)**, who moves into the centre of defence to fill the gap that has been created.

With these defensive reactions, it means that Atlético can still defend with 3 players inside the box and avoid being outnumbered by their opponents.

Tactical Situation 12 - Rear Block's Defensive Reactions After Wide Players Receive

CONTROLLING THE FULL BACK WHO RECEIVES IN AN ADVANCED POSITION AGAINST THE 4-2-3-1

The Full Back Defends the Space to Play for Time and Manage the Gap in the Defensive Line

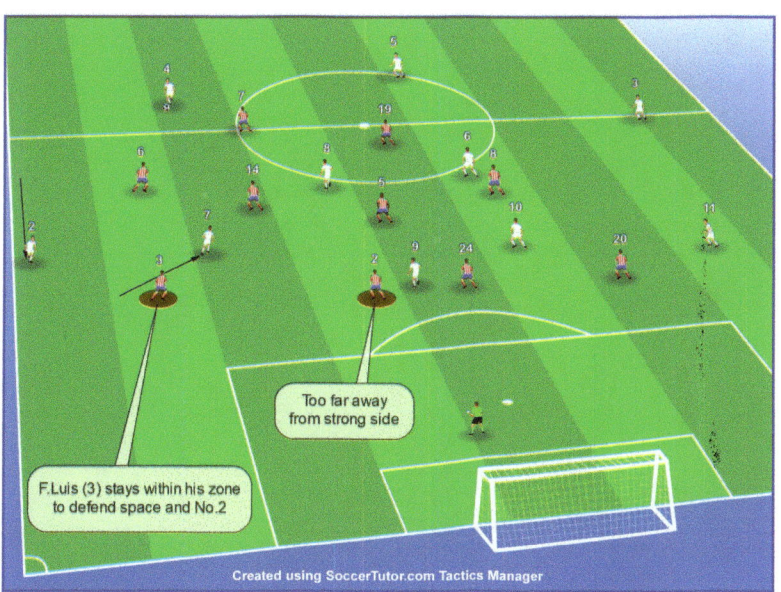

When the centre back **Godín (2)** was not close enough to the full back **F. Luis (3)**, the Atlético defenders had to react in a different way.

Godín (2) is focused on marking the forward No.9 and is too far away from the left back **F. Luis (3)**.

This positioning prevents him from taking over the marking of the white winger No.7 immediately, especially as he could make a run into the space behind **F. Luis (3)**.

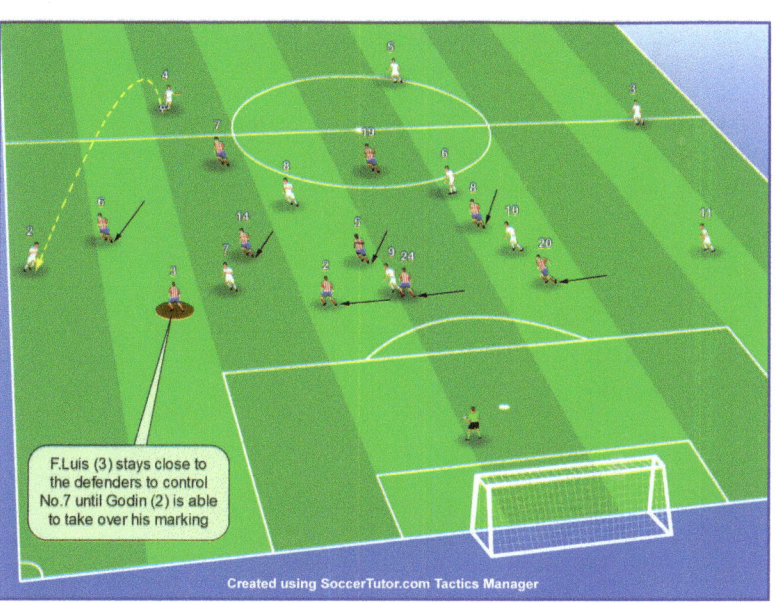

The pass is played to the advanced right back No.2, but the Atlético left back **F. Luis (3)** doesn't move forward to press him, and instead plays for time.

This reaction is used to control the opposing winger No.7 and a potential run behind his back, as well as allow time for the centre back **Godín (2)** to shift across and take over the marking of No.7.

DIEGO SIMEONE'S DEFENDING TACTICS

Tactical Situation 12 - Rear Block's Defensive Reactions After Wide Players Receive

Variation 1: The Opposing Winger DOES Make a Run into the Space Behind the Full Back

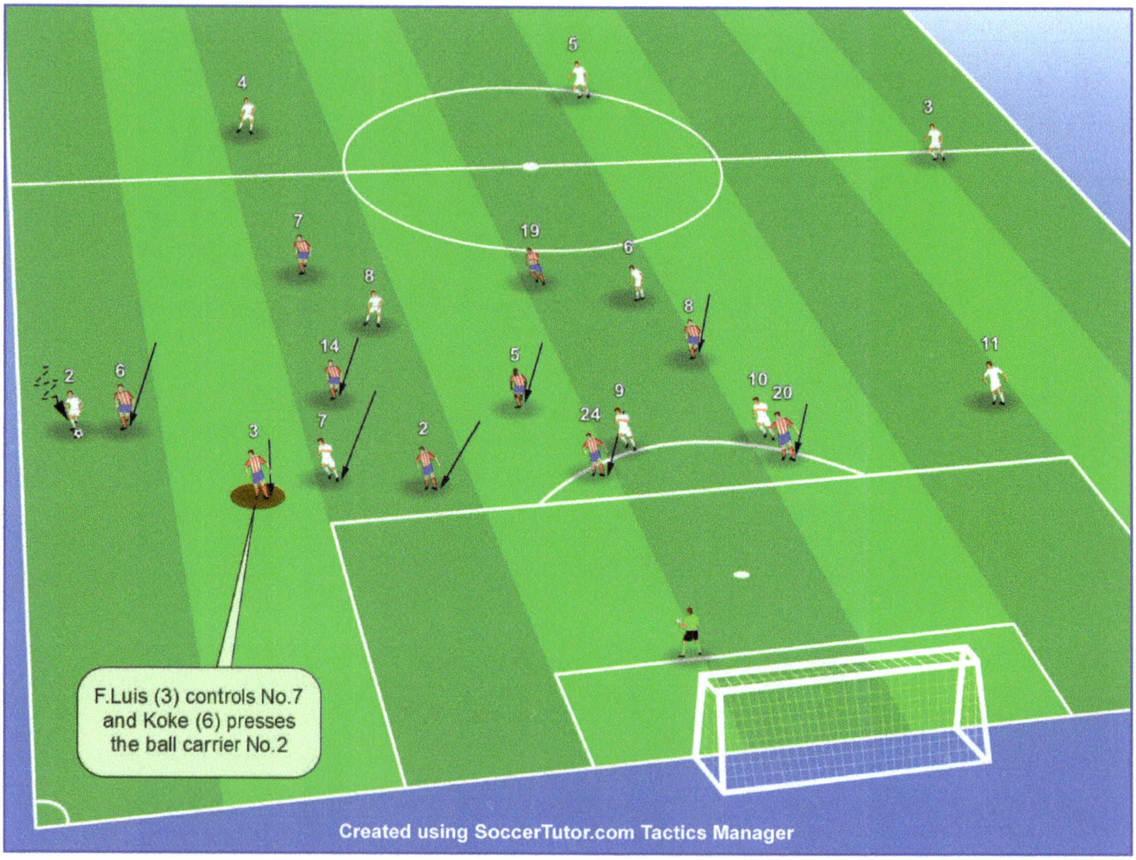

F.Luis (3) controls No.7 and Koke (6) presses the ball carrier No.2

If the winger No.7 runs in behind **F. Luis (3)**, he drops deeper to control him and leaves the closing down of the ball carrier to the left midfielder **Koke (6)**.

Balance is retained and the run of white No.7 into the potential gap between the full back and centre back can be controlled.

Additionally, the centre back **Godín (2)** has time to shift across and get closer to No.7.

On the next page, we show what happens when the opposing winger No.7 does not make a run into the space behind F. Luis (3)...

Tactical Situation 12 - Rear Block's Defensive Reactions After Wide Players Receive

Variation 2: The Opposing Winger DOES NOT Make a Run into the Space Behind the Full Back

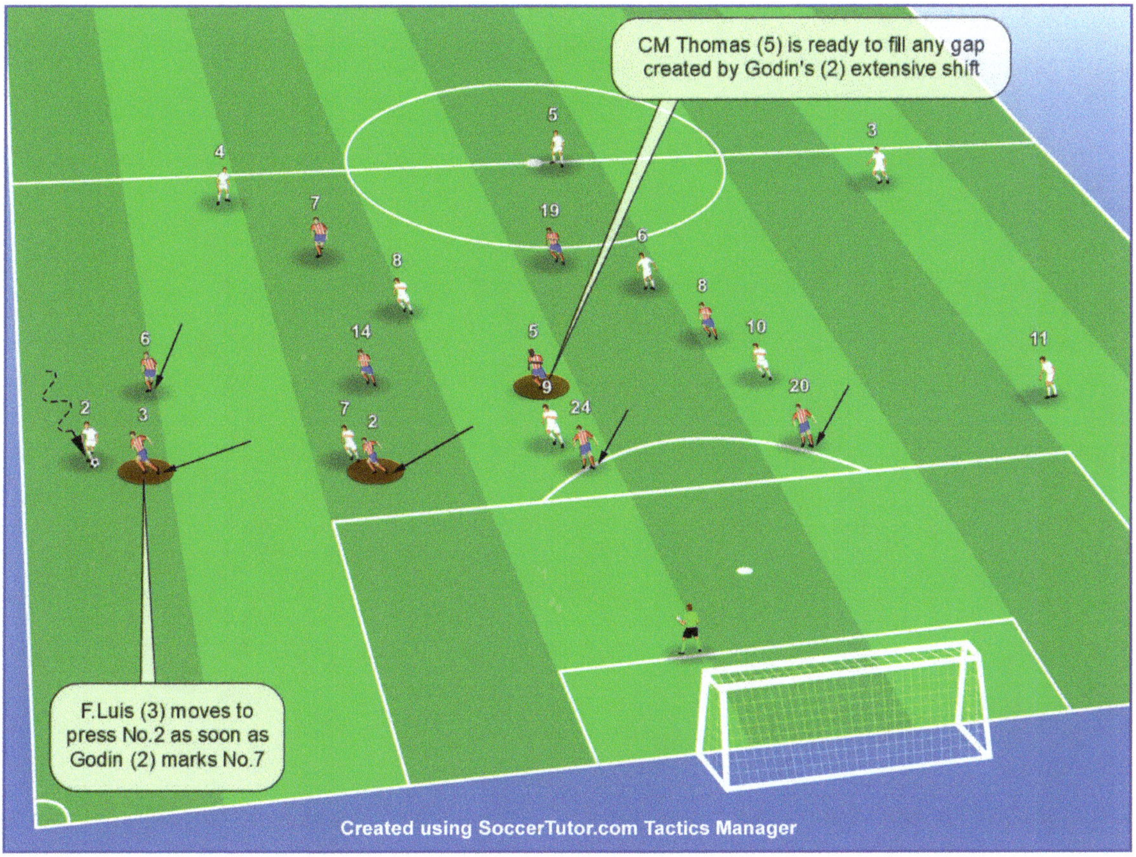

In this second variation, the white winger No.7 does not make a run in behind **F. Luis (3)** and instead stays in a central position.

In this situation, the Atlético full back **F. Luis (3)** waits until the centre back **Godín (2)** shifts across enough to take over No.7's marking. As soon as this takes place, **F. Luis (3)** moves to close down the man in possession (white No.3) and the left midfielder **Koke (6)** moves to apply double marking.

The central midfielder on the weak side **Thomas (5)** is ready to fill the gap in the defensive line if **Godín (2)** is forced to follow No.7 towards the side-line.

 **ASSESSMENT**

Atlético are playing against the 4-2-3-1 in the examples, but the reaction would be similar against the 4-4-2 formation too, as the No.10 would take the role of the second forward.

©SOCCERTUTOR.COM

DIEGO SIMEONE'S DEFENDING TACTICS

Tactical Situation 12 - Rear Block's Defensive Reactions After Wide Players Receive

CONTROLLING THE WINGER WHEN THE CENTRE BACK IS CLOSE TO THE STRONG SIDE

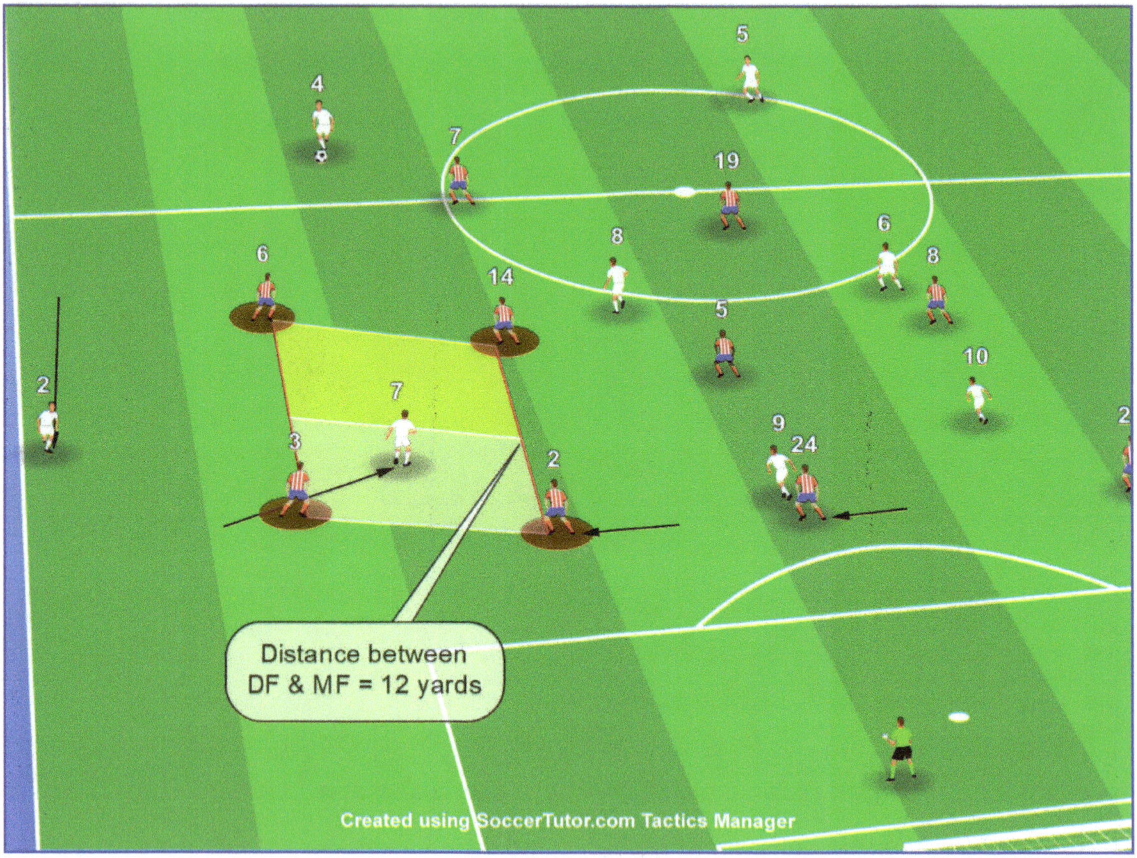

Distance between DF & MF = 12 yards

The situations on the previous pages show the pass to the advanced full back because Atlético blocked the through pass towards the central positioned winger. However, Atlético have mechanisms to react to every potential situation. So, when there was a successful through pass towards the winger in the centre, the players reacted according to the tactical situation.

When the opposing winger moves inside and the full back moves forward, Atlético's wide midfielder passes responsibility of the opposing full back to the full back, who then has 2 players within his zone of responsibility.

The **2 Key Factors** are:

1. The positioning of Atlético's centre back (close or away from the strong side).

2. Whether the opposing winger is in an **advanced** (white area) **or deep position** (yellow area).

The distance between the players in the rear block should be no more than 12 yards. For the best possible cooperation between the players, the space between the lines is divided into 2 equal parts (6 yards each).

©SOCCERTUTOR.COM

DIEGO SIMEONE'S DEFENDING TACTICS

Tactical Situation 12 - Rear Block's Defensive Reactions After Wide Players Receive

1. Controlling the Opposing Winger Who Moves Inside to Receive in an **Advanced Position**

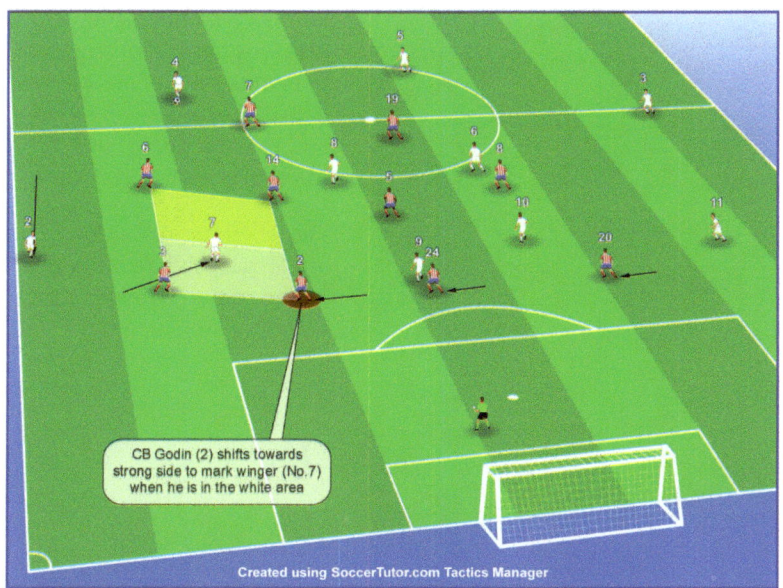

The white winger No.7 is in an advanced position (white area) and the centre back **Godín (2)** has shifted close to the strong side.

Therefore, it is **Godín (2)** who takes over the marking of white No.7.

The left back **F. Luis (3)** is responsible for marking the opposing right back No.2, who moves forward into an advanced position.

As soon as the pass is directed to the winger, **Godín (2)** moves to press him and the deepest central midfielder **Thomas (5)** moves to apply double marking.

Godín (2) presses in a way to prevent the turn inside and **Thomas (5)** ensures that No.7 is unable to turn towards the **Crucial Central Area**.

Potentially dangerous passes to white No.9, No.10 and No.11 are blocked.

©SOCCERTUTOR.COM   DIEGO SIMEONE'S DEFENDING TACTICS

Tactical Situation 12 - Rear Block's Defensive Reactions After Wide Players Receive

2. Controlling the Opposing Winger Who Moves Inside to Receive in a Deep Position

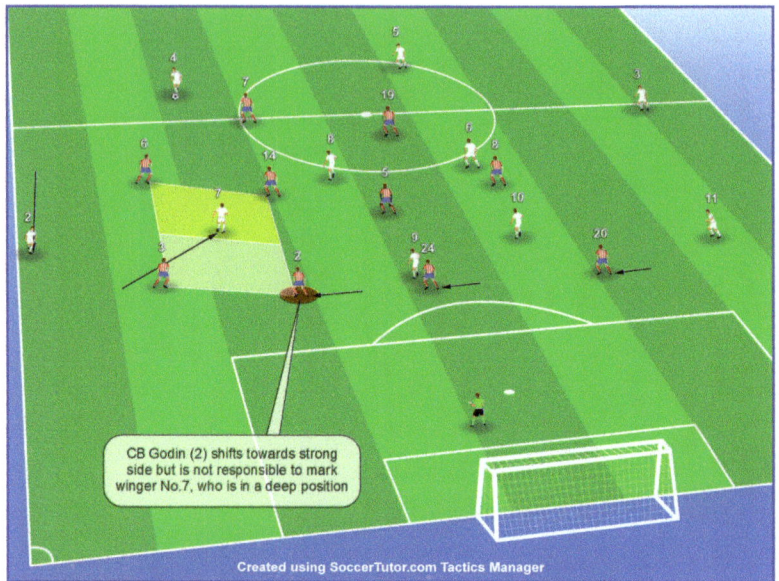

CB Godin (2) shifts towards strong side but is not responsible to mark winger No.7, who is in a deep position

In this variation of the previous tactical example, the white winger No.7 is in a **deeper position** (yellow area), and the reaction of the Atlético players is different.

The Atlético midfielders are responsible to close the winger down if he receives.

The midfielders (6, 14 & 5) take over the immediate pressing of the winger

As soon as the pass is directed to the winger, the left midfielder **Koke (6)** and the central midfielder on the strong side **Rodri (14)** take over the role of closing him down.

The central midfielder on the weak side **Thomas (5)** has the important role of preventing No.7 dribbling or passing towards the **Crucial Central Area**, where both white No.9 and No.10 can receive.

Tactical Situation 12 - Rear Block's Defensive Reactions After Wide Players Receive

Variation: The Opposing Winger is Able to Receive in a Deep Position, Turn and Dribble Forward

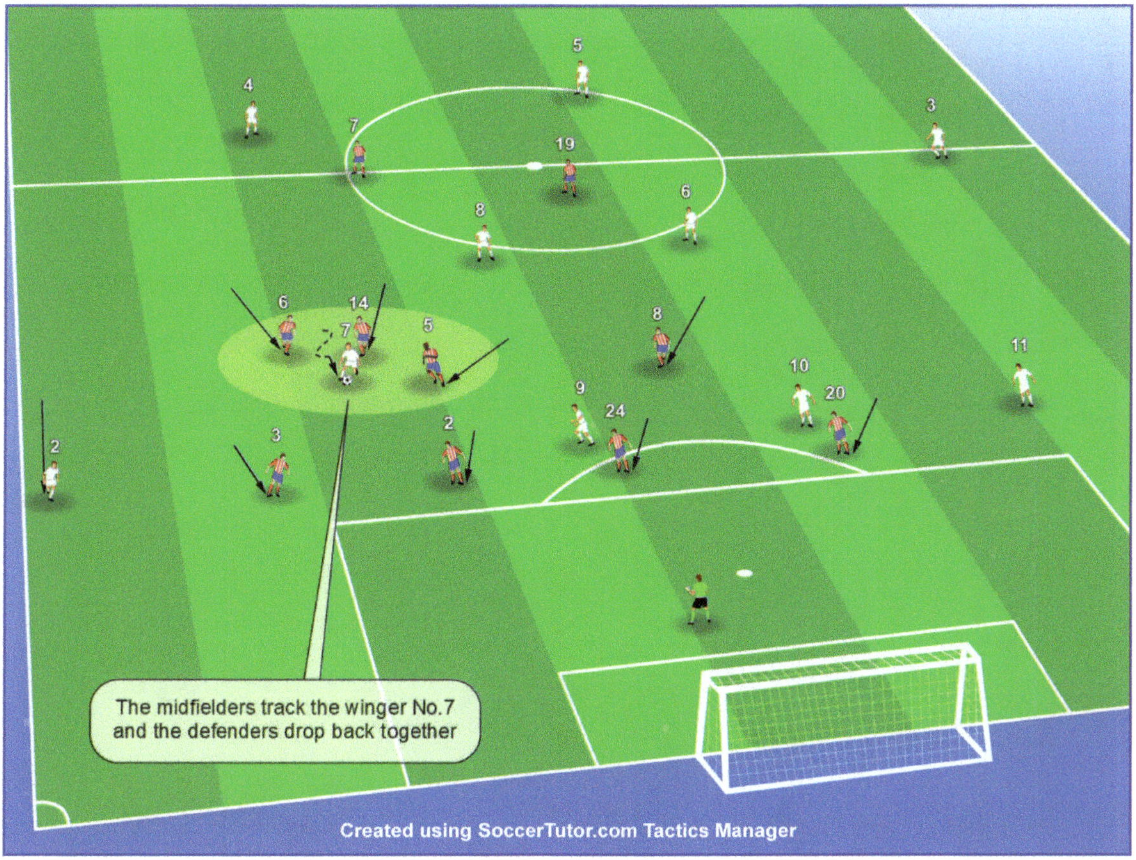

The midfielders track the winger No.7 and the defenders drop back together

In this variation of the previous example, the white winger No.7 is able to receive between the lines and turn.

As white No.7 dribbles forward, the Atlético defenders all drop back (open ball situation).

This gives time for the Atlético midfielders to track the winger's run and close him down.

The central midfielder on the weak side **Thomas (5)** again plays the important role of preventing No.7 dribbling or passing towards the **Crucial Central Area**, where both white No.9 and No.10 can receive.

Once this is achieved, the opposition's attacking play becomes predictable because the only choice for No.7 is the pass to the full back No.2 near the side-line.

Tactical Situation 12 - Rear Block's Defensive Reactions After Wide Players Receive

CONTROLLING THE WINGER WHEN THE CENTRE BACK IS AWAY FROM THE STRONG SIDE

The Opposing Winger is Able to Receive in an Advanced Position, Turn and Dribble Forward

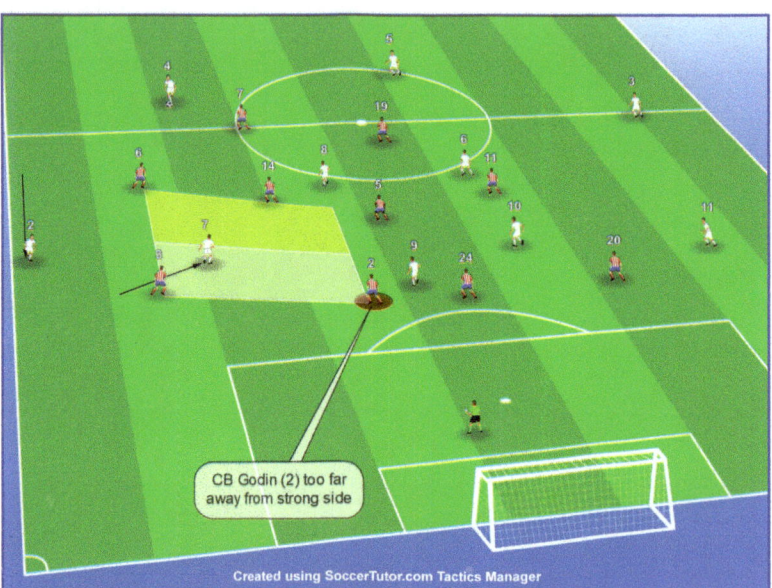

In this example, the centre back **Godín (2)** is too far away from the strong side to take over the marking of the white winger No.7, even when he is in an advanced position (white area).

As soon as the pass is directed to the winger, responsibility of closing down white No.7 is passed to the midfielders. The defenders drop back and get more compact, giving time for the midfielders to close No.7 down.

The central midfielder on the weak side **Thomas (5)** again makes the opposition's attack predictable by blocking any path into the **Crucial Central Area**.

©SOCCERTUTOR.COM   DIEGO SIMEONE'S DEFENDING TACTICS

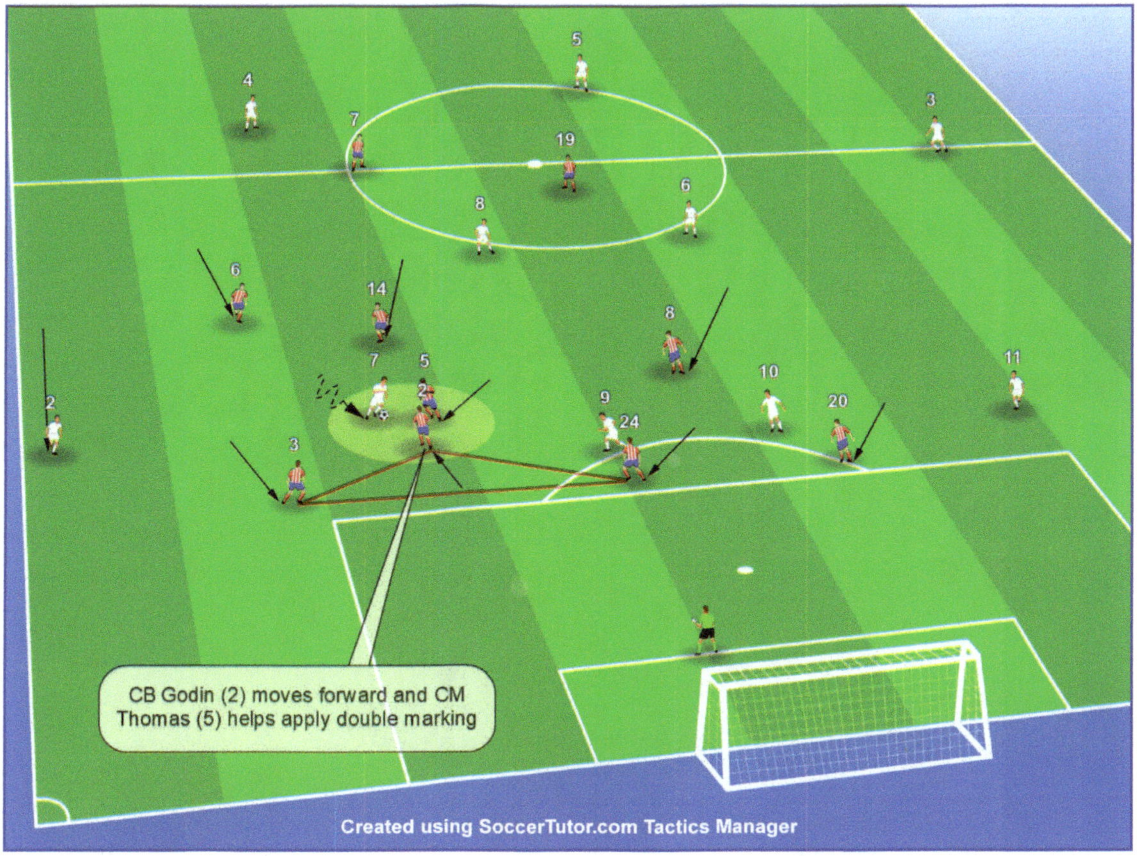

Tactical Situation 12 - Rear Block's Defensive Reactions After Wide Players Receive

CB Godín (2) moves forward and CM Thomas (5) helps apply double marking

If the central midfielder **Thomas (5)** catches the winger No.7 before he reaches shooting range, the centre back **Godín (2)** doesn't have to step forward.

However, if **Thomas (5)** is unable to catch No.7 before he reaches shooting range and he continues his forward run with the ball, **Godín (2)** moves forward to close him down, while **Thomas (5)** helps apply double marking from the inside.

In order for this reaction to be successful, it is important that the defenders have firstly obtained the appropriate compactness and a **defensive triangle** (see red lines in diagram) is created effectively.

The opposition's attacking play again becomes predictable and the only option for the winger No.7 is to play a pass towards the right back No.2 near the side-line.

ASSESSMENT

Atlético are playing against the 4-2-3-1 in the examples, but similar situations can be created by teams using the 4-3-3 or 4-4-2 formation. The most important thing for the appropriate reaction by the Atlético players is the reading of the tactical situation.

SESSION (2 PRACTICES FOR) "REAR BLOCK'S DEFENSIVE REACTIONS AFTER WIDE PLAYERS RECEIVE"

Tactical Situation 12 - Rear Block's Defensive Reactions After Wide Players Receive

SESSION FOR THIS TACTICAL SITUATION (2 PRACTICES)
1. Rear Block's Defensive Reactions After Wide Players Receive in a Structured Functional Practice

Scenario A: The Full Back Moves to Receive in an Advanced Position

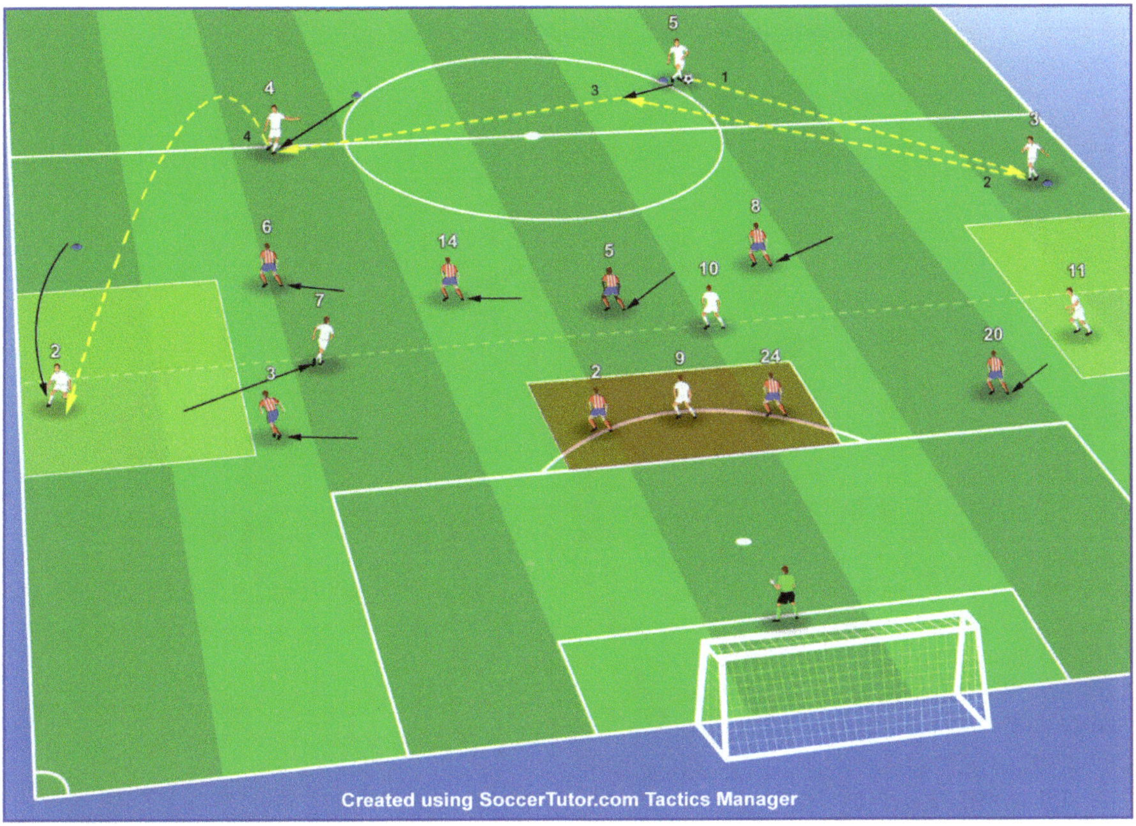

Description (Scenario A)
- Mark out an area on each side (12 yards long) and divide it into 2 equal areas, which indicate deep and advanced positions.
- The 4 white defenders pass the ball between each other, while the red players shift according to the ball position. As soon as a white centre back (No.4 in diagram) receives in an advanced position, the full back on that side (No.2) moves forward and the winger (No.7) moves inside.
- In this first example, the centre back No.4 passes to the full back No.2 in an advanced position (white area) and the whites try to score.
- Please see the **analysis on pages 170-175** for how the red players should react.
- The key is the positioning of the centre back on the strong side and whether or not he has managed to shift to the strong side in time.

©SOCCERTUTOR.COM

DIEGO SIMEONE'S DEFENDING TACTICS

Tactical Situation 12 - Rear Block's Defensive Reactions After Wide Players Receive

Scenario B: The Winger Moves Inside to Receive Between the Lines

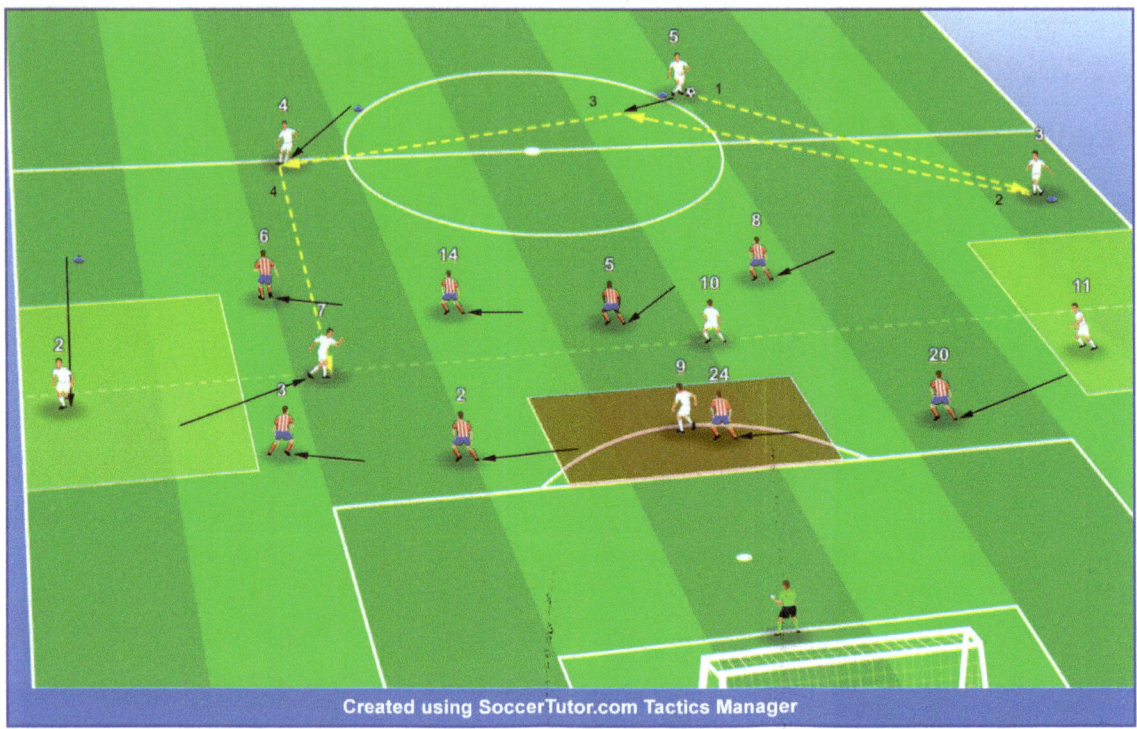

Description (Scenario B)

- In this second scenario, the white centre back (No.4) plays a through pass to the winger on the weak side (No.7), who has moved inside to receive in between the lines.

- The white winger (No.7) tries to receive, turn, and then play forward. The white team aim to score past the GK.

- Firstly, the red players react differently depending on whether their centre back is close (outside red area) or far away from the strong side (inside the red area).

- The red players also react differently depending on whether the opposing winger (No.7) receives in a deep position (behind the line) or in an advanced position (in front of the line).

- Please see the **analysis on pages 176-181** for how the red players should react in each situation.

Restriction: The red midfielders do not block the through pass to the white winger.

Coaching Points

1. Communication is very important, and the centre back should inform his team-mate about his positioning.
2. The full back needs to have a good open body shape for a full view of his opponents and team-mates' positions.
3. Make the correct decision based on the specific tactical situation and movements of the opponents.

Tactical Situation 12 - Rear Block's Defensive Reactions After Wide Players Receive

PROGRESSION
2. Rear Block's Defensive Reactions After Wide Players Receive in a Dynamic Game

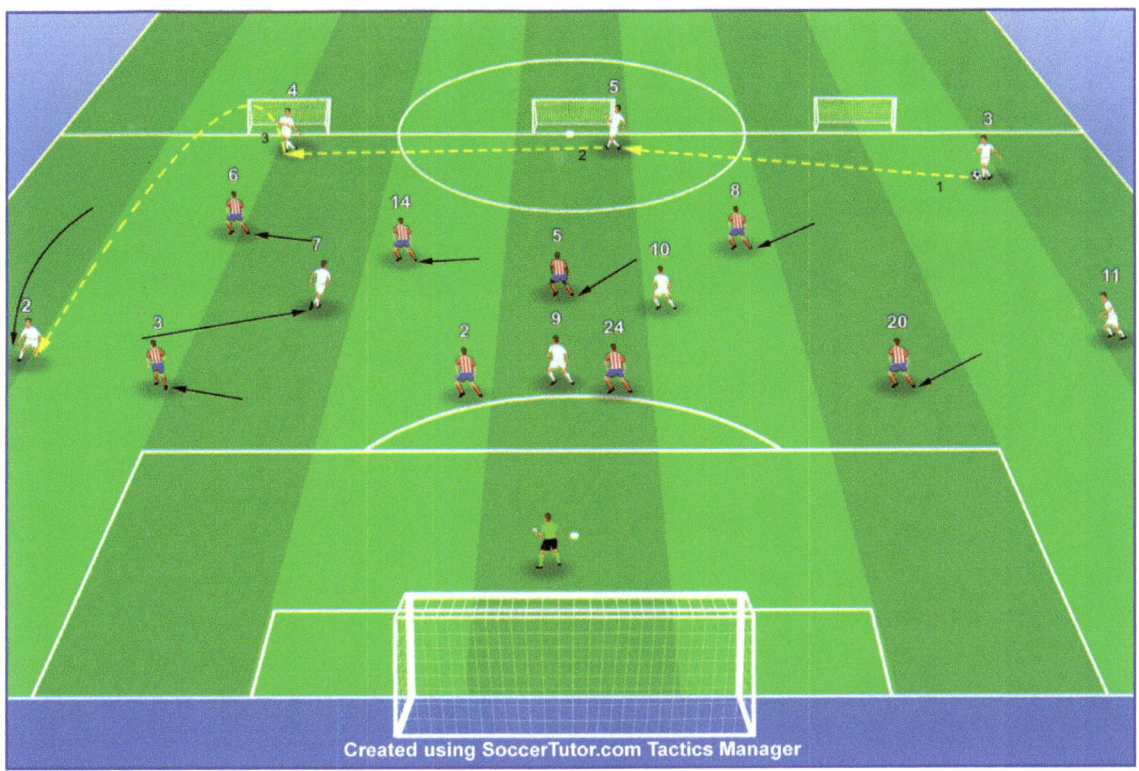

Description
- The 2 teams play a normal 8 (+GK) v 9 game. The aim for the whites is to score but if they score after synchronised movements of the full back and winger, they score 2 goals.
- The reds defend according to the situation (**see analysis pages**), try to win the ball and counter attack to score in the 3 mini goals.

Progression
11 v 11 game using 2/3 of pitch. The whites can score in any way but if they do it after a pass to the forward moving full back or a through pass to the centrally positioned winger, they score 3 goals. The reds try to win the ball and score with a counter attack within a set amount of time.

ASSESSMENT
Both practices in this session show the reds playing against the 4-2-3-1, but they can be easily adapted to play against the 4-4-2.

TACTICAL SITUATION 13

How the Centre Backs Defend the Forwards' Movements (Rear Block)

The content in this section is from analysis of Diego Simeone's Atlético Madrid teams during the 2017/2018 and 2018/2019 seasons.

The analysis is based on recurring patterns of play observed within the Atlético Madrid team. Once the same phase of play occurred several times (at least 10), the tactics would be seen as a pattern. The analysis on the following pages are examples of the team's tactics being used effectively.

Each action, pass, individual movement with or without the ball, and the positioning of each player on the pitch including their body shape, are presented.

The analysis is then used to create a session to coach this specific tactical situation.

Tactical Situation 13 - How the Centre Backs Defend the Forwards' Movements (Rear Block)

HOW THE CENTRE BACKS DEFEND THE FORWARDS' MOVEMENTS

Winning the Aerial Duel and Creating a Defensive Triangle when the Opposition are Forced to Play a Long Pass

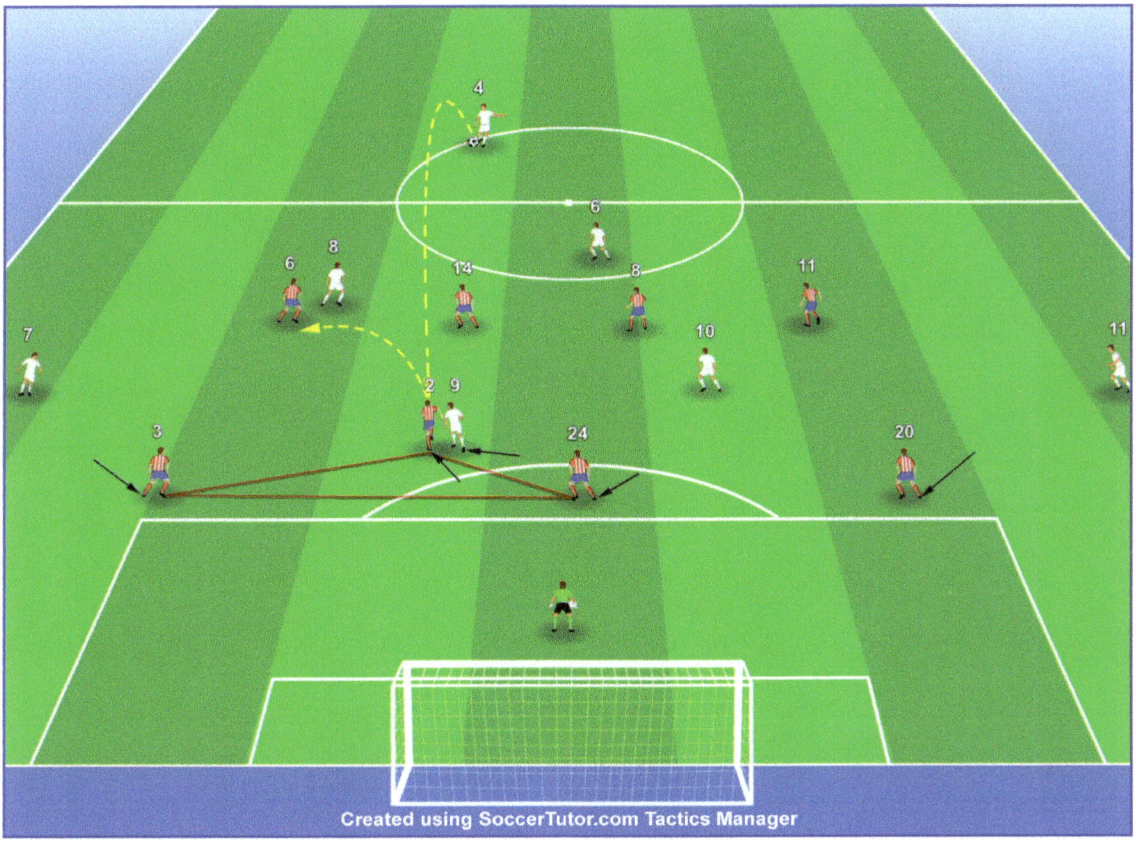

In previous sections, it was mentioned that the distance between the defenders depends on the positioning of the opposing forwards. However, as the Atlético midfielders retain a very compact formation, their opponents are often forced to move the ball to the forwards by playing long balls that bypass the midfield line.

Long passes are relatively easy for the Atlético defenders, who are strong and very good in aerial duels.

In the diagram example, the Atlético centre back **Godín (2)** applies tight marking against the white forward No.9 and stays close to him.

When a long ball is played towards the white forward, **Godín (2)** is able to intervene successfully and reach the ball first. At the same time, the left back **F. Luis (3)** and the other centre back **Giménez (24)** create a defensive triangle to provide support and cover.

©SOCCERTUTOR.COM

DIEGO SIMEONE'S DEFENDING TACTICS

Tactical Situation 13 - How the Centre Backs Defend the Forwards' Movements (Rear Block)

Defending the "Crucial Central Area" when the Opposition Play a Through Pass

[Diagram: Distance between DF & MF = 12 yards]

However, during a 90 minute match, there will be situations when successful through passes are played into the **Crucial Central Area**. A player receiving a pass unmarked and turning within this area can cause problems to any team and Atlético Madrid's defending tactics focus on preventing this.

The distance between the 2 lines should be no more than 12 yards, so opponents between the lines can be more easily controlled.

This space is further restricted by the central midfielder on the weak side **Saúl (8)** dropping back. This also enables him to apply double marking easier and fill potential gaps in the defensive line.

The distance between the centre backs and the most advanced central midfielder **Gabi (14)** is divided into 2 equal 6 yard areas.

The yellow area is the Atlético midfield's zone of responsibility. The opposing forwards or whoever enters it should be closed down by Atlético midfielders. The white area is the Atlético defence's zone of responsibility. The opposing forwards or whoever enters it should be closed down by Atlético defenders.

NOTE: During a competitive match, these boundaries can be altered by 1-2 yards.

©SOCCERTUTOR.COM

DIEGO SIMEONE'S DEFENDING TACTICS

Tactical Situation 13 - How the Centre Backs Defend the Forwards' Movements (Rear Block)

Solution 1: Opposing Forward Drops Back and the Centre Back Moves Forward into a Balanced Position

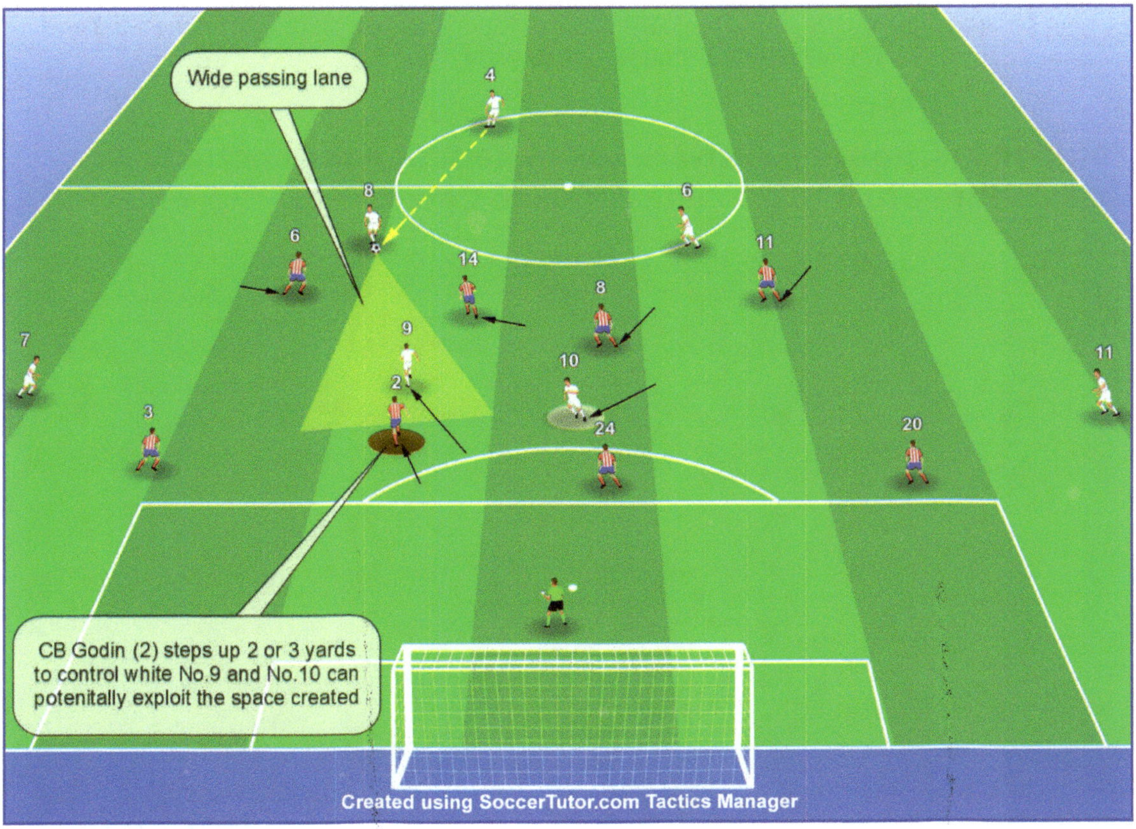

NOTE: When an opposing forward who is positioned between the lines of the rear block is unable to receive a through pass, there is no need for the centre backs to move forward to follow him if he drops back.

However, when there is an available passing lane towards the forward, the centre backs need to act.

In this example, the white central midfielder No.8 receives and turns. It is highly likely that he will be able to make a forward pass through the wide available passing lane (yellow highlighted area).

The white forward No.9 moves to receive and the closest centre back **Godín (2)** has to read the tactical situation, then react accordingly. In this situation, **Godín (2)** steps forward only 2-3 yards in order to control the forward. This way, he avoids creating space behind him which white No.10 can exploit.

A very important element in this situation is the deeper positioning of the Atlético central midfielder on the weak side **Saúl (8)**, as he is the player who controls the space between the lines and provides support to the defenders.

Tactical Situation 13 - How the Centre Backs Defend the Forwards' Movements (Rear Block)

ASSESSMENT

In the diagram on the previous page, Atlético are playing against the 4-2-3-1 formation and it is the attacking midfielder (white No.10) who moves to exploit the potential free space behind the centre back. The same situation can take place against the 4-3-3 and the 4-4-2, where it might be the second forward.

Solution 2: Opposing Forward Drops Back and the Centre Back Presses Him while Team-mates Provide Cover

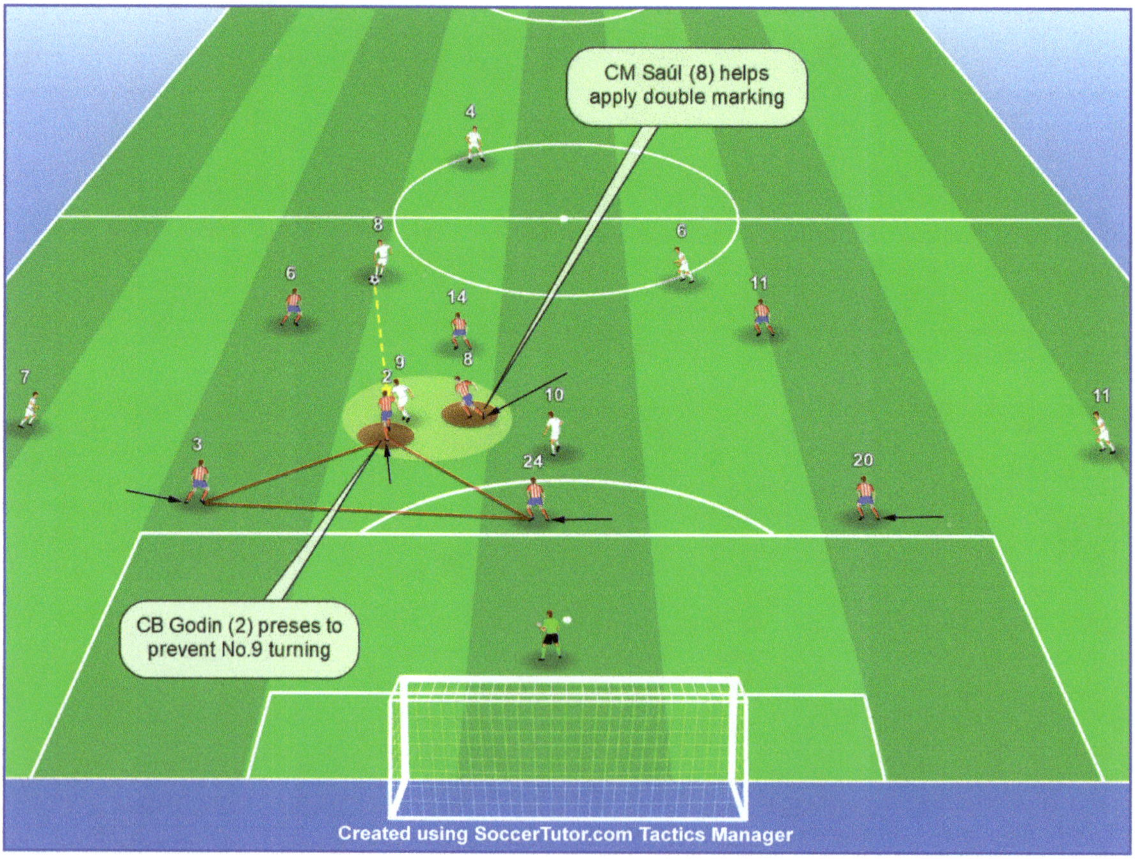

As soon as the pass is played towards the white forward No.9, the centre back **Godín (2)** moves to put press him and prevent the turn.

At the same time, the left back **F. Luis (3)** and the other centre back **Giménez (24)** create a defensive triangle to provide support and cover.

The weak side central midfielder **Saúl (8)** moves to apply double marking and stop No.9 turning towards the centre, as well as block the potential pass to white No.10. So, No.9 only has one option, which is to move towards the outside where there is less danger and it is easier to defend.

Tactical Situation 13 - How the Centre Backs Defend the Forwards' Movements (Rear Block)

Solution 3: Opposing Central Midfielder Attempts an Aerial Pass in Behind and the Centre Back Drops Back to Intercept

If the white central midfielder chooses to play a long pass behind the centre back, **Godín's (2)** positioning is highly likely to enable him to drop back and get to the ball.

Solution 4: Opposing Central Midfielder Attempts an Aerial Pass in Behind and the Centre Back is Able to Provide Support

Even if **Godín (2)** is not able to get to the ball in behind him, his positioning close to the other defenders enables him to drop back immediately into a supporting position and prevent the white forward from creating a dangerous situation for Atlético.

Tactical Situation 13 - How the Centre Backs Defend the Forwards' Movements (Rear Block)

Solution 5: Opposing Forward Drops Back Deeper and the Centre Back Follows Him when there is No Danger Behind

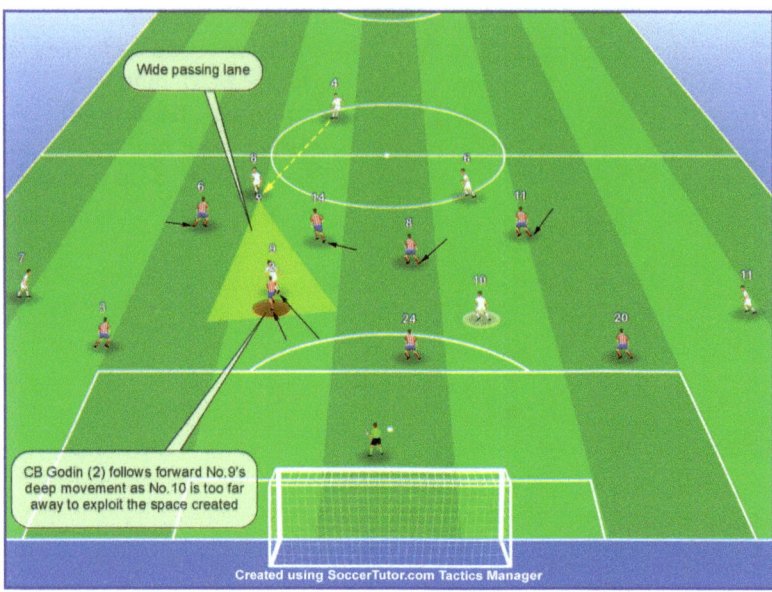

In this variation, the white forward drops further back.

There is no opponent in a suitable position to exploit the free space behind **Godín (2)**, so he follows No.9 into a **deeper position** (even into yellow highlighted area shown on page 188).

Solution 6: Opposing Forward Drops Back Even Deeper and the Midfielders Take Over His Marking

In this last example, the forward No.9 drops even deeper and enters the zone of responsibility of the midfielders and responsibility of marking him is passed to the midfielders.

The midfielders close down the forward as soon as he receives.

The Atlético centre back **Godín (2)** drops back and recovers into his starting position.

©SOCCERTUTOR.COM   DIEGO SIMEONE'S DEFENDING TACTICS

SESSION (2 PRACTICES) FOR "HOW THE CENTRE BACKS DEFEND THE FORWARDS' MOVEMENTS (REAR BLOCK)"

Tactical Situation 13 - How the Centre Backs Defend the Forwards' Movements (Rear Block)

SESSION FOR THIS TACTICAL SITUATION (2 PRACTICES)
1. The Centre Backs Defend the Forwards' Movements in a Structured Functional Practice

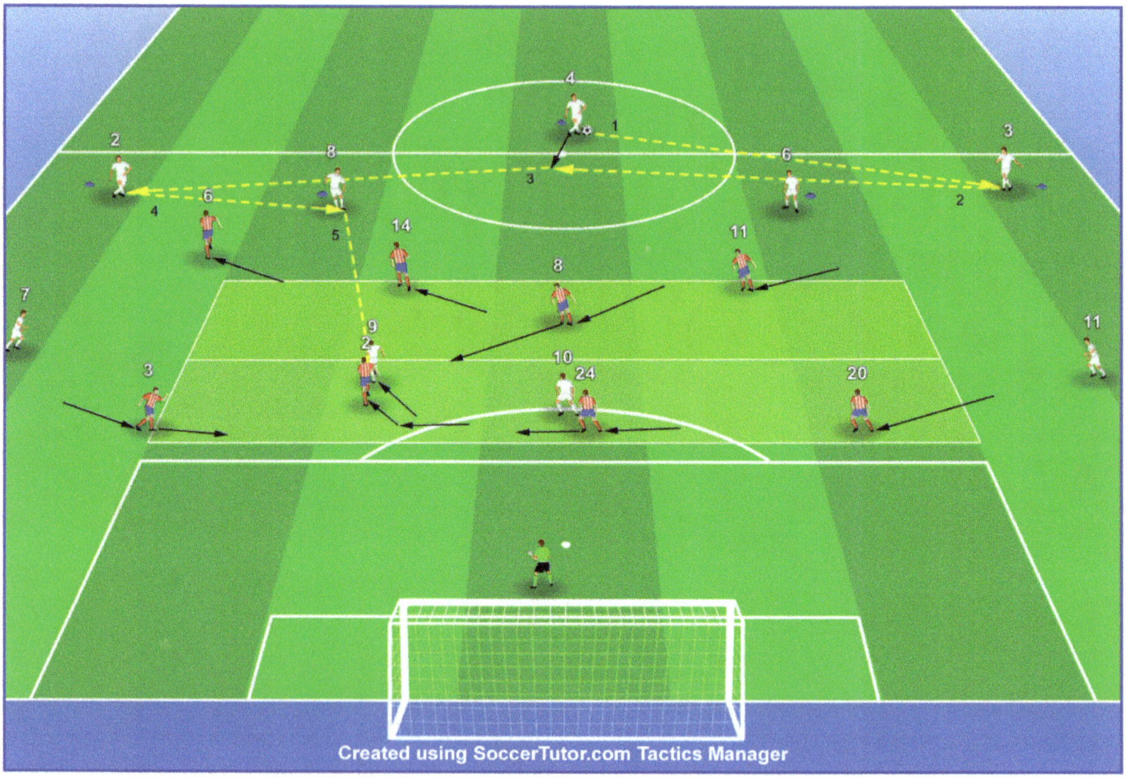

Description

- There are 2 areas that are the width of the box and 6 yards long, which help the centre backs read the positioning of the forwards.

- The 4 white defenders pass the ball between each other, while the red players shift according to the ball position.

- As soon as the ball is passed to the central midfielder (No.8 in diagram), a through pass can be played.

- The white forward on the strong side (No.9) moves to receive either in an advanced position (within the white area) or in a deep position (yellow area).

- The respective red centre back (No.2 in diagram) has to read the tactical situation to react accordingly and the reds try to prevent the whites from scoring.

- Please **see the analysis pages** for how the red centre back and other players should react.

- The key points are whether the first white forward is high or deep and if the second forward is close enough to exploit space in behind the red centre back or not.

Restriction: The red midfielders do not block the through pass to the white forward.

DIEGO SIMEONE'S DEFENDING TACTICS

Tactical Situation 13 - How the Centre Backs Defend the Forwards' Movements (Rear Block)

PROGRESSION
2. The Centre Backs Defend the Forwards' Movements in a Dynamic Game

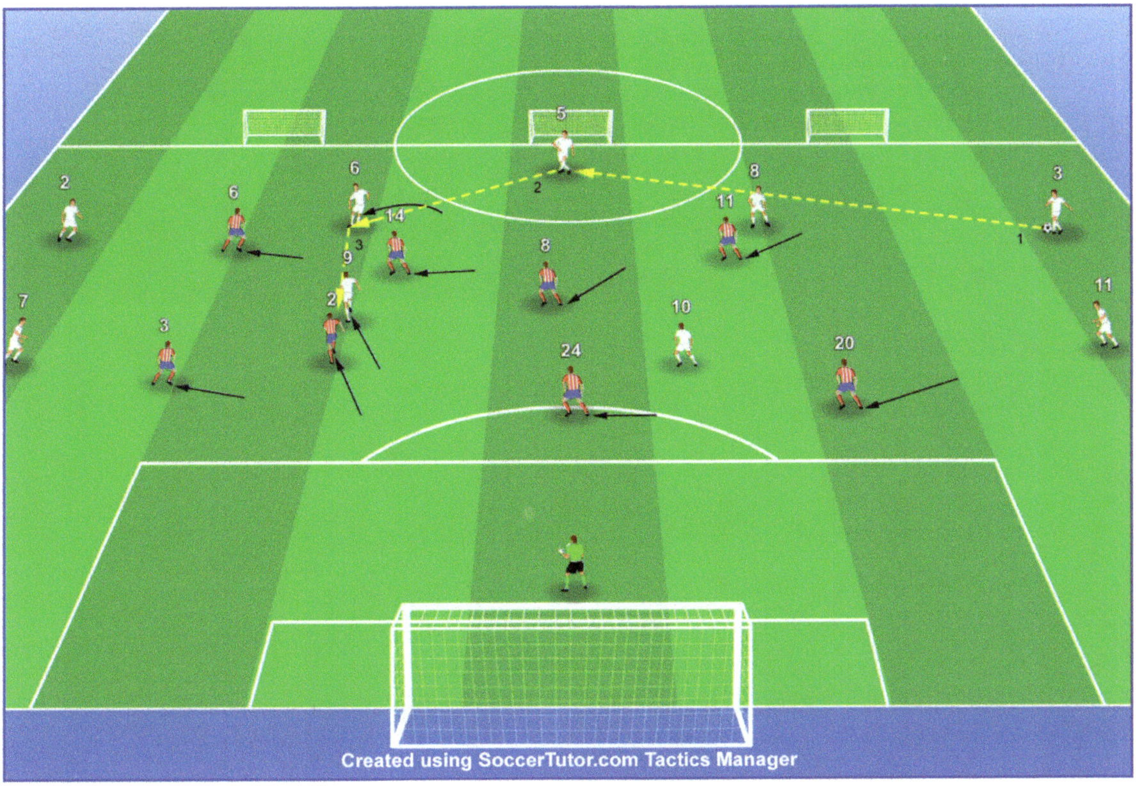

Description

- The 2 teams play a normal 8 (+GK) v 9 game.
- The aim for the whites is to score but their focus is on playing through the central area.
- If they score after passing to the forward who drops back to receive or by exploiting space created behind a red centre back, they score 2 goals.
- The reds team use the correct defensive reactions (**see analysis pages**), try to win the ball and counter attack to score in the 3 mini goals within a set amount of time e.g. 10 seconds.

Progression: The same game can be played with the whites also using synchronised movements of the full back and winger as a tactic. This way, the rear block has to deal with more potential situations and react accordingly.

Coaching Points

1. Read the tactical situation.
2. Communication between players is key.
3. Focus on the positioning of the first and second forward.

TACTICAL SITUATION 14

Pressing High Up the Pitch (from the Goalkeeper)

The content in this section is from analysis of Diego Simeone's Atlético Madrid teams during the 2017/2018 and 2018/2019 seasons.

The analysis is based on recurring patterns of play observed within the Atlético Madrid team. Once the same phase of play occurred several times (at least 10), the tactics would be seen as a pattern. The analysis on the following pages are examples of the team's tactics being used effectively.

Each action, pass, individual movement with or without the ball, and the positioning of each player on the pitch including their body shape, are presented.

The analysis is then used to create a practice to coach this specific tactical situation.

Tactical Situation 14 - Pressing High Up the Pitch (from the Goalkeeper)

PRESSING HIGH UP THE PITCH (FROM THE GK) AGAINST THE 4-3-3

1. Match-up of Atlético Madrid's 4-4-2 Formation Against the 4-3-3

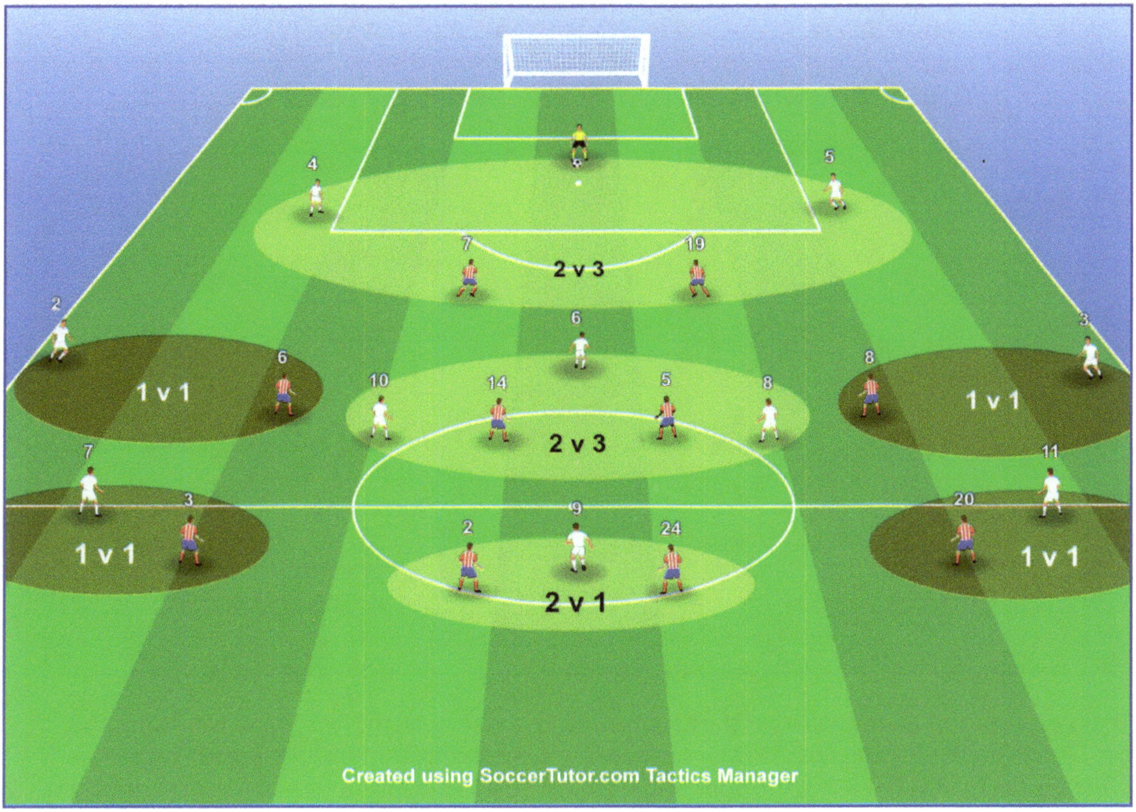

To analyse Atlético's pressing application properly, it is important to take the opposition's formation into account. The focus should be on the players rather than the space. The numerical situations in different areas affect the way the pressing is applied.

Against the 4-3-3, there is a numerical equality of 2v2 in the high part of the pitch, but the presence of the GK makes it 2v3. When building up from the back, the GK is the extra player for the opposing team.

There is a 2v3 numerical disadvantage in the centre of midfield. The opposing defensive midfielder (No.6) is in a deep position and is the extra player.

In the centre of defence, Atlético have a 2v1 advantage, with 2 centre backs against the 1 forward.

In the wide areas, there is a 1v1 on both sides in midfield (wide midfielders) and in defence (full backs).

Tactical Situation 14 - Pressing High Up the Pitch (from the Goalkeeper)

2. Positioning of the Players when Pressing High Up the Pitch

[Diagram: D.Costa (19) creates a strong side. LM Koke (6) and CM Thomas (5) have balanced positions to control 2 players. RM Saúl (8) controls white LB No.3 and in some cases, the pass to CB No.5]

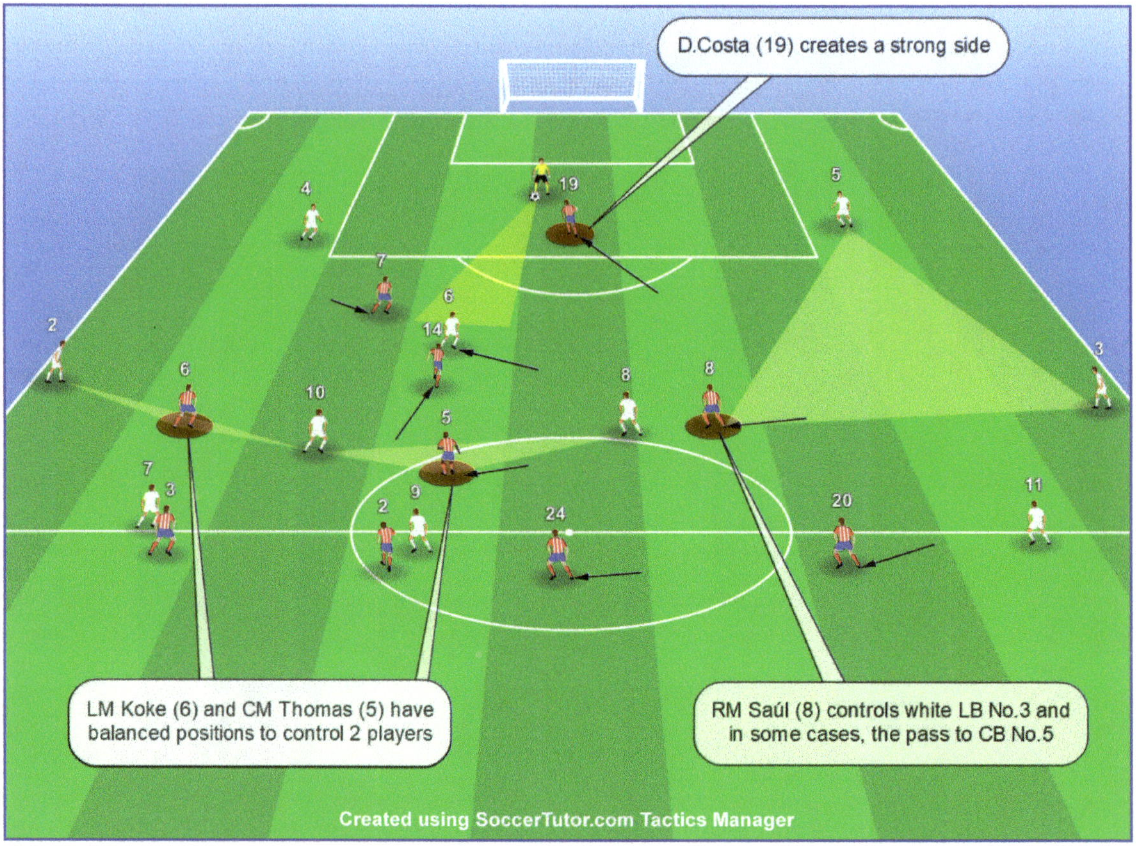

The pressing application can either start against the GK or after the GK's first pass. When Atlético press the GK against the 4-3-3, the opposition have a 2v3 numerical advantage.

One of the Atlético forwards (**D. Costa 19** in diagram) uses intelligent positioning and body shape to block the path to white No.5 and force the play to one side. This creates a strong side and the numerical disadvantage is eliminated.

As soon as a strong side is created, the Atlético players shift towards the strong side so they have a numerical advantage within the area where a potential pass will be played.

As the white defensive midfielder No.6 is in a deep position and can act as a link player to move the ball to No.5 on the weak side, the closest central midfielder **Rodri (14)** moves into a more advanced position to control him. Additionally, **D. Costa (19)** and **Griezmann (7)** keep the through passing lane towards him as narrow as possible.

The other central midfielder **Thomas (5)** and the left midfielder **Koke (6)** are in balanced positions to control 2 players.

The right midfielder **Saúl (8)** shifts towards the strong side to mark white No.8 and provide support to **Thomas (5)** but he must retain a balanced position so he can also control the white left back No.3, and be aware of a potential pass by No.6 towards No.5.

©SOCCERTUTOR.COM   DIEGO SIMEONE'S DEFENDING TACTICS

Tactical Situation 14 - Pressing High Up the Pitch (from the Goalkeeper)

3. Potential Passing Options for the Opposing GK

The potential passing options for the opposing GK in this situation are:

1. Short pass towards the right centre back No.4.
2. Short (but risky) pass to the defensive midfielder No.6.
3. Long pass to the full back No.2.
4. Long pass to the attacking midfielder No.10.
5. Long pass to the winger No.7.

Even though the Atlético Madrid players are in balanced positions, it is highly likely that any long passes will be neutralised before they reach an opposing player. This is because they have more time to react compared to short passes.

Of the 2 short passing options, the one to the defensive midfielder No.6 is the most dangerous.

This is because the opposition will have the chance to move the ball to the free player on the weak side (centre back No.5), thus eliminating the strong side which Atlético had created.

Tactical Situation 14 - Pressing High Up the Pitch (from the Goalkeeper)

4. Controlling the GK's Through Pass to the Defensive Midfielder

The passing lane towards the weak side gets narrow

Saúl (8) gets ready to anticipate the pass

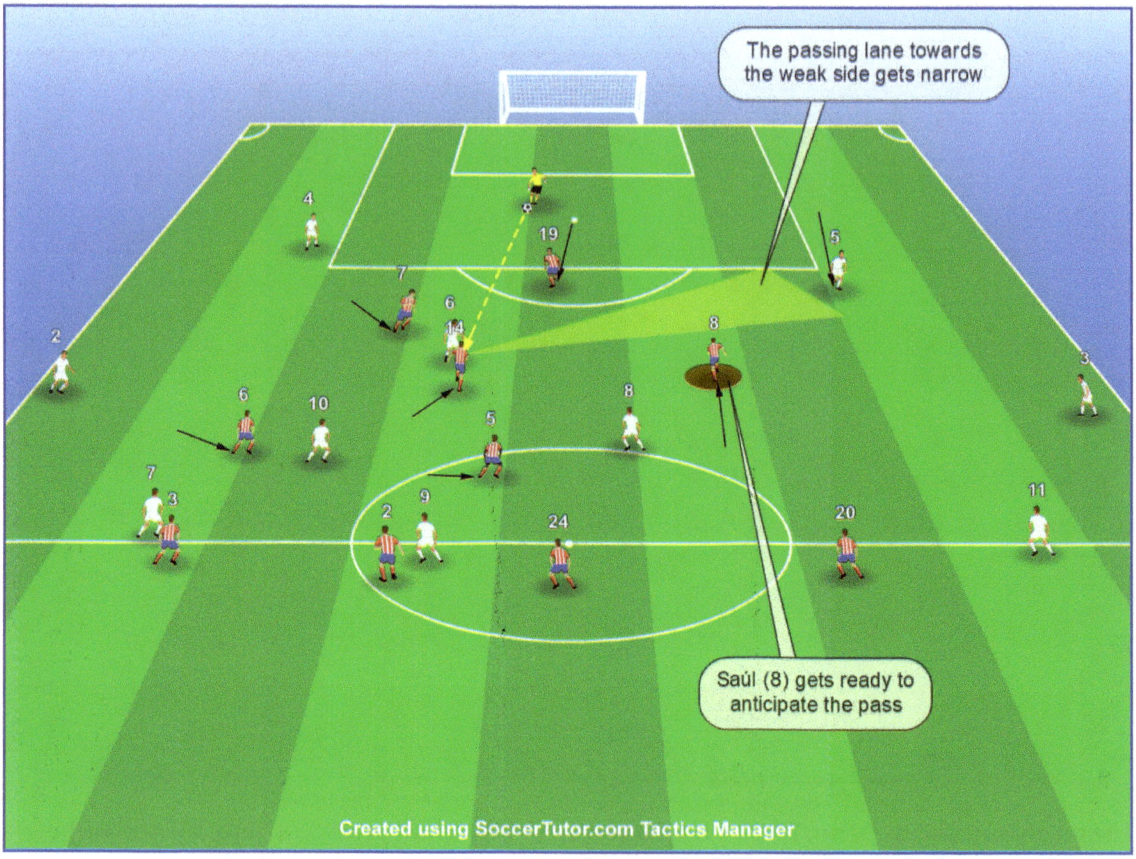

The pass to the defensive midfielder No.6 is the most dangerous and should be avoided by making the passing lane towards him very narrow. If the pass towards No.6 is made impossible, the wide midfielder on the weak side **Saúl (8)** can be totally focused on supporting the central midfielder **Thomas (5)** by moving inside and close to the white attacking midfielder No.8.

However, If the pass to white No.6 is played, Atlético are ready to react accordingly. As soon as the pass is made and No.6 receives, the central midfielder **Rodri (14)** moves to close him down and prevent him from turning. In particular, allowing No.6 to turn towards the weak side needs to be avoided, as the opposition will find available space and time on the ball.

Additionally, both forwards **D. Costa (19)** and **Griezmann (7)** move close to the ball area to take advantage if there is a bad first touch.

Griezmann (7) moves to prevent the turn towards the strong side, while **D. Costa (19)** drops back and narrows the passing lane towards the weak side and centre back No.5, who moves forward to provide a passing option.

Saúl (8) moves forward to further narrow the passing lane and anticipates the pass to No.5. As white No.6 is facing his own goal, he is unable to see **Saúl (8)** and can't foresee an intervention by him. When this reaction is successful, No.6 can only make a risky pass back to the GK.

©SOCCERTUTOR.COM · DIEGO SIMEONE'S DEFENDING TACTICS

Tactical Situation 14 - Pressing High Up the Pitch (from the Goalkeeper)

5. Collective Shifting After the GK's Pass to the Centre Back

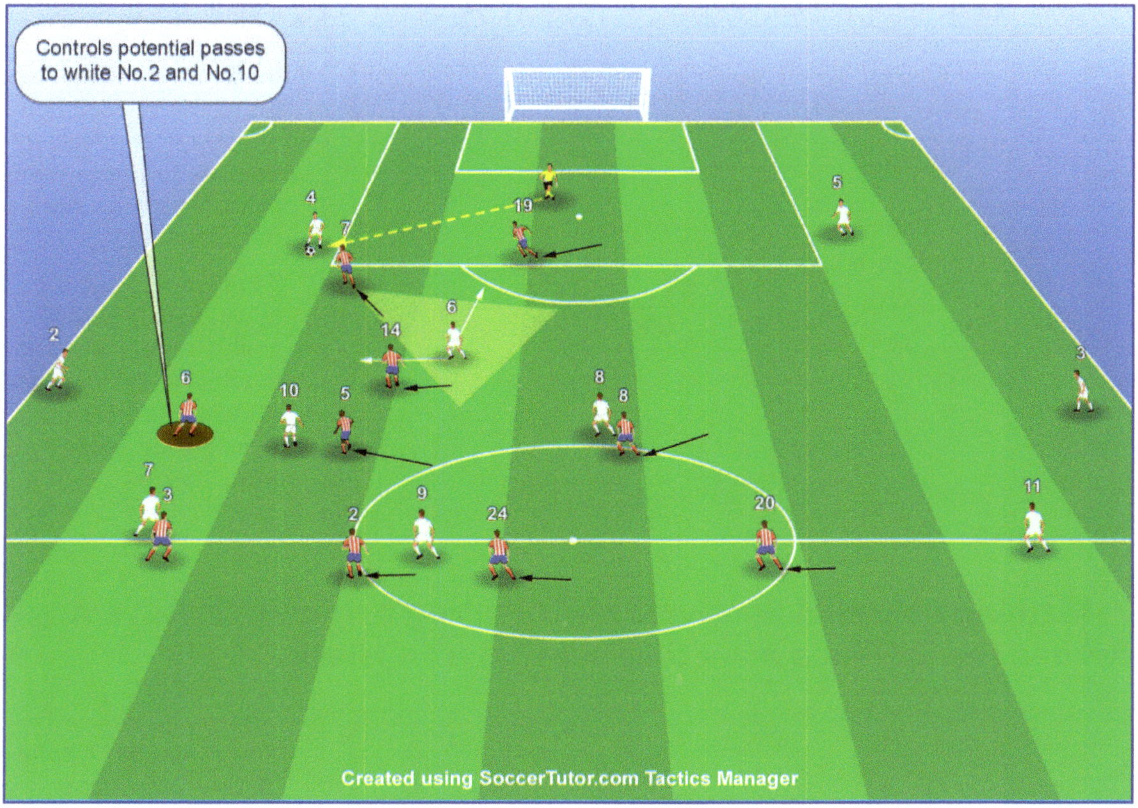

If the GK's pass is directed to the centre back No.4, the forward **Griezmann (7)** presses him. He doesn't have to create a strong side, as the back pass to the GK is controlled by **D. Costa (19)**.

Additionally, the pass to the defensive midfielder No.6 is now blocked, so the Atlético central midfielder **Rodri (14)** doesn't have to stay close to him and instead shifts towards the side-line to help create a numerical advantage around the area the ball is likely to be directed.

If white No.6 attempts to move out of **Griezmann's (7)** shadow, he will be controlled by **D. Costa (19)** or **Rodri (14)** depending on the direction of his movement (see white arrows).

Potential passes for No.4 are towards No.2, No.10 and No.7. The long pass to No.7 can be easily cut out as there is more time to react. Passes to No.2 and No.10 should be under control.

The pass to No.10 can be dangerous if he is able to receive and turn. **Koke (6)** is in a balanced position to control No.2 and No.10, but his focus should be on No.10.

Thomas (5) initially takes up a balanced position to control 2 players (No.8 and No.10) and would be able to shift in time to close down white No.10 as soon as the pass is made.

If **Koke (6)** notices that **Thomas (5)** has shifted to mark No.10 (see diagram), he can focus more on the pass to No.2. However, he should not shift extensively towards the side-line as he will open the passing lane for a through pass to No.7.

Tactical Situation 14 - Pressing High Up the Pitch (from the Goalkeeper)

6. Double or Triple Marking the Receiver After a Through Pass

If the centre back No.4 attempts a pass towards the attacking midfielder No.10, the best solution is for the left midfielder **Koke (6)** to intercept the pass before it reaches the opponent.

If this is not possible, he moves to help double mark the new ball carrier together with **Thomas (5)**, while **Rodri (14)** drops back to make it triple marking.

7. Marking Potential Receivers and Creating a Numerical Advantage Around the Ball Area After the Pass to the Full Back

If the pass is directed to the full back No.2, **Koke (6)** takes advantage of the transmission phase to press the ball immediately, while the rest of the Atlético players shift towards the strong side.

Potential receivers No.7, No.10 and No.4 are tightly marked. **Rodri (14)** blocks the path to No.6 and helps create a numerical advantage near the ball. These conditions are ideal for winning the ball and there are many passing options for a potential counter attack.

PRACTICE FOR "PRESSING HIGH UP THE PITCH (FROM THE GOALKEEPER)"

Tactical Situation 14 - Pressing High Up the Pitch (from the Goalkeeper)

PRACTICE FOR THIS TACTICAL SITUATION
Pressing High Up the Pitch (from the GK) and Forcing Play Wide in a Dynamic Game with a Central Zone

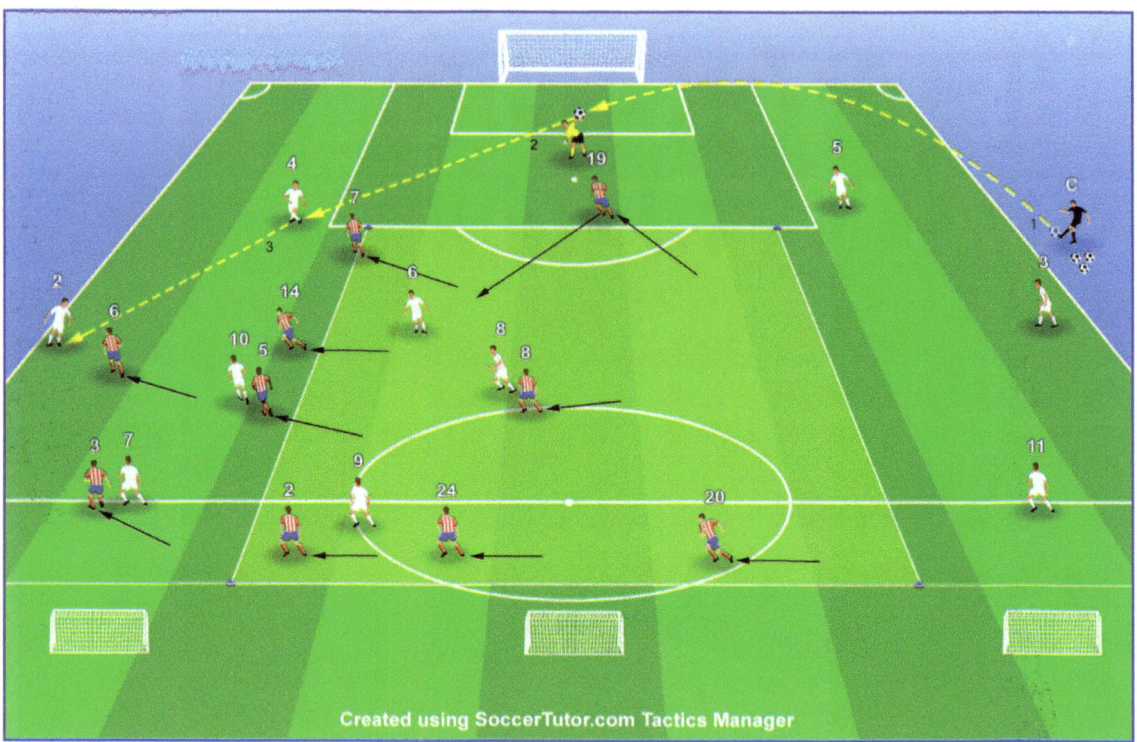

Description
- The 2 teams play a 10 v 10 (+GK) game and the Coach starts the practice with a long pass to the GK.
- The white team's aim is to try build up play through the red's pressure and score in any of the 3 mini goals. If a goal is scored from within the central zone, the whites score 3 goals.
- The red players apply pressing straight away (from the GK), with the aim of keeping the ball out of the large central zone.
- The red team's aim is to force the play to one side (create a strong side), mark all potential receivers and create a numerical advantage around the ball area if possible.
- Please **see the analysis pages in this section** for how the red players should apply their pressing as a team.
- If the ball is passed to a player inside the central zone, the reds have to either block the pass or win possession within 3-5 seconds.

Coaching Points
1. Force the ball wide and create a strong side.
2. Prevent opponents from moving the ball to the weak side.

©SOCCERTUTOR.COM   DIEGO SIMEONE'S DEFENDING TACTICS

TACTICAL SITUATION 15

Pressing After the Goalkeeper's Pass

The content in this section is from analysis of Diego Simeone's Atlético Madrid teams during the 2017/2018 and 2018/2019 seasons.

The analysis is based on recurring patterns of play observed within the Atlético Madrid team. Once the same phase of play occurred several times (at least 10), the tactics would be seen as a pattern. The analysis on the following pages are examples of the team's tactics being used effectively.

Each action, pass, individual movement with or without the ball, and the positioning of each player on the pitch including their body shape, are presented.

The analysis is then used to create a practice to coach this specific tactical situation.

Tactical Situation 15 - Pressing After the Goalkeeper's Pass

PRESSING AFTER THE GOALKEEPER'S PASS AGAINST THE 4-3-3

a. Positioning of the Players when the Aim is Pressing After the GK's First Pass

If the aim of Atlético is to apply pressing after the first pass from the GK, the players take up appropriate positions. The 2 forwards **Griezmann (7)** and **Torres (9)** are in balanced positions. They should not be too wide as they need to control the white defensive midfielder No.6, who is in a deep position. They must also not be too narrow as they need to control both centre backs No.4 and No.5.

This doesn't completely prevent the pass to the white midfielder No.6, which is why central midfielder **Gabi (14)** moves into a more advanced position to help control him. However, **Gabi (14)** doesn't move too far forward, as he has to also control the white attacking midfielder No.10.

If white No.6 moves even deeper, he is left under the control of the forwards.

This positioning of the Atlético players forces the GK to play a wide pass to one of the centre backs.

Tactical Situation 15 - Pressing After the Goalkeeper's Pass

b. Pressing and Collective Shifting Across to Create a Strong Side After the GK's First Pass

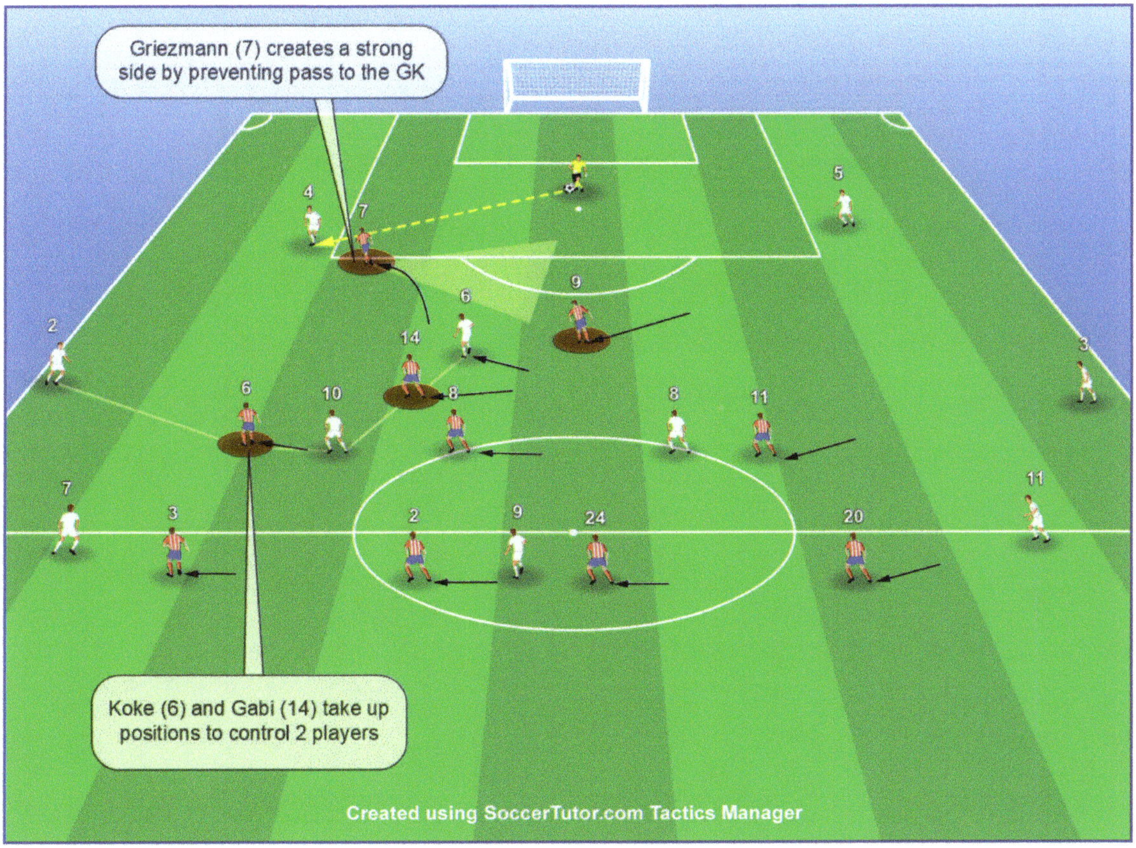

[Diagram: Griezmann (7) creates a strong side by preventing pass to the GK. Koke (6) and Gabi (14) take up positions to control 2 players]

As soon as the pass is directed to the centre back No.4, the forward on that side **Griezmann (7)** moves to create a strong side by preventing the back pass to the GK.

However, the positioning of **Griezmann (7)** leaves the inside passing lane towards the defensive midfielder No.6 open.

As there is no way for No.4 to switch play by passing to the GK, the other forward **Torres (9)** moves towards the strong side. This action helps create a numerical advantage near the strong side and control the white defensive midfielder No.6 if possible.

The central midfielder **Gabi (14)** shifts towards the strong side but has to control 2 players (No.10 and No.6).

At the same time, the left midfielder **Koke (6)** shifts towards the side-line but stays in a balanced position to control both No.2 and No.10.

The focus for both **Gabi (14)** and **Koke (6)** has to be on No.10, who is the most dangerous option. This is because the other central midfielder **Saúl (8)** is too far away from controlling him.

Tactical Situation 15 - Pressing After the Goalkeeper's Pass

c. Defensive Reactions After the Centre Back's Inside Pass to the Defensive Midfielder

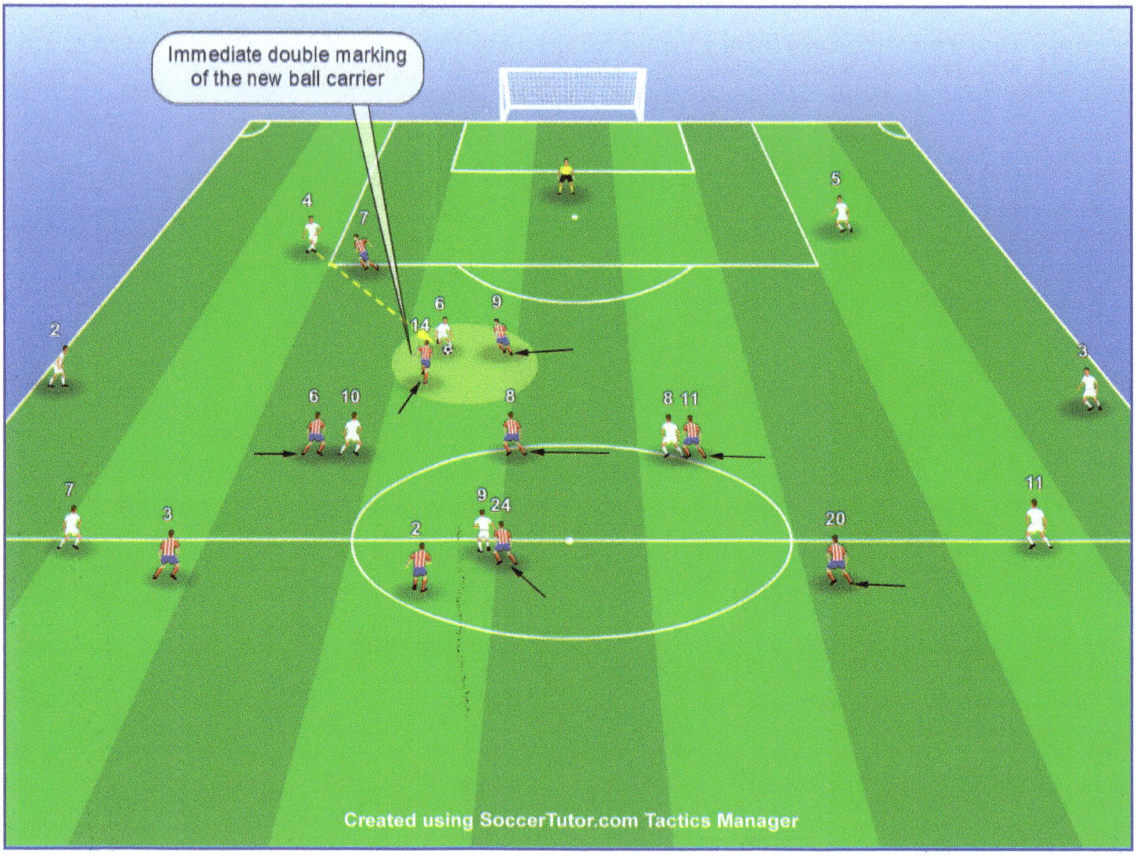

As soon as the pass is directed to the white defensive midfielder No.6, the new ball carrier is immediately pressed by the forward **Torres (9)** and central midfielder **Gabi (14)**.

Diego Simeone's Atlético team look to apply double marking in this crucial area. If they win the ball, they will be able to quickly counter attack with a short distance to goal.

In addition, they want to prevent No.6 passing back to the GK, as this could lead to a switch of play and the opponents successfully breaking through Atlético's pressing.

Tactical Situation 15 - Pressing After the Goalkeeper's Pass

d. The Second Forward Takes Up a Balanced Position when the First Forward Has Not Yet Been Able to Create a Strong Side

![Diagram showing Griezmann (7) is not in a suitable position to create a strong side yet; Torres (9) controls the GK and No.6]

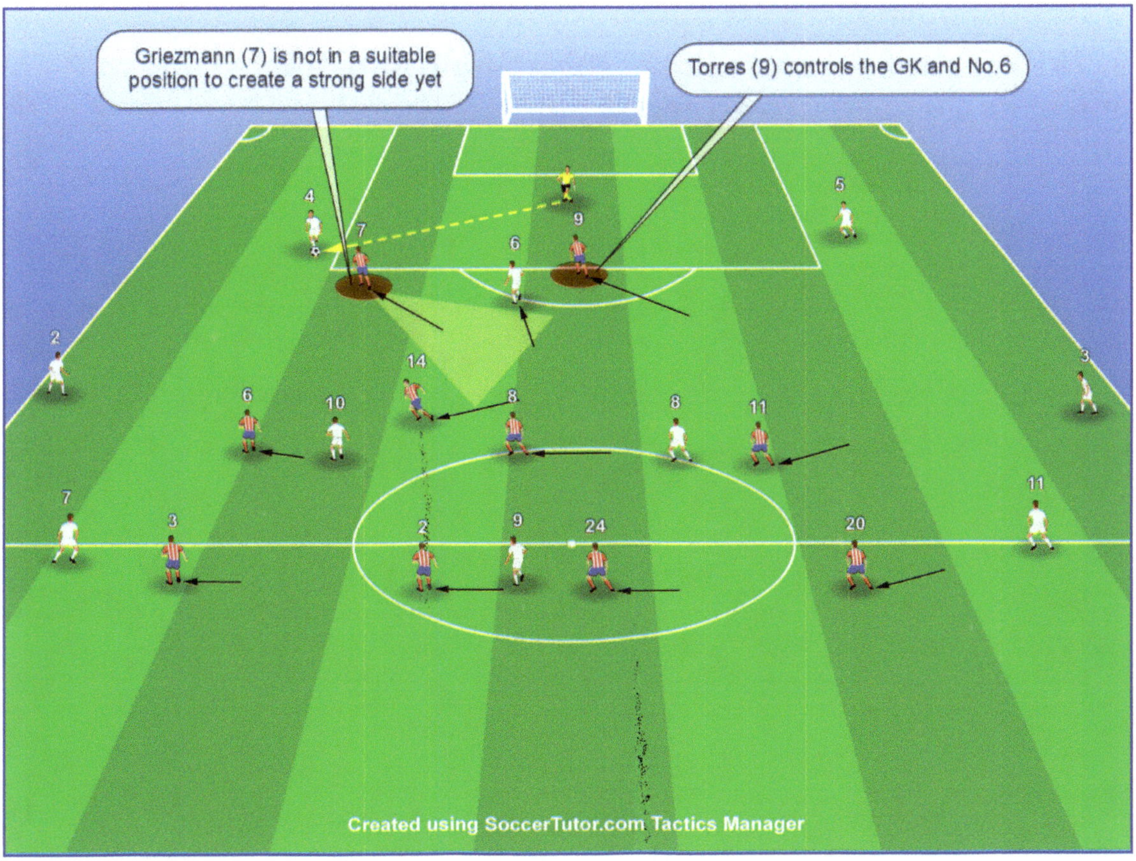

If the forward **Griezmann (7)** hasn't been able to create a strong side, the second forward **Torres (9)** should be in a balanced position.

Torres (9) needs to control the potential passes to the GK and the defensive midfielder No.6, who is initially blocked by **Griezmann (7)** but then drops into a deep position to create a passing lane. If No.6 doesn't drop back, **Torres' (9)** focus should be exclusively on the GK.

If the pass is directed to the GK, **Torres' (9)** should press him in a way that forces him to play the ball to one specific side, as shown in the previous section "Tactical Situation 14 - Pressing High Up the Pitch (from the Goalkeeper)."

However, as soon as **Griezmann (7)** gets into a position that prevents the back pass to the GK, **Torres (9)** should drop back and towards the strong side, as he did in the previous example.

DIEGO SIMEONE'S DEFENDING TACTICS

Tactical Situation 15 - Pressing After the Goalkeeper's Pass

FORCING PLAY TO ONE SIDE AND CREATING AN IDEAL PRESSING SITUATION AGAINST THE 4-3-3

a. The Forward Uses Intelligent Positioning and Body Shape to Force the GK to Play to a Specific Side

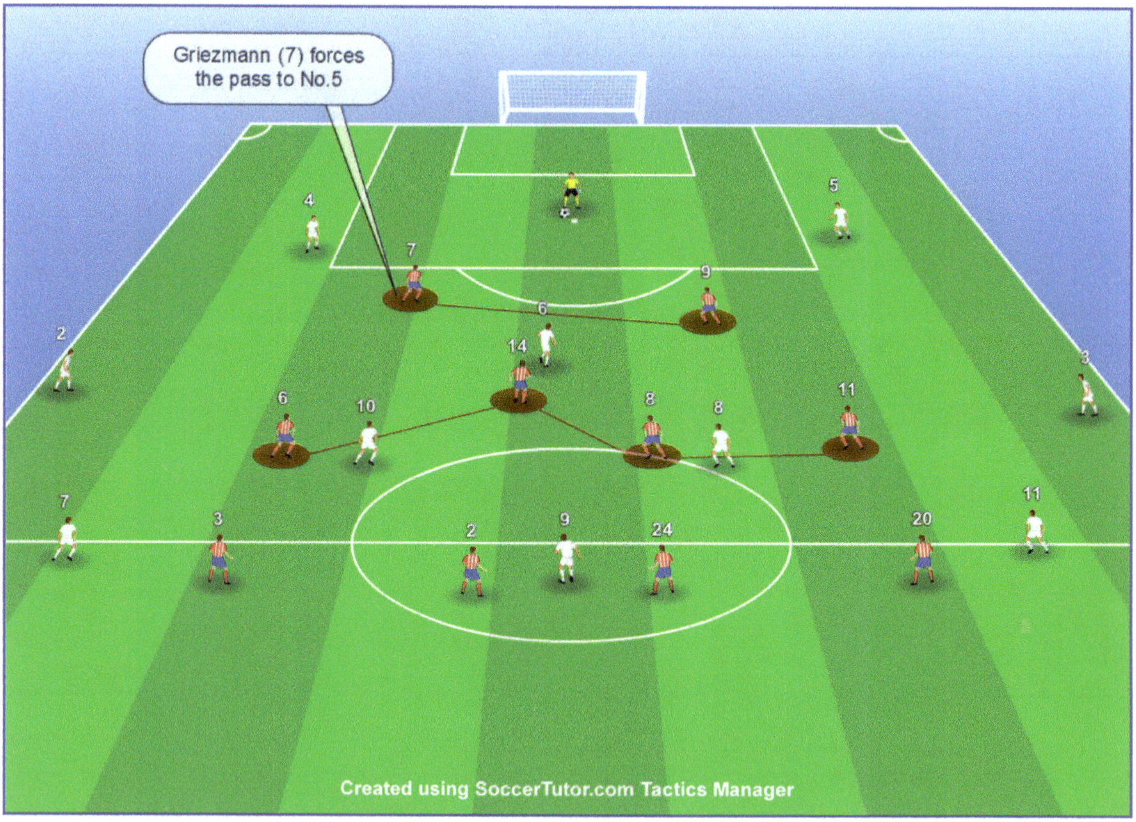

(Diagram: Griezmann (7) forces the pass to No.5)

When there is good communication between the Atlético players, an ideal pressing situation can occur.

The central midfielder **Gabi (14)** moves into an advanced position to mark the white defensive midfielder No.6 and informs the forward **Griezmann (7)** about his positioning.

This enables the forward **Griezmann (7)** to take a more advanced position too and force the play to the other side (towards white No.5).

If the ball is directed to the left centre back No.5, all potential receivers can be tightly marked.

This is partly because the Atlético central midfielder **Saúl (8)** on that side is close to his direct opponent (white No.8), compared to the respective situation on the other side.

Tactical Situation 15 - Pressing After the Goalkeeper's Pass

b. Positioning of the Players and Shifting Across Movements After the GK's Pass to the Centre Back

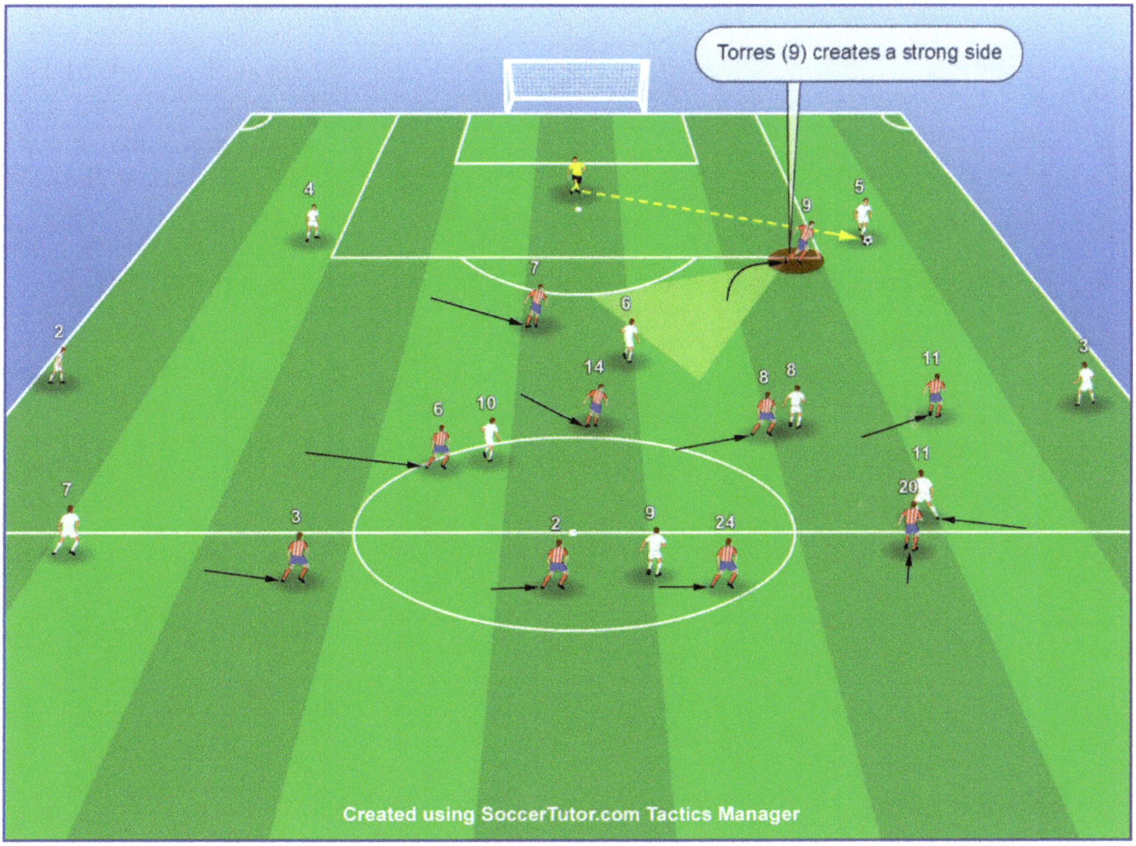

As soon as the pass is directed to the left centre back No.5, the forward **Torres (9)** creates a strong side with a curved run and also blocks the passing lane to the defensive midfielder No.6.

Both white No.8 and No.11 are tightly marked by their direct opponents.

Atlético's right midfielder **Correa (11)** makes sure not to move too wide so he can block a potential through pass. He also controls the white left back No.3 and presses him immediately if the next pass is directed to him.

ASSESSMENT

If **Torres (9)** hasn't managed to create a strong side and the back pass to the GK is still possible, the other forward **Griezmann (7)** doesn't move into a deeper position. Instead, he stays in a high and balanced position to control both the pass to the GK and the potential pass to No.6, as it was described in a similar situation on the other side.

DIEGO SIMEONE'S DEFENDING TACTICS

Tactical Situation 15 - Pressing After the Goalkeeper's Pass

c. Intercepting the Attempted Through Pass by the Centre Back

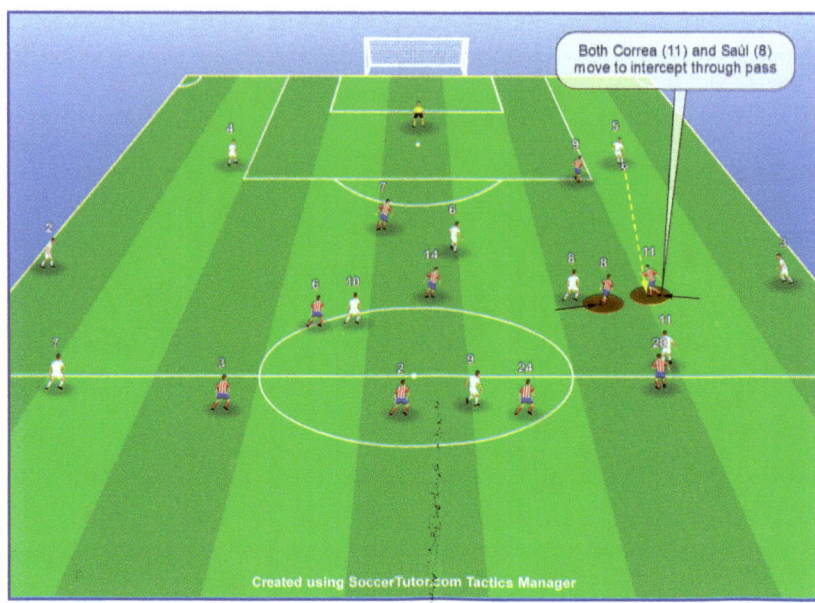

As shown in the previous diagram, the right midfielder **Correa (11)** is in a balanced position and not too wide.

If a through pass is attempted, both **Correa (11)** and the central midfielder **Saúl (8)** move to intercept the pass.

d. Marking All Potential Receivers After the Pass to the Full Back

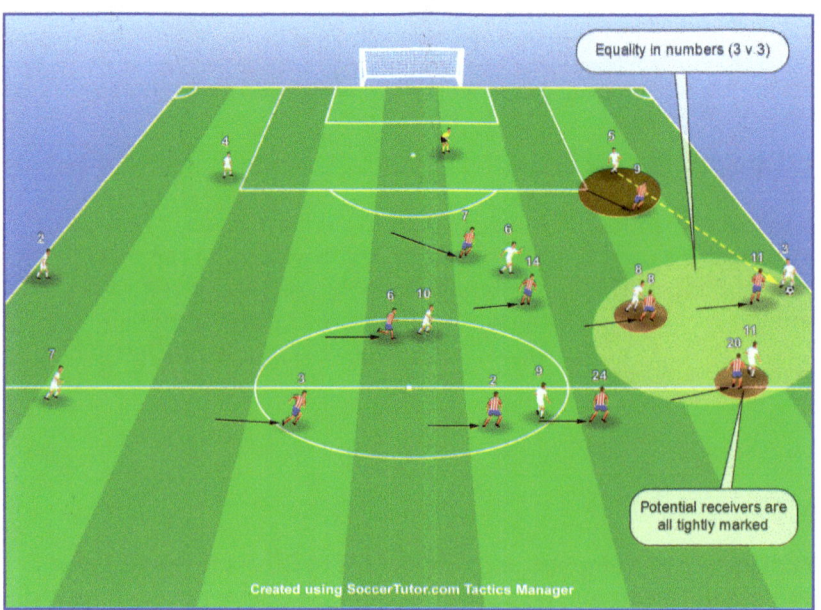

If the pass is directed to No.3, **Correa (11)** takes advantage of the transmission phase (time the ball takes to travel) to press him immediately and restrict his time and space. There is no numerical advantage around the ball area (3v3), but all potential receivers are tightly marked.

The only pass left for No.3 is the inside pass to No.6, who can be pressed by **Gabi (14)** and **Griezmann (7)**.

Tactical Situation 15 - Pressing After the Goalkeeper's Pass

e. Double Marking the Defensive Midfielder After an Inside Pass from the Full Back

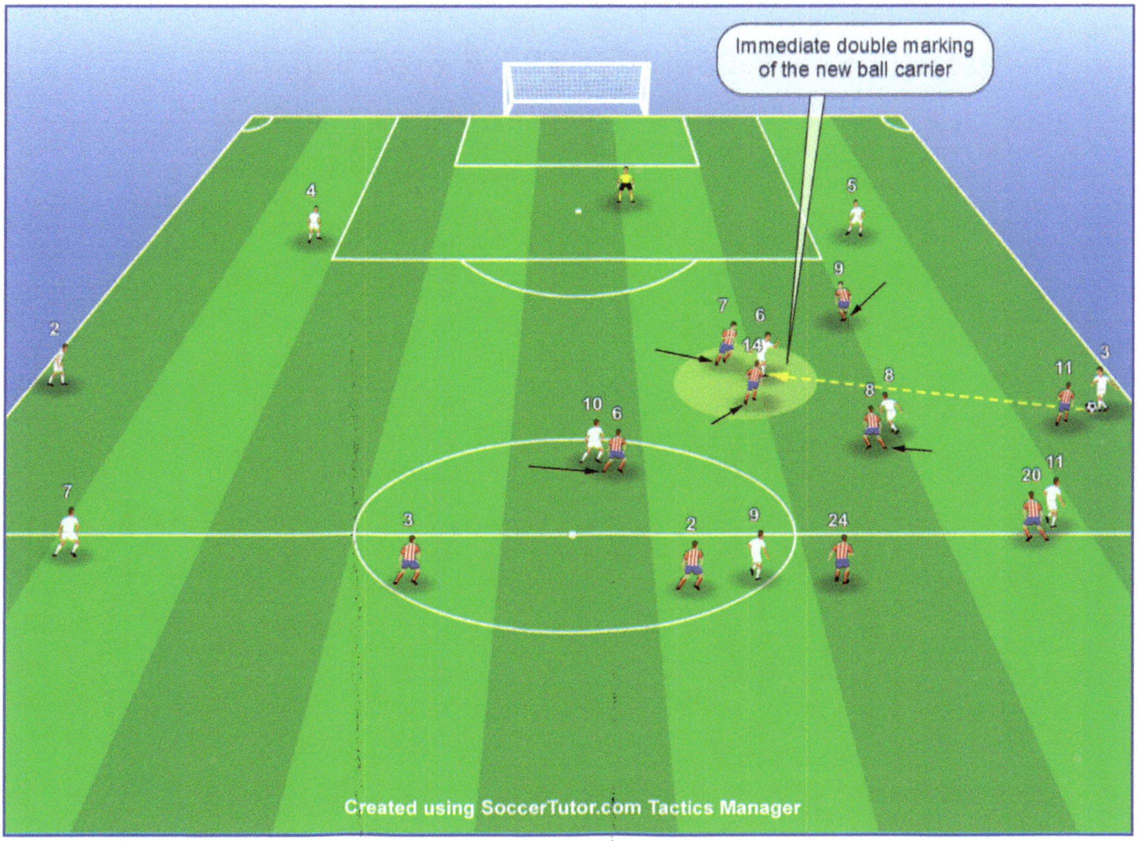

The white left back No.3 passes inside to the defensive midfielder No.6, as it is the only available option.

The forward on the weak side **Griezmann (7)**, who has already shifted towards the ball area and the central midfielder **Gabi (14)**, who was in charge of controlling No.6 initially, move to press the new ball carrier and apply double marking.

Diego Simeone's Atlético team look to apply double marking in this crucial area. If they win the ball, they will be able to quickly counter attack with a short distance to goal.

Griezmann (7) blocks the ball being played back to the GK and the other forward **Torres (9)** moves to block the pass back to the centre back No.5.

The other potential receivers around the ball area (No.3, No.8, No.10 and No.11) are all tightly marked.

Tactical Situation 15 - Pressing After the Goalkeeper's Pass

PRESSING WHEN THE DEFENSIVE MIDFIELDER DROPS VERY DEEP AGAINST THE 4-3-3

1a. The Defensive Midfielder Drops Back into a Very Deep Position

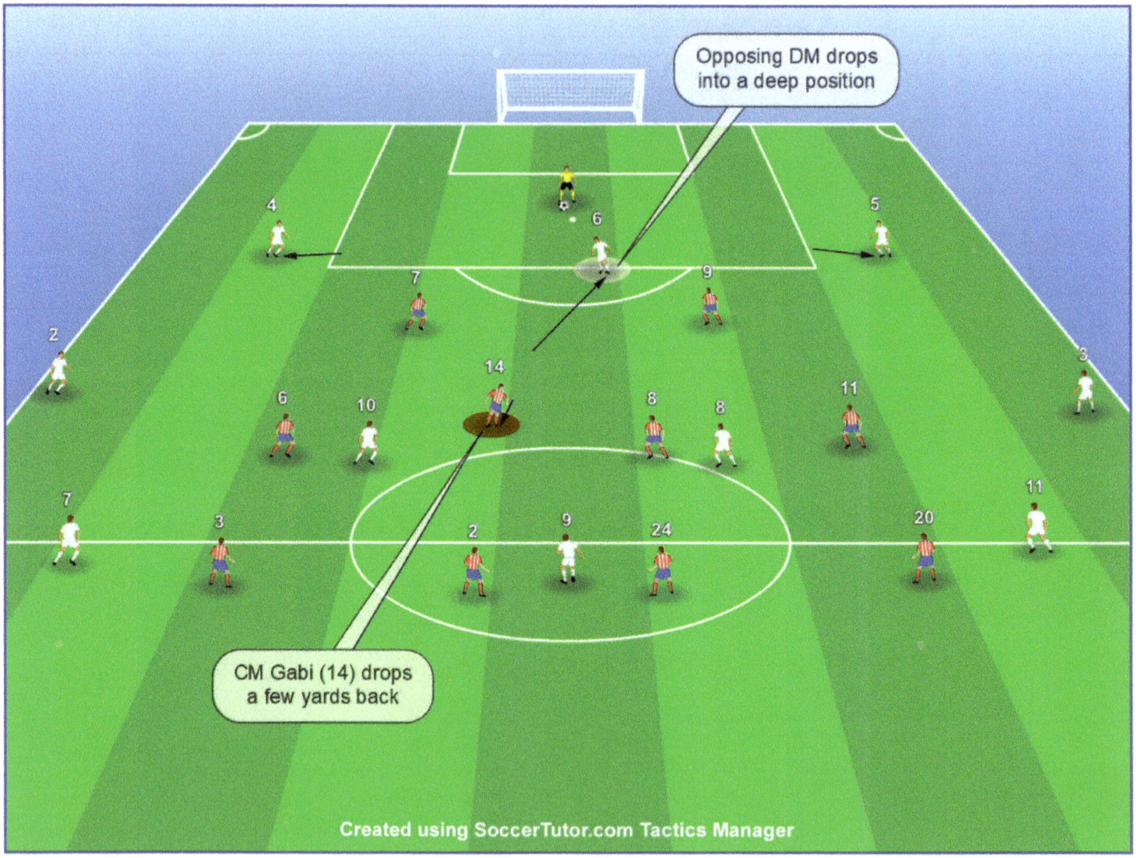

If the opposing defensive midfielder No.6 drops into a very deep position to create a back 3, the responsibility of controlling him is passed onto the 2 forwards **Griezmann (7)** and **Torres (9)**.

The central midfielder **Gabi (14)**, who normally controls the opposing defensive midfielder against the 4-3-3, drops a few yards back but stays in a higher position than the other central midfielder **Saúl (8)**.

This movement of the defensive midfielder No.6 creates a favourable 3 (+GK) v 2 situation at the back for the white team.

DIEGO SIMEONE'S DEFENDING TACTICS

Tactical Situation 15 - Pressing After the Goalkeeper's Pass

1b. Creating a Strong Side Against a 3 Man Defence and Preventing a Numerical Disadvantage

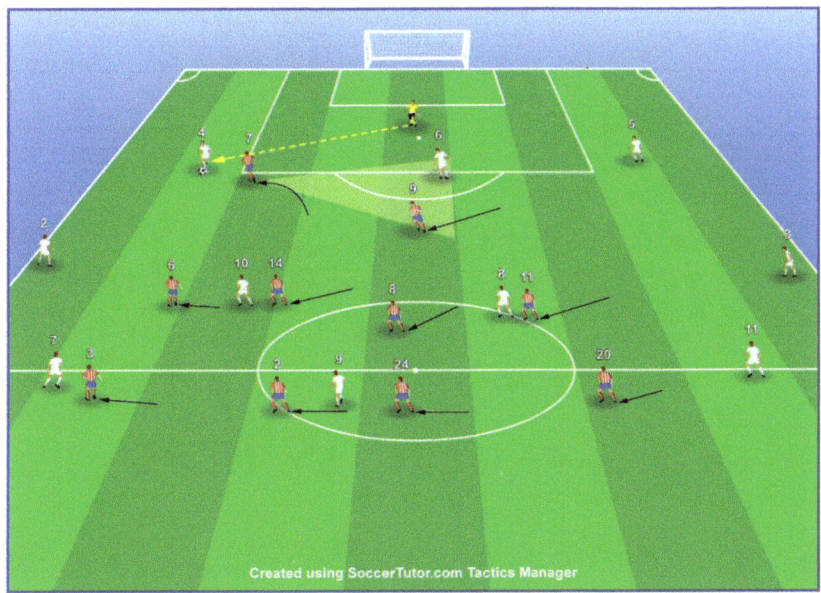

If the pass is directed to one of the centre backs, the closest forward creates a strong side. This eliminates the numerical advantage at the back for the white team. There is no way for No.4 to pass back to the GK or No.6.

As **Griezmann (7)** blocks these passes, the other forward **Torres (9)** is able to move towards the strong side, as do the Atlético midfielders like in previous situations.

2a. Forcing Play to One Side After the Defensive Midfielder Receives

In this second example, the GK passes to the very deep defensive midfielder No.6.

This time, **Torres (9)** forces play towards one side in order to make the opposition's build-up play predictable, for which Atlético are well prepared.

The other forward **Griezmann (7)** drops back and towards the centre but must also be ready to press No.4, who is the only passing option available for No.6.

Tactical Situation 15 - Pressing After the Goalkeeper's Pass

2b. Creating a Strong Side After the Defensive Midfielder is Forced to Pass to the Wide Centre Back

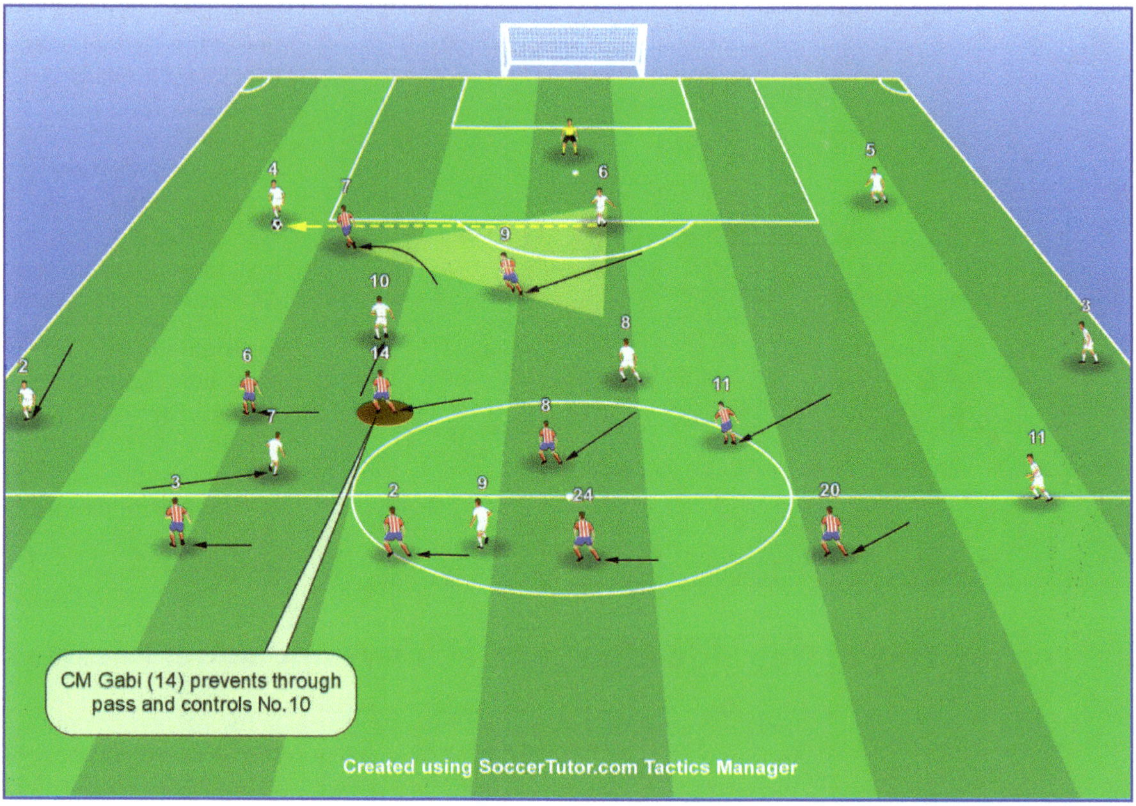

CM Gabi (14) prevents through pass and controls No.10

As soon as the pass is played towards the right centre back No.4, the forward on that side **Griezmann (7)** moves to close him down and create a strong side for Atlético at the same time.

If this attempt is successful, the other forward **Torres (9)** moves back and towards the strong side because the pass to the defensive midfielder No.6 is blocked by **Griezmann (7)** and there is no way for No.4 to pass the ball back to the GK.

If there is a possibility for a pass back to the GK, then **Torres (9)** has to stay in a high position.

As white No.4 receives, the right back No.2 moves forward, the winger No.7 moves inside, and the attacking midfielder No.10 drops back to get free of marking.

In this situation, the key player is the central midfielder on the strong side **Gabi (14)**, who has to defend with these **2 Objectives**:

1. Block the through pass towards the winger No.7, because a 2v1 situation will be created if he receives, with white No.2 and No.7 vs Atlético's left back **F. Luis (3)**.

2. Control the white attacking midfielder No.10 and prevent him from receiving and turning.

Tactical Situation 15 - Pressing After the Goalkeeper's Pass

2c. Applying Double Marking After the Wide Centre Back's Pass to the Attacking Midfielder

(Diagram: Immediate double marking of new ball carrier)

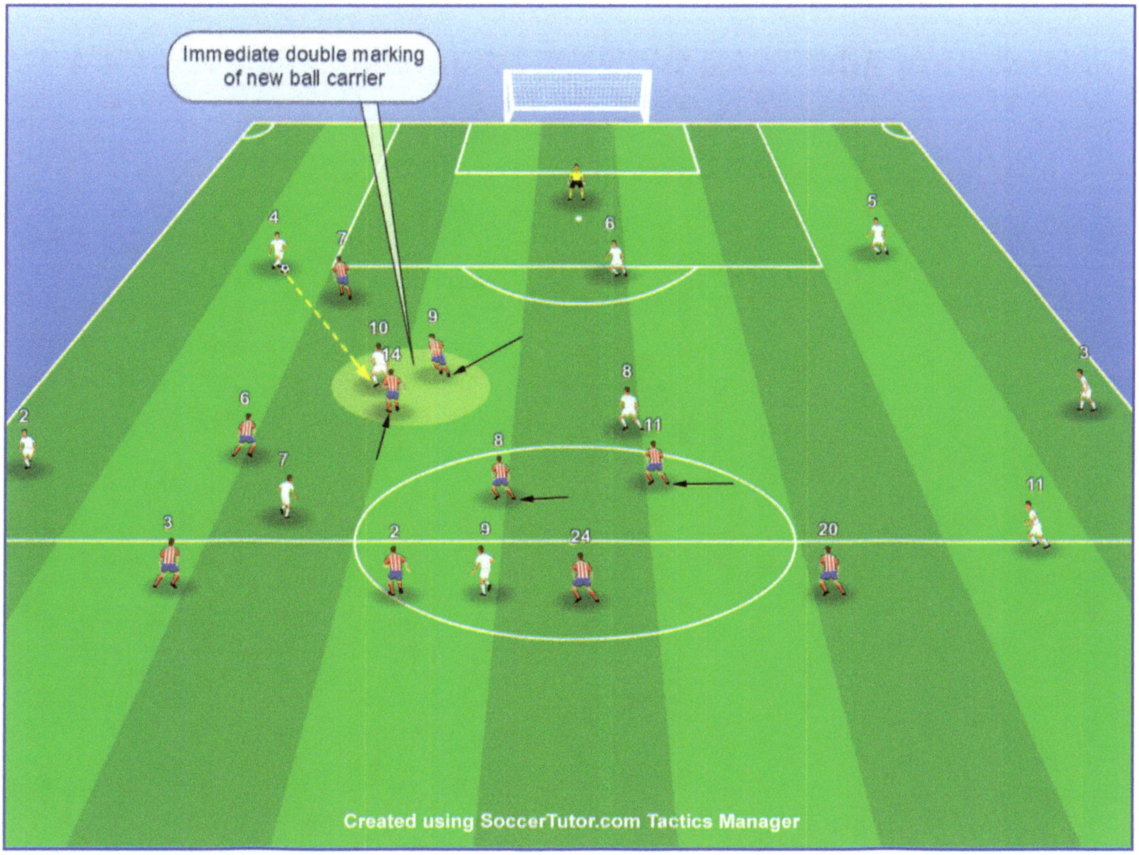

In the diagram example above, we show one of the options for the white centre back No.4.

When No.4's pass is directed to the attacking midfielder No.10, 2 Atlético players move to close him down and prevent him from turning. They also try to force him into a bad first touch which will lead to winning possession.

If white No.4 had attempted to play a through pass towards the winger No.7, then Atlético's left midfielder **Koke (6)** and the central midfielder **Gabi (14)** should easily be able to react and block it.

For when No.4 plays a pass to the advanced full back No.2 or is able to successfully play a through pass to the winger No.7, see the section "Tactical Situation 12 - Rear Block's Defensive Reactions After Wide Players Receive" for Atlético's defensive reaction.

DIEGO SIMEONE'S DEFENDING TACTICS

Tactical Situation 15 - Pressing After the Goalkeeper's Pass

PRESSING AFTER THE GOALKEEPER'S PASS AGAINST THE 4-4-2

1. Match-up of Atlético Madrid's 4-4-2 Formation Against the 4-4-2

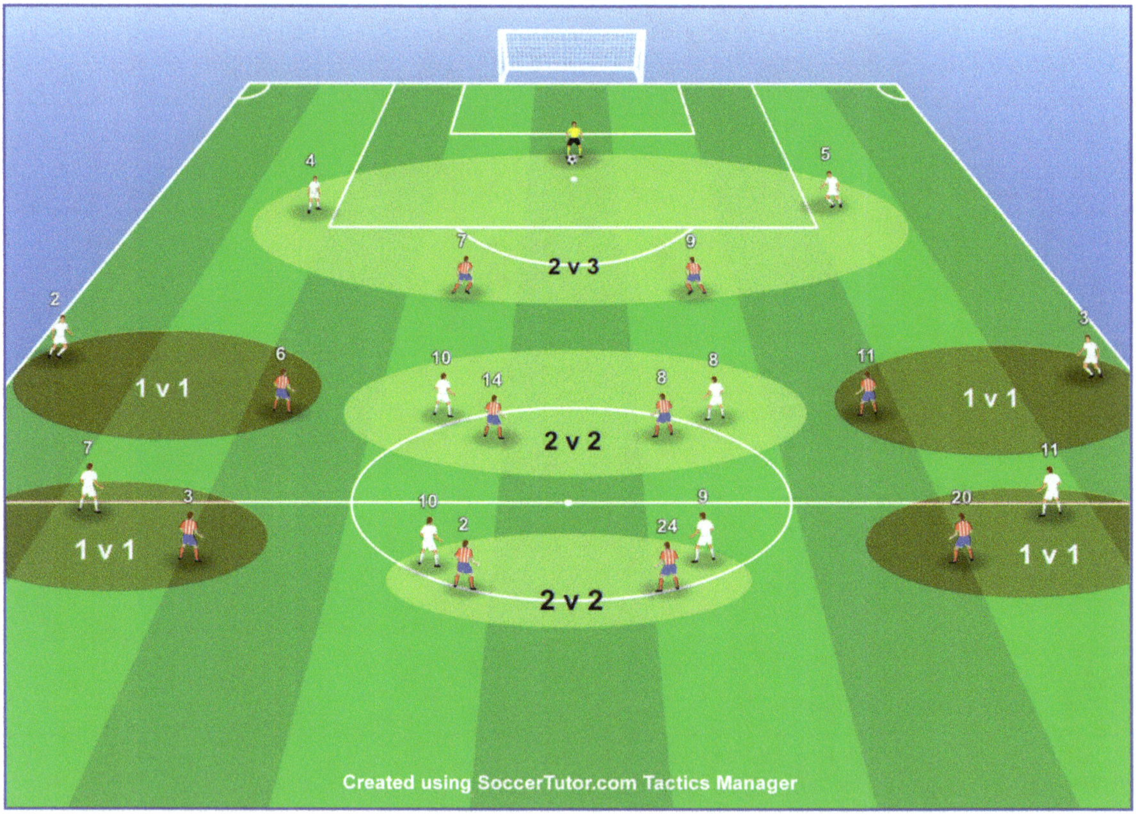

To analyse Atlético's pressing application properly, it is important to take the opposition's formation into account.

The focus should be on the players rather than the space. The numerical situations in different areas affect the way the pressing is applied.

Against the 4-4-2, there is a perfect match-up with numerical equality in most areas of the pitch, with many 1v1s.

There is a numerical equality of 2v2 in the high part of the pitch, but the presence of the GK makes it 2v3. When building up from the back, the GK is the extra player for the opposing team.

DIEGO SIMEONE'S DEFENDING TACTICS

Tactical Situation 15 - Pressing After the Goalkeeper's Pass

2. Pressing the Opposition in their Conventional 4-4-2 Shape After the GK's First Pass

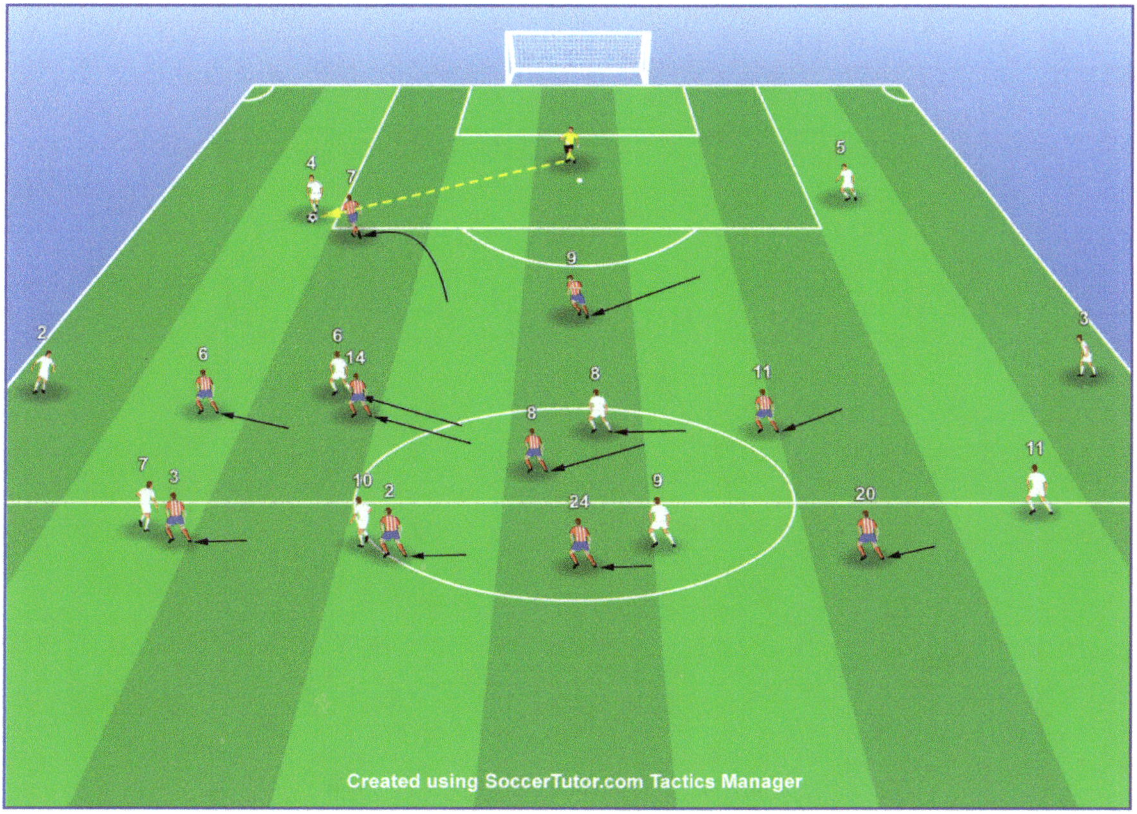

If the opposing team try to build up play from the back in a rigid 4-4-2 formation without changing their shape, it is not difficult for Diego Simeone's Atlético team. It is relatively easy for the players to deal with the situation, as they simply have to focus on their direct opponents.

The diagram above shows Atlético's pressing application against the 4-4-2 after the goalkeeper's first pass to the centre back No.4.

The central midfielder on that side **Gabi (14)** shifts across to mark the white central midfielder No.6, who is a potential receiver. The right midfielder **Koke (6)** is ready to put the white right back No.2 under pressure if he receives.

Additionally, both **Gabi (14)** and **Koke (6)** keep the through passing lane towards white No.7 or No.10 very narrow.

The rest of the Atlético players retain a good defensive shape, while the forward on the weak side **Torres (9)** drops back and shifts towards the strong side to help create a numerical advantage.

Tactical Situation 15 - Pressing After the Goalkeeper's Pass

PRESSING AFTER THE GOALKEEPER'S PASS
AGAINST THE 4-2-3-1

Match-up of Atlético Madrid's 4-4-2 Formation Against the 4-2-3-1

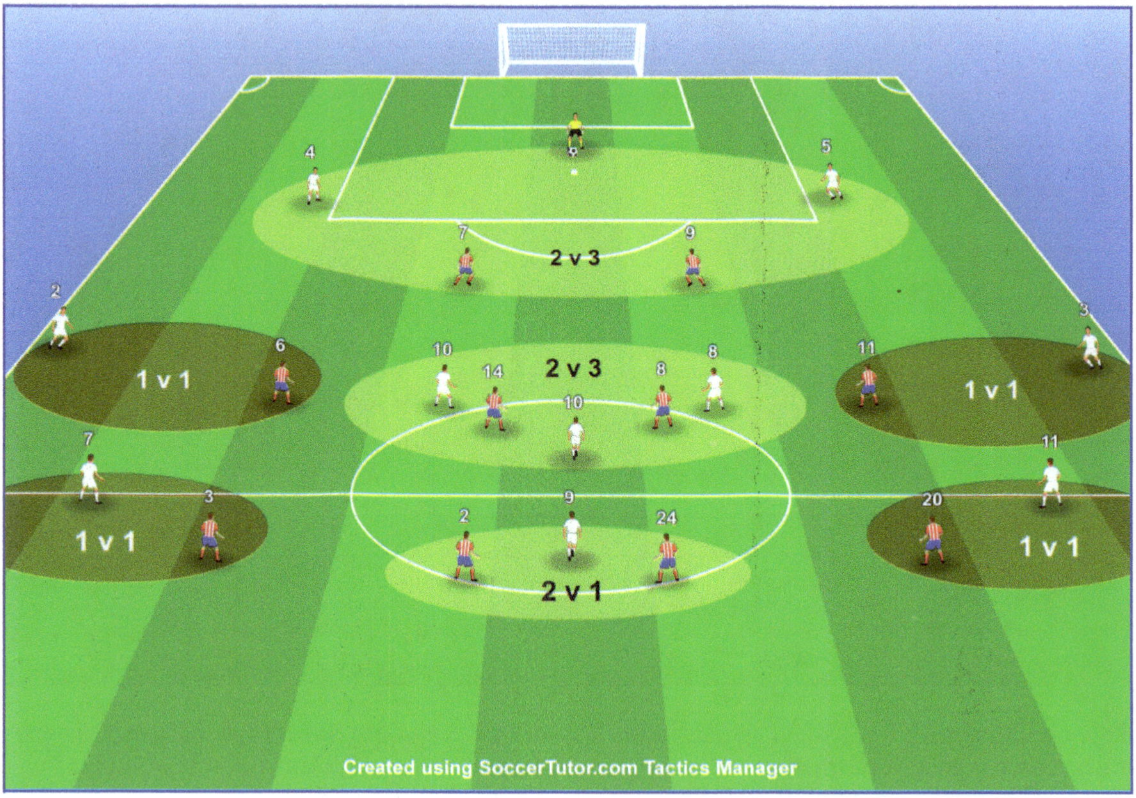

Against the 4-2-3-1 formation, there is a numerical advantage of 3v2 in midfield for the opposition due to the presence of the No.10.

However, this numerical advantage does not affect the pressing application, as the white No.10 is unable to provide a direct passing option for the GK or one of the centre backs.

Similarly to the pressing application against the 4-4-2 (**see previous page**), if the opposition do not change their shape at all and play with a rigid 4-2-3-1 to build up play, Atlético will again have few problems to deal with this situation.

However, if one of the white central midfielders drops deeper, their formation changes and the Atlético players have to react and apply their pressing accordingly.

DIEGO SIMEONE'S DEFENDING TACTICS

Tactical Situation 15 - Pressing After the Goalkeeper's Pass

THE CENTRAL MIDFIELDER DROPS INTO A DEEP POSITION AGAINST THE 4-4-2

1. The Opposing Central Midfielder Drops into a Deep Position and Creates Space in the Centre of Midfield

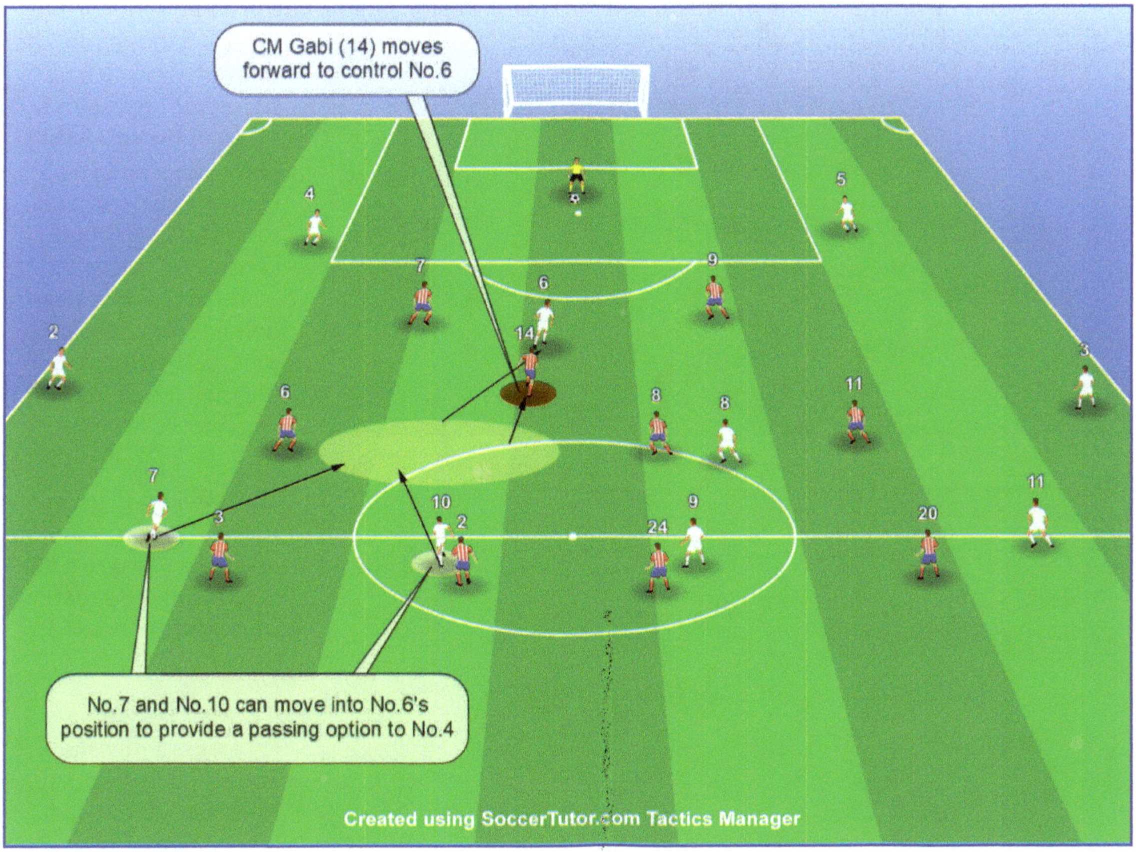

When pressing against the 4-4-2, one of the central midfielders may drop back into a deep position to create a numerical advantage in the low zone for the initial build-up play.

In this situation, it is the closest Atlético central midfielder **Gabi (14)** who has to control him.

This then creates a 1v1 situation in the centre of midfield with **Saúl (8)** vs white No.8.

The space created (highlighted area) by the forward movement of **Gabi (14)** can be occupied by the white wide midfielder No.7 or forward No.10.

If the GK passes to the right centre back No.4 in this situation, he will now have an extra passing option available.

DIEGO SIMEONE'S DEFENDING TACTICS

Tactical Situation 15 - Pressing After the Goalkeeper's Pass

2. The Opposing Wide Midfielder Moves to Occupy the Free Space in Midfield and Provide a Passing Option

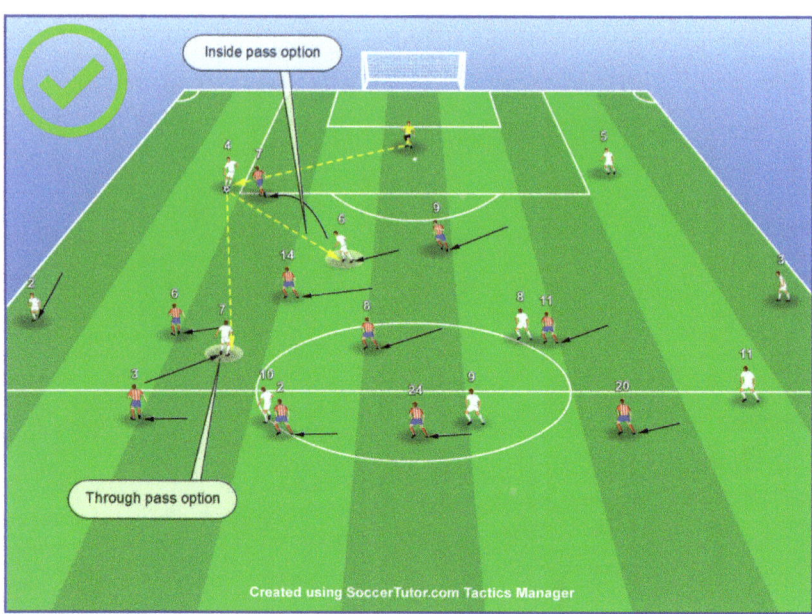

If the pass is directed to No.4 and white No.7 moves to provide a passing option, the Atlético players react the way they do against the 4-3-3 formation. The through passing lane should be kept narrow by **Koke (6)** and **Gabi (14)**, who should also control the inside pass to white No.6. **F. Luis (3)** doesn't follow white No.7 and instead defends the space and gets ready to take over the marking of No.2, who moves forward.

The previous diagram shows Atlético's correct reactions to make sure they avoid the situation shown in this second diagram.

If the left back **F. Luis (3)** makes a mistake and follows white No.7, available space is created for the opponents in behind.

This space can either be exploited by the white full back No.2 or the forward No.10.

©SOCCERTUTOR.COM   DIEGO SIMEONE'S DEFENDING TACTICS

Tactical Situation 15 - Pressing After the Goalkeeper's Pass

3. The Opposing Forward Moves to Occupy the Free Space in Midfield and Provide a Passing Option

If the forward No.10 is the player who drops back to provide a passing option to No.4, the centre back **Godín (2)** steps forward a few yards but doesn't follow him deeper to avoid creating space behind.

Koke (6) and **Gabi (14)** focus on blocking the potential through pass. If the pass is directed to white No.6, double marking should be applied by **Gabi (14)** and **Torres (9)**, as in previous examples.

The previous diagram shows Atlético's correct reactions to make sure they avoid the situation described in this second diagram.

If the centre back **Godín (2)** makes a mistake and follows white No.10 too far, available space is created for the opponents in behind.

This space can either be exploited by the white right midfielder No.7 or the other forward No.9.

PRACTICE FOR "PRESSING AFTER THE GOALKEEPER'S PASS"

©SOCCERTUTOR.COM

DIEGO SIMEONE'S DEFENDING TACTICS

Tactical Situation 15 - Pressing After the Goalkeeper's Pass

PRACTICE FOR THIS TACTICAL SITUATION
Pressing After the Goalkeeper's Pass in a Dynamic Game with Central Zones vs the 4-3-3

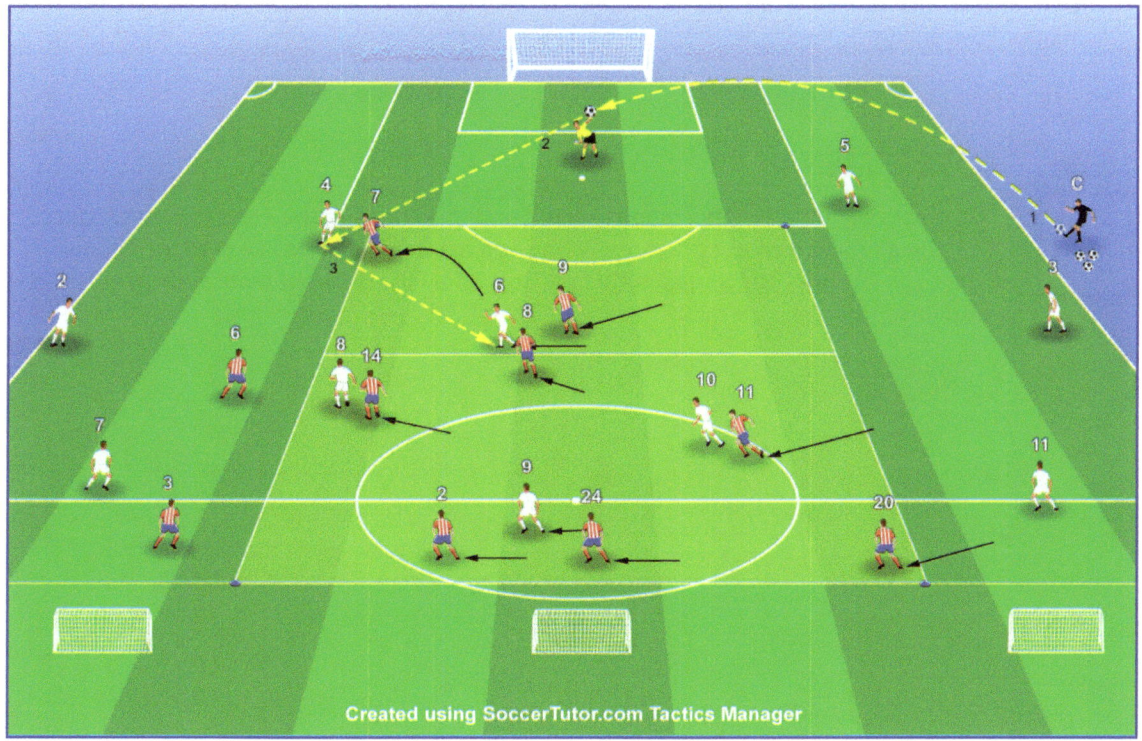

This is a **similar practice to Page 204**, but the central area is divided into 2 zones - the yellow zone is where the white defensive midfielder moves and should be controlled by the red team.

Description

- The 2 teams play a 10 v 10 (+GK) game and the Coach starts the practice with a long pass to the GK.

- The white team's aim is to build up play through the red's pressing and score in any of the 3 mini goals. If a goal is scored from within the central zone, the whites score 3 goals.

- The red players apply pressing after the GK's first pass (or throw), with the aim of keeping the ball out of the white central zone.

- Please **see the analysis pages in this section** for how the red players should apply their pressing as a team.

- If the ball is passed to the white defensive midfielder No.6 inside the yellow zone from an outfield player (not GK), the reds close him down immediately, preventing a switch of play or forward pass into the white zone.

- If the GK passes directly to No.6, the reds force play wide or backwards.

- If the ball is passed towards a player inside the white central zone, the red players have to either block the pass or win possession within 3-5 seconds.

©SOCCERTUTOR.COM   DIEGO SIMEONE'S DEFENDING TACTICS

Tactical Situation 15 - Pressing After the Goalkeeper's Pass

Variations

1. The white defensive midfielder No.6 drops into a very deep position to create a 3 man defence and the reds must make the correct defensive adjustments for the situation.
2. The white team use the 4-4-2 or 4-2-3-1 formation (see analysis).

Coaching Points

1. Force the ball wide and create a strong side.
2. Stop the ball moving to the weak side.
3. Control the defensive midfielder.

ASSESSMENT

This practice shows the opposition (white team) playing with the 4-3-3 formation but it can be adapted easily to practice playing against the 4-4-2 and 4-2-3-1 formations. Please **see the analysis pages in this section** for all the different tactical situations and solutions.

THE TRANSITION FROM ATTACK TO DEFENCE

The Transition from Attack to Defence

THE TRANSITION FROM ATTACK TO DEFENCE (NEGATIVE TRANSITION)

DEFINITION

The transition from attack to defence (or negative transition) is the phase which starts as soon as possession is lost and ends when the defending team manages to achieve good defensive organisation. After this moment, the defensive phase starts.

ATLÉTICO MADRID'S DEFENSIVE PHASE

Atlético Madrid's success under Diego Simeone is mainly based on their tactics in the defensive phase and the transition from defence to attack.

The basic elements of Atlético Madrid's defensive phase are fully described on **Page 18**.

ATLÉTICO MADRID'S TRANSITION FROM ATTACK TO DEFENCE

There are also many more details about Atlético's defensive play in the transition from attack to defence. These are fully analysed and presented in this section of the book with 4 different tactical situations:

1. Retaining a Numerical Advantage at the Back During Build-up Play
2. Negative Transition After Losing Possession from a Long Pass
3. Negative Transition After Losing Possession During a Switch of Play
4. Counter-Pressing After Losing Possession During Combination Play

TACTICAL SITUATION 1

Retaining a Numerical Advantage at the Back During Build-up Play

The content in this section is from analysis of Diego Simeone's Atlético Madrid teams during the 2017/2018 and 2018/2019 seasons.

The analysis is based on recurring patterns of play observed within the Atlético Madrid team. Once the same phase of play occurred several times (at least 10), the tactics would be seen as a pattern. The analysis on the following pages are examples of the team's tactics being used effectively.

Each action, pass, individual movement with or without the ball, and the positioning of each player on the pitch including their body shape, are presented.

The analysis is then used to create a session to coach this specific tactical situation.

Tactical Situation 1 - Retaining a Numerical Advantage at the Back During Build-up Play

RETAINING A NUMERICAL ADVANTAGE AT THE BACK DURING BUILD-UP PLAY

THE ATTACKING PHASE

Diego Simeone makes sure his Atlético Madrid players take up appropriate positions during the attacking phase to make sure:

1. They are effective in creating scoring chances.
2. Retain balance in preparation for the transition from attack to defence (negative transition).

THE TRANSITION FROM ATTACK TO DEFENCE

With Simeone's principles in the attacking phase, the Atlético players are always able to defend effectively after losing possession.

Atlético Madrid are one of the best teams in the world and Diego Simeone is one of the best defensive coaches.

RETAINING BALANCE

An important element when retaining balance during the attacking phase is to always have a spare player (numerical advantage) at the back.

Retaining a numerical advantage at the back is very important in reducing the likelihood of conceding a goal from a potential counter attack by the opposition.

It was mainly the role of the defenders and the central midfielders to carry out these tactics, which are fully analysed on the following pages.

Tactical Situation 1 - Retaining a Numerical Advantage at the Back During Build-up Play

RETAINING A NUMERICAL ADVANTAGE AT THE BACK DURING BUILD-UP AGAINST THE 4-4-2

1. Creating a 3v2 Numerical Advantage at the Back when Building Up Play Against the 4-4-2 with Full Back in a Deep Position

When playing against the 4-4-2 formation, Atlético had to create a 3v2 situation at the back which made building up play and the transition from attack to defence much easier. This is because Diego Simeone's team would always have a spare man.

The 3v2 situation is created in 2 ways. Either the full back on the weak side dropped into a deep position (**diagram above**) or the central midfielder did (**see next page**).

In this example, the centre back **Giménez (24)** has the ball, and the full back on the strong side **Juanfran (20)** is in a very high position. This position was taken because the central midfielder on the strong side **Thomas (5)** is in a suitable position to provide safety and control white No.11 in case possession is lost.

The full back on the weak side **F. Luis (3)** drops into a deep position to ensure that a 3v2 numerical advantage at the back is created.

©SOCCERTUTOR.COM   DIEGO SIMEONE'S DEFENDING TACTICS

Tactical Situation 1 - Retaining a Numerical Advantage at the Back During Build-up Play

2. Creating a 3v2 Numerical Advantage at the Back when Building Up Play Against the 4-4-2 with Central Midfielder in a Deep Position

This second example shows another option which Diego Simeone's Atlético Madrid team used to create a 3v2 numerical advantage at the back when building up play.

This time it is the dropping back movement of the central midfielder on the weak side **Rodri (14)**, which creates a numerical advantage at the back against the 2 white forwards No.9 and No.10.

This action by **Rodri (14)** enables the full back **F. Luis (3)** to stay in a high position.

However, **F. Luis' (3)** positioning (in line with white No.7) should allow him to control the white winger in case possession is lost.

Tactical Situation 1 - Retaining a Numerical Advantage at the Back During Build-up Play

3. The Central Midfielder Drops Back and into a Wide Position to Retain Balance at the Back when the Centre Back Switches Play

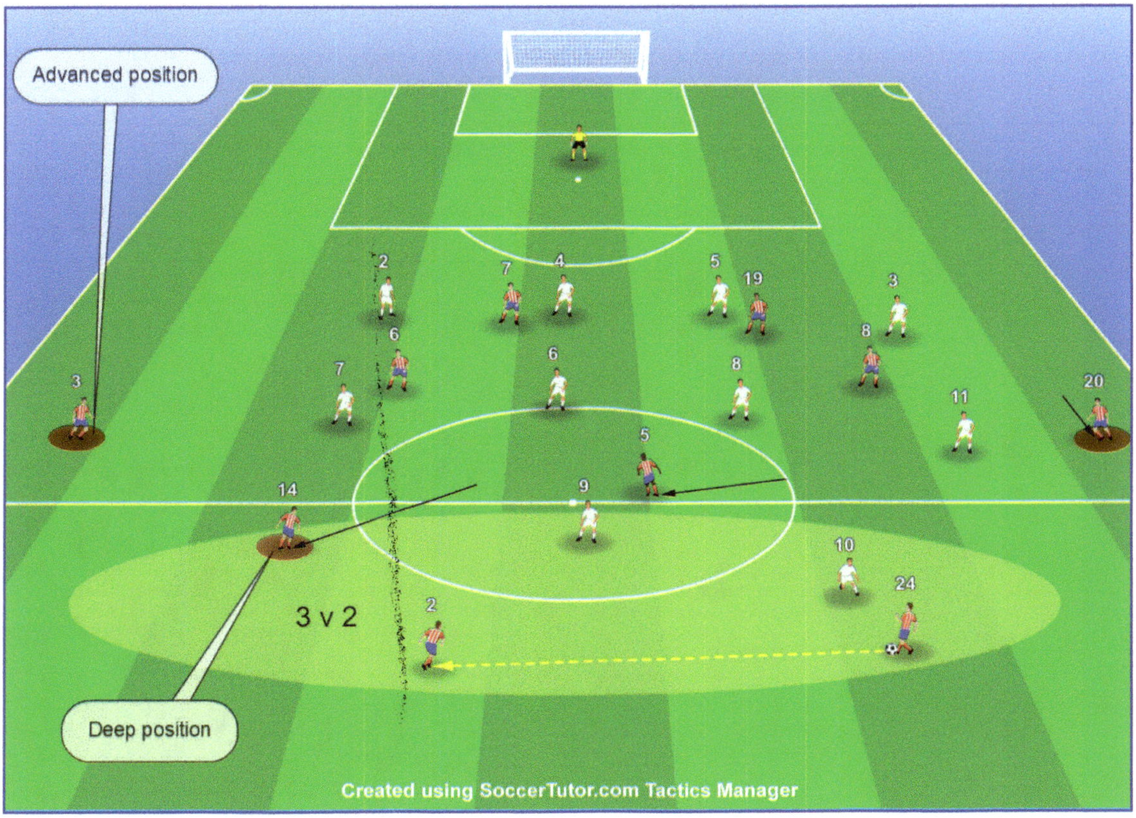

Following on from the previous page, if the centre back **Giménez (24)** switches play, the Atlético players readjust their positioning.

Giménez (24) passes to his centre back partner **Godín (2)**. One central midfielder **Rodri (14)** moves into a wider position, while the other central midfielder **Thomas (5)** moves towards the centre to retain balance.

Due to the central positioning of **Thomas (5)**, controlling No.11 is no longer possible.

This forces the full back on the strong side **Juanfran (20)** to drop a few yards back and take up a high position (instead of very high). This enables him to control white No.11 in case possession is lost.

 **ASSESSMENT**

In situations when moving the ball forward to one of the central midfielders was easy (low pressure from opposing forwards and easy possession), both full backs took up high positions. However, as soon as the ball was passed into an area where losing possession was possible, balance and a numerical advantage at the back was ensured.

©SOCCERTUTOR.COM   DIEGO SIMEONE'S DEFENDING TACTICS

Tactical Situation 1 - Retaining a Numerical Advantage at the Back During Build-up Play

4a. Building Up Play with Both Full Backs in Advanced Positions and the Central Midfielders Deep

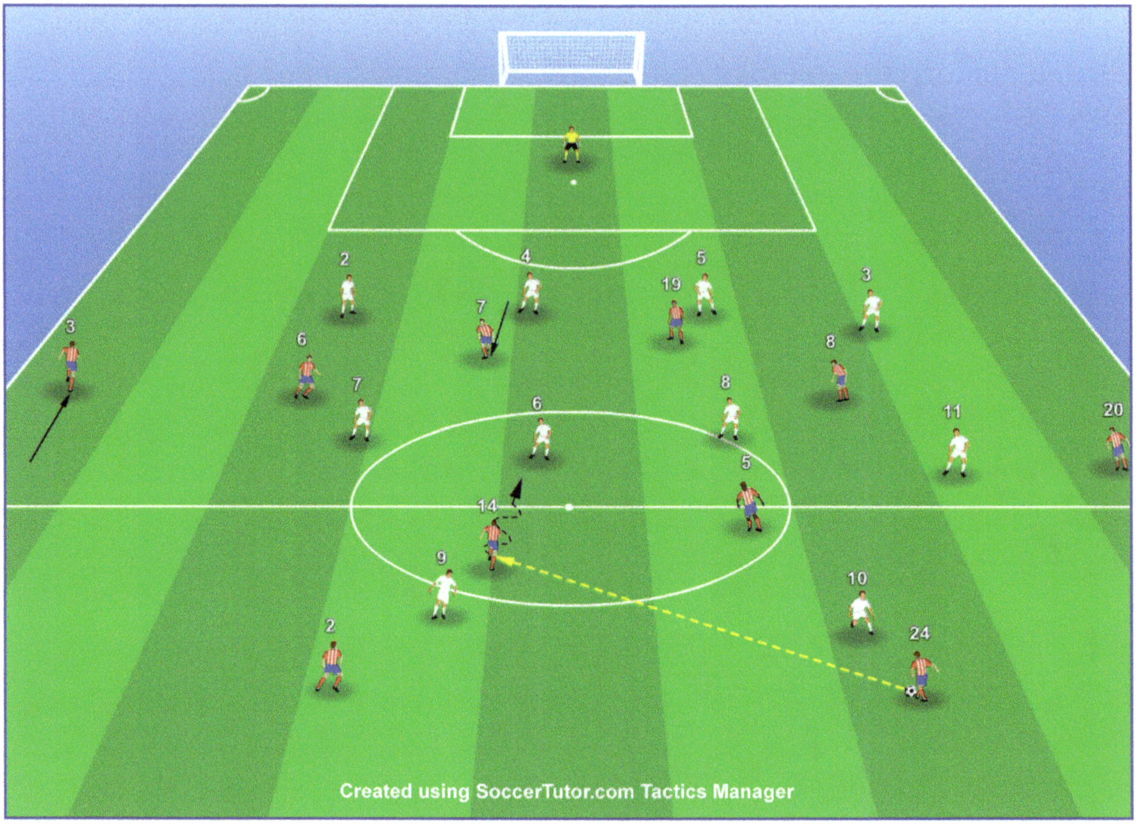

In this situation, **Giménez (24)** knows that the pass played to one of the central midfielders should be a safe pass, as both full backs and both central midfielders are in high enough positions.

If the ball carrier in this situation is under heavy pressure, he won't risk a forward pass but will play back to the GK and the players will readjust positions.

After **Giménez's (24)** pass to **Rodri (14)**, the left back **F. Luis (3)** moves forward into a very high position, as he is highly likely to receive a pass.

Rodri (14) is able to control white No.7 if possession is lost.

DIEGO SIMEONE'S DEFENDING TACTICS

Tactical Situation 1 - Retaining a Numerical Advantage at the Back During Build-up Play

4b. The Full Back Drops Back to Retain Balance at the Back when the Ball is Moved to an Area Where Possession Could be Lost

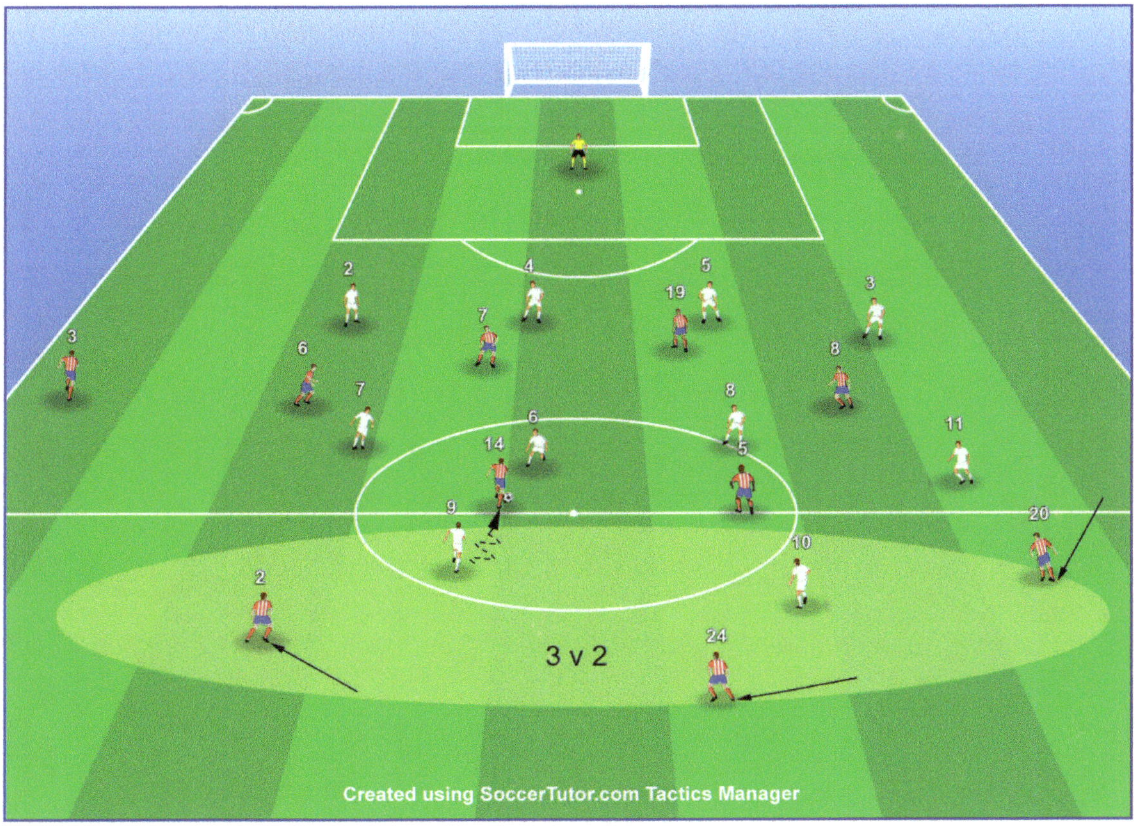

As soon as **Rodri (14)** receives and moves forward to make the next pass, the Atlético defenders get ready to react in case the team lose possession.

Therefore, the right back **Juanfran (20)** drops back to create a 3 man defence and retain a 3v2 numerical advantage against the 2 white forwards.

DIEGO SIMEONE'S DEFENDING TACTICS

Tactical Situation 1 - Retaining a Numerical Advantage at the Back During Build-up Play

RETAINING A NUMERICAL ADVANTAGE AT THE BACK DURING BUILD-UP AGAINST THE 4-2-3-1

Creating a Numerical Advantage at the Back when Building Up Play Against the 4-2-3-1 when the No.10 is in a Deep Position

When playing against the 4-2-3-1 formation and the opposing No.10 was in a relatively deep position, there is no need for the Atlético full back or central midfielder on the weak side to drop back into a deep position, like shown on the previous pages against the 4-4-2.

This is because there is already a 2 v 1 numerical advantage against the 1 white forward No.9.

However, if the white No.10 takes up a more advanced position, then the Atlético players have to react as if they were playing against a team with 2 forwards (**see previous 5 pages**).

Tactical Situation 1 - Retaining a Numerical Advantage at the Back During Build-up Play

RETAINING A NUMERICAL ADVANTAGE AT THE BACK DURING BUILD-UP AGAINST THE 4-3-3 OR 4-1-4-1

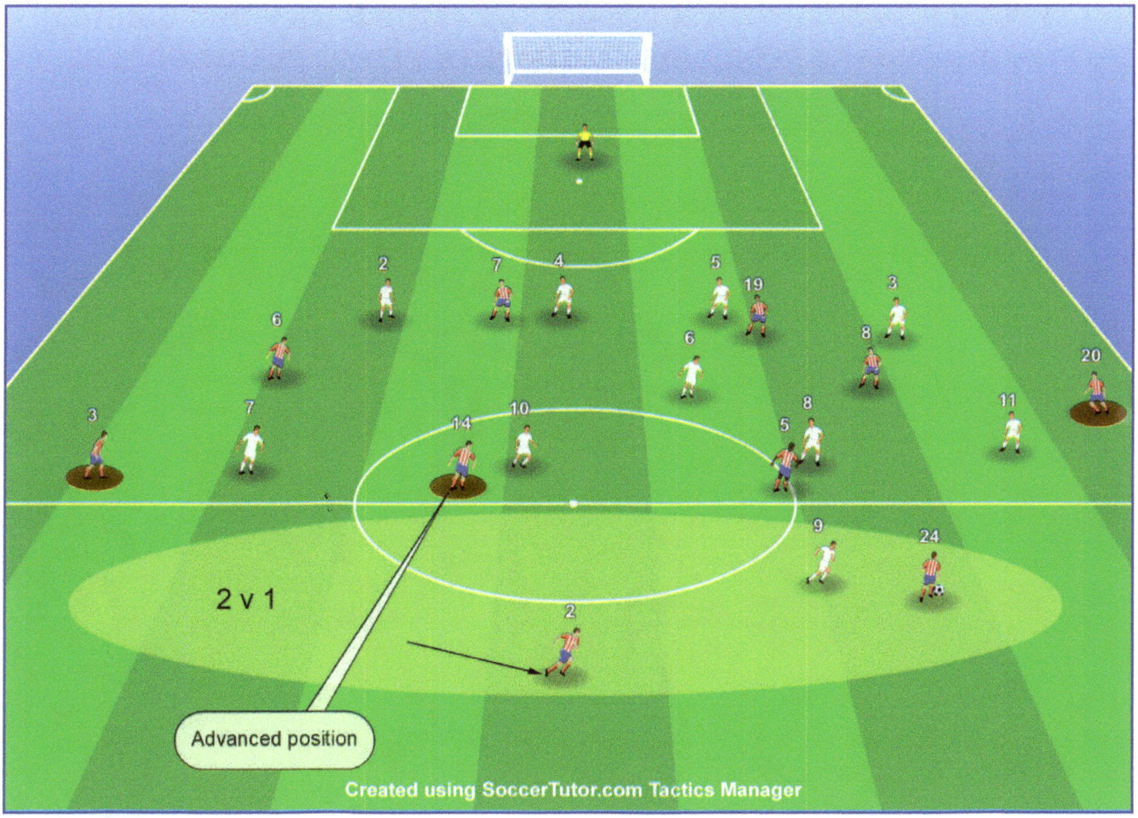

When playing against the 4-3-3 or 4-1-4-1 formations, there is again no need for the Atlético full back or central midfielder on the weak side to drop back into a deep position.

This is because there is already a 2v1 numerical advantage against the 1 white forward No.9.

The Atlético full backs and central midfielders can all be in high positions. The right back **Juanfran (20)** is in a very high position as central midfielder **Thomas (5)** can provide cover for him if possession is lost.

Tactical Situation 1 - Retaining a Numerical Advantage at the Back During Build-up Play

RETAINING A NUMERICAL ADVANTAGE AT THE BACK DURING BUILD-UP AGAINST THE 3-5-2

1. Creating a 3v2 Numerical Advantage at the Back when Building Up Play Against the 3-5-2 with Full Back in a Deep Position

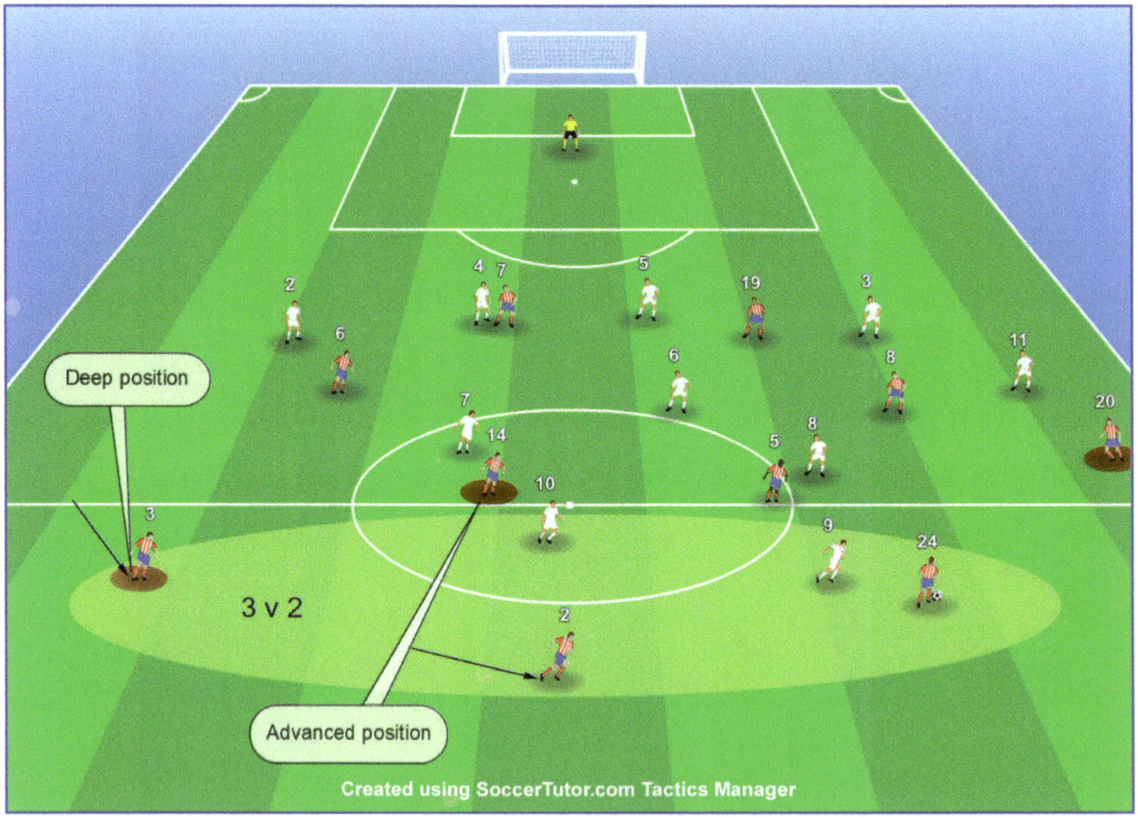

When playing against the 3-5-2 formation, Atlético create a 3v2 situation at the back in the same way as they do against the 4-4-2.

The 3v2 situation is created in 2 ways. Either the full back on the weak side dropped into a deep position (**diagram above**) or the central midfielder did (**see next page**).

In this example, the centre back **Giménez (24)** has the ball, and the full back on the strong side **Juanfran (20)** is in a high position.

The full back on the weak side **F. Luis (3)** drops into a deep position to ensure that a 3v2 numerical advantage at the back is created.

©SOCCERTUTOR.COM

DIEGO SIMEONE'S DEFENDING TACTICS

Tactical Situation 1 - Retaining a Numerical Advantage at the Back During Build-up Play

2. Creating a 3v2 Numerical Advantage at the Back when Building Up Play Against the 3-5-2 with Central Midfielder in a Deep Position

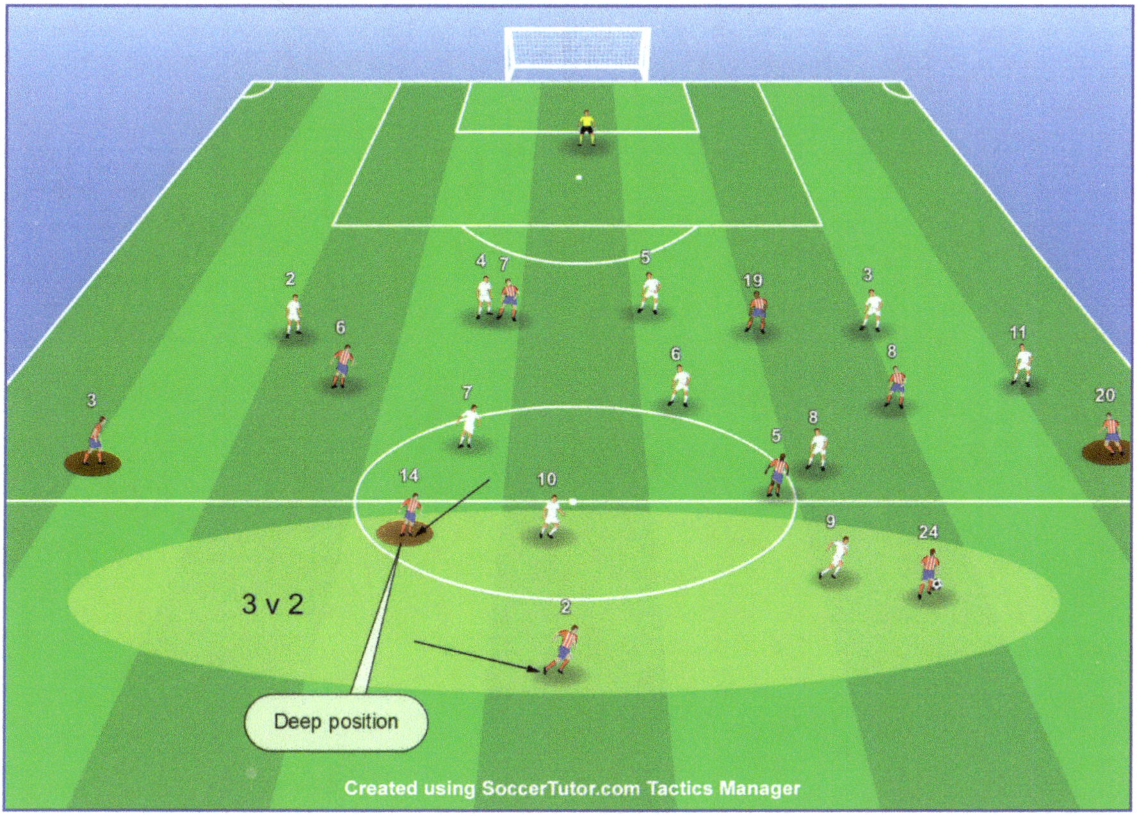

This second example shows another option which Diego Simeone's Atlético Madrid team used to create a 3v2 numerical advantage at the back when building up play.

This time it is the dropping back movement of the central midfielder on the weak side **Rodri (14)** which creates a numerical advantage at the back against the 2 white forwards.

This action by **Rodri (14)** enables the full back **F. Luis (3)** to stay in a high position.

ASSESSMENT

Retaining a numerical advantage at the back during the attacking phase enabled the Atlético Madrid defenders to defend actively and more effectively against passes directed straight to the forwards if the opposing team won the ball (counter attack).

©SOCCERTUTOR.COM — DIEGO SIMEONE'S DEFENDING TACTICS

SESSION (2 PRACTICES) FOR "RETAINING A NUMERICAL ADVANTAGE AT THE BACK DURING BUILD-UP PLAY"

Tactical Situation 1 - Retaining a Numerical Advantage at the Back During Build-up Play

SESSION FOR THIS TACTICAL SITUATION (2 PRACTICES)

1. Retaining a Numerical Advantage at the Back During Build-up Play in a Passive Practice

Scenario A: Weak Side Full Back Drops Back into Deep Position

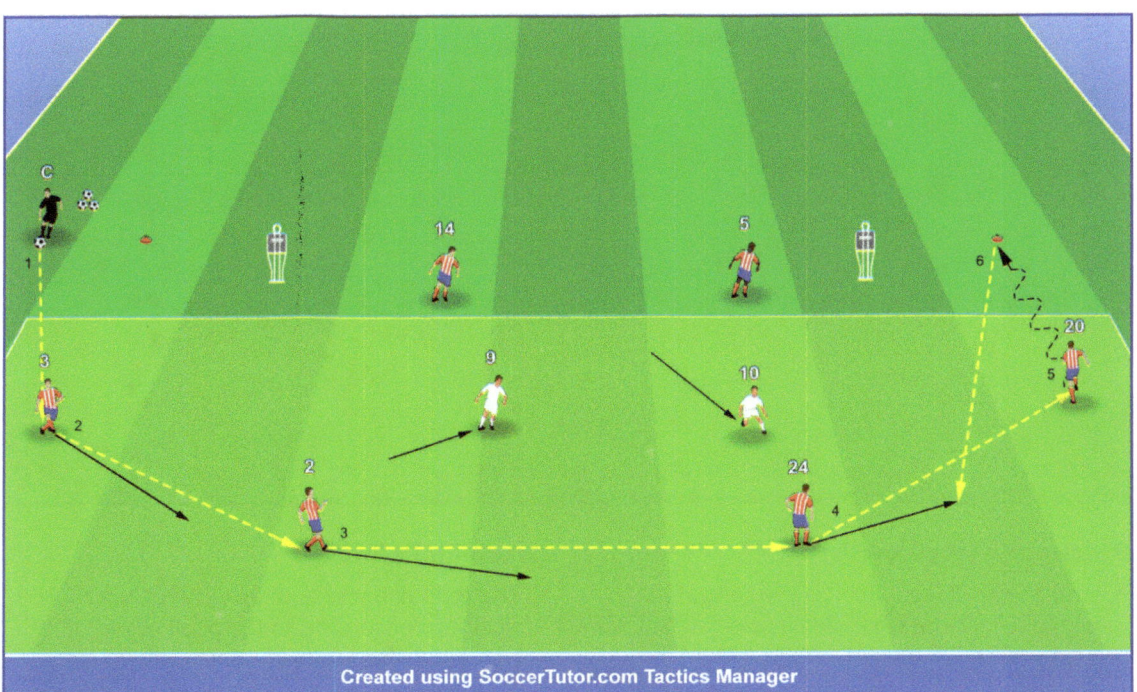

Description (Scenario A)

- Within the 40 x 20 yard area, there are 4 red defenders and 2 white forwards. Just outside, there are 2 red central midfielders and 2 mannequins.

- The practice starts with the red defenders and the 2 white forwards press in a passive way.

- The red players pass the ball around and move it to the full back on the strong side **(20)**, who dribbles up to the red cone.

- The red team need to always retain a 3 v 2 numerical advantage inside the area.

- As the full back on the strong side dribbles outside of the area, either the full back drops back into a deep position (**diagram above**) or the central midfielder drops back (**see diagram on next page**).

- In this example, the red full back on the weak side **(3)** drops back after the other full back **(20)** moves forward.

- The reds can switch from one option to the other, but this should be done in synchronisation and without ever being unbalanced.

DIEGO SIMEONE'S DEFENDING TACTICS

Tactical Situation 1 - Retaining a Numerical Advantage at the Back During Build-up Play

Scenario B: Weak Side Central Midfielder Drops Back into Deep Position

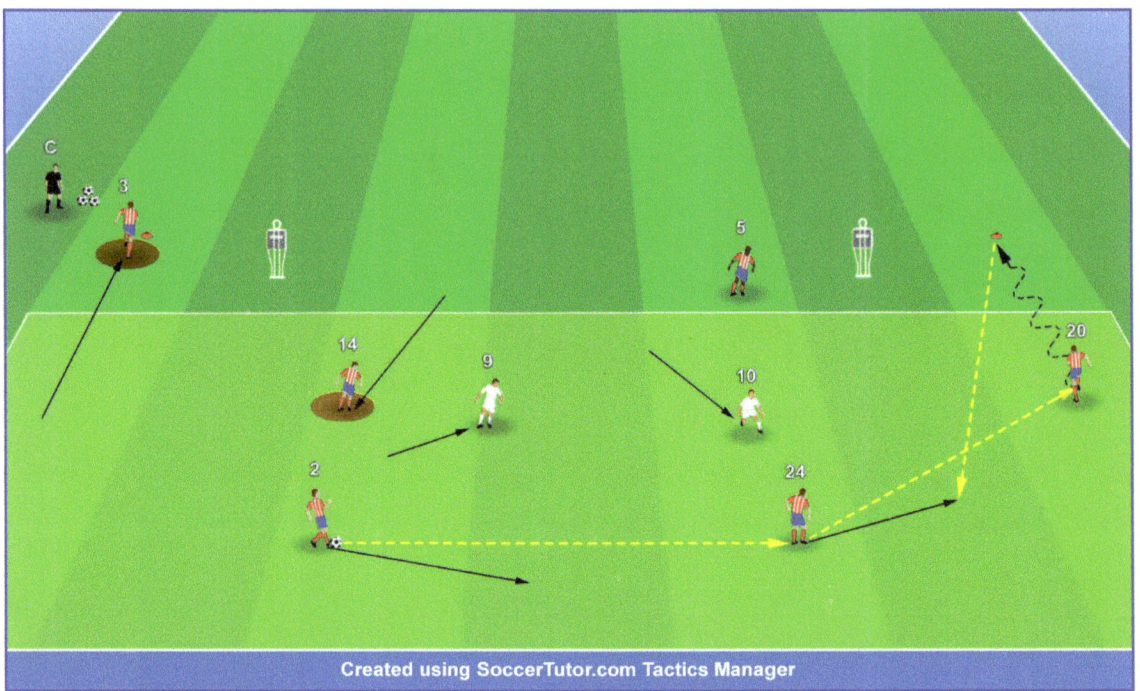

Description (Scenario B)
- In this second scenario, it is the central midfielder on the weak side instead of the full back who drops back.
- The red central midfielder (**14**) drops back after the full back (**20**) moves forward and the red team retain a 3v2 numerical advantage at the back against the 2 white forwards.

Coaching Points
1. The red full backs take up very high or high positions according to the positioning of the respective white central midfielders (mannequins).
2. Synchronisation is needed for the players movements and good communication.

ASSESSMENT
This practice can be used to play against any possible formation (4-4-2, 4-2-3-1, 4-3-3, 3-5-2 etc).

©SOCCERTUTOR.COM

DIEGO SIMEONE'S DEFENDING TACTICS

Tactical Situation 1 - Retaining a Numerical Advantage at the Back During Build-up Play

PROGRESSION
2. Retaining a Numerical Advantage at the Back During Build-up Play in a Conditioned 7 v 8 (+GK) Game

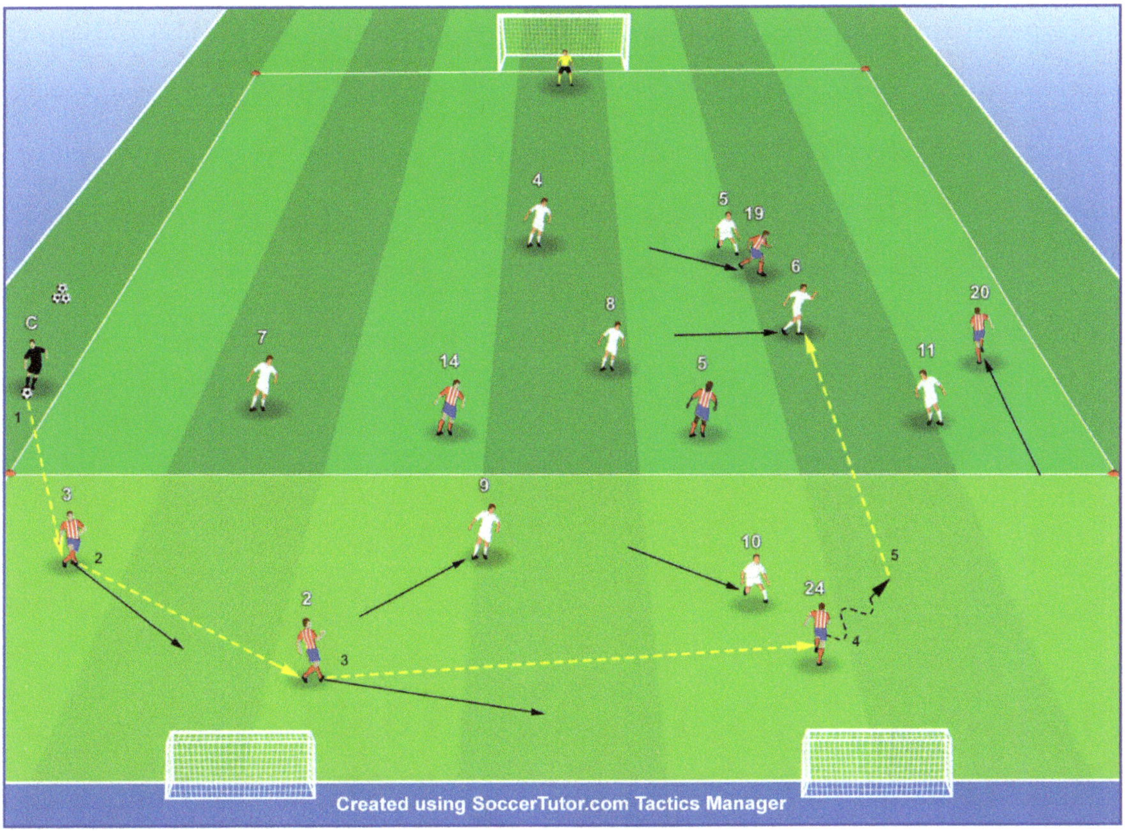

Description
- In this progression, we mark out a 40 x 20 yard low zone within the total playing area, which is 40 x 60 yards.
- 4 white midfielders, 2 white centre backs and 1 red forward are added.
- The reds start and build up play while retaining a 3 v 2 advantage in the low zone (in case possession is lost), then try to play forward and score past the GK.
- The whites try to win the ball and then score in the 2 mini goals (counter attack).

Restriction
During the red's build up play, the 2 white forwards are only allowed inside the low zone. If the whites win the ball, the 2 forwards can then move freely.

Coaching Points
1. The red full backs take up very high or high positions according to the positioning of the respective white central midfielder.
2. Synchronisation is needed for the players movements and good communication.

©SOCCERTUTOR.COM   DIEGO SIMEONE'S DEFENDING TACTICS

TACTICAL SITUATION 2

Negative Transition After Losing Possession from a Long Pass

The content in this section is from analysis of Diego Simeone's Atlético Madrid teams during the 2017/2018 and 2018/2019 seasons.

The analysis is based on recurring patterns of play observed within the Atlético Madrid team. Once the same phase of play occurred several times (at least 10), the tactics would be seen as a pattern. The analysis on the following pages are examples of the team's tactics being used effectively.

Each action, pass, individual movement with or without the ball, and the positioning of each player on the pitch including their body shape, are presented.

The analysis is then used to create a practice to coach this specific tactical situation.

NEGATIVE TRANSITION AFTER LOSING POSSESSION

SHORT PASSING STYLE AND COUNTER-PRESSING

The reactions of a team during the transition from attack to defence (negative transition) depend largely on the playing style during the attacking phase.

If a team uses short passing with triangle shapes and they try to create a numerical advantage around the ball when attacking, then counter-pressing is easy to be carried out and possession can be regained immediately.

This is the playing style that Pep Guardiola and Jürgen Klopp try to adapt with their respective Manchester City and Liverpool teams at the moment.

DIRECT ATTACKING STYLE DOES NOT ENABLE COUNTER-PRESSING

If a team uses long passing or directs the ball into areas where not many attacking players are positioned compared to defending players, the possibility of applying counter-pressing after losing possession is limited.

In these situations, tactics such as dropping back, shifting across, forcing the play wide, reorganising and becoming compact are used.

ATLÉTICO MADRID'S PLAYING STYLE: A MIX OF SHORT PASSING AND DIRECT ATTACKING

Diego Simeone's playing style with Atlético Madrid during the attacking phase combines a mixture of short passing combination play and more direct passing (long passes or switches of play).

Therefore, there were situations when Atlético used combination play with short passing in tight spaces where many attacking players were positioned, and there were situations when the ball was played to the forwards directly using long passes.

This is the reason why Diego Simone's Atlético Madrid team do not have a specific way of carrying out the transition from attack to defence (negative transition phase), but instead adjust their reactions according to the specific tactical situation.

In the last 3 sections of this book, we analyse the transition from attack to defence for all of Atlético's different attacking playing styles:

- **Tactical Situation 2:**
  Negative Transition After Losing Possession from a Long Pass

- **Tactical Situation 3:**
  Negative Transition After Losing Possession During a Switch of Play

- **Tactical Situation 4**:
  Counter-Pressing After Losing Possession During Combination Play

Tactical Situation 2 - Negative Transition After Losing Possession from a Long Pass

NEGATIVE TRANSITION AFTER LOSING POSSESSION FROM A LONG PASS

a. Possession is Lost After the Central Midfielder's Unsuccessful Long Pass to the Forward

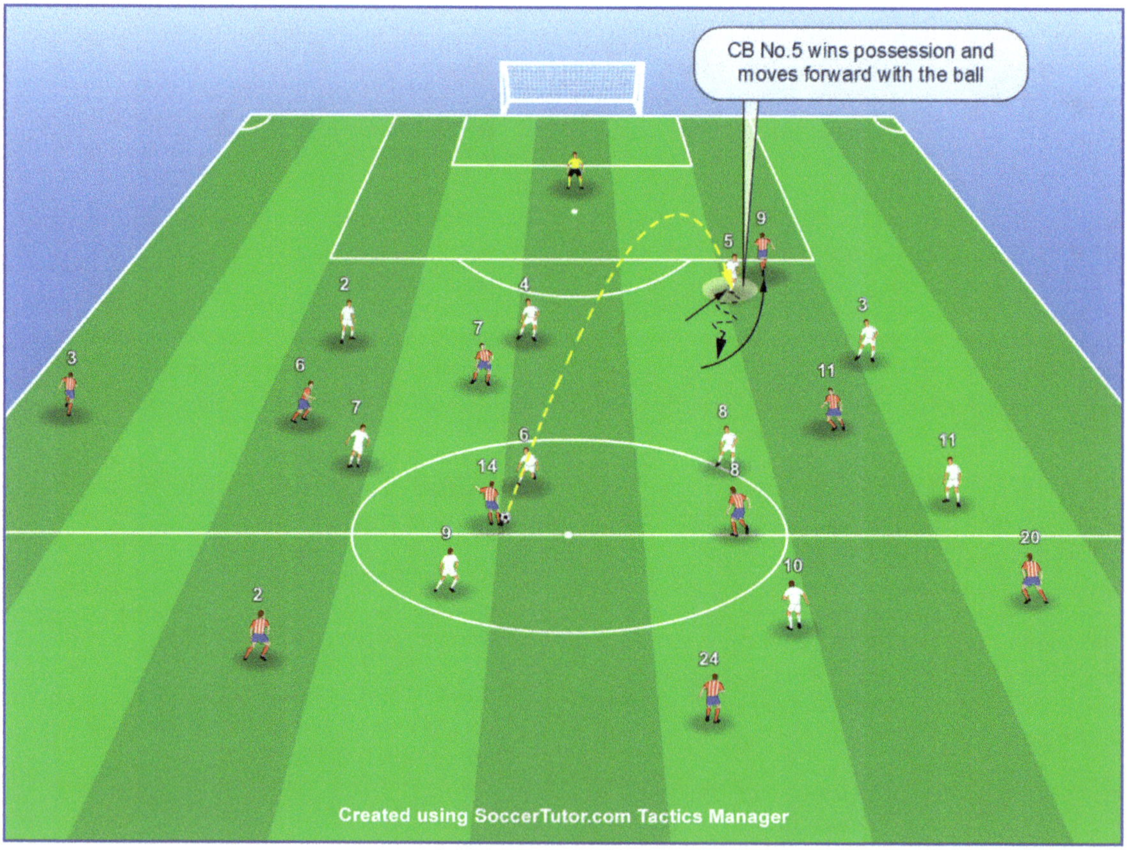

When Atlético Madrid used long passes to move the ball quickly to the forwards and possession was lost with no Atlético player close enough to put immediate pressure on the ball, the defenders aim to recover into effective defensive positions. The midfielders get compact, prevent through passes and force play wide.

As mentioned in the previous section, Atlético always retain a numerical advantage at the back. In this situation, we have 3 v 2.

In the diagram example, the central midfielder **Gabi (14)** plays a long pass towards the forward **Torres (9)**, who makes a run on the blind side of the white centre back No.5.

White No.5 intercepts the long pass and moves forward with the ball.

The description of this situation continues on the next page...

DIEGO SIMEONE'S DEFENDING TACTICS

Tactical Situation 2 - Negative Transition After Losing Possession from a Long Pass

b. Creating a Compact Formation and Forcing the Ball Wide After the Opposing Centre Back Gains Possession

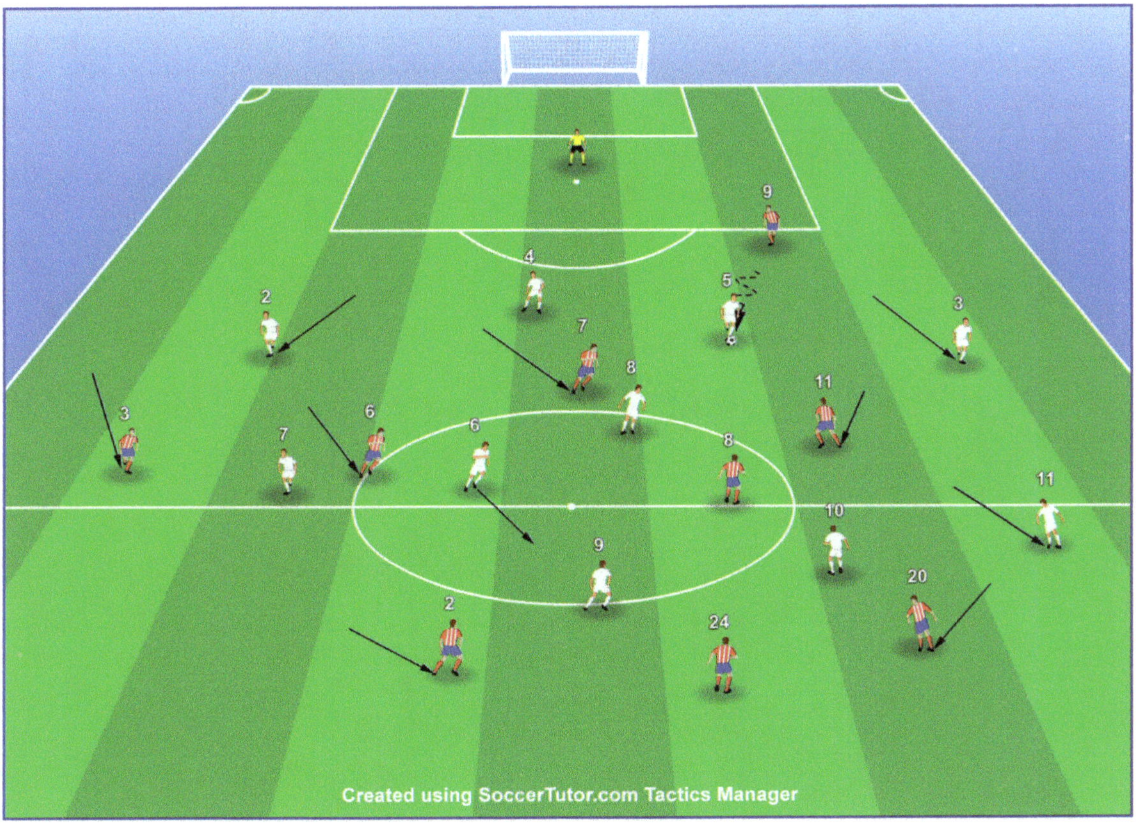

As soon as the white centre back No.5 wins possession and dribbles the ball forward, the deep positioned forward **Griezmann (7)** moves back and across to take up a central position close to the midfielders.

Griezmann's (7) aim is to prevent a switch of play and make the opposition's attacking play more predictable.

The Atlético midfielders move towards the centre and try to regain a compact defensive shape. This reaction enables them to prevent through passes and force the ball towards the side-line.

Forcing the ball wide doesn't only make the white team's play predictable, it also gives time to the advanced positioned players, such as the left back **F. Luis (3)**, to recover back and provide defensive balance to the team.

Tactical Situation 2 - Negative Transition After Losing Possession from a Long Pass

c. The Centre Back's Pass to the Full Back Gives the Atlético Players Time to Become Organised and Compact

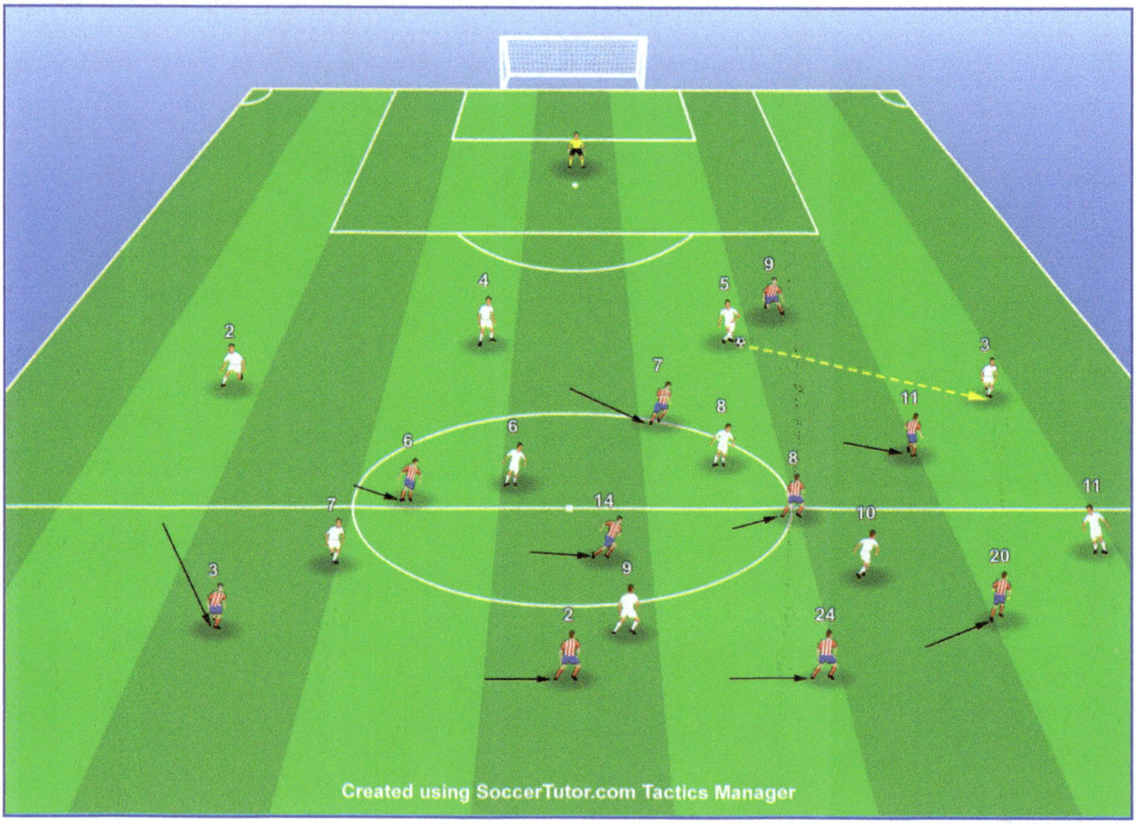

After the pass from the white centre back No.5 to the left back No.3, Atlético are well balanced near the ball area and time has been created for the full back **F. Luis (3)** on the weak side to recover back and take up an effective defensive position.

The most obvious passing option for white No.3 is the one towards No.11.

However, the white wide midfielder No.11 would receive within limited space and Atlético are highly likely to be able to apply double marking.

PRACTICE FOR "NEGATIVE TRANSITION AFTER LOSING POSSESSION FROM A LONG PASS"

Tactical Situation 2 - Negative Transition After Losing Possession from a Long Pass

PRACTICE FOR THIS TACTICAL SITUATION (1 PRACTICE)
Negative Transition After Losing Possession from a Long Pass in a Conditioned Game with a Central Zone

Description
- The 2 teams play an 11v11 game in 2/3 of a full pitch with 3 zones marked out as shown.
- The practice starts with the red team's GK and the reds build up play. Either the full back or central midfielder on the weak side drops back to create a back 3 (retain a 3v2 numerical advantage), so the reds are ready to defend effectively in case possession is lost.
- A red defender or central midfielder must play a long pass (from within low zone) towards the yellow zone for one of the forwards.
- This ball should be intercepted by a white centre back and the reds then have to carry out the negative transition phase properly (red arrows show the movements) and prevent their opponents from scoring.
- Through passes towards the central white zone should be blocked and play should be forced towards the wide areas - **please see analysis pages for the correct reactions**.

Coaching Points
1. The red full backs take up very high or high positions according to the positioning of the respective white central midfielder.
2. Progress to 11v11 on a full sized pitch with the same emphasis when losing possession.

DIEGO SIMEONE'S DEFENDING TACTICS

TACTICAL SITUATION 3

Negative Transition After Losing Possession During a Switch of Play

The content in this section is from analysis of Diego Simeone's Atlético Madrid teams during the 2017/2018 and 2018/2019 seasons.

The analysis is based on recurring patterns of play observed within the Atlético Madrid team. Once the same phase of play occurred several times (at least 10), the tactics would be seen as a pattern. The analysis on the following pages are examples of the team's tactics being used effectively.

Each action, pass, individual movement with or without the ball, and the positioning of each player on the pitch including their body shape, are presented.

The analysis is then used to create a practice to coach this specific tactical situation.

Tactical Situation 3 - Negative Transition After Losing Possession During a Switch of Play

NEGATIVE TRANSITION AFTER LOSING POSSESSION DURING A SWITCH OF PLAY

a. Possession is Lost After the Central Midfielder's Unsuccessful Switch of Play Towards the Advanced Full Back

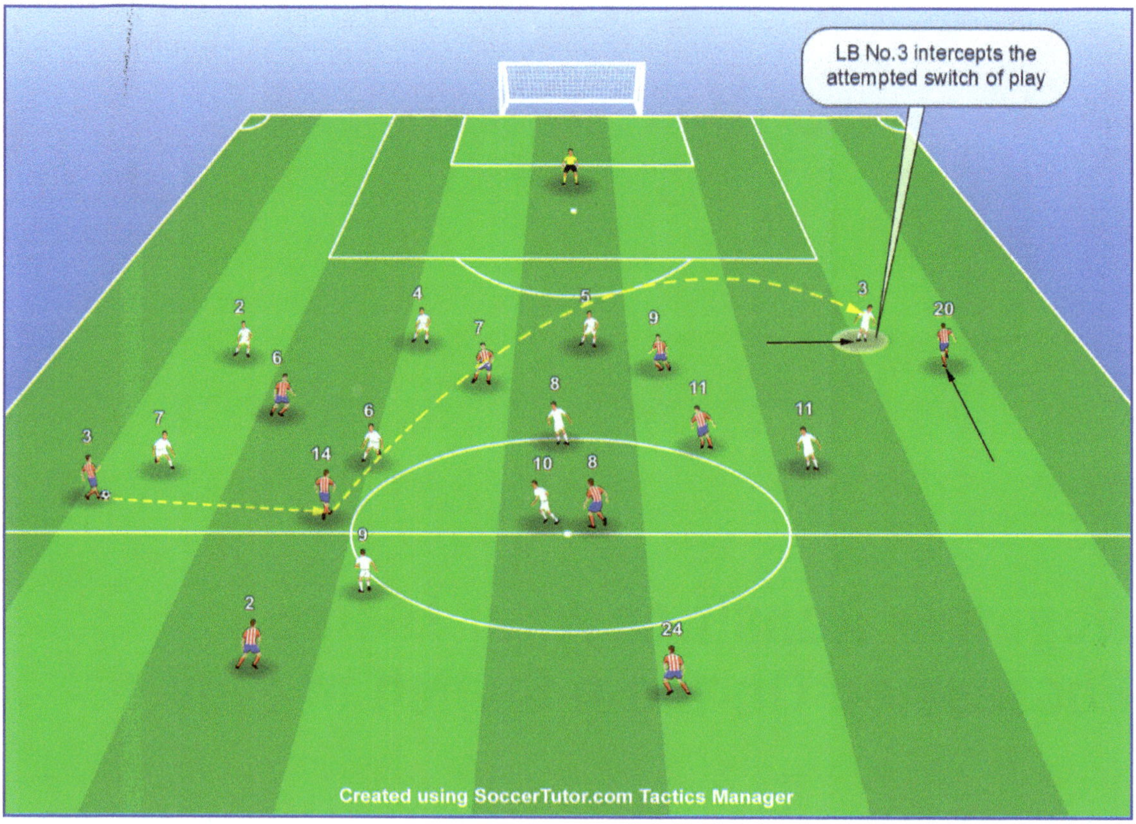

LB No.3 intercepts the attempted switch of play

In this tactical example, we show how Diego Simeone's Atlético Madrid react to losing possession after an attempted switch of play.

As mentioned previously, Atlético always retain a numerical advantage at the back. In this situation, we have 2 v 1.

The central midfielder **Gabi (14)** receives from the left back **F. Luis (3)** and tries to switch play towards the right back **Juanfran (20)**, who has made a forward run into an advanced position.

The switch of play is intercepted by the white left back No.3 and the Atlético players have to react in the appropriate way for the transition from attack to defence to be successful.

The description of this situation continues on the next page...

©SOCCERTUTOR.COM

DIEGO SIMEONE'S DEFENDING TACTICS

Tactical Situation 3 - Negative Transition After Losing Possession During a Switch of Play

b. Shifting to Create a Strong Side with a Numerical Advantage Around the Ball when the Full Back Intercepts and Dribbles Forward

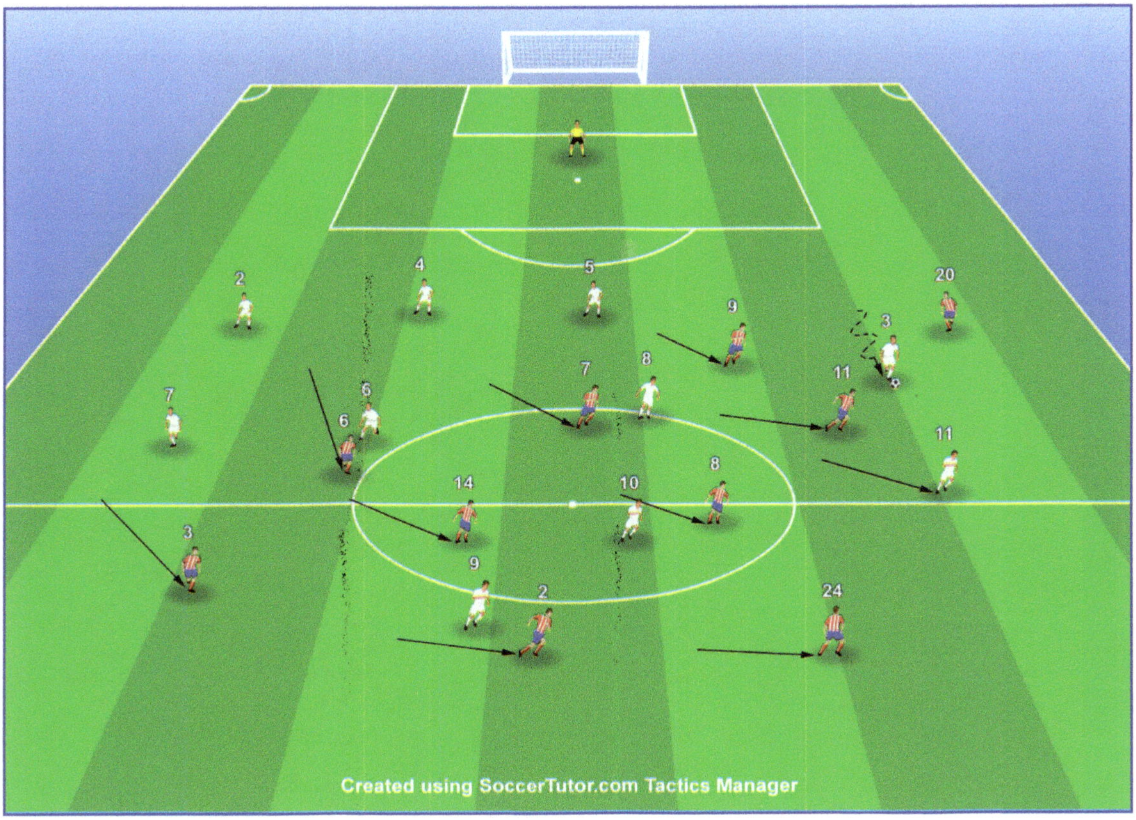

White No.3 moves forward and the Atlético players drop back in an attempt to create a compact formation.

The full back **Juanfran (20)** is in an advanced position and the centre back **Giménez (24)** has to shift towards the side-line to restrict space for white No.11 and restore balance on the right.

This is because Atlético are missing one player from their defensive line: **Juanfran (20)**.

Tactical Situation 3 - Negative Transition After Losing Possession During a Switch of Play

c. Defensive Reactions to Compensate for the Extensive Shift of the Centre Back After the Full Back's Pass to the Winger

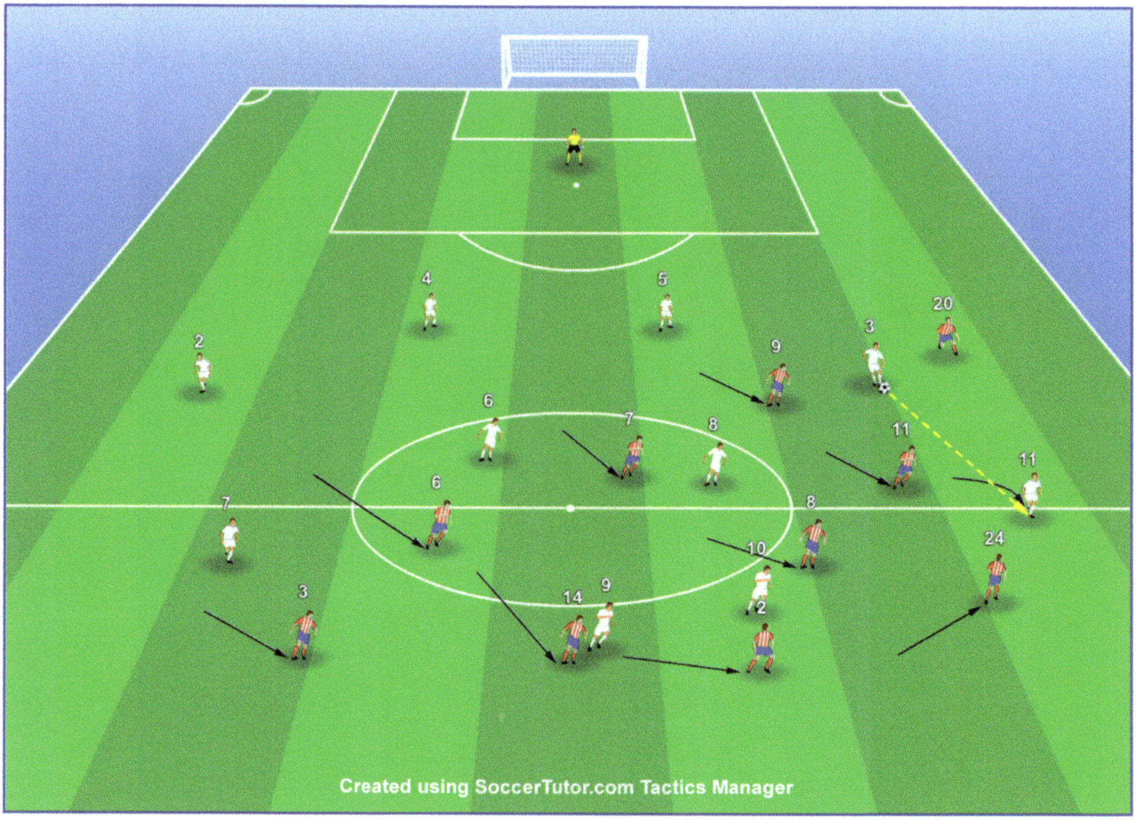

The shifting towards the strong side should not affect the numerical advantage at the back.

As soon as the ball is passed to white No.11, the centre back **Giménez (24)** shifts extensively to close him down and the central midfielder **Gabi (14)** drops back into a very deep position to compensate this, retaining balance and the numerical advantage at the back.

The right midfielder **Correa (11)** moves to apply double marking.

If the defensive midfielder **Gabi (14)** is not in an appropriate position to drop back and fill the gap in the defensive line, the centre back **Giménez (24)** doesn't move to close No.11 down and instead stays in a central position to play for time.

DIEGO SIMEONE'S DEFENDING TACTICS

PRACTICE FOR "NEGATIVE TRANSITION AFTER LOSING POSSESSION DURING A SWITCH OF PLAY"

Tactical Situation 3 - Negative Transition After Losing Possession During a Switch of Play

PRACTICE FOR THIS TACTICAL SITUATION
Negative Transition After Losing Possession During a Switch of Play in a Conditioned Game vs 4-4-2

Description
- The 2 teams play an 11v11 game in 2/3 of a full pitch. There is a 30 yard low zone for the red's build up play and 2 side zones which are 10 x 15 yards.

- The practice starts with the red team's GK and the reds build up play. The central midfielder on the weak side **No.8** drops back to create a back 3 (retain a 3v2 numerical advantage), so the reds are ready to defend effectively in case possession is lost.

- A red defender or central midfielder must switch play (from within low zone) towards the wide area for one of the full backs.

- This ball should be intercepted by a white full back and the reds then have to carry out the negative transition phase properly (red arrows show the movements) and prevent their opponents from scoring.

- Please **see the analysis pages in this section** for the correct defensive reactions.

Coaching Points
1. The red full backs take up high or very high positions according to the positioning of the opposing wide midfielder.
2. This practice can be adjusted to various opposition formations (4-2-3-1, 4-3-3 etc).

©SOCCERTUTOR.COM

DIEGO SIMEONE'S DEFENDING TACTICS

TACTICAL SITUATION 4

Counter-Pressing After Losing Possession During Combination Play

The content in this section is from analysis of Diego Simeone's Atlético Madrid teams during the 2017/2018 and 2018/2019 seasons.

The analysis is based on recurring patterns of play observed within the Atlético Madrid team. Once the same phase of play occurred several times (at least 10), the tactics would be seen as a pattern. The analysis on the following pages are examples of the team's tactics being used effectively.

Each action, pass, individual movement with or without the ball, and the positioning of each player on the pitch including their body shape, are presented.

The analysis is then used to create a practice to coach this specific tactical situation.

Tactical Situation 4 - Counter-Pressing After Losing Possession During Combination Play

COUNTER-PRESSING AFTER LOSING POSSESSION DURING COMBINATION PLAY IN THE CENTRE

a. Creating Triangle Shapes and Maintaining Short Distances Between Players During the Attacking Phase

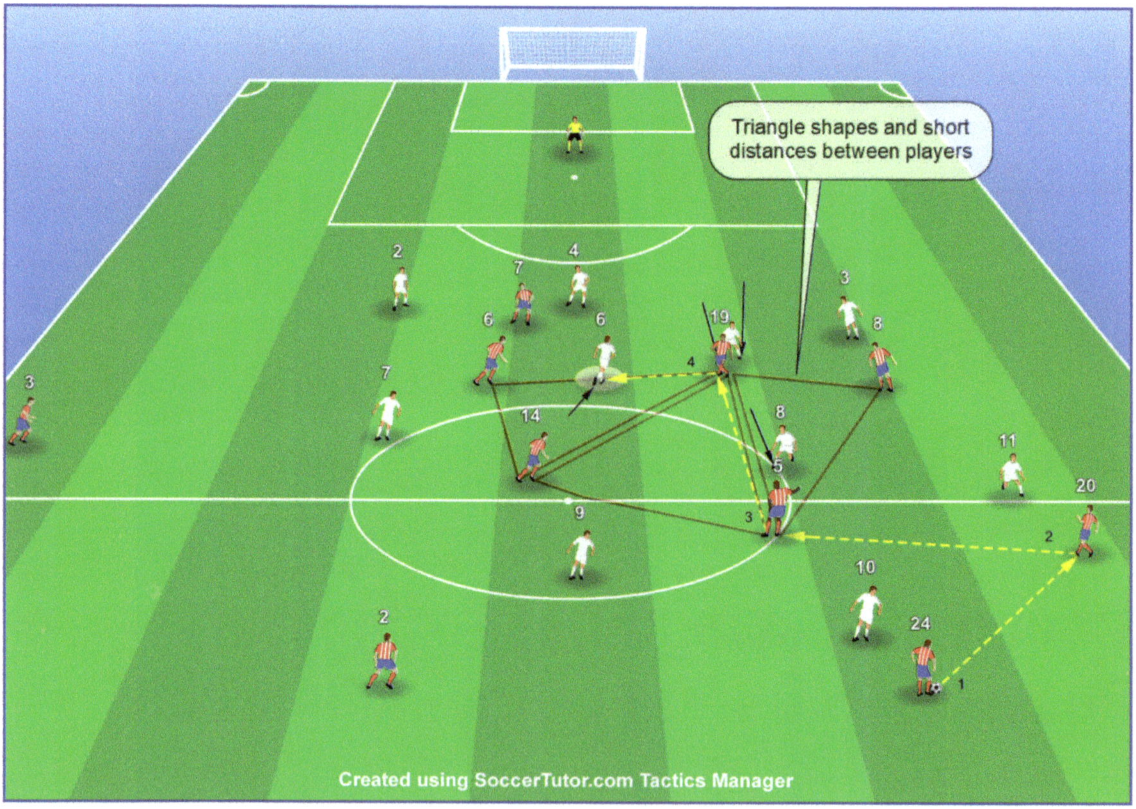

For Atlético Madrid to use short combination play, specific elements must first exist. The distances between the players need to be short and there should be triangle shapes set up. If an opponent wins the ball, they can then be immediately pressed.

When Atlético use combination play in tight spaces, the distance between the players is short. If there are also triangle shapes, there are good conditions for Simeone's team to use counter-pressing to win the ball back immediately.

In this example, the forward **D. Costa (9)** drops back to receive or create space and the white centre back No.5 follows him, thus creating space for **Saúl (8)** to exploit in behind via a pass from **Koke (6)**.

However, the pass towards **Koke (6)** is intercepted by the white central midfielder No.6 and the Atlético players have to react in the appropriate way for the transition from attack to defence to be successful. The description of this situation continues on the next page...

©SOCCERTUTOR.COM   DIEGO SIMEONE'S DEFENDING TACTICS

Tactical Situation 4 - Counter-Pressing After Losing Possession During Combination Play

b. Applying Counter-Pressing Immediately After Losing the Ball to Win it Back as Quickly as Possible

The reaction of the players is immediate, and the new ball carrier is pressed by 3 Atlético players from different directions, who create a pressing triangle.

The aim for **Rodri (14)**, who is at the base of the triangle, is to apply pressure immediately and prevent the ball carrier from having any time and space on the ball.

The other 2 players in the triangle are the left midfielder **Koke (6)** and the forward **D. Costa (19)**. They move to press from behind and win the ball if white No.6 hesitates or tries to change direction.

Most of the white players are eliminated as passing options because the passing lanes towards them are blocked.

In addition, potential receivers white No.8 and No.10 are marked by the central midfielder **Thomas (5)** and centre back **Giménez (24)** respectively.

At the same time, there is safety with a 3v2 numerical advantage at the back. Atlético have their two centre backs **Godín (2)** and **Giménez (24)**, and right back **Juanfran (20)** against the two white forwards No.9 and No.10.

DIEGO SIMEONE'S DEFENDING TACTICS

Tactical Situation 4 - Counter-Pressing After Losing Possession During Combination Play

COUNTER-PRESSING AFTER LOSING POSSESSION DURING COMBINATION PLAY OUT WIDE

a. Creating Triangle Shapes and Maintaining Short Distances Between Players During the Attacking Phase

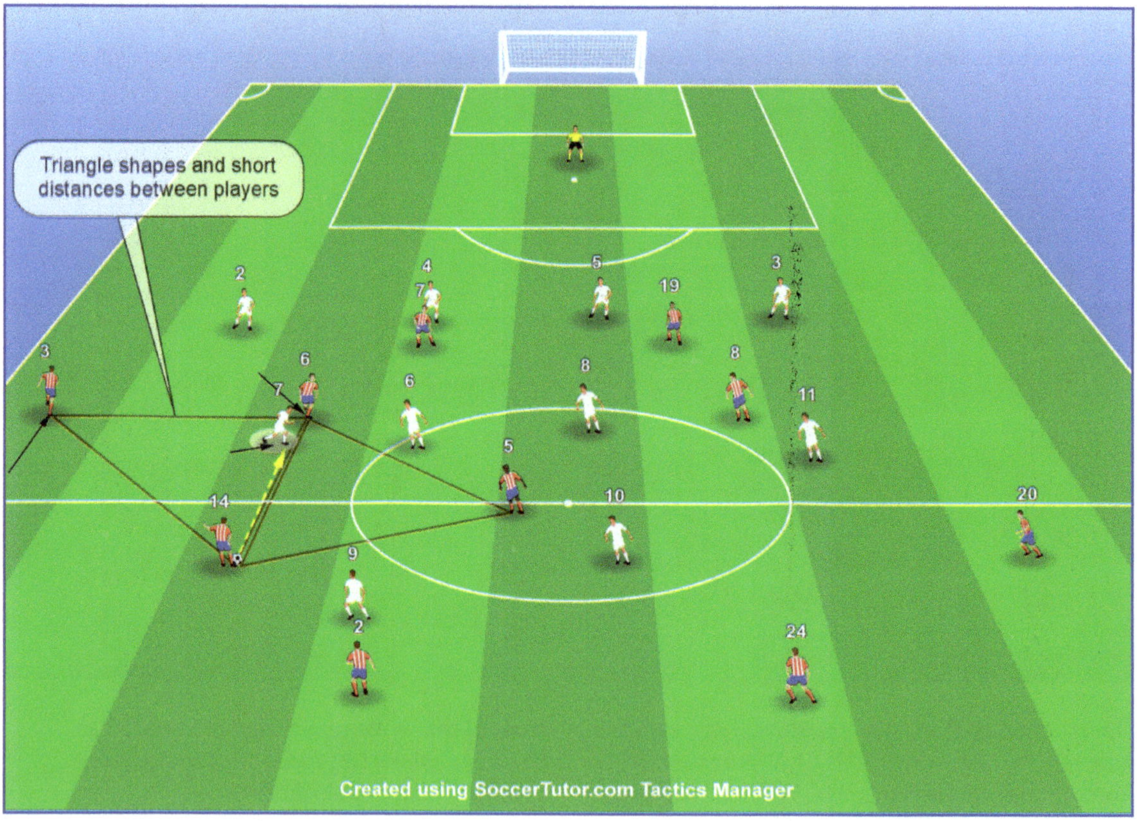

This tactical example shows Atlético Madrid using combination play away from the centre and towards the side of the pitch.

If the distances between the players are short enough (10-12 yards) and there are triangle or diamond shapes, the opponents can then be immediately pressed when possession is won.

The central midfielder **Rodri (14)** attempts a forward pass but possession is lost because the white No.7 moves across to intercept the ball.

The description of this situation continues on the next page...

Tactical Situation 4 - Counter-Pressing After Losing Possession During Combination Play

b. Applying Counter-Pressing Immediately After Losing the Ball to Win it Back as Quickly as Possible

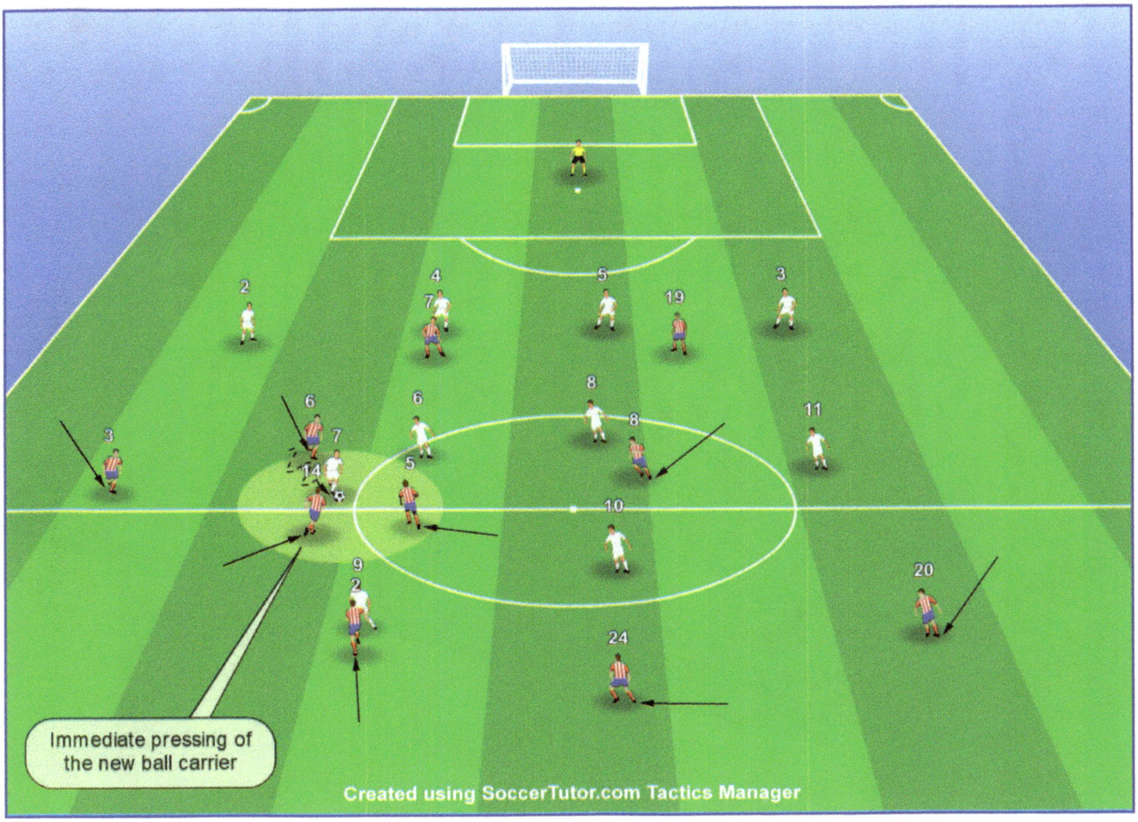

Immediate pressing of the new ball carrier

Simeone's Atlético players react immediately when white No.7 intercepts and moves forward with the ball.

The new ball carrier No.7 is pressed by 3 Atlético players from different directions, who create a pressing triangle.

The aim for the central midfielder **Rodri (14)** is to press in a way that blocks forward passes and force the play towards one side (Atlético's left side) to make the opposition's attack predictable.

Left midfielder **Koke (6)** and the other central midfielder **Thomas (5)** move to press white No.7 from behind and try to win the ball if he hesitates or tries to change direction.

The centre back **Godín (2)** moves forward and marks the forward No.9 tightly.

The other centre back **Giménez (24)** and the right back **Juanfran (20)** retain the 3v2 numerical advantage at the back by moving towards the left side.

PRACTICE FOR "COUNTER-PRESSING AFTER LOSING POSSESSION DURING COMBINATION PLAY"

Tactical Situation 4 - Counter-Pressing After Losing Possession During Combination Play

PRACTICE FOR THIS TACTICAL SITUATION
Counter-Pressing After Losing Possession During Short Combination Play in a Conditioned Game

Description
- The 2 teams play an 11 v 11 game in 2/3 of a full pitch and there is a 30 yard low zone for the red's build up play.
- The practice starts with the red team's GK and the reds attack by using passes no longer than 10-15 yards. If this is difficult to apply, you can divide the pitch into small areas as shown.
- The red players are only allowed to pass to team-mates in neighbouring areas. They try to create triangle shapes and score using short combination play. The white players try to win the ball and then score with a counter attack.
- If the reds lose the ball, they should have players close enough to the ball to apply counter-pressing immediately.
- Please **see the analysis pages in this section** for the correct defensive reactions.

Coaching Points
1. Good off the ball movement is essential to create triangle shapes.
2. Synchronisation is needed for the players movements and good communication.

DIEGO SIMEONE'S DEFENDING TACTICS

FREE TRIAL

TACTICS MANAGER
Create your own Practices, Tactics & Plan Sessions!

www.SoccerTutor.com/TacticsManager
info@soccertutor.com

PC Mac iPad Tablet Web

Football Coaching Specialists Since 2001

Available in Full Colour Print and eBook!
PC | Mac | iPhone | iPad | Android Phone/Tablet | Kobo | Kindle Fire

www.SoccerTutor.com
info@soccertutor.com

Football Coaching Specialists Since 2001

MARCELO BIELSA

Coaching Build Up Play Against High Pressing Teams

Terzis Athanasios

Available in Full Colour Print and eBook!
PC | Mac | iPhone | iPad | Android Phone/Tablet | Kobo | Kindle Fire

www.SoccerTutor.com
info@soccertutor.com

Football Coaching Specialists Since 2001

Available in Full Colour Print and eBook!
PC | Mac | iPhone | iPad | Android Phone/Tablet | Kobo | Kindle Fire

www.SoccerTutor.com
info@soccertutor.com

www.ingramcontent.com/pod-product-compliance
Lightning Source LLC
Chambersburg PA
CBHW061128010526
44117CB00023B/2992